KU-102-466

contemporary research in the sociology of education

A selection of contemporary research papers
together with some of the formative
writings of the recent past

First published in 1974 by
Methuen & Co Ltd
11 New Fetter Lane London EC4P 4EE
Editorial material © 1974 S. John Eggleston
Reprinted 1976

Set IBM by Tek-Art,
London SE20
Printed in Great Britain at the University Printing House, Cambridge

ISBN 0 416 78780 0 hardbound
ISBN 0 416 78790 8 paperback

*This title is available in both hard and paperback editions. The
paperback edition is sold subject to the condition that it shall not,
by way of trade or otherwise, be lent, re-sold, hired out, or otherwise
circulated without the publisher's prior consent in any form of binding
or cover other than that in which it is published and without a similar
condition including this condition being imposed
on the subsequent purchaser.*

Distributed in the USA by
HARPER & ROW PUBLISHERS, INC.
BARNES & NOBLE IMPORT DIVISION

CONTEMPORARY RESEARCH IN THE SOCIOLOGY OF EDUCATION

Edited by
John Eggleston

Methuen

CONTENTS

Acknowledgements

The editor and publishers would like to thank the following for permission to reproduce the articles in this book:

P. Bellaby for 'The distribution of deviance among 13-14 year old students'; G. Bernbaum and the *Sociological Review* for 'Headmasters and schools: some preliminary findings'; B. Bernstein and Dorothy Henderson and the Clarendon Press for 'Social class differences in the relevance of language to socialization'; P. Bourdieu and Editions of the National Centre of Scientific Research, Paris, for 'The conservative school'; P. Bourdieu and Monique de Saint-Martin and *Annales* for 'Scholastic excellence and the values of the educational system': D.S. Byrne and W. Williamson and the Clarendon Press for 'Some intra-regional variations in educational provision and their bearing upon educational attainment – the case of the north east'; M. Craft for 'Talent, family values and education in Ireland': *New Society* for 'Going comprehensive: a case study of secondary reorganization' by John Eggleston; *Comparative Education* and the Carfax Publishing Company for 'Some environmental correlates of extended secondary education in England' by John Eggleston; Jean Floud and *Forum* for 'Reserves of ability'; Julienne Ford and Routledge and Kegan Paul and Humanities Press Inc., New York, for 'Ability and opportunity in a comprehensive school' from *Social Class and the Comprehensive School:* G.R. Grace and Routledge and Kegan Paul for 'Vulnerability and conflict in the teacher's role' from *Role Conflict and the Teacher;* A.H. Halsey and Her Majesty's Stationery Office for 'The EPAs and their schools' from *Educational Priority;* C. Lacey for 'Destreaming in a "pressured" academic environment'; J. Lehtinen and the National Planning Office, Helsinki, for 'The differentiation of the educational structure: a location analysis on secondary education in Finland'; U.P. Lundgren for 'Pedagogical roles in the classroom'; K.M. Marjoribanks and *Teacher Education* for 'Home environment and mental abilities'; R. Nash and *New Society* for 'Camouflage in the classroom'; J. Patrick and Eyre Methuen for extracts from *A Glasgow Gang Observed;* P.E.D. Robinson for 'An ethnography of classrooms'; M.D. Shipman and the *Journal of Curriculum Studies* for 'The impact of a curriculum project'; R.W. Witkin and the Clarendon Press for 'Social class influence on the amount and type of positive evaluation of school lessons'.

Notes on contributors

BELLABY, Paul — Lecturer in Sociology, University of Keele.

BERNBAUM, G. — Senior Lecturer in Education, University of Leicester.

BERNSTEIN, Basil — Professor of the Sociology of Education, University of London Institute of Education, and Head of the Sociological Research Unit.

BOURDIEU, Pierre — Director of Studies of the École Pratique des Hautes Études, Paris and Deputy Director of its Centre for European Sociology.

BYRNE, D.S. — Lecturer in Department of Sociology and Social Administration at the University of Durham.

CRAFT, Maurice — Professor of Education, Goldsmith's College, University of London. Previously Senior Lecturer in Education, University of Exeter.

EGGLESTON, John — Professor of Education and Head of Education Department, University of Keele.

FLOUD, Jean — Principal, Newnham College, Cambridge. Previously Fellow of Nuffield College, Oxford and Reader in the Sociology of Education at the University of London.

FORD, Julienne — Senior Lecturer in Sociology at Middlesex Polytechnic.

GRACE, Gerald R. — Lecturer in Sociology of Education, King's College, London.

HALSEY, A.H. — Director of Department of Sociology and Administrative Studies, University of Oxford and Director of the research

	project on Educational Priority sponsored by the Department of Education and Science and the Social Science Research Council.
HENDERSON, Dorothy	Research Officer, Sociological Research Unit, University of London, Institute of Education.
LACEY, C.	Professor of Education, University of Sussex, and Director of Research, Schools Council.
LEHTINEN, Jukka	Senior Officer, Planning Unit of the Finnish Ministry of Education. Previously Research Officer, Finnish National Planning Office.
LUNDGREN, Ulf P.	Research Fellow, School of Education, University of Göteborg, Sweden.
MARJORIBANKS, K.M.	Professor of Education, University of Adelaide, previously Lecturer in Sociology, Department of Educational Studies, Oxford.
NASH, Roy	Lecturer in the Sociology of Education, University College of North Wales, Bangor.
PATRICK, James	Lectures in Social Psychology in an English University.
ROBINSON, Philip E.D.	Lecturer in the Sociology of Education, University of Keele.
De SAINT—MARTIN, Monique	Assistant Professor, École des Hautes Études, Paris.

SHIPMAN, M.D.

Director of Research and
Statistics, Inner London
Education Authority. Previously
Senior Lecturer in Education at
the University of Keele.

WILLIAMSON, W.

Lecturer in Department of
Sociology and Social
Administration, University of
Durham.

WITKIN, Robert W.

Lecturer in Sociology,
University of Exeter. Seconded
as Director of Research
on Schools Council study on
'The arts and the adolescent' at
the University of Exeter.

EDITORIAL INTRODUCTION
The contemporary context of research in the sociology of education

The purpose of this collection of papers is to present evidence of the contemporary contribution of research in the sociology of education to the understanding of education and of society. The output of research in the sociology of education is probably greater and certainly as great as that in any field of sociology. In the past decade support from the research foundations has been generous and the number of individual studies has increased rapidly. Yet the contribution of this output has been minimized by a concentration of attention on a limited range of widely quoted studies; by a theoretical orientation that is implicit rather than explicit and, at times, an excessive and distorting use of its findings by pressure groups. Notwithstanding these problems, however, the potential contribution of findings from research in the sociology of education is considerable, and increasingly decisions on such matters as school organization, teachers' roles, curriculum content and the like are made in the belief that they are supported, or at least legitimated, by sociologically oriented research. The fact that such legitimation may be assumed rather than actual presents a further justification for the publication of this collection which, it is hoped, will help to reduce the uncertainties and uninformedness about the nature and standing of research in the field and draw attention to the complex interrelationship between educational research and policy. It is not a guide for those who wish to produce educational research; but rather a guide for those who seek access to the intellectual and emotional core of research and, in so doing, wish to use it critically.

The collection contains a range of research studies that include a number that have not been published previously and others that have been virtually unobtainable outside their countries of origin (France, Finland and Sweden). A consideration of their context, content and contribution forms the remainder of this general introduction to the volume; there are also specific editorial introductions to the various sections of the book in which the individual papers are discussed.

A dominant feature of the context of all contemporary research in the sociology of education is the controversy between scientific positivism and the reaction to it, notably from phenomenological and ethnomethodological approaches; the conflict between the 'normative' and 'interpretative' perspectives. Alongside this there is the closely related conflict between 'value free' and 'value oriented' sociology. Both of these conflicts are central to the nature of research and its understanding and use. But they are conflicts which dominate sociology as a whole and not just the sociology of education. Accordingly it is necessary to consider briefly the condition of sociological research generally before exploring the particularly educational connotations of research in the discipline.

The establishment of sociological research

'Pure' research in sociology is currently beset by a paradox; it has become both established and disestablished more or less concurrently. The establishment is unquestionable — recognition in universities and colleges throughout most of the world for sociology as a subject with academic standing and with legitimate research functions; a rapid growth in the range of accredited and well-funded research institutes; definitive recognition through direct sponsorship from major funding organizations and through public grant-awarding bodies.

The establishment of research in sociology has been a necessary condition of the establishment of the discipline itself. Only by demonstrating, empirically, that there are laws governing human behaviour in societies could sociology substantiate its claim for a legitimate separate existence either from literature with its established capacity to describe and interpret human interaction, or from history with its established strategies of analysing unique events and their consequences.[1] The battle for scientific recognition of this kind was first fought by the psychologists, successfully but at considerable cost to the development of the subject — where the crudities of behaviourism, having the manner of approved scientific method, were tolerated, while the exciting but largely untestable hypotheses in the field of psychoanalysis presented continuous embarrassment. The rigorous formalism of the British Psychological Society, still largely modelled on the prestigious pure science organizations, points to a continuing belief in a need for scientific respectability.

Sociology was spared some of these traumas. The recognition of psychology opened the path for the recognition of sociology even though it was along a path that had been laid down by the psychologists. But at least some of the exertions to establish it could be avoided by sociologists who were able to devote somewhat more of their time to exploring sociological as opposed to scientific perspectives. In this they were helped by the standing of anthropological study as a distinct and acceptable even if somewhat remote area of study. Yet the influence of the psychological interpretation of the pure science model on sociology is regularly to be seen, and Swift (1973) has noted that sociologists in Britain still find themselves 'forced into doing social psychology'. He suggests that many of the problems in the way of a fruitful relationship between sociology and psychology spring from the psychologically determined path of recognition that has had to be trodden by sociologists. There are many examples in present day sociology that reaffirm this history. The almost universal use of Durkheim's *Suicide*[2] and the compulsory statistical course, both of which form part of the routine socialization of first year sociology undergraduates, and the disfavour with which 'applied' social work students are often viewed, are well-known phenomena.

Yet there is no doubt that the presentation of a 'pure science' model of research with its reliable definitions, order and control of materials, detached and rational behaviour by investigators, as a model that is applicable to sociology has greatly facilitated even if it has not largely been responsible for the establishment of sociology as a subject of university study.[3]

The reaction to 'scientific positivism'

It is precisely the emphasis on pure science method that has led to a powerful reaction against the relevance and appropriateness of research of this 'normative' kind of sociology. It springs from a revived concern for the fundamental distinction between the material of the scientists and of the social scientists. Human beings are neither consistently logical nor reliably predictable in their behaviour. Unlike the subjects of the natural science researchers they are able to understand the purposes of the investigation, respond to them and even to mislead the researchers. The arrival of sociology within the ranks of social science research made the problem inescapable. While the relatively small scale 'experiments' of psychologists using animals or small groups of respondents (often psychology students) were still able to match up to the form of pure science, the development of sociology, with its exploration of whole life situations of larger populations in their everyday context, made this pure form distinctly less feasible. This in turn made it clear that the 'scientific' conception of the everyday world that had to be adopted in order to act in a scientific way was at variance with the subtle, shifting and often covert everyday conceptions of the world and the responses to it that were at the heart of what was being studied. The dissonance between methodology and subject matter became manifest. It was seen that even the attempt to act in a scientific way led to a necessary exclusion of some data and an ensuing overweighting of other data. Research findings in sociology, far more than those in natural science, must not only present findings but must also carry an interpretation that is not only in the 'conclusions' but also in the very collection and analysis of the data. As Swift (1973) reminds us, 'it is not so much that there is something "out there" which is sociological as that we perceive something sociological about that which is "out there".'

This is not to say that the methods of the natural sciences are in themselves all that are claimed by the natural scientists. An important critique by Kuhn (1970) suggests that natural scientists themselves are limited by their paradigms of scientific knowledge which have an important influence on their choice of problems, research methodology and their analysis of results. For Kuhn the development of scientific knowledge comes largely through scientific revolutions when the old paradigms are discarded and the new ones adopted. In the opinion of many sociologists it is just such a revolution that is now taking place in sociology.

Symbolic interactionism, phenomenology and ethnomethodology

In an attempt to break through the barriers established as a result of the pure science/psychological research model, sociologists have been attracted by the newly prominent 'interpretative' approaches; symbolic interactionism and phenomenology and ethnomethodology. Symbolic interactionism is concerned to explore the ways in which human beings defend and benefit themselves in the way in which they present themselves to others and the constant process of adjustment made by them in this presentation. Goffman's work, for example, observes the presentation of the self in a variety of social situations such as shops, restaurants, leisure activities, as well as in closed institutions. In all he is concerned to explore the pattern of negotiations or interactions, frequently by asking such apparently simple minded but essentially complex questions as 'how do people avoid bumping into each other on the street?' Such inquiries, though undeniably 'research', are fundamentally different from the controlled research design of the natural sciences, being concerned not with apparently rational, general and ordered behaviour, but with non-rational, specific and often disordered modes of behaviour. Linked with symbolic interactionism is a more general phenomenology, concerned with the manner in which the individual perceives reality in social situations and responds to his perceptions. For the phenomenologists the 'social constructions of reality' of individuals are in fact social knowledge which is seen not as having a permanent 'out there' nature but rather to be an essentially subjective artefact as are the qualities of 'truth' and 'objectivity' associated with it. It is this 'rediscovery' and reinterpretation of the sociology of knowledge that forms an important part of phenomenology which goes on to explore the processes whereby individuals obtain or are denied access to knowledge — in fact the social control of knowledge. The exploration requires the examination of all that is 'taken for granted'.

So far much that has been said about phenomenology would appear to characterize a psychologist accustomed to exploring individual emotional characteristics with a thematic appreciation test or Rorschach 'ink-blots'. But the phenomenologist is essentially a sociologist, for he is concerned with the regularities that may exist in individual perceptions and behaviours; his distinction from many other sociologists is his starting point with the individual rather than with some concept of 'society'.

Yet a further development of the reaction to positivism have been the ethnomethodological approaches concerned with 'indexicality' developed by Garfinkel (1967) and others, in which researchers are charged with a kind of experimental 'deviant participant role' in which their 'normal' patterns of response and interaction in a group are deliberately broken and violated in a way that may lead to modification, interruption or even breakdown in human interaction in the group.

The reaction to the positivism of the natural scientists has not only challenged the relevance of the natural science methodology and the results likely to be obtained from it, but it has also demonstrated in the social sciences the importance of the investigator's own perceptions and views on social reality. The work of two phenomenologists, Berger and Luckmann (1971), is of particular importance in suggesting that the way in which reality is perceived in social situations is an artefact;

a construction of all the participants of a social situation which, however permanent it may appear to be, may be redefined and therefore changed. It follows that the social scientist himself must take a part in defining reality in any social situation in which he is involved. When it is also seen that his presence as an interrogator or observer may significantly change the situation he is studying, forcing to some extent all participants to redefine it and modify their actions accordingly, it is clear that the work of social science researchers has to depart still further from any aspired natural science model in a way that transcends the differences in subject matter previously noted (Mayo in his identification of the 'Hawthorne' effect early alerted social scientists to this range of possibilities of distortion in social scientific research).

It is clear then that the position of the anti-positivists is likely to be as 'ambiguous' as that of the positivists they reject. Shipman (1972 ii) has alleged that 'the new perspectives, whilst rejecting conventional scientific methods and forms of proof, do not advance any alternatives' In the same publication he also reminds us that the phenomenological view that man constructs social reality must logically preclude the acceptance of any general concept such as 'social class' as a given fact of life.[4] Commenting on 'the failure of phenomenologists to recognise this limitation' he asserts that:

> In practice, those using phenomenological and interactionist perspectives should be the first to acknowledge publicly that their evidence is the joint product of the scenes they observe and the eyes with which they do the observing. Social phenomenologists in particular, having exposed the ideological bias in the Sociology of Education and among teachers, have then used phenomenology as a screen for their own slanted views.

Berger and Berger (1971 p. 295) have also suggested that one attraction of the phenomenological approach lies in its capacity to apparently legitimize almost any argument to overthrow existing behavioural norms. Indeed it is in its relativistic nature that phenomenology faces its greatest dilemma.

Gouldner (1971 p.495) sees this as a 'reflexive sociology'. He writes:

> A reflexive sociology, then, is not characterised by *what* it studies. It is distinguished neither by the persons nor the problems studied nor even by the techniques and instruments used in studying them. It is characterised, rather, by the *relationship* it establishes between being a sociologist and being a person, between the role and the man performing it. A reflexive sociology embodies a critique of the conventional conception of segregated scholarly roles and has a vision of an alternative. It aims at transforming the sociologist's relation to his work.[5]

The 'liberation' of the phenomenological approach has led a number of sociologists to an enthusiasm to go beyond a latent level of interpretation of data and analysis and to undertake a research in which their own value orientations are manifest; in which, in fact, their views are part of the subject matter of the research. This leads to a research that is likely to support their own values and aspirations in, say, social policy on matters such as industrial co-operation, social security and rehousing or, more generally, to undertake research that is likely to justify arguments in favour of 'changing the system'. An outstanding recent example is to be found in Halsey (1972) where, using to the full the concept of 'action research', the investigation is progressively developed to further a desired social change — the achievement of greater fairness in the distribution of educational resources within the educational priority areas. The work is notable however not only for the advocacy but also for the quality of the research presentation.

All this is not wholly new; it has been a longstanding appraisal of much sociological research that, almost predictably, its findings tend to justify the further development of 'socialist' policies. It is arguable that the structural functionalist approach that has dominated sociology in the past (and which has the doubtful advantage of compatibility with the 'pure science model') has a persistent though latent value assertion. What is new is the open conflict between those sociologists who believe that they can minimize and, hopefully, eradicate investigator variables of this nature and those who are willing to espouse them and to use them to their advantage. Certainly the concept of research with the concepts and theories that guide it has broadened during the debate: even to the point where it may be seen as subjective and arbitrary rather than definitive and absolute. Such a view, as the more perceptive phenomenologists realize, can only mean that the new approaches themselves may also be ephemeral and transitory.

The conflict in education

This brief résumé of some of the major aspects of the current conflict in research in sociology has been a necessary prelude for consideration of the present state of research in the sociology of education. For not only are all these positions found in educational research; the sociology of education provides major examples of all of them.

Of the establishment of research in the sociology of education there can be little doubt. The only two incumbents of the DES post of Research Adviser established in the early 1960s have both been sociologists with substantial research interests in education. Both the past and the present Directors of Research of the Inner London Education Authority, Britain's largest education authority, have been sociologists. The University of London Institute of Education has its own major research unit in the sociology of education and has recently appointed a sociologist as the Director of the Institute. Substantial research projects in the field exist in many institutions. The number of members of the British Sociological Association citing education as a field of interest outnumbers all other named research areas. Major educational research organizations such as the Committee for Educational Research and Innovation of the OECD (OECD 1971) have regularly staffed research groups with sociological personnel; the International Sociological Association has recently established a research group in the sociology of education.

There are many reasons for this apparent position of strength. The school system represents one of the last surviving institutions in modern societies which all are obliged to experience. Moreover, its duration is extending with recent extensions to the compulsory attendance period in many countries and a growing enthusiasm to experience voluntary continuation in schools, colleges, universities, polytechnics and other institutions, culminating in the concept of *l'éducation permanante*. Schooling has an undeniable effect on human behaviour and on the interaction of its members, as Shipman has demonstrated in his study of childhood (Shipman 1972 ii). Moreover, that it can be seen to modify or reinforce behaviour patterns, roles and status opportunities, values and structures at both micro and macro levels is hardly surprising.

But another fundamental source of strength in the sociology of education is its long established tradition of research – a tradition of possibly greater duration than in any other field of sociological investigation. The political arithmetic studies of Gray and Moshinsky (1938) themselves sprang from the analyses of earlier government statistics on educational distribution and achievement. From these developed the studies of Glass (1954) and others on social mobility using social survey techniques in which the sections on the distribution of educational opportunity formed a major part. Here the early work of Floud, Halsey, Martin and others on social class and educational opportunity emerged – work that was to dominate developments in the sociology of education in the 1950s and subsequently. A range of important work sprang from these beginnings, including the researches of Jackson and Marsden (1962), of Douglas and his colleagues (1964) and of many other investigators who were intrigued by the social factors that appear to influence if not even govern access to education, achievement in it and the consequences of it.

This area of study, with others, will be considered later in the book with reference to the specific papers in its appropriate section. Here it is of importance to recognize its major sociological importance. Its methodology for the most part assisted the development of sociology in its bid for scientific respectability, but at the same time it genuinely furthered new sociological understandings. Particularly, it emphasized the significance of social structure and the individual's relationship to it. It allowed the development of new and recognizably sociological concepts concerning matters such as social mobility – for example, Turner's two concepts of sponsored and contest mobility (Turner 1961) which have attracted continued debate ever since (Hopper 1971). In doing so it enabled the sociologists in education to establish an alternative framework to the previously dominant psychology of individual differences with their assumed predictive nature.

The 'social class and educational opportunity' era was essentially one of structural functionalism with theoretical orientations of economic determinism and cultural discontinuity.[6] In 1961 Halsey, Floud and Anderson, introducing a representative collection of papers in the sociology of education, were able to write:

> Thus modern industrial societies are distinguished in their structure
> and development from others of comparable complexity,
> principally by the institutionalization of innovation — that is to
> say by the public and private organization on an increasingly
> large scale of scientific research in the service of economic and
> military growth. Their occupational structures are characteristic-
> ally diversified with relatively high educational qualifications for
> employment at all levels but the lowest. Education attains
> unprecedented economic importance as a source of technological
> innovation and the education system is bent increasingly to the
> service of the labour force, acting as a vast apparatus of
> occupational recruitment and training.

The use of sociological research in education

The implications of certainty and predictability that can be glimpsed
even in this quotation certainly helped to lead to the rapid exploitation
of 'sociological research evidence' by a range of pressure groups
advocating social and educational policies, in some ways in anticipation
of the explicit value commitment of subsequent sociologists. The social
distribution of education identified by the research of sociologists
became reidentified as the social maldistribution of educational
opportunity. Their evidence was used to particularly powerful effect
by the advocates of secondary school reorganization. An even more
striking example of the use, or even abuse, of research finding in
education is on the topic of streaming. Here again the work of
sociologists and psychologists had been used to lend legitimacy to
arguments against ability streaming in primary and, later, in secondary
schools — arguments that have in many areas been won even though the
research findings in the matter are, at best, inconclusive.[7]

Yet out of all this confusion and uncertainty new approaches in the
sociology of education have flourished. The more dynamic approaches
of European sociologists such as Bourdieu and Luscher (1971) in their
analyses of European systems were matched by a growing concern in
Britain and America to recognize that conflict theories offered a more
realistic framework than structural functionalism. The conflicting use
made of existing research reports made the point readily; the use of
similar sociological evidence to support the arguments in both the
'Black Papers' and the 'Red Paper' alerted many sociologists to the
oversimplifications of the consensus view implicit in many functionalist
approaches.[8] An important by-product of the development of conflict
approaches was that they enabled sociologists to understand more fully
the ways in which pressure groups acted and in this way they were able
to anticipate more usefully the likely uses that were to be made of
their findings. This has had its own important consequences on the
presentation of results.

Interactionist and phenomenological perspectives in education

The study of conflict in schools was facilitated by the development, in
other areas of sociological research, of new techniques for organization-

al analysis and role studies which had a ready application to the study of schools and which will be considered later in this volume. But matters were taken still further by the development in sociology of interactionist and phenomenological approaches which opened up a potentially rich and rewarding field of strategies for examining school and classroom behaviour. Writing on this theme Gorbutt (1972 p.8) has noted:

> Clearly teachers' subject and pedagogical perspectives have implications for the way in which they organize children's learning, assess their success and so on. If we take the notion that intelligence is not an intrinsic quality of the child but is imputed to him by others then we can ask questions like how does the teacher define an intelligent child? What is the implicit concept of intelligence being used by the teacher and where did he acquire it? Are the teacher's judgments about intelligence linked to his belief about social class? Through an understanding of the socially constructed nature of teachers' subject and pedagogical perspectives and their constituent categories we can gain new insights into the determinants of teaching and learning activities in classrooms.

But the emergence of these new perspectives also alerted sociologists in education to the manner in which research problems had been taken up. Young (1971) points out that researchers in education, including socio- logists, have 'taken' educators' problems as given and in their inquiries on these 'given' problems, such as the achievement of working class children, the content of the curriculum, the attainment of curriculum objectives and the like, have accepted the educators' definition of the situation with all its assumptions and interpretations unchallenged. Certainly the early research on the determinants of 'educational opportunity' treated as unproblematic the concept of 'what it is to be educated' or the nature of the education pupils fail at.

Brandis and Henderson made this clear in concluding their research study *Social Class, Language and Communication* (1971):

> In all work concerned with comparative socialisation within a society, there is always a danger that the differences such studies reveal will be transformed into statements of 'better' or 'worse'. This is particularly the case where the groups involved are social class groups and the socialisation is into the school. Once such judgments are made, implicitly or explicitly, that one form of socialisation is 'better' than another it is but a short step to consider how we can transform the 'worse' into the 'better'. Can we make the working-class as the middle-class? This question is based upon the dubious premise that socialisation within contemporary middle-class strata and the education we offer in the schools represents the acme of three quarters of a million years of civilisation. It equally and inevitably leads on to a view of the child as a deficit system, his parents as inadequate and their culture as deprived. The very form our research takes reinforces this view. It shows nearly always what the middle-class *do* and what the working-class do *not* do in relation to the middle-class.

For Young (1971) and his co-authors the important task facing researchers in the sociology of education is to 'make' rather than 'take' problems. An essential part of this task is to regard 'what it is that counts as educational knowledge as problematic'. Bernstein writing in the same volume points out that 'how a society selects, classifies, distributes, transmits and evaluates the educational knowledge it considers to be public reflects both the distribution of power and the principles of social control'. He goes on to identify as an important yet previously largely unexamined research area these processes of selection, classification, distribution, transmission and evaluation of knowledge.

The phenomenological contribution to the sociology of education as to sociology in general has been to reaffirm the importance of the study of the sociology of knowledge as a central research area. In particular this leads to a focusing of interest on the sociology of the curriculum with the realization, for example, that the curriculum of the comprehensive school may be far more powerful in its selective effects than separate secondary schools ever were.[9] (An indication of the possible nature of the outcome of the new approaches is given in the introduction to section I of this volume.)

These new and often relativistic approaches with their important implications for earlier research in the sociology of education are being given wide diffusion, notably through the medium of the Open University courses in education. The result has been the generation of a very great degree of uncertainty and, in places, the suspension of judgement on research finding in the sociology of education. The realization that the very concept of research is itself arbitrary and subjective and that the theories and concepts that guide it may be transitory and unstable is deeply disturbing to many.

This is not necessarily a harmful state of affairs; indeed, it may be healthy. Yet it would be unfortunate and wasteful if the long research tradition in the sociology of education came to be ignored or abandoned. Not only does it provide the platform on which the present debate stands (in that it provides legitimation for it) but it also provides the base for development of understanding by providing a still continuing series of major new studies that can be illuminated by the new approaches. The point may be made by citing two of the major ongoing programmes (both represented in this volume). The work of Hargreaves (1967) and Lacey (1970) both springing from a major research initiative at the University of Manchester have unquestionably added to our knowledge of life in classrooms. The work of the Sociological Research Unit directed by Bernstein (Brandis and Henderson 1970; Gahagan and Gahagan 1971; Turner and Mohan 1971; Bernstein 1971, 1972; Robinson and Rackstraw 1972) has revealed much that was previously unknown of the subtle links between language, values and schooling. Both programmes, though rooted in the 'normative' paradigms, are widely regarded as making important contributions to the 'interpretative' paradigm. In short the relationship between the two paradigms is incremental rather than destructive (Eggleston 1973).

Theory and method in the sociology of education [10]

Each of these studies as well as those in this volume may be viewed from a narrow perspective. Seen by functionalists they may be regarded as illustrating the essential selective mechanisms required by society and operated through the school system. By phenomenologists they may be seen to offer important evidence of the capacity of the individual, in various social situations, to achieve different constructions of reality arising from different definitions of the system. Yet a careful reading of each of the research studies presented in this volume will make it clear that these or any other 'blinkered' interpretations are not only insufficient but also misleading. If the new approaches to the sociology of education can be seen as complementary rather than destructive to those that preceded them then this can only do good and enhance the sensitivity with which research is hypothesized, conducted and interpreted. The range of theoretical orientations now available in sociology and the sociology of education runs from structural functionalism (with its Marxist variations of functional conflict) through conflict theories to the full range of interactionist perspectives offering the opportunity to explore not only macro questions but also micro ones using techniques of role study and organizational and interactive analyses in the schools. [11]

In a similar way extensions in the range of the methodologies of research enhance the research potential in the field. Bruyn (1966) has suggested that there are two polar modes of scientific inquiry in sociology. One is traditional empiricism and the other participant observation. The full range of research strategies within this spectrum can be seen in the papers in this volume. They include survey techniques and questionnaire approaches, documentary and comparative studies, case studies, sociometric and participant observation studies. All have major disadvantages as well as advantages, as Shipman has noted (1972 i), but for an area of human interaction so complex as education, the use of the fullest range of techniques available is not only appropriate but also necessary. No one methodology is likely to be sufficient to explore any major area of inquiry and any attempt to prescribe a single strategy can only lead to unnecessary restriction. Sociologists who wish to wait, for example, for the development of 'proper phenomenological research methodologies' that will give 'proper phenomenological research' are making a mistake just as great as did the singleminded functionalists whom they criticize. Both have a model of research purity that is as inappropriate for the data as it is for their orientations and, indeed, for sociology.

It will now be clear that the range of papers that follow in this volume range widely in perspective, methodology and theory. The presentation would have been incomplete if it were otherwise and the purposes outlined at the start of this chapter would have been made unattainable. But another important purpose has been emphasized in the subsequent discussion. There is a real danger that enthusiasm for new approaches may lead to the discredit of older ones,and, conversely, that sociologists committed to the longer established approaches may ignore the insights afforded by the new ones. Neither sociology nor the sociology of education can afford to waste its still limited assets in this way. Still less can it survive a situation in which a succession of changing orientations regularly call for the abandonment of most of what has been achieved before. As has already been noted, revolutions are predominantly incremental rather than annihilistic in character. This collection seeks to identify even more sharply the conflict so that the debate is enhanced and made more fruitful. But it also seeks to communicate the importance of the various kinds of research activities in a way that will show their continuing utility to all participants in the sociology of education, researchers, students, clients and combatants and above all to the teachers and students in the schools. The importance of effective communication cannot be overemphasized. It would be a tragedy if sociologists came to know more about the school and yet be understood less by those who work there.

The book is divided into five sections: the distribution of educational achievement, the availability of educational provision, the organization of the school, roles and interaction in the school, and values and learning. Each section is preceded by a brief editorial introduction to the papers. Although the selection is designed to be both developmental and representative it must also be arbitrary and partial. In particular several major areas of work have not been covered. These include the study of social change which, although of fundamental importance in the field of education, is handicapped by the theoretical uncertainty and the practical difficulty of formulating and testing useful hypotheses. Also omitted is the important and rapidly developing field of socio-linguistic studies in education, partly because of the impossibility of adequately representing such an open ended area in a volume of this nature and also because of the ready availability of extensive reading in this field (see for example the volumes in the Penguin Modern Linguistics Readings series; Pride and Holmes (1972) and Laver and Hutcheson (1972)). Historical research in the sociology of education has been omitted for similar reasons even though it was with particular regret that the work of writers such as Vaughan and Archer (1971) was excluded.

In conclusion it should be mentioned that though the volume is concerned with both theory and methodology, major discussions of these areas have been avoided as they are properly the scope of other volumes, In particular the developments in the theory of the sociology of education have recently been explored in the contributions to a reader edited by Hopper (1971). Methodology is adequately covered by the proliferation of readers in this field, a notable source being the annual volumes on sociological methodology published for the American Sociological Association (in particular Borgatta 1969, Costner 1972) that provide valuable sources for the discussion of recent methodological issues applicable to the sociology of education.

Notes

[1] The restrictive legitimacy of the arts subjects is itself an important but relatively unstudied field of sociological inquiry (the work of Bourdieu (1967) is of particular importance here).

[2] Interestingly Durkheim's *Suicide* is itself an example of institutionalized constraints on research and its definition.

[3] The writings of Schutz (1964) contain valuable extended discussions of pure science models of research in the social sciences, particularly of 'second order' constraints.

[4] Though one of the achievements of phenomenology is the new approach it offers to 'social class' that springs from the work of Runciman (1964).

[5] The nature of phenomenology is valuably explored in the debate between Gouldner and Becker in Goulas (1970).

[6] An interesting reappraisal of the theoretical orientations of the period is to be found in a recent paper by Halsey (1971).

[7] For a discussion on research and the streaming controversy see Shipman (1971 i pp.117-21). Education indeed has a history of the selective and 'self-sustaining' use of research findings. The response to research on class size is an often quoted cautionary tale (Hajnal 1972, pp.178-80). Another characteristic problem is the willingness of advocates to mix research with non-research findings, notably the use of works by writers such as Holt which are seldom supported by identifiable evidence. Of interest is the number of pressure groups that have established their own research departments or committees — there are many examples including the sponsors of the Initial Teaching Alphabet and the Comprehensive Schools Committee, as well as the teachers' organizations which not only have research departments but also 'commission' research on major political issues. Acland (1973) has attempted to classify educational research into two models, 'direct' and 'indirect'. In direct research the questions are formulated by the researcher and are therefore likely to be researchable questions: in indirect research the questions are fomulated by policymakers and may not necessarily be researchable. Though the models are useful conceptual tools, Acland's subsequent analysis indicates the extreme difficulty of categorizing existing educational research in this way and emphasizes the problem of applying a pure science research model in this field.

[8] Yet elsewhere in education the simple faith in a consensus model persists — as, for instance, in the model generally adopted to explore curriculum development, in which teachers are assumed to be able to act unanimously in setting their objectives and often in developing teaching methods as well. Yet such a model can be seen to be not only misleadingly simplified but also out of touch with the reality of the day-to-day thinking of teachers, as any observer who has spent even a brief period of time in a school

staffroom comes to realize. For a discussion of this issue see Eggleston (1976).

[9] A fuller discussion of the sociology of the curriculum is to be found in Eggleston (1976).

[10] The distinction between theory and method is itself an arbitrary and arguable one as phenomenologists have noted (Cicourel 1964, Phillipson 1972).

[11] Swift (1973) presents a valuable typology of theoretical orientations in the sociology and psychology of education in which the theoretical distinctions and complementarities between and within the two disciplines are explored. In this collection several papers, notably those by Lundgren and Marjoribanks, illustrate the possibilities of a complementary approach between the two disciplines.

References

ACLAND, H., 1973, *Social Determinants of Educational Achievement.* Oxford: unpublished D.Phil.thesis.

BERGER, P.L., and BERGER, B., 1972, *Sociology, a Biographical Approach.* New York: Basic Books.

BERGER, P.L. and LUCKMAN, T., 1971, *The Social Construction of Reality.* London: Penguin.

BERNSTEIN, B.B. (ed.), 1971, 1973, *Class, Codes and Control. Volume I: Theoretical Studies towards a Sociology of Language. Volume II: Applied Studies towards a Sociology of Language.* London: Routledge and Kegan Paul.

BORGATTA, E.F. (ed.), 1969, *Sociological Methodology.* San Francisco: Jossey Bass.

BOURDIEU, P., 1967, 'Systems of education and systems of thought'. *International Social Science Journal,* 19(3).

BRANDIS, W., and HENDERSON, D., 1970, *Social Class, Language and Communication.* London: Routledge and Kegan Paul.

BRUYN, P., 1966, *The Human Perspective in Sociology.* New York: Prentice-Hall.

CICOUREL, A.V., 1964, *Method and Measurement in Sociology.* Glencoe, Ill.: Free Press.

CICOUREL, A.V., and KITSUSE, J.I., 1963, *The Educational Decision Makers.* Indianapolis: Bobbs-Merrill.

COSTNER, H.L. (ed.), 1971, *Sociological Methodology.* San Francisco: Jossey Bass.

DOUGLAS, J. 1970, *The Relevance of Sociology.* New York: Appleton-Century-Crofts.

DOUGLAS, J.W.B., 1964, *The Home and the School.* London: MacGibbon and Kee.

EGGLESTON, J., 1973, 'Knowledge and the school curriculum'. *Education for Teaching,* 91

EGGLESTON, J., 1976, *The Sociology of the School Curriculum.* London: Routledge and Kegan Paul.

FLOUD, J., HALSEY, A.H., and MARTIN, P., 1956, *Social Class and Educational Opportunity.* London: Heinemann.

GAHAGAN, D.M. and GAHAGAN, G.A., 1971, *Talk Reform.* London: Routledge and Kegan Paul.

GARFINKEL, H., 1967, *Studies in Ethnomethodology.* Englewood Cliffs: Prentice-Hall.

GLASS, D.V. (ed), 1954, *Social Mobility in Britain.* London: Routledge and Kegan Paul.

GORBUTT, D., 1972, 'The new sociology of teaching'. *Education for Teaching,* 89

GOULDNER, A., 1971, *The Coming Crisis in Modern Sociology.* London: Heinemann.

GRAY, J.L., and MOSHINSKY, P., 1938, in Hogben, L.T. (ed.), *Political Arithmetic.* London: Gollancz.

HAJNAL, J., 1971, *The Student Trap.* London: Penguin.

HALSEY, A.H., 1971, 'Theoretical advance and empirical challenge' in Hopper, E., (ed.), *Readings in the Theory of Educational Systems.* London: Hutchinson.

HALSEY, A.H. (ed.), 1972, *Educational Priority.* London: HMSO.

HALSEY, A.H., FLOUD, J., and ANDERSON, C.A. (eds.), 1961, *Education, Economy and Society.* Glencoe, Ill.: Free Press.

HARGREAVES, D.H., 1967, *Social Relations in a Secondary School.* London: Routledge and Kegan Paul.

HOPPER, E., 1971, *Readings in the Theory of Educational Systems.* London: Hutchinson.

JACKSON, B. and MARSDEN, D., 1962, *Education and the Working Class.* London: Routledge and Kegan Paul.

KUHN, T.S., 1970, *The Structure of Scientific Revolutions.* Chicago: University Press.

LACEY, C., 1970, *Hightown Grammar.* Manchester: University Press.

LAVER, J.G., and HUTCHESON, S., 1972, *Communication in Face to Face Interaction.* London: Penguin.

LUSCHER, K., 1971, 'Sociology and educational research'. *Education,* Hamburg: Institute for Scientific Co-operation, 4, pp.22-30.

OECD, 1971, *Centre for Educational Research and Innovation.* Paris: OECD

PHILLIPSON, M., 1972, 'Theory, methodology and conceptualisation' in Filmer, P., Phillipson, M., Silverman, D. and Walsh, D., *New Directions in Sociological Theory.* London: Collier-Macmillan.

PRIDE, J.B., and HOLMES, J., 1972, *Sociolinguistics.* London: Penguin.

RUNCIMAN, W.G., 1964, 'Embourgeoisement, self-rated class and party preference'. *Sociological Review,* 12(2).

ROBINSON, W.P., and RACKSTRAW, S.J., 1972, *A Question of Answers.* London: Routledge and Kegan Paul.

SCHUTZ, A., 1964, *Collected Papers.* The Hague: Martinus Nijhoff.

SHIPMAN, M.D., 1972 (i), *The Limitations of Social Research.* London: Longmans.

SHIPMAN, M.D., 1972 (ii), *Childhood, a Sociological Perspective.* Slough; NFER.

SWIFT, D.F., 1973, 'Sociology and educational research' in Taylor, W. (ed.), *Research Perspectives in Education.* London: Routledge and Kegan Paul.

TURNER, R.H., 1961, 'Modes of social ascent through education: sponsored and contest mobility', in Halsey, A.H., Floud, J. and Anderson, C.A. (eds.), *Education, Economy and Society*. Glencoe, Ill.: Free Press, pp.121-30.

TURNER, G.J., and MOHAN, B.A., 1971, *A Linguistic Description and Computer Program for Children's Speech*. London: Routledge and Kegan Paul.

VAUGHAN, M., and ARCHER, M.S., 1971, *Social Conflict and Educational Change in England and France 1789-1848*. Cambridge: University Press.

YOUNG, M.F.D. (ed.), 1971, *Knowledge and Control*. London: Collier-Macmillan.

I The distribution of educational achievement

INTRODUCTION

Papers in this section represent some of the major contributions by sociologists to the exploration of the relationship of environmental differences to such differences as access to schools, the duration of school life, success in examinations, entry to higher education — in short the study of differences in educational opportunity. This field has attracted countless researchers and many major studies exist. Yet at first glance it appears to fall neatly into the category of 'taken problems' identified by Young (1971) in that it takes as given the educators' definition both of success and the desirability of success in the educational system. It is a definition that goes on to identify those who do not succeed as in some way deficient and calls for strategies to eliminate or at least to alleviate these deficiencies (increasingly seen as 'cultural') so that children may be 'restored to their rightful place in the socialization and selective process' and thereby 'compete on equal terms'. Such views embody a range of assumptions about the nature and desirability of both achievement and non-achievement and the ways in which they occur and can be modified. They appear to leave unquestioned such concepts as 'success' and 'deficiency' and the processes whereby they are defined. In doing so they allow a major value judgement to remain in what is normally regarded as a value free area of investigation.

It is in the appraisal of studies of the distribution of educational achievement that the new 'interpretative' paradigms of the phenomenologists appear to have made their greatest impact on the traditional or 'normative' paradigms within which most of the work was undertaken. Yet it is precisely in this area that the case may be made for regarding the new paradigms as restructuring rather than destructuring devices. (It is useful to remember that Kuhn's (1970) model of scientific revolutions, often quoted by phenomenologists, is just such a process of restructuring, and does not imply the dismissal of previous knowledge but rather the incremental nature of understanding.)

The incremental characteristics of the new perspectives may perhaps be illustrated by the three models in the diagram overleaf. These models are not only incremental in that (2) springs from (1), and (3) springs from (2), but also in that they demonstrate the new contributions of the new approaches.

In the 'pre-sociological' model (1) the distribution of opportunity and achievement were not so much 'taken problems' as non-problems until the investigations of sociologists took place. Certainly in England and Wales the educator's problem was expressed in terms that were

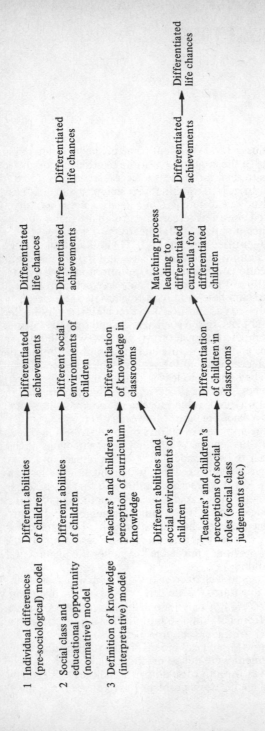

1 Individual differences (pre-sociological) model

Different abilities of children → Differentiated achievements → Differentiated life chances

2 Social class and educational opportunity (normative) model

Different abilities of children → Different social environments of children → Differentiated achievements → Differentiated life chances

3 Definition of knowledge (interpretative) model

Teachers' and children's perception of curriculum knowledge → Differentiation of knowledge in classrooms

Different abilities and social environments of children → Differentiation of knowledge in classrooms

Teachers' and children's perceptions of social roles (social class judgements etc.) → Differentiation of children in classrooms

Differentiation of knowledge in classrooms → Matching process leading to differentiated curricula for differentiated children

Differentiation of children in classrooms → Matching process leading to differentiated curricula for differentiated children

Matching process leading to differentiated curricula for differentiated children → Differentiated achievements → Differentiated life chances

notably different; the task was seen to be one of ensuring that
children could receive an education appropriate to their measured
aptitude and ability. Indeed subsequent events could be interpreted in
a way that suggests that educators have 'taken' the sociologists'
problems.

The 1944 Education Act and the reorganization of selective
secondary education that followed it led to the establishment of a
major selective mechanism, designed to identify and select children,
that ranged from streaming in the primary school through to school
leaving examinations and differentiated higher education. The centre
piece of this mechanism was the 'eleven plus' examination. Representing possibly the zenith of psychological influence on educational
administration it claimed, to within a generally estimated tolerance
of 5 per cent, accuracy of assessments of capacity for secondary
schooling, and above all, predictability.

The early years after 1944 did indeed present dramatic changes
in the pattern of entry to selective secondary schools. Many more
working class children came to enter them now that the entry
requirements were solely expressed in terms of eleven plus
selection and, apart from the direct grant grammar schools, no fees
were required. The changes were sufficient to reassure a Labour
government and the population at large that a sufficient — possibly
even an excessive — move to egalitarianism had taken place. It was left
to Floud and her colleagues in Watford and Middlesborough, in work
springing from the London School of Economics social mobility
studies, to show that there still remained a substantial difference
in class chances of access to the selective secondary schools (Floud
1958, p.43). She was able to show, for instance, that the sons of
professional workers had a chance of entry to selective schooling
at eleven plus that was some ten times greater than that of the sons of
manual workers.

In this stage of certainty about eleven plus procedures figures of
this order were seen as no more than an anticipated class distribution
of ability and appeared to confirm the general pattern of expectations
about the genetic superiority of middle class children. It was the
secondary modern schools that, with their student populations defined
as of average and below average ability and both unable and unsuitable
to take public examinations and achieve high occupational and social
status, made the major challenge to these assumptions. In the 1950s a
number of these schools found ways of enabling their students to enter
and succeed in these examinations and, as Taylor (1963) showed, they
were able to contract back into the competitive world of educational
and social advancement from which they had been excluded at eleven.
Yet one of the most convincing and, possibly, ingenious demonstrations
of the sociological point was made by Floud in her re-analysis of some
of the unprecedented range of statistical evidence accrued by the
Crowther Committee (Crowther Report 1958). In a brief paper
reprinted in this collection she shows that ability to pass the eleven plus
was socially differentiated but that ability itself appeared to be far less
so. A picture emerges from her figures of middle class environments in

which the development of ability, or at least that kind of ability needed to pass the eleven plus, appears to take place more rapidly than in working class homes, but that by eighteen plus differences in this ability are far less socially differentiated. To put it simply, the working class children had in many cases 'caught-up' — but too late to 'benefit' from an age and ability linked selective educational system. Work of this nature firmly established the second model (the normative paradigm) indicated in the diagram.

The political implications of these and similar findings were immense. Much of the relative success of the campaign for comprehensive education must be attributed to the legitimation of the arguments allowed by such evidence. But, perhaps more importantly, the potential of the work of the individual teacher was seen to be substantially enhanced by the realization that environmental factors appear to affect the distribution and development of ability.

The point has been simply put by Husén (1972) when he says:

Since it is the task of the educator to bring about worthwhile changes in a growing up or grown up individual, and since modifications due to environmental influences, and not those due to genetical influences, are the ones that are accessible to direct observation and measurement, it would seem that the burden of proof as to how genetic factors act as restraints to educational endeavours rests with the advocate of the hereditarian, not the environmental, view.

Yet the implications for sociological research were less successful. Enthusiasm to explore environmental factors leading to different intellectual and educational attainments led to a rash of studies, many of indifferent quality, that explored every environmental variable from furniture and floor covering to newspaper reading, often with a very incomplete perception of social class as a cultural factor.[1] Unfortunate attempts to investigate correlations with environmental aggregates that had little meaning in terms of individual human environment were made using 'pure' and sociologically insensitive scientific methodology (see, for example, Wiseman (1964)). The opportunity to develop the somewhat limited functionalist theoretical basis of the early studies based upon 'the thesis of a tightening bond between education and occupation in advanced industrial societies' (Halsey 1971) with its strong Durkheimian implications was not always taken. But, as Halsey goes on to record, more recent studies in the past decade have demonstrated the considerable remaining potential for well-conceived and soundly based research in this area.

Some assistance in helping research to escape from its preoccupation with access and achievement in selective secondary schooling came from the gradual moves to comprehensive schooling that demonstrated, as did subsequent moves to destreaming, that labels such as 'grammar' and 'A-stream' were themselves somewhat unreliable and even mis-leading guides to social reality (Ford 1969, Barker Lunn 1970). But the main breakthrough occurred when sociologists came more clearly to concern themselves with identifiable causal factors rather than correlated categories. It was at this stage that the most important contributions of the normative paradigm occurred and the insights that were to give rise to the interpretative paradigm came to be available. The critical event was the identification of the importance of value patterns, of family, community and school, and the associated language structures that carry them. In the detailed analysis of environmental values and their transmission, the work of Bernstein and his colleagues in the Sociological Research Unit (which has already been mentioned in the introduction to this volume) is outstanding and an important example of this work is presented in the final section. Another central figure is Bourdieu. Like Bernstein, much of Bourdieu's work springs firmly from the 'normative' paradigm yet is of central importance in the 'interpretative' paradigm. In this section one of Bourdieu's early papers illustrates his conceptualization of the problems of the distribution of ability and his recognition of the causal influence of values — particularly those of the school. Though not strictly a research paper it is included because of its outstanding development of research hypotheses which have been explored in Bourdieu's later work. The publication of this relatively inaccessible paper will make available an important contribution to the appraisal of Bourdieu's work.

Subsequently the paper by Craft illustrates the fruitfulness of the research that can now be developed in the exploration of differential achievements and values, here demonstrated in work on the school system of Ireland. Both papers illustrate the particular importance of the values of the school system itself in the development of opportunity; a theme that is referred to more fully in section III of this volume.

A further development of causal analyses is the intensive detailed study of small populations. Papers of this kind are now appearing from most educational systems. One example of many is *Social Disadvantage and Educational Opportunity* (Uildriks 1972). This is a case study of fifty individual cases from two working class neighbourhoods in Holland. A brief, unpretentious, but valuable example of this category of paper is included here. In it Marjoribanks, using a relatively simple statistical technique, indicates effectively that, in his population, the family value factors are of greater significance in educational achievement than either those of family status or family structure. The inclusion of Marjoribanks's paper serves a further purpose in that it offers a useful demonstration of the contribution that 'psychological approaches' can make when they are sociologically sensitive.[2] As Swift has reminded us, the cross-fertilization of psychological and sociological research offers one of the more effective ways forward towards the understanding of educational arrangements (Swift 1973).

But it is not only the values of the home and the school that are critical in the experience of schooling; there are also those that spring from peer group and community. There is a long literature here still dominated by seminal works such as Coleman's *Adolescent Society* (1961), and Rogoff's study of local community structure (1961). Yet research findings in this area like those on social class and the family must be treated with some suspicion (see for example the discussion by Jahoda and Warren (1965)) — suspicion springing in part from the realization that youth groups and communities may be at times no more than statistical aggregates which, like others referred to earlier, may have little meaning in terms of human environment. More recent work, like the Swedish studies of Andersson (1970) in the Youth in Göteborg project, have benefited from the critiques of early researches.[3]

But it is to participant studies that we must still look for the greatest illumination on the values of groups of young people and of the community. Since the early work of Thrasher (1927) this has continued to be a major source of information and the recent attentions of social interactionists have underlined its significance. The recent study of Patrick (1973) on the values and interactions of a Glasgow gang, with its particular sensitivity to the values of teachers, is an impressive new example of this genre and parts of the study are included in section V of this volume.

An important feature of such studies and the papers by Bourdieu and Craft is that, though they appear in part to 'take the educator's problems', they also 'take' the problems of parents, students and other involved members of the community. If it happens, for whatever reason, that the ways in which educators define their problems have similarities with the ways in which parents, adolescents and the community define theirs, then it is important for sociologists to recognize this similarity even though they may properly go on, as do Bourdieu and Craft, to ask how and why the similarity of definition exists.

This is not to say that the reformulations indicated by the phenomenologists have already been taken account of in research in this field. Many of the assumptions of cultural dissonance which define working class children not only as different but also as deprived and their social environment as inadequate are still deeply embedded in both hypotheses and interpretation. We have yet to experience in this field fully developed research which explores hypotheses that spring from a realization of the importance of the definition of knowledge that dominates the 'interpretative' paradigm. Such studies, as the diagram indicates, would explore the ways in which the teachers' and childrens' perception of curriculum knowledge and of the social system, acting through differentiated classroom situations, leads to differentiated achievements.[4]

It is clear that, in the exploration of educational achievement, the new paradigm offers vast research potential; research that has yet to be undertaken but that will spring logically from the best of the work of the normative paradigm that is exemplified in this section.

Notes

[1] Readers who seek a comprehensive and up-to-date guide to some of the more reliable research in this field are recommended to Husen's OECD survey *Social Background and Educational Career* (1972).

[2] A further development of Marjoribanks's work is to be found in 'Ethnicity and learning patterns' (1972).

[3] Work of this nature may offer a useful corrective to studies that may appear to overemphasize social class variables in education. Musgrove

(1967) discussing his own work with adolescent students writes:

> I found no differences in attitude to school (or home) among children of different social background. Middle class children were as critical of the constraints and bureaucratic features of their grammar schools as working class children. At least with regard to the values I am talking about — personal and domestic values, concern for genuineness and dislike of impersonal organisation — we seem to have few social class differences. The main social class difference appears to be in levels of social and occupational aspirations; and it is in this sphere that schools appear to be most effective in reducing social class differences.

Witkin's paper (section V of this volume) is relevant in this connection.
[4] Important preliminary work on school interaction has occurred however and is discussed in section V of this volume.

References

ANDERSSON, B.E., 1969, *Studies in Adolescent Behaviour*. Stockholm: Almqvist and Wiksell.

BARKER LUNN, J.C., 1970, *Streaming in the Primary School*. Slough: NFER.

BERNSTEIN, B., 1971, 'On the classification framing of educational knowledge' in Young, M.F.D., *Knowledge and Control*. London: Collier-Macmillan.

COLEMAN, J., 1961, *The Adolescent Society*. Glencoe, Ill.: Free Press.

'CROWTHER REPORT', 1959, Central Advisory Council for Education (England), 15 to 18. London: HMSO volumes 1 and 2.

FLOUD, J., 1958, in Judges, A.V., *Looking forward in education*. London: Faber and Faber.

FORD, J., 1969, *Social Class and the Comprehensive School*. London: Routledge and Kegan Paul.

HALSEY, A.H., 1971, 'Theoretical advance and empirical challenge' in Hopper, E., (ed.), *Readings in the Theory of Educational Systems*. London: Hutchinson.

HUSEN, T., 1972, *Social Background and Educational Career*. Paris: OECD.

JAHODA, M. and WARREN, N., 1965, 'The myth of youth'. *Sociology of Education*, 38, pp. 138-49.

KUHN, T.S., 1970, *The Structure of Scientific Revolutions*. Chicago: University Press.

MARJORIBANKS, K., 1972, 'Ethnicity and leaving patterns'. *Sociology*, 6(3), pp. 417-31.

MUSGROVE, F., 1967, 'Childhood and adolescence' in Schools Council Working Paper No. 12, *The Educational Implications of Social and Economic Change*. London: HMSO.

PATRICK, J., 1973, *A Glasgow Gang Observed*. London: Eyre Methuen.

ROGOFF, N., 1961, 'Local structure and educational selection' in Halsey, A.H., Floud, J., and Anderson, C.A., (eds.), *Education, Economy and Society*. Glencoe, Ill.: Free Press.

SWIFT, D.F., 1973, 'Sociology and educational research' in Taylor, W. (ed.), *Research Perspectives in Education*. London: Routledge and Kegan Paul.

TAYLOR, W., 1963, *The Secondary Modern School*. London: Faber and Faber.

THRASHER, F.M., 1927, *The Gang*, Chicago: University Press.

UILDRIKS, G., 1972, *Social Disadvantage and Educational Opportunity*. Gent: Laboratorium Voor Experimentele, Differentiele en Genetische Psychologie.

WISEMAN, S., 1964, *Education and Environment*. University of Manchester Press.

YOUNG, M.F.D. (ed.), 1971, *Knowledge and Control*. London: Collier-Macmillan.

JEAN FLOUD

Reserves of ability *

'The pool of ability', as the notion is usually invoked, is not a fact,
but a point of view. It is important to be clear about this. There is no
Iron Law of the national intellect imposing an upper limit on what can
be done by education. What only the outstanding could do yesterday,
the great many can do today (e.g. read, write, multiply); so that
although the gap between the outstanding and the average does not
widen, the educational threshold of mediocrity is continually rising.
Moreover, the challenge produces the response, and the response itself
is self-consolidating. (There is a nice elaboration of this pedagogical
platitude, with reference to the teaching of mathematics, in volume II
of the Crowther Report, p. 206.)

As soon as we can bring ourselves to acknowledge these common-
places we can share the profound and liberating educational
optimism which is the *leitmotiv* of the Crowther Report. But
confidence in the potential yield of the educational plough (to use a
Crowther metaphor) does not make it unnecessary to gauge the task
or estimate the harvest; and this the report does, in striking fashion,
with the aid of three substantial surveys presented in some detail in
volume II. The result is to provide us with the most up-to-date account
available of the social distribution of educational opportunity for boys
in Britain, and a valuable analysis of some of the major social influences
of educability. This short review is confined to some aspects of the
former question of the distribution of educational opportunity.

The report offers a rough-and-ready analysis of the distribution of
what is termed 'latent ability'. This is based on the results of objective
tests administered to recruits to the Armed Forces between eighteen
and twenty-one years of age, in order to decide which of them it will
be more profitable to train for the more skilled, responsible or exacting
tasks. These tests, says the report, are intended to be dependent to the
least extent on the amount of education beyond the minimum that the
recruit has had, and dependent to the greatest extent on his natural
talent. To the degree that this has been achieved, 'the tests serve as an
indication not only of *developed* ability but of ability where it is
latent — that is, where it has not shown itself, in the recruit's progress
up the ladder of formal education' (II, p.114).

* Reprinted from Jean Floud, 'Reserves of ability' 3(2) Forum (spring
  1961) pp. 66-8 (originally published as a review of 15 to 18 (Crowther
  Report)), by kind permission of the author and publishers.

The test battery comprises a non-verbal test of reasoning ability; tests of mechanical knowledge and aptitude, simple arithmetic and mathematics, spelling, comprehension and verbal facility; and a test of ability to understand complex instructions and to carry them out rapidly and accurately. The sum of his scores on all these tests allocates the recruit to one of six so-called 'summed selection groups' dubbed by Crowther (I think unnecessarily and somewhat misleadingly) 'ability groups'. The highest group 1 accounts for approximately 10 per cent of recruits, groups 2 to 5 for another 20 per cent or so each, and group 6 for a final 10 per cent.

The second ability group

In its brief commentary on a valuable series of tables analysing the educational level achieved by boys in these ability groups, the report makes clear its view that the largest pocket of latent ability is of the second order, and located in the main among the 'very important group of skilled workers' sons who provide about half the sampled population and nearly half of the two highest ability groups' (II, p. 127). Most recruits falling into the highest order of ability, it points out, stayed at school at least until the age of sixteen, and sat the 'O' level examinations for the GCE but for the second order of ability the position is different. Of boys in this group, two thirds left school at the minimum age. Only 24 per cent sat the 'O' level GCE examinations; but of these 56 per cent sat in four or more subjects, and the average number of passes per candidate is 3.7. The potential yield is therefore considerable; but it is unevenly distributed among the broad social groups into which recruits were divided on the basis of a conventional classification of their fathers' occupations. One half of the 15 year old leavers in ability group 2 were the sons of skilled manual workers; but within all the ability groups at each educational level 'the distribution by the occupational group of the recruit's father suggests that the educational yield depends very much upon the climate of opinion in each group' (p,117).

It is worth trying to get a more detailed picture from a closer look at the evidence. Of the entire group of recruits, only 2 per cent were graduates or had achieved a comparable educational qualification. This élite accounted for less than one in five (18 per cent) of the young men in the top ability group, and for a minute proportion (1 per cent) of those in the second. Underlying these figures, moreover, are marked social differences. Thus, in ability group 1 the son of a non-manual (professional, managerial or clerical) father is at least twice as likely to have graduated as the son of a manual worker. In ability group 2 the sons of professional and managerial fathers are three times as likely as the sons of skilled workers to have graduated, and at a lower level, three times as likely to have got a good 'A' level GCE (two or more passes) and twice as likely to have got a good 'O' level GCE (four or more passes).

These facts reflect the social distribution of educational opportunity as the following figures show:

Social class differences in the schooling of army recruits (1956-8) at two levels of ability

Secondary schooling	Fathers' occupation									
	Professional and managerial		Clerical and other non-manual		Skilled manual		Semi-skilled manual		Unskilled manual	
	Group 1	Group 2	Group 1	Group 2	Group 1	Group 2	Group 1	Group 2	Group 1	Group 2
	%	%	%	%	%	%	%	%	%	%
Independent or Grammar	89.4	58.6	86.8	32.4	76.0	22.1	77.0	18.0	55.0	14.0
Technical	6.8	10.5	7.5	14.2	10.8	11.0	9.0	11.3	22.2	12.3
All selective	96.2	69.1	94.3	46.6	86.8	33.1	86.0	29.3	77.2	26.3

Source: Compiled from Table 2a, The Crowther Report, volume II, p. 120.

In the second order of ability, 58.6 per cent of recruits whose fathers were of the professional and managerial class have attended grammar or independent schools. At the same level of ability, only 22 per cent of the sons of skilled workers have done so — and it is not the case, as might be hoped, that more of them had attended technical schools instead. Even in the first order of ability, the social differences in schooling are marked. Crowther makes a point (I, p. 199) of emphasizing the similarity of the maintained and independent schools in the ability of their pupils. Yet, as is well known, there is a tremendous difference in the proportion staying on for advanced work in two types of school.

Of recruits in the Crowther sample who attended independent efficient schools, 60 per cent had stayed on to eighteen plus as against 24 per cent of those from maintained schools; the corresponding figures for 17 year old leavers were 23 per cent and 16 per cent respectively. This contract reflects the difference in social composition of the two types of school. Only 6 per cent of recruits from independent efficient schools were the sons of manual workers, as compared with 56 per cent of those from the maintained schools, of whom 70 per cent left before they were seventeen.

In short, then, the post-war movement of educational reform has brought the abler sons of skilled workers into the grammar and technical schools. However, the proportion of working class recruits even in the highest ability groups with a selective secondary education is below that for the sons of non-manual workers; and at the second ability level, and for the sons of semi- and unskilled workers in particular, it is very much lower. Moreover, the propensity for all working class boys to leave school well before the sixth form is very marked.

That there is a substantial reserve of uneducated ability in the offspring of working class fathers cannot be doubted. It is worth adding, however, that any calculations based on the Crowther distributions would underestimate its size. Tests administered at eighteen or twenty-one are only in a limited sense tests of ability. Even more than is the case with tests of the same kind administered at eleven, they are tests of attainment rather than potential. Part of the differences they reveal are attributable to differences in the kind and amount of formal schooling, and in occupational experiences after school. Thus, the graduates and others similarly qualified among the Crowther sample of recruits were being tested immediately on, or shortly after, leaving an institution of full-time education; whereas those who had left school earlier were at a disadvantage with regard to the capacities measured by the test, and even probably at a varied disadvantage according to the kind of occupation they had followed between leaving school and being called up.

Assessments of 'latent ability' based on intelligence test or other attainment test scores probably have diagnostic value; but they are at best poor guides for long-term educational policy, which had much better be based on some operational definition of 'equality of opportunity'. Thus, one can aim at abolishing social, as distinct from academic, selection in education, searching for and eliminating particular manifestations, as, for example, the 'early leaving' problem in secondary schools: or one can aim at equalizing educational chances at all social levels, by providing a highly differentiated secondary and further system of education, such that the social composition of students in each of its branches approximates closely to that of the relevant population at large, and the differential 'class chances' for achieving a given educational level are eliminated.

Admittedly, 'equality of educational opportunity', like 'the pool of ability', is a point of view and not a fact; but it has the advantage (quite apart from its undeniable social philosophical merits as a principle of distributive justice) that it can be translated into valid operational terms from which can be derived propositions for concrete investigations, of which the findings can serve as a basis for educational policy.

PIERRE BOURDIEU

The school as a conservative force: scholastic and cultural inequalities

(translated by J.C. Whitehouse) *

It is probably cultural inertia which still makes us see education in terms of the ideology of the school as a liberating force ('l'école libératrice') and as a means of increasing social mobility, even when the indications tend to be that it is in fact one of the most effective means of perpetuating the existing social pattern, as it both provides an apparent justification for social inequalities and gives recognition to the cultural heritage, that is, to a *social* gift treated as a *natural* one.

As processes of elimination occur throughout the whole of the period spent in education, we can quite justifiably note the effects they have at the highest levels of the system. The chances of entering higher education are dependent on direct or indirect selection varying in severity with subjects of different social classes throughout their school lives. The son of a manager is eighty times as likely to get to university as the son of an agricultural worker, forty times as likely as the son of a factory worker and twice as likely as even the son of a man employed in a lower-salaried staff grade.[1] It is striking that the higher the level of the institution of learning, the more aristocratic its intake. The sons of members of managerial grades and of the liberal professions account for 57 per cent of students at the Polytechnique, 54 per cent of those at the École Normale Supérieure (noted for its 'democratic' intake), 47 per cent of those at the Ecole Normale and 44 per cent of those at the Institut d'Etudes Politiques.

However, simply stating the fact of educational inequality is not enough. We need a description of the objective processes which continually exclude children from the least privileged social classes. Indeed, it seems that a sociological explanation can account for the unequal achievement usually imputed to unequal ability. For the most part, the effects of cultural privilege are only observed in their crudest forms — a good word put in, the right contacts, help with studies, extra teaching, information on the educational system and job outlets. In fact, each family transmits to its children, indirectly rather than directly, a certain *cultural capital* and a certain *ethos*. The latter is a system of implicit and deeply interiorized values which, among other things, helps to define attitudes towards the cultural capital and educational institutions. The cultural heritage, which differs from both points of view according to

* Reprinted from Pierre Bourdieu, 'l'école conservatrice', Revue française de sociologie, 7(1966), pp. 225-6, 330-42, 346-7, by kind permission of the author and publishers.

social class, is the cause of the initial inequality of children when faced with examinations and tests, and hence of unequal achievement.

Choice of options

The attitudes of the members of the various social classes, both parents and children, and in particular their attitudes towards school, the culture of the school and the type of future the various types of studies lead to, are largely an expression of the system of explicit or implied values which they have as a result of belonging to a given social class. The fact that different social classes send, despite equal attainment, a different proportion of their children to *lycées* is often explained by such vague terms as 'parental choice'. It is doubtful whether one can meaningfully use such expressions except metaphorically, as surveys have shown that 'in general there is a massive correlation between parental choice and options taken' — in other words, parental choice is in most cases determined by real possibilities.[2] In fact, everything happens as if parental attitudes towards their children's education — as shown in the choice of sending them either to a secondary school or leaving them in the upper classes of an elementary school, and of sending them to a *lycée* (and thus accepting the prospect of prolonged studies, at least, to the *baccalauréat)* or to a *collège d'enseignement général* (and thus accepting a shorter period of education, until the *brevat,* for example) — were primarily the interiorization of the fate objectively allotted (and statistically quantifiable) as a whole to the social category to which they belong. They are constantly reminded of their fate by a direct or indirect intuitive grasp of the statistics of the failures or partial successes of children of the same kind, and also less directly, by the evaluation of the elementary school teacher who, in his role as a counsellor, consciously or unconsciously takes into account the social origin of his pupils and thus, unwittingly and involuntarily, counterbalances the over-theoretical nature of a forecast based purely on performance. If members of the lower middle and working classes take reality as being equivalent to their wishes, it is because, in this area as elsewhere, aspirations and demands are defined in both form and content by objective conditions which exclude the possibility of hoping for the unobtainable. When they say, for example, that classical studies in a *lycée* are not for them, they are saying much more than that they cannot afford them. The formula, which is an expression of internalized necessity, is, we might say, in the imperative indicative as it expresses both an impossibility and a taboo.

The same objective conditions as those which determine parental attitudes and dominate the major choices in the school career of the child also govern the children's attitude to the same choices and, consequently, their whole attitude towards school, to such an extent that parents, to explain their decision not to let the child go to secondary school, can offer as a close runner-up to the cost of study the child's wish to leave school. But, at a deeper level, as the reasonable wish to get on through education will not materialize as long as the real chances of success are slim, and although working class people may well be unaware of their children's 2 in 100 chance of getting to university, their behaviour is based on an empirical evaluation of the real hopes common to all individuals in their social group. Thus it is understandable that the lower middle class — a transitional class — lays more emphasis on educational values as the school offers them reasonable chances of achieving all they want by mixing the values of social success and cultural prestige. In comparison with working class children, who are doubly disadvantaged as regards facilities for assimilating culture and the propensity to acquire it, middle class children receive from their parents not only encouragement and exhortation with regard to their school work but also an ethos of 'getting on' in society and an ambition to do the same at and by means of school, which enables their keen desire for the possession of culture to compensate for cultural poverty. It also seems that the same self-denying ethos of social mobility which gives rise to the prevalence of small families in certain sections of the lower middle classes also underlies their attitude towards the school.[3]

In the most fertile social groups, such as agricultural workers, farmers and factory workers, the chances of going into the *sixième* decrease clearly and regularly as a further unit is added to the family, but they fall drastically for less fertile groups such as artisans, small tradesmen, clerks and lower-salaried personnel, in families of four and five children (or more) — i.e., in families distinguished from others in the group by their high fertility — so that instead of seeing in the number of children the causal explanation of the sharp drop in the percentage of children attending school, we should perhaps suppose that the desire to limit the number of births and to give the children a secondary education are a sign, in groups where *both* these traits are noted, of the same inclination to make sacrifices.[4]

In general, children and their families make their own choices by reference to the contraints which determine them. Even when the choices seem to them to follow simply from taste or vocational sense, they nevertheless indicate the roundabout effects of objective conditions. In other words, the structure of the objective chances of social mobility and, more precisely, of the chances of a social mobility by means of education conditions attitudes to school (and it is precisely these attitudes which are most important in defining the chances of access to education, of accepting the values of norms of the school and of succeeding within the framework and thus rising in society) through subjective hopes (shared by all individuals defined by the same objective future, and reinforced by the group's pressure for conformity), which are no more than objective chances intuitively perceived and gradually internalized.[5]

A description of the logic of the process of internalization, at the end of which objective chances have become subjective hopes or lack of hope, would seem necessary. Can that fundamental dimension of class ethos, the attitude to the objective future, be in fact anything but the internalization of the objective future course of events which is gradually brought home to and imposed on every member of a given class by means of the experience of successes and failures? Psychologists have observed that the level of aspiration of individuals is essentially determined by reference to the probability (judged intuitively by means of previous successes or failures) of achieving the desired goal.

'A successful individual', writes Lewin, 'typically sets his next goal somewhat, but not too much, above his last achievement. In this way he steadily raises his level of aspiration... . The unsuccessful individual on the other hand, tends to show one of two reactions: he sets his goal very low, frequently below his past achievement... or he sets his goal far above his ability.'[6] It is quite clear that a circular process occurs: 'If the standards of a group are low an individual will slacken his efforts and set his goals far below those he could reach. He will, on the other hand, raise his goals if the group standards are raised.'[7] If we also accept that '... both the ideals and the action of an individual depend on the group to which he belongs and upon the goals and expectation of that group',[8] it can be seen that the influence of peer groups — which is always relatively homogeneous from the point of view of social origin as, for example, the number of children going to *collèges d'enseignement général, collèges d'enseignement technique* and *lycées,* (and, within these, their spread through the various types of education offered by each) is very much a function of the social class of the children — reinforces, among the least privileged children, the influence of the family milieu and the general social environment, which tend to discourage ambitions seen as excessive and always somewhat suspect in that they imply rejection of the individual's social origins. Thus, everything conspires to bring back those who, as we say, 'have no future' to 'reasonable' hopes (or 'realistic' ones, as Lewin calls them) and in fact, in many cases, to make them give up hope.

The cultural capital and the ethos, as they take shape, combine to determine behaviour in school and the attitude to school which make up the differential principle of elimination operating for children of different social classes. Although success at school, directly linked to the cultural capital transmitted by the family milieu, plays a part in the choice of options taken up, it seems that the major determinant of study is the family attitude to the school which is itself, as we have seen, a function of the objective hopes of success at school which define each social category. M. Paul Clerc has shown that, although both scholastic attainment and the rate of entry into the *lycée* depend closely on social class, the overall inequality in the rate of entry to the *lycée* depends more on the inequality in the proportion of those of equal attainment who enter the *lycée* rather than on inequality of attainment itself.[9]

That means in fact that the handicaps are *cumulative,* as children from the lower and middle classes who overall achieve a lower success rate must be more successful for their family and their teachers to consider encouraging further study. The same method of double selection also comes into operation with the age criterion: children from peasant and working class homes, usually older than children from more privileged homes, are more severely eliminated, at an equal age, than children from the latter. In short, the general principle which leads to the excessive elimination of working and middle class children can be expressed thus: the children of these classes, who because of a lack of cultural capital have less chance than others of exceptional success, are nevertheless expected to achieve exceptional success to reach secondary education. But the process of double selection becomes increasingly important as one rises to the higher levels of secondary establishments and, ascends the socially selective hierarchy of subject departments within them. There, once again, given equal achievement, the children of privileged classes go more often than others both to the *lycée*, and the classics side of the *lycée*, the children of underprivileged strata mostly having to pay for their entry to the *lycée* by relegation to a *collège d'enseignement général*, while the children of well-to-do classes, who are not clever enough to go to a *lycée*, can find a suitable alternative in a private school.

It will be seen that here too advantages and disadvantages are cumulative, because the initial choices (of school and subject department determine the school future irreversibly. Indeed, one survey has shown that results obtained by arts students over a series of exercises aimed at measuring the comprehension and manipulation of language and in particular of the language of education were directly related to the type of secondary establishment attended and to knowledge of Greek and Latin. Choices made when entering the *lycée* thus close the options once and for all so that the child's part of the cultural heritage is determined by his previous school career. In fact, such choices, which are a commitment of a whole future, are taken with reference to varying images of that future. 31 per cent of the parents of children at *lycées* want their children to go on to higher education, 27 per cent to the baccalauréat, only a tiny proportion of them wanting the children to proceed to a technical diploma (4 per cent) or to BEPC (2 per cent): 27 per cent of parents of children at *collèges d'enseignement général* on the other hand want to see them obtain a technical or professional diploma, 15 per cent the BEPC, 14 per cent the *baccalauréat*, and 7 per cent want them to go on to higher education.[10]

Thus, overall statistics which show an increase in the percentage of children attending secondary school hide the fact that lower class children are obliged to pay for access to this form of education by means of a considerable diminution in the area of their choices for the future.

The systematic figures which still separate, at the end of their school career, students from different social milieux owe both their form and their nature to the fact that the selection that they have undergone is not equally severe for all, and that *social* advantages or disadvantages have gradually been transformed into *educational* advantages and disadvantages as a result of premature choices which, directly linked with social origin, have duplicated and reinforced their influence. Although the school's compensating action in subjects directly taught explains at least to some extent the fact that the advantage of upper class students is increasingly obvious as the areas of culture directly taught and completely controlled by the school are left behind, only the effect of compensation combined with over-selection can explain the fact that for a behavioural skill such as

the scholastic use of scholastic language, the differences tend to
lessen to an overwhelming extent and even to be inverted, since,
highly selected students from the lower classes obtain results
equivalent to those of the higher social classes who have been less
vigorously selected and better than those of the middle classes, who
are also penalized by the linguistic atmosphere of their families, but
are also less rigorously selected.[11]

Similarly, all the characteristics of a school career, in terms of
schools attended or subjects taken, are indices of the direct influence
of the family milieu, which they reflect within the logic of the
scholastic system proper. For example, if greater mastery of language is
always encountered, in our present state of pedagogical traditions and
techniques among arts students who have studied classical languages, this
is because pursuit of a classical education is the medium through which
other influences are exerted and expressed, such as parental information
on subjects of study and careers, success in the first stages of a school
career, or the advantage conferred by entry into those classes in which
the system recognizes its élite.

In seeking to grasp the logic by which the transformation of the social
heritage into a scholastic heritage operates in different class situations,
one would observe that the choice of subjects or school and the results
obtained in the first year of secondary education (which themselves are
linked to these choices) condition the use which children from different
milieux can make of their heritage, be it positive or negative. It would no
doubt be imprudent to claim to be able to isolate, in the system of
relations we call school careers, determining factors and, *a fortiori,* a
single predominant factor. But, if success at the highest level of a school
career is still very closely connected to the very earliest stages of that
career, it is also true that very early choices have a great effect on the
chances of getting into a given branch of higher education and succeeding in it. In short, crucial decisions have been taken at a very early stage.

The functioning of the school and its role as a socially conservative force

It will be easy — perhaps too easy — to accept what has been said so
far. To stop there, however, would mean not questioning the responsibility of the school in the perpetuation of social inequalities. If that
question is seldom raised, it is because the Jacobin ideology which
inspires most of the criticism levelled at the university system does not
really take inequality with regard to the school system into account,
because of its attachment to a formal definition of educational equity.
If, however, one takes socially conditioned inequalities with regard to
schools and education seriously, one is obliged to conclude that the
formal equity, which the whole education system is subject to, is in
reality unjust and that in any society which claims to have democratic
ideals it protects privileges themselves rather than their open transmission.

In fact, to penalize the underprivileged and favour the most privileged,
the school has only to neglect, in its teaching methods and techniques

and its criteria when making academic judgements, to take into account the cultural inequalities between children of different social classes. In other words, by treating all pupils, however unequal they may be in reality, as equal in rights and duties, the educational system is led to give its *de facto* sanction to initial cultural inequalities. The formal equality which governs pedagogical practice is in fact a cloak for and a justification of indifference to the real inequalities with regard to the body of knowledge taught or rather demanded. Thus, for example, the 'pedagogy' used in secondary or higher education is, objectively, an 'arousing pedagogy', in Weber's words, aimed at stimulating the 'gifts' hidden in certain exceptional individuals by means of certain incantatory techniques, such as the verbal skills and powers of the teacher. As opposed to a rational and really universal pedagogy, which would take nothing for granted initially, would not count as acquired what some, and only some, of the pupils in question had inherited, would do all things for all and would be organized with the explicit aim of providing all with the means of *acquiring* that which, although apparently a natural gift, is only *given* to the children of the educated classes, our own pedagogical tradition is in fact, despite external appearances of irreproachable equality and universality, only there for the benefit of pupils who are in the *particular position* of possessing a cultural heritage conforming to that demanded by the school. Not only does it exclude any questions as to the most effective methods of transmitting to all the knowledge and the know-how which it demands of all and which different social classes transmit very unequally; it also tends to disparage as 'elementary' (with undertones of 'vulgar') and paradoxically, as 'pedantic', pedagogical methods with such aims. It is not by chance that higher elementary education, when it was in competition with the *lycée* in its traditional form, unsettled working class pupils less and attracted the scorn of the élite precisely because it *was* more explicitly and technically methodical. We have here two concepts of culture and of the techniques of transmitting it which, in the form of corporate interests, are still visible in the clash between teachers emerging from the elementary schools and those following the more traditional route through the secondary system.[12] We should also have to examine the role played for teachers by the pious horror of cramming for examinations as opposed to 'general education'. Cramming is not an absolute evil when it consists simply of realizing that pupils are being prepared for an examination and of making them aware of this. The disparagement of examination techniques is merely the corollary of the exaltation of intellectual prowess which is structurally akin to the values of culturally privileged groups. Those who have by right the necessary *manner* are always likely to dismiss as laborious and laboriously acquired values which are only of any worth when they are innate.

Teachers are the products of a system whose aim is to transmit an aristocratic culture, and are likely to adopt its values with greater ardour in proportion to the degree to which they owe it their own academic and social success. How indeed could they avoid unconsciously bringing into play the values of the milieu from which they come, or to which they now belong, when teaching and assessing their pupils? Thus, in higher education, the working or lower middle class student will be judged according to the scale of values of the educated classes which many teachers owe to their social origin and which they willingly adopt, particularly, perhaps, when their membership of the élite dates from their entry into the teaching profession. As soon as the lower middle class ethos is judged from the point of view of the ethos of the élite, and measured against the dilettantism of the well-born and well-educated man, the scale of values is reversed and, by means of a change of sign, application becomes pedantry and a respect for hard work grinding, limited pettiness, with the implication that it is intended to compensate for a lack of natural talents. On the other hand, of course, the dilettantism of students from privileged social classes, which is apparent in many aspects of their behaviour and in the very style of their relationship with a culture which they never owe exclusively to school, corresponds to what – often unconsciously – is expected of them by their teachers and even more by the objective and explicit demands of the school. Even minor signs of social status such as 'correct' dress and bearing and the style of speech and accent are minor class signs and – again most often without their knowledge – help to shape the judgement of their teachers.[13] The teacher who, while appearing to make judgements on 'innate gifts', is in fact measuring by reference to the ethos of the cultivated élite conduct based on a self-sacrificing ethos of hard and painstaking work is setting one type of relationship to culture against another, and all children are born into one or the other. The culture of the élite is so near to that of the school that children from the lower middle class (and *a fortiori* from the agricultural and industrial working class) can only acquire with great effort something which is *given* to the children of the cultivated classes – style, taste, wit – in short, those attitudes and aptitudes which seem natural in members of the cultivated classes and naturally expected of them precisely because (in the ethnological sense) they are the *culture* of that class. Children from the lower middle classes, as they receive nothing from their family of any use to them in their academic activities except a sort of undefined enthusiasm to acquire culture, are obliged to expect and receive everything from school, even if it means accepting the school's criticism of them as 'plodders'.

What the education system both hands on and demands is an aristocratic culture and, above all, an aristocratic relationship with it.[14] This is particularly clear in the relationship of teachers to language. Moving to and fro between charismatic use of the word as a lofty incantation whose function is to create in the pupil a suitable receptivity to grace, and a traditional use of university language as the consecrated vehicle of a consecrated culture, teachers assume that they already share a common language and set of values with their pupils, but this is only so when the system is dealing with its own heirs. By acting as if the language of teaching, full of allusions and shared understanding, was 'natural' for 'intelligent' and 'gifted' pupils, teachers need not trouble to make any technical checks on their handling of language and the students' understanding of it, and can also see as strictly fair academic judgements which in fact perpetuate cultural privilege. As language is the most important part of the cultural heritage because, as syntax, it provides a system of transposable mental postures which themselves completely reflect and dominate the whole of experience, and as the gap between university language and that spoken in fact by the different social classes varies greatly, it is impossible to have pupils with equal rights and duties towards university language and use of language without being obliged to hold the gift responsible for a number of inequalities which are primarily social. Apart from a lexis and a syntax, each individual inherits from his milieu a certain attitude towards words and their use which prepares him, to a greater or lesser extent, for the scholastic games which are still to some extent, in the French tradition of literary studies, games with words. This relationship with words, whether reverent or emancipated, assumed or familiar, thrifty or extravagent, is never more obvious than in oral examinations, and teachers consciously or unconsciously distinguish between 'natural' ease of expression composed of fluency and elegant lack of constraint, and 'forced' ease, common among lower middle and working class students, which reflects the effort to conform, at the price of not getting quite the right note, to the norms of university discourse, indicating some anxiety to impress, and too evidently an attempt to create the right impression to be free of all taint of self-seeking vulgarity. In short, the teachers' *certitudo sui*, which is never more clearly seen than in the high eloquence of a lecture, is based on class ethnocentrism which authorizes both a given usage of academic language and a certain attitude to the use which students make of language in general and of academic language in particular.

Thus, implicit in these relationships with language, there can be seen the whole significance allotted by the educated classes to learned culture and the institution responsible for transmitting it — the latent functions which they give to educational institutions, i.e. the task of organizing the cult of a culture which can be offered to all because in fact it is reserved for the members of the class whose culture it is, the hierarchy of intellectual values which gives the impressive manipulators of words and ideas a higher rank than the humble servants of techniques, and the inner logic of a system whose *objective* function is to *preserve* the values which are the basis of the social order. More deeply, it is because traditional education is objectively addressed to those who have obtained from their social milieu the linguistic and cultural capital that it *objectively* demands that it cannot openly declare its demands and feel itself obliged to give everyone the means of meeting them. Like common law, the university tradition merely specified infringements and punishments without ever openly stating the principles underlying them. Thus, to take examinations as an example, it is quite clear that the more vaguely what they ask for is defined, whether it be a question of knowledge or of presentation, and the less specific the criteria adopted by the examiners, the more they favour the privileged. Thus, the nearer written examinations come to the more traditional kind of 'literary' exercise, the more they favour the exhibition of imponderable qualities in style, syntax of ideas or knowledge marshalled, the *dessertatio de omni re scribili* which dominates the great *concours* in literary subjects (and still plays an important part in scientific ones), the more clearly they divide candidates of differing social classes. In the same way, the 'inheritors' are more favoured in oral examinations than in written ones, particularly when the oral becomes *explicitly* the test of distinguished and cultivated manners which it always *implicitly* is.[15] It is quite clear that such a system can only work perfectly as long as it can recruit and select students capable of satisfying its objective demands, that is as long as it can be directed towards individuals possessing a cultural capital (and able to make it pay off) which it presupposes and endorses without openly demanding it or transmitting it methodically. The only test to which it can really be put is not, it is clear, that of numbers, but that of the *quality* of students. 'Mass education', about which we talk so much nowadays, is the opposite of both education reserved for a small number of inheritors of the culture demanded by the school and of education reserved for any small number of students of any *kind whatever*.

In fact, the system can take in an increasingly large number of pupils, as happened during the first half of this century, without having to change profoundly, provided that the newcomers are also in possession of the socially acquired aptitudes which the school traditionally demands.

On the other hand, it is bound to experience crises (which it will describe as 'a lowering of standards') when it takes in an increasingly large number of pupils who have not acquired the same mastery as their predecessors of the cultural heritage of their social class (as happens when there is a continuous increase in the percentage of children undergoing secondary and higher education from the classes which have traditionally enjoyed it, if there is a similar drop in the rate of selection) or who, coming from culturally underprivileged classes, have no cultural heritage. A number of changes now taking place within the education system can be ascribed to determining factors which can properly be described as *morphological*. It is therefore clear that they affect nothing essential, and that there is very little question, either in programmes of reform or in the demands of teachers and students, of anything affecting specifically the traditional system of education or its working. It is true that enlarging the social basis of recruitment to the *sixième* would no doubt be a decisive test entailing very probably major changes in the functioning of the system in its most specific form, if the segregation of children according to the hierarchy of types of schools and 'sides' (ranging from the *collèges d'enseignement général* or the *collèges d'enseignement technique* to the classical 'sides' of the *lycées*) did not afford the system a protection tailored to its own inner logic, in that lower class children, who do not bring to their school work either the keenness to learn of lower middle class children or the cultural capital of upper class children, take refuge in a kind of negative withdrawal which upsets teachers, and is expressed in forms of disorder previously unknown. It is of course obvious that in such cases it is enough to let matters take their own course to bring crude social handicaps into play and for everything to return to normal. To meet this challenge in a really effective way, the education system should have at its disposal the means to carry out systematic and widespread educational priority programmes of the kind that it can dispense with as long as it is aimed at children from the privileged classes.[16]

It would therefore be ingenuous to expect that, from the very way of working of a system which itself defines its methods of recruitment by imposing demands which are all the more effective for being implicit, there should arise the contradictions capable of determining a basic change in the logic of its own working and of preventing the institution responsible for the conservation and transmission of culture from carrying out its task of social conservation. By giving individuals educational aspirations strictly tailored to their position in the social hierarchy, and by operating a selection procedure which, although apparently formally equitable, endorses real inequalities, schools help both to perpetuate and legitimize inequalities. By awarding allegedly impartial qualifications (which are also largely accepted as such) for socially conditioned aptitudes which it treats as unequal 'gifts', it transforms *de facto* inequalities into *de jure* ones and *economic and social* differences into *distinctions of quality,* and legitimates the transmission of the cultural heritage. In doing so, it is performing a confidence trick. Apart from enabling the élite to justify being what it is, the *ideology of giftedness,* the cornerstone of the whole educational and social system, helps to enclose the underprivileged classes in the roles which society has given them by making them see as natural inability things which are only a result of an inferior social status, and by persuading them that they owe their social fate (which is increasingly tied to their educational fate as society becomes more rationalized) to their individual nature and their lack of gifts. The exceptional success of those few individuals who escape the collective fate of their class apparently justify educational selection and give credence to the myth of the school as a liberating force among those who have been eliminated, by giving the impression that success is exclusively a matter of gifts and work. Finally those whom the system has 'liberated' — teachers in elementary, secondary and higher education — put their faith in *l'école libératrice* at the service of the school which is in truth a conservative force which owes part of its power of conservation to that myth. Thus by its own logic the educational system can help to perpetuate cultural privileges without those who are privileged having to use it. By giving cultural inequalities an endorsement which formally at least is in keeping with democratic ideals, it provides the best justification for these inequalities.

At the end of *The Republic* Plato describes how souls about to start another life had to make their own choice of lots among patterns of lives, all possible animal and human lives, and how, once the choice was made, they had to drink the water of the River of Forgetfulness before returning to earth. The theodicy Plato's myth assumes devolves, in our societies, on university and school examiners. But we can quote Plato further,

> Then a prophet first marshalled them in order, and then taking lots and patterns of lives from the lap of Lachesis, mounted upon a high pulpit and spoke: 'The word of the daughter of Necessity, maid Lachesis. Souls of a day, here beginneth another circle that bears the mortal race to death. The angel will not cast lots for you, but you shall choose your angel. Let him whose lot falls first have first choice of a life to which he shall be bound by Necessity... The responsibility is on him that chooseth. There is none on God.[17]

In order to change fate into the choice of freedom, the school, the prophet of Necessity, need only succeed in convincing individuals to rely on its judgement and persuading them that they themselves have chosen the fate that was already reserved for them. From that point there is no questioning the divinity of society. We could consider Plato's myth of the initial choice of lots with that proposed by Campanella in *La Città del Sole:* to set up immediately a situation of perfect mobility and to ensure the complete independence of the position of fathers and sons, one thing only is necessary — the separation of children from their parents at birth.[18]

Statisticians are in fact implicitly invoking the myth of perfect mobility when they refer the empirically observed situation to a situation of total independence between the social position of inheritors and that of parents. We should no doubt allow a critical role to this myth and the clues it enables us to create, as they help to expose the gap between democratic ideals and social reality. But even the most cursory examination would make it clear that considering these abstractions presupposes ignorance of the social costs and of the conditions in which a high degree of mobility would be possible.[19]

But is not the best way of judging to what extent the reality of a 'democratic' society conforms to its ideals to measure chances of entering the institutionalized instruments of social elevation and cultural salvation open to individuals of different social classes?[20] If so we are then led to the conclusion that a society which allows the most privileged social classes to monopolize educational institutions — which, as Max Weber would say, hold a monopoly of the manipulation of cultural goods and the institutional signs of cultural salvation — is rigid in the extreme.

Notes

1 Cf. P. Bourdieu and J.C. Passeron, *Les Héritiers* (Éditions de Minuit, 1964), pp. 14-21.
2 Correlation frequently occurs between the wishes expressed by parents with children finishing the *cours moyen,* opinions given later on the choice of a particular school, and the real choice. 'By no means all parents want their children to go to a lycée ... .Only 30 per cent of parents with children in *collèges d'enseignement général* or

fin d'études say yes, whatever the previous achievement of the child may have been', P. Clerc, 'La famille et l'orientation scolaire au niveau de la sixième. Enquête de juin 1963 dans l'agglomeration Parisienne', *Population,* 4 (August-September 1964), pp.635-6.

[3] Cf. P.Bourdieu and A. Darbel, 'La fin d'un mathusianisme' in Darras, *Le Partage des bénéfices* (Editions de Minuit, 1966) (*Le Sens Commun*).

[4] Analysing the differential influence (exerted by the dimension of the family in various milieux) on the access to secondary education, A. Girard and H. Bastide write, 'Although two-thirds of the children of officeworkers and skilled craftsmen and traders go into the *lycées,* the proportion is highest in the smallest families (i.e. of one or two children). With these groups, however, children from large families (i.e. of four or more) do not enter the *lycée* in greater numbers than those of families of factory workers having only one or two brothers and sisters', A. Girard and H. Bastide, 'La stratification sociale et la démocratisation de l'enseignement', *Population* (July-September 1963), p.458.

[5] There is a presupposition in this system of explanation by means of the common perception of objective and collective chances that the advantages or disadvantages perceived are the functional equivalent of the advantages or disadvantages really experienced or objectively verified in that they influence behaviour in the same way. This does not imply that we underestimate the importance of objective chances. In fact, every scientific observation, in very different social and cultural situations, has tended to show that there is a close correlation between *subjective hopes* and *objective chances,* the latter tending to effectively modify attitudes and behaviour by working through the former (cf. P. Bourdieu, *Travail et travailleurs en Algérie* (Mouton, 1962), part 2, pp. 36-8; Richard A. Cloward, and Lloyd E.Oulir, *Delinquency and Opportunity: a theory of delinquent gangs* (New York, Free Press of Glencoe, 1960); Clarence Schrag, 'Delinquency and opportunity: analysis of a theory', *Sociology and Social Research,* 46 (January 1962), pp. 167-175.

[6] Kurt Lewin, 'Time, perspective and morale' in *Resolving Social Conflicts* (New York, 1948), p.113.

[7] Ibid., p.115.

[8] Ibid., p.115.

[9] P.Clerc, op.cit. p.646.

[10] It is probably by reference to a *social definition* of a reasonably obtainable diploma that individual career projects and hence attitudes to school are determined. This social definition clearly varies from class to class: while, for many of the lower strata of the middle class, the *baccalauréat* still appears to be seen as the normal end of studies — as a result of cultural inertia and lack of information but also probably because office workers and the lower grades of supervisory personnel are more likely than others to experience the effectiveness of this barrier to promotion — it still appears more to the upper reaches of the middle classes and to the upper classes as a sort of entrance examination to higher education. This image of the scholastic career perhaps explains why a particularly large

proportion of the sons of office workers and lower grades of salaried staff do not go on to study after the *baccalauréat*.

[11] Cf. P.Bourdieu, J.C. Passeron and M.de Saint-Martin, op. cit. In order to have a complete measurement of the effect of the linguistic capital, it would be necessary to find out, by means of experimental studies similar to those carried out by Bernstein, whether there are any significant links between the syntax of the spoken language (e.g. its complexity) and success in fields other than that of literary studies (where the link has been shown) — for example, in mathematics.

[12] See V.Isambert-Jamati, 'La rigidité d'une institution: structure scolaire et systèmes de valeur', *Revue française de sociologie,* 7 (1966), p.306.

[13] Similarly elementary school teachers, who have fully absorbed the values of the middle classes from which they increasingly come, always take into account the *ethical colouring* of conduct and attitudes towards teachers and disciplines when making judgements on their pupils.

[14] At the heart of the most traditional definition of culture there lies no doubt the distinction between the contents of the culture (in the subjective sense of an interiorized objective culture) or, perhaps, *knowledge,* and the characteristic means of possessing that knowledge, which gives it its whole meaning and value. What the child received from an educated milieu is not only a *culture* (in the objective sense), but also a certain *style* of relationship to that culture, which derives precisely from *the manner of acquiring it.* An individual's relationship with cultural works (and the mode of all his cultural experiences) is thus more or less easy, brilliant, natural, difficult, arduous, dramatic or tense according to the conditions in which he acquired his culture, the osmosis of childhood in a family providing good conditions for an experience of familiarity (which is the source of the illusion of charisma) which schooling can never completely provide. It can be seen that by stressing the relationship with culture and setting great value on the most aristocratic style of relationship (ease, brilliance) schools favour the most privileged children.

[15] The resistance of teachers to *docimology* and their even greater resistance to any attempt to rationalize testing (one has only to think of the indignant protests at the use of closed questionnaires) is unconsciously based on the same aristocratic ethos as the rejection of all pedagogical science, even though a 'democratic' excuse for it is found in the ritual denunciation of the danger of technocracy.

[16] Can the pressure of economic demand impose decisive changes? It is possible to imagine industrialized societies managing to meet the need for trained personnel without any major widening of the basis of recruitment from secondary, and more particularly from higher education. If we use only criteria of cost, or rather, of formal rationality, it is perhaps preferable to recruit — in the face of all the claims of educational equality — from those classes whose social culture is the nearest to educational culture, and thus dispense with the need for any educational priority programme.

[17] Plato, *The Republic*, Book 10, 617 (Everyman, 1942), p.322.

[18] Cf. Marie Skodak, 'Children in foster homes. A study of mental development' in *Studies in Child Welfare*, University of Iowa Studies, 16(1) (January 1939), pp. 1-56; B. Wellmar, 'The fickle IQ', *Sigma XI Quarterly*, 28(2) (1940), pp.52-60.

[19] Apart from the difficulty of obtaining a precise assessment of mobility, and the discussions on the point in the careers of father and son which should be taken to obtain a relevant comparison, mention should be made of the fact that, as Bendix and Lipset have pointed out, 'perfect mobility' (in the sense of completely equal chances of mobility), and 'maximum mobility' are not necessarily linked, and that a distinction should be made between forced and intentional 'rigidity' or 'mobility'.

[20] We should also take into account the differential chances of social elevation given identical use of institutional means. We know that, at an equivalent level of instruction, individuals from different social classes reach varying levels in the social hierarchy.

MAURICE CRAFT

Talent, family values and education in Ireland *

A persistent focus of attention in commentaries on the development of school systems is a concern with talent, its identification, conservation and development. The process by which societies industrialize, and by which the lives of their members become gradually more urban, more based on contract rather than on custom, more 'secular' and less 'sacred', seems to be inseparable from an increasingly intensive cultivation of individual ability.

As many have pointed out, these urban-rural dichotomies paint an oversimplified picture, and sometimes embody implicit value judgements about the direction of change. But none the less, the parallel accompaniment of industrializaton by increasingly complex educational bureaucracies, devoted to the cultivation of those cognitive, affective and normative capacities of most relevance to the needs of more technical, more differentiated and more achievement oriented societies seems everywhere apparent. Initially, greatest attention is paid to the young, to basic literacy, to an introduction to less diffuse and more specific social roles, to the deferment of impulsive behaviour, to equality of treatment rather than particularism, and to a preference for what a man can do rather than what he is. As societies become more complex they show an increasing concern with post-primary, with higher, and then with continued, in-service education and retraining, and the emphasis is then turned to the development of more advanced cognitive and social skills. Loss of talent, at whatever age, through misidentification, inadequate social policies, inept pedagogy or differential educability becomes a foremost political and professional issue; and attention is called to defects in selective and grouping procedures, to the range and effectiveness of the curriculum, and to the extent and quality of staffing and of teacher education.

At first sight, there appears to be a fairly straightforward connection between the demand for education and *economic need,* and the world-wide expansion of educational systems seems to run alongside a worldwide rise in skill levels as primary industries attract progressively less manpower and tertiary industries progressively more. In Table I, for example, Vaizey shows the relationship of education and skill in Japan.[1]

*This paper is published for the first time in this collection. The author gratefully acknowledges the support of the SSRC in financing the research which it partly reports.

TABLE I Education and skill in Japan

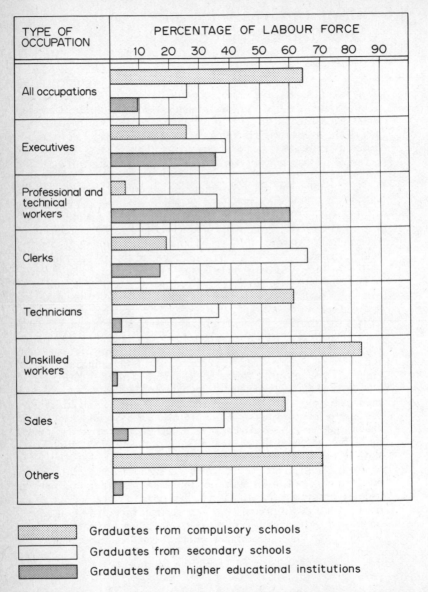

Source: Vaizey (1967), p.59. Data derived from *Education in Japan*
(Tokyo, Ministry of Education, 1964)

As Husén (1969) has described the situation:

> In developed countries with highly advanced economies, the
> qualification and social status structure . . . increasingly resembles
> the shape of an egg. At the bottom of the status hierarchy is a
> diminishing number of occupations that require a modest amount
> of formal schooling and vocational training over a considerable
> time. In the middle a rapidly increasing number of occupations
> require formal education to the age of 16-18 after which a
> specialised vocational training is being sought. At the top, finally,
> the number of persons with higher educational and professional
> occupations also increases rapidly. (Husén 1969, p.71)

But on the other hand the pattern is not a tidy one and it cannot be
claimed that there is a simple one-to-one response in the education-
occupation relationship. Competition for higher-status jobs, and
commercial and political prestige, have also been known to inflate
educational requirements for employment; and the geographical and
social distribution of educational opportunities, the soaring costs of
educational provision and the appropriateness of curriculum content
have frequently been demonstrated to be seriously dysfunctional to
the economy (Coombs 1968). Secondly, educational expansion has
been a response also to the rising levels of individual aspiration which
have accompanied the progressive democratization of industrial societies.
Naturally, this source of demand, as Bereday (1969) says, is 'partly noble
and partly expedient': '[Men] want to know the meaning of existence,
how things are ordained and how nature can be harnessed. But they also
want to know how to get a job and advance in it' (p.xi). So ideological
and economical concerns are interrelated here. The same might also be
said of the possible contribution of educational 'progressives', of
social scientists and of the mass media to the expansion of school
systems, in any assessment of the relationship of industrialization and
talent development. Has the paperback revolution and an expanding
market in higher education aided the rapid dissemination of proposals
for educational change? Or are such proposals attracting increasing
attention because the economic gain from more flexible curricula is now
easier to propound? As Hoyle (1969) has put it, 'is the economic demand
[for flexible and creative manpower] being exploited by educationists
as an argument for institutionalising ideas which have long appealed to
progressives, but which have not been institutionalised hitherto because
they have offered no economic pay-off?'

Educational development in Ireland

In the Irish Republic, recent educational development has exemplified
a number of these issues. The continuing *democratization* of Irish
society has been accompanied by a steeply rising demand for post-
primary education, and by a number of far-reaching policy measures
designed to extend educational opportunities. A higher school leaving
age and free post-primary education, increased financial assistance for
students, and greater flexibility in curricular offerings are among a large

number of such measures. The relationship of recent educational change to *economic* development has been even more striking. In 1958, the Republic launched its First Programme for Economic Expansion, and in 1962 undertook a complete and thoroughgoing review of the educational system under the aegis of the OECD, with the specific objective of appraising existing and future skilled manpower needs. In 1965 this massive study reported serious shortcomings in the output of trained manpower, in equality of post-primary enrolments socially and regionally, in the efficiency, for example, of very small schools, and in the length and curriculum content of the school week (OECD 1965, 1966). The outcome of these recommendations included the establishment of a Development Branch to facilitate long-term government planning in education, the amalgamation of large numbers of small schools and the introduction of comprehensive schools, an expansion of regional technical provision, and detailed reviews of teacher training and higher education (OECD 1969, Craft 1970).

At much the same time a considerable expansion of social science research, and particularly research in education, some of it arising directly from OECD (1969) and UN recommendations (Friis 1965), and from the establishment of an educational research centre in Dublin, began to focus upon differential educability with particular reference to post-primary education. As in other countries, most of this early work has been demographic in nature and has outlined the clear social class gradients familiar in all Western and westernized school systems. The OECD (1965) Report itself, for example, showed that not only do working class children in Ireland have a greater propensity to leave school at the earliest permitted age, and a far smaller chance of reaching university, but they are also more likely to drop out from the secondary (i.e. grammar) schools, and numerous subsequent studies have documented these findings in urban and rural areas in different parts of the country.[2] Other researches have related school attainment and verbal reasoning ability to home background variables, and have identified associations between higher performance and middle class status, higher levels of parental or sibling education, smaller families, higher ordinal position, less poverty, or parents rated by teachers as being 'interested' in their child's education.[3] Craft (1972), for example, found that working class children in south Dublin were more likely to drop out even where ability and type of school were controlled (Table II).

All these findings corroborate those of similar researches into educability in other industrial societies, but they do little more than offer useful predictors, broad indications perhaps of the deeper assumptions governing aspirations and behaviour at different social levels. However, a growing number of recent Irish studies have attempted to shed some light on these patterns of assumptions, beginning with *locality* differences. The Rutland Street Project,[4] for example, a detailed study of a disadvantaged district in central Dublin, revealed, like those of Burt, Mays and Wiseman, a familiar cluster of environmental, educational and personality variables, interrelated, mutually reinforcing, and self-perpetuating; the 'culture of poverty' perhaps, but with indications of subcultural variations.[5] Others have identified

TABLE II School leaving in south Dublin, analysed by age, non-verbal ability, type of school and social class

	Primary (%)						Secondary (%) (including secondary tops)						Vocational (%)					
	Middle class			Working class			Middle class			Working class			Middle class			Working class		
	AA	A	BA	AA	A	BA	AA	A	BA	AA	A	BA	AA	A	BA	AA	A	BA
Left at 14	-	21	62	-	43	73	-	-	-	-	4	10	50	30	-	-	18	44
Stayed on	100	79	38	100	57	27	100	100	100	100	96	90	50	70	-	100	82	55
Totals	100	100	100	100	100	100	100	100	100	100	100	100	100	100	-	100	100	99
(N)	N=1	N=33	N=13	N=11	N=158	N=37	N=33	N=75	N=5	N=26	N=69	N=10	N=2	N=10	-	N=9	N=44	N=9
Left at 15	-	-	-	-	60	-	3	2	29	10	8	23	50	35	100	41	31	18
Stayed on	-	-	-	-	40	-	97	98	71	90	92	77	50	65	-	59	69	82
Totals	-	-	-	-	100	-	100	100	100	100	100	100	100	100	100	100	100	100
(N)	-	-	-	-	N=5	-	N=33	N=88	N=7	N=29	N=88	N=13	N=2	N=20	N=3	N=17	N=98	N=11
Left at 16	-	-	-	-	-	-	-	6	50	29	20	55	100	64	75	40	68	88
Stayed on	-	-	-	-	-	-	100	94	50	71	80	45	-	36	25	60	32	12
Totals	-	-	-	-	-	-	100	100	100	100	100	100	100	100	100	100	100	100
(N)	-	-	-	-	-	-	N=32	N=84	N=4	N=26	N=78	N=11	N=1	N=14	N=4	N=10	N=72	N=8
Left at 17	-	-	-	-	-	-	3	7	50	24	30	25	100	100	100	100	74	71
Stayed on	-	-	-	-	-	-	97	93	50	76	70	75	-	-	-	-	26	29
Totals	-	-	-	-	-	-	100	100	100	100	100	100	100	100	100	100	100	100
(N)	-	-	-	-	-	-	N=30	N=75	N=2	N=21	N=54	N=4	N=2	N=8	N=1	N=1	N=31	N=7
Left at 18	-	-	-	-	-	-	7	49	100	50	69	67	-	57	-	50	92	-
Stayed on	-	-	-	-	-	-	93	51	-	50	31	33	-	43	-	50	8	-
Totals	-	-	-	-	-	-	100	100	100	100	100	100	-	100	-	100	100	-
(N)	-	-	-	-	-	-	N=28	N=61	N=1	N=16	N=32	N=3	-	N=7	-	N=2	N=12	-

Notes:

1 Primary schools offer basic education, normally to the minimum school leaving age only. Secondary schools (including the few 'secondary tops' in primary schools) offer an academic (i.e. grammar-type) curriculum to eighteen/nineteen years. Vocational schools offer a vocationally oriented curriculum to fifteen/sixteen years.

2 Social class groupings are based on father's occupation and the Irish Census.

3 'A' = average ability for this sample (i.e. ±1 SD from the mean of the raw scores on Raven's Progressive Matrices). 'AA' = above average, and 'BA' below average.

a 'roughs-respectables' continuum in urban family norms (O'Neill 1971), and marked inter-locality variations in attitudes to education and to parent-teacher contact in Dublin (Kelly 1970, McCluskey 1970, Nevin 1970).

Subcultural studies of educability which are less *contextually* oriented are still very few, and have begun the painstaking task of sketching the outlines of educational aspirations and attitudes in different social groups.[6] Nevin (1970), for example, described behavioural and attitudinal differences between skilled manual and white collar parents in an attempt to explain differences in university recruitment from these two social groups; and Humphreys' (1966) study of the effects of urbanization on Irish family structure produced a good deal of data on attitudes to education at four social class levels. Humphreys' research is of particular interest in demonstrating that attitudes to education are an aspect of life style, a function of family values, and have no independent existence, and it was with this hypothesis in view that the writer's study of school leaving in Dublin was undertaken (Craft 1972).

Values analysis and education

A concern with values is central to the thought and activity of industrial societies because of the rapidity of social change in such societies. Established assumptions are constantly under review, in turn requiring the prevailing ethic of inquiry, change and achievement to justify its persistent dynamic. The value conflicts generated by the political, economic and social upheavals in England and Europe from the late eighteenth century onwards are reflected in the work of early social theorists who have bequeathed a vocabulary of basic concepts to help explain the changing quality of human relationships and the changing criteria of human actions: Marx's 'alienation', Durkheim's 'anomie' and Weber's rationalization', for example. Successive theories of urban-rural contrast have been formulated, down to the present time, and the status/contract, military/industrial, gemeinschaft/gesellschaft, mechanical/organic dichotomies of Maine, Spencer, Tonnies and Durkheim are perhaps among the best-known of these modes of analysis. As Becker (1950) and others have cogently argued, these are over-simplifications, and more recent models have tended to utilize more complex patterns of variables (e.g. Kahl 1968); but all reflect a continuing preoccupation with the nature of industrial man, and it is curious that the educational process has been so little subjected to cultural analysis at this level.

As suggested earlier, the demographic predictors associated with school success (i.e. social class, family size, income and so on) are now well known, and the generally greater responsiveness of middle class schoolchildren is increasingly being interpreted in terms of higher family aspirations, greater parental support and encouragement, and a closer congruence with the ethos and objectives of the school system (Bynner 1972). But few studies, even where they involve a detailed analysis of the child-rearing practices associated with high achievement

(Heckhausen 1967), have sought to relate style of socialization to the occupational and social structure,[7] and fewer still to a family's fundamental attitudes, say, to *time,* or to *kin* or to *mastery* of the environment. It is true that a good deal of psychological research has considered deferred gratification patterns in children, impulsiveness, attention span and the like, but rarely as part of an individual's total world view, despite the volume of work relating personality and culture and the various psychological studies of cultural systems (Triandis 1972).[8] Just as whole societies may be subjected to ideal-type analysis, so too can social class, religious or ethnic groups, and such an approach might well contribute something to the understanding of differential educability, the value transmission function of school systems, and other educational problems.

A cultural typology which readily lends itself to this kind of application and which avoids the simplistic dichotomy of many other theorists is that of Kluckhohn and Strodtbeck (1961), who argued that five major problems confront all peoples at all times and that solutions to them must be found: these relate to the character of innate *human nature,* to the relationship of *man to nature,* to man's view of *time* and of *activity,* and to man's *relationship to other men.* The five problems and a conceptualization of their possible solutions are outlined in Table III, below.

TABLE III   Five basic value orientations, and the range of variations postulated for each*

Orientation	Postulated range of variations		
Human nature	Evil	Neutral/Mixture of good and evil	Good
	mutable/immutable	mutable/immutable	mutable/immutable
Man-nature	Subjugation to nature	Harmony with nature	Mastery over nature
Time	Past	Present	Future
Activity	Being	Being-in-becoming	Doing
Relational	Lineality	Collaterality	Individualism

Source: Kluckhohn and Strodtbeck (1961), p.12

*It is important to note the assumption that all combinations are possible, e.g. collaterality, doing, present, harmony, good (mutable).

The schema is not without its critics, but it would seem to have some validity; most of its dimensions appear frequently in other values analyses,[9] and, with its derivatives, it has already been successfully used in numerous sociological researches, including studies of talent wastage. Rosen (1956), for example, utilized a values scale embodying

Kluckhohn and Strodtbeck's man-nature, time, and man-other men dimensions, which successfully discriminated between middle class and working class adolescents and between high and low educational aspirers in the north-east United States,[10] and later between various ethnic groups in the same region (Rosen 1959).[11] In Japan, Caudill and Scarr (1962), following closely the methodology of Kluckhohn and Strodtbeck, completed a detailed study of 18 year olds and their parents in urban and rural areas, and identified relatively little inter-generational value change. In Newfoundland, Kitchen (1965) used a values instrument modelled on that of Kluckhohn and Strodtbeck to discriminate between adolescents from urban or rural districts, on the man-nature dimension;[12] in Brisbane, Watts (1969) carried out a similar study with aborigine and white Australian adolescent girls (and their mothers) and identified a number of significant differences;[13] and in Alberta, Gue (1971), also using a values instrument based on Kluckhohn and Strodtbeck, found important differences between Indians (adolescent pupils and their parents) and non-Indian teachers and administrators on the relational dimension.[14]

In London, Jayasuriya (1960) used an extended version of the Rosen values instrument with secondary schoolboys and, like Rosen, related high values scores to middle class status.[15] Sugarman (1966) used a slightly revised version of Jayasuriya's values scale, also with London secondary schoolboys, and found a significant relationship (particularly with the future orientation component) between high scores and school achievement, conduct and father's occupation.[16]

The Dublin study

The values studies reported above are of course by no means without their contradictions. But despite occasional inconsistencies, they seemed to justify the adoption of a methodology which had proved useful in the investigation of life orientations and talent wastage in several continents and with widely differing samples, in a study of school leaving in Dublin. It seemed likely that the relationship between educational/vocational aspirations and activistic/future oriented/ individualistic values, indicated for example by Rosen and Jayasuriya, might well be reproduced by the parents of Dublin adolescents. But in this case controls for social class and religion would be applied to add stringency to the hypothesis. It was now being proposed that even in those social groups (i.e. those of working class status, and of RC religion) which elsewhere had demonstrated *lower* values scores on the man-nature ('mastery'), time, and man-other men dimensions, the parents whose children stay on beyond the minimum school leaving age would tend to score more highly than those whose children leave.

1. Methodology

This hypothesis dictated a matched groups model, and the research design was briefly as follows.[17] In *stage 1* all the schools in south Dublin except two[18] (i.e. a total of thirty-nine schools) with boys or girls aged between thirteen years eight months and fourteen years were visited, and several standardized ability and attainment tests and a questionnaire were administered to each eligible group of children. Each child's teacher also completed a rating. In *stage 2,* some months later (autumn 1966), two groups were chosen from this universe of 557 children for more intensive study. One group had now become leavers[19] while the second had stayed on, and both were matched for ability,[20] social class,[21] religion,[22] family size,[23] sex,[24] and of course age (all were now just over fourteen). The home of each of these 118 children was now visited, and each mother and father was separately interviewed using a schedule incorporating several attitude probes. *Stage 3* has consisted of an annual follow-up to ascertain the occupational or educational whereabouts of each child, and the cohort (now aged over twenty) is still under surveillance.

Of several attitude measures used, the values instrument was considered to be the most probing. It consisted of eighteen items, six for each of Rosen's three components: the activistic-passivistic orientation,[25] the present-future orientation[26] and the familistic-individualistic orientation.[27] Of the eighteen items, eleven were taken from Sugarman and the remainder were added. The scale was administered, as part of the stage 2 schedule, to each father and mother separately;[28] the responses were individually scored by the interviewer on a pre-coded schedule, on a six-point scale ('strongly agree' to 'strongly disagree', and including 'no views'),[29] and were subsequently analysed item by item by computing mean scores for the sample as a whole and for each of the eighteen subgroups.[30] In addition to this treatment of *individual items,* each of the three *subgroups* of six items (i.e. Rosen's three components), were tested for homogeneity by the method of summated ratings (Edwards 1957) and were found to intercorrelate satisfactorily. It is therefore possible to make comparisons not only in terms of the eighteen individual statements, but also in terms of the three components of the values scale. Thirdly, as regards the *total* scale, this too was tested by the method of summated ratings and with the exception of two items was found to intercorrelate satisfactorily. Comparisons of *total* values scores have therefore also been computed, but excluding the two rejected items.

2. Findings[31]

An initial finding was that the total sample of parents scored rather more than halfway along the continuum for the full scale; but whether this would have been different with, say, a rural or a middle class or a Protestant sample, or whether this is simply one of the possible draw-backs of using a five-point Likert-type scale[32] it is impossible to say. The mean for the *time* dimension (future-present subscale) was a shade higher than that for either the *activity* (activistic-passivistic subscale) or the *relational* (familistic-individualistic subscale) dimensions, but the differences are marginal.

When the scores of fathers and mothers are compared, however, some important differences emerge: fathers were significantly more future oriented than mothers,[33] and significantly more activistic,[34] but both score at much the same levels on the relational dimension. On the total

TABLE IV Analysis of fathers' and mothers' values scores

Future-present subscale

	Fathers						item	Mothers					
	L/S	BL/BS	GL/GS	B/G	BL/GL	BS/GS		L/S	BL/BS	GL/GS	B/G	BL/GL	BS/GS
							item (l)	$p<.02$					
							item (g)			$p.002$			$p<.02$
	$p<.02$	$p<.05$					item (a)	$p<.02$	$p<.05$				
							item (i)	$p<.02$		$p<.05$			
							item (d)						
							item (q)						
		$p<.05$					TOTALS	$p<.01$		$p<.01$			

Activistic-passivistic subscale

	Fathers						item	Mothers					
	L/S	BL/BS	GL/GS	B/G	BL/GL	BS/GS		L/S	BL/BS	GL/GS	B/G	BL/GL	BS/GS
							item (h)						
							item (o)			$p<.05$			
							item (m)						
							item (e)						
							item (b)						
							item (r)						
							TOTALS						

Familistic-individualistic subscale

	Fathers						item	Mothers					
	L/S	BL/BS	GL/GS	B/G	BL/GL	BS/GS		L/S	BL/BS	GL/GS	B/G	BL/GL	BS/GS
		$p<.05*$		$p<.02$	$p.001$		item (k)						
							item (n)						
							item (f)						
			$p<.05*$				item (j)						
	$p<.05$						item (c)	$p<.01$		$p<.01$			
							item (p)						
	$p<.05$						TOTAL	$p<.05$		$p<.01$			
	$p<.05$						TOTAL V–SCALE	$p<.05$		$p<.05$			

*These were significant differences, but *not* in the predicted direction values scale fathers scored at a significantly higher level than mothers.[35] These results may be indicative both of segregated conjugal roles and of a prevailing familism in this urban, Catholic, working class sample.

When fathers' and mothers' responses are broken down in terms of leaving/staying, a second important finding emerges. Despite the generally more future oriented and activistic values of fathers, it is where these characteristics occur in *mothers* that they are likely to be associated with children's staying on (and in particular with daughters' staying on). In Table IV a summary of these inter-group findings is presented: the table is divided horizontally into three sections relating to the three subscales, and the vertical divisions (L/S, BL/BS etc.) refer to the parents of leavers compared with those of stayers, boy leavers compared with boy stayers and so on. Right at the bottom of the table the probabilities of <.05 in the L/S and GL/GS columns indicate the overall significant differences in the mothers' scores.[36] The upper section of the table shows that whereas (as mentioned earlier) fathers are significantly more future oriented than mothers, it is *mothers'* future orientation which is more likely to be associated with staying on at school, and much the same may be said of the lower section of the table which reports on the relational dimension. The middle section suggests that whereas (as was also mentioned earlier) fathers are generally the more activistic, activism in *neither* parent is likely to be associated with staying on at school and it may be a wider cultural fatalism that is being reflected here.[37]

The basic finding that it is *mothers'* values which appear to relate to school leaving may, of course, be due to methodological factors: the inadequate sensitivity of the research instrument (the values scale) in a fairly tightly controlled sample, perhaps; or possibly even defects in the sample itself. On the other hand, the possibility of a matriarchal family structure in this working class area[38] seems not unlikely, and these findings are reinforced by those reported below.

The analysis of fathers' and mothers' values scores also scrutinized *combinations* of parental responses, and here a third important finding emerged. Where both parents have high values scores, a child is far more likely to stay on than where both have low scores; and, further, the F low/M high combination is far more likely to be associated with staying on than the F high/M low combination. This finding not only supports the basic hypothesis that high parental values scores will tend to be associated with staying on and low with leaving, but it also confirms the earlier finding that *mothers'* values are crucial in this sample. A possible 'special relationship' between mothers' values and daughters' staying on, and between fathers' values and sons' staying on could not be fully substantiated. But when the sex of child variable is removed, the pattern of values combinations outlined above was confirmed at a statistically significant level except on the activistic-passivistic dimension. This might again suggest that while passivism is a fairly common attribute in this Irish, Catholic, working class sample, future orientation varies more sharply in its occurrence (Table V).

TABLE V Parental values and school leaving

Parents' F-P scores*	Leavers N	%	Stayers N	%
F and M low	13	39	4	10
F high/M low	11	33	7	17
F low/M high	6	18	13	32
F and M high	3	9	16	40
	33	99	40	99

Result: $\chi^2 = 16.60875$ 3d.f. p <.001

Parents F-I scores*	Leavers N	%	Stayers N	%
F and M low	13	39	11	27
F high/M low	11	33	6	14
F low/M high	3	9	13	32
F and M high	6	18	10	25
	33	99	40	98

Result: $\chi^2 = 9.12908$ 3d.f. p<.02

Parents' A-P scores*	Leavers N	%	Stayers N	%
F and M low	13	39	10	25
F high/M low	9	27	8	20
F low/M high	4	12	12	30
F and M high	7	21	10	25
	33	99	40	100

Result: $\chi^2 = 5.17515$ 3d.f. Not significant

Parents' total scores*	Leavers N	%	Stayers N	%
F and M low	13	39	3	7
F high/M low	8	24	5	12
F low/M high	3	9	17	42
F and M high	9	27	15	36
	33	99	40	97

Result: $\chi^2 = 18.59477$ 3d.f. p<.001

*A straight dichotomy of scores into 'high' and 'low', using each respective mean

TABLE VI   Parental values and progressive dropout :I

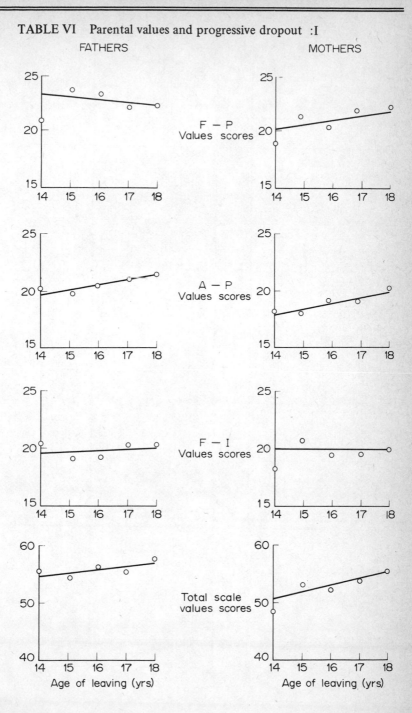

FATHERS

MOTHERS

F — P
Values scores

A — P
Values scores

F — I
Values scores

Total scale
values scores

Age of leaving (yrs)

TABLE VII Parental values and progressive dropout: II (F-P subscale)*

	F and M low		F high/M low		F low/M high		F and M high	
	N	%	N	%	N	%	N	%
Left at 14	13	76 } 88%	11	61 } 89%	5	26 } 73%	3	16 } 58%
Left at 15	–	–	1	6	4	21	2	10
Left at 16	2	12	4	22	5	26	6	32
Left at 17	1	6 } 12%	2	11 } 11%	3	16 } 26%	3	16 } 42%
Left at 18	1	6	–	–	1	5	5	26
Still in full time education†	–	–	–	–	1	5	–	–
	17	100	18	100	19	99	19	100

* The cells in this table are thought to be too small for meaningful significance testing

† In 1972.

TABLE VIII   Parental values and progressive dropout: III

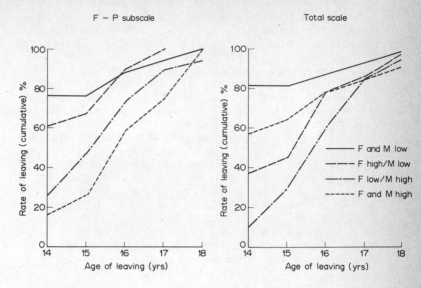

Finally, the data was examined to see whether parental values scores which were recorded when children were aged fourteen years have any bearing on dropout at later ages,[39] bearing in mind the small size of the stage 2 sample. The results of this analysis tended to support the hypothesis, and in general it seemed that the higher his/her parents' values scores (and particularly in the case of mothers' scores) the later a child in this sample left school (Table VI).

When the *combinations* of parental values scores are related to progressive dropout, it appears that the same patterns of parental influence operate not only at fourteen years but at later ages too: where a father and mother both have low values scores, children were far more likely to drop out by the age of sixteen years than where both have high values scores, and the intermediate combinations also follow the earlier pattern;[40] but of the three dimensions examined, the results are clearest for future-present orientation (Table VII).

When plotted graphically over time, the importance of the F low/M high combination becomes even more apparent; and of the three dimensions of the values scale, *time* again appears to be the most effective in demonstrating the differential functioning of the various parental combinations, and *activity* the least effective (Table VIII).

Summary and conclusions

This paper began with the talent needs of complex societies, and has briefly reviewed educational development in the Irish Republic in the context of recent economic and ideological change. An aspect of this has been the considerable expansion of social science research in the Republic, and in research into educability in particular, research which has outlined all the familiar performance/environment gradients. A number of contextual studies have also been undertaken; but sub-cultural studies which place greater emphasis on attitudinal features have yet to develop, and particularly those which interpret perceptions of education as an integral part of life style.

The sociological analysis of life style has a lengthy past, but such insights as have been developed have so far not found their way into the study of the educational process to the extent, perhaps, that they might (despite the quite extensive discussion of psychological correlates such as deferred gratification). The cultural typology of Kluckhohn and Strodtbeck (1961) is felt to have been a most seminal starting point for work of this kind, and Craft (1972) reports a values analysis of school leaving in Dublin which has followed similar researches in the United States, Japan, Canada, Australia and London, all of which have utilized Kluckhohn and Strodtbeck's fundamental hypotheses.

In two groups of Dublin adolescents, matched for social class, religion, ability, family size, sex and age, those who stayed on beyond the minimum school leaving age were found to have parents (and particularly mothers) who scored at a significantly higher level on a values scale incorporating activity, time and relational dimensions. Future orientation was particularly effective in discriminating between the parents of leavers and stayers. *Mothers'* values proved to be influential even when in combination with those of fathers; indeed, the F low/M high combination was often as effective as F and M high.

The Dublin study, as a pilot inquiry, has indicated what might be revealed with a comparable methodology in a variety of other social and ethnic groups. There is also plainly much scope for exploring the wide range of possible occupational and other contextual correlates of these basic value orientations. Does a father's entrepreneurial or supervisory work role, for example, generate a particular pattern of values (Pearlin and Kohn 1966)? Or does it attract functionaries who already possess them? Do some curriculum strategies have greater potential in this respect than others? Is there any scope for *changing* the values of schoolchildren, either technically, or ethically (Breer and Locke 1965, OECD 1971)? Should such programmes focus less on children than on parents, and particularly mothers?

A far bigger question, perhaps, and one on which it is impossible to embark here, is the place which the kinds of values discussed in this paper (activistic, future oriented and individualistic) should in future take in industrial societies. As Gouldner (1970) writes:

> Since 1945 and the end of World War II we have seen the beginnings of a new international resistance against a society organised around utilitarian values, a resistance, in short, against industrial, not merely capitalist, society .... [The new culture] ... rejects the value of conforming usefulness, counterposing to it, as a standard, that each must 'do his own thing'. (p.78)

This puts the identification, conservation and development of talent referred to at the beginning of this paper into a different perspective, questioning traditional pedagogies, the value content of the curriculum, even the worth of extended education itself. For some, these changes promise to liberate home, school and society; for others utopia is thought to be a little farther off. In the meantime, a careful analysis of means and ends (of the values parents and teachers actually transmit to children, and of the educational and social objectives we have in view) may prove enlightening, and will evidence no less profound a concern for individual freedom and fulfilment.

Notes

[1] Table 16 (p.60) in Central Statistical Office (1971) illustrates the 1961-70 figures for GB.

[2] e.g. Hannan 1966, Mulligan 1967, Nevin 1968, O'Sullivan 1969, Irvine 1970, Kellaghan and Greaney 1970, Craft 1972.

[3] e.g. Halligan 1963, Cullen 1969, Kellaghan and Neuman 1971, Kellaghan and Macnamara 1971, Craft 1972, Rudd 1972.

[4] Carney 1970, Chamberlain 1970, Garvey 1970, McGee 1970, Quinn 1971.

[5] McGee (1970) notes, for example, that more favourable attitudes to teachers and to education are associated with more toys in the home, with a husband who married at a less young age and with more favourable attitudes to the police.

[6] Jackson 1967, Ward 1969, Cullen 1969, Irvine 1970, McCluskey 1970.

[7] As, for example, have Kohn (1969) and Pearlin (1972).

[8] Similarly, work in political science which is concerned with 'powerlessness' and political alienation, or that in social administration which deals with 'fatalism' and poverty also often lacks a broader theoretical framework.

[9] e.g. Getzels 1958, Doob 1967, Kahl 1968, Inkeles 1969, Williams 1970.

[10] High school boys who were middle class and/or were planning to continue their education had higher values scores (i.e. they were more mastery oriented (or 'activistic'), more future oriented and more individualistic.

[11] Adult Jews, Protestants and Greeks achieved the highest mean scores, and RCs (the Italians and French Canadians) the lowest. The values scale was also found to discriminate strongly between different social class levels, but not to the exclusion of ethnicity.

[12] The higher the mastery score, the more likely were pupils to be from larger and more industrialized communities, and to be less religious, of higher social status and with better-educated parents.

[13] For example, less strong preferences among aborigines for future over present time, and for individualism over collaterality; and a tendency to prefer harmony-with-nature to mastery. But there was also much acculturation to white Australian value orientations.

[14] The Indians gave significantly greater preference to *lineality*(i.e. the importance of family relations over time) rather than to *individualism*.

[15] He also related high scores to vocational ambition, plans for continuing at school, and aims in further and higher education for both grammar and secondary modern boys.

[16] The more activistic, future oriented and individualistic the child, the better his school work and conduct was likely to be, and the higher his father's occupational status.

[17] Discussed more fully in Craft (1972).

[18] Neither was willing to participate.

[19] The statutory leaving age at that time was fourteen years.

[20] Children achieving grades 3- to 4- only on Raven's Progressive Matrices. (This range of scores overlapped almost exactly with those falling within ± 1 SD of the mean for the total sample, and were regarded as being of 'average' ability.) The Irish Drumcondra verbal reasoning test had not yet become available.

[21] Upper and lower working class, using father's occupation and deriving basic groupings from the Irish Census.

[22] RC only.

[23] No small families (i.e. 1-3 children, in this sample). The mean family size was 5.6, and 'medium' family size was taken to be 4-7 children.

[24] Twenty-one boy leavers and twenty-eight boy stayers; thirty-four girl leavers and thirty-five girl stayers.

[25] e.g. (item o) 'You must accept life as it is, for there is nothing much you can do to alter things.'

[26] e.g. (item l) 'Enjoy the present and let the future take care of itself.'

[27] e.g. (item n) 'Keeping in contact with friends and relations is more important than moving up in the world.'

[28] Each statement was read out slowly and was simultaneously shown on a typewritten card to make the maximum impact. (All instruments used in stages 1 and 2 were piloted before the main fieldwork, in each case.)

[29] In scoring, the 'no view' responses were eliminated and the remainder were scored 1 to 5.

[30] The mothers of boys, of girls, of leavers, of stayers, etc. etc.

[31] A more extensive account will appear in *Social Class, Values and Education* (Longman, forthcoming).

[32] i.e. the tendency for responses to cluster at the centre of the scale.

[33] Comparison of means by t test, $p < .01$

[34] Comparison of means by t test, $p < .01$

[35] Comparison of means by t test, $p < .01$

[36] All probability ratings in Table IV indicate the levels of significance in the differences between the means, as calculated by t test.

[37] An item-by-item analysis elaborates on these findings and shows that, in general, higher parental values scores are associated with children's staying on.

[38] The research was centred on a large corporation estate in south Dublin.

[39] An annual follow-up has charted precisely the progressive dropout of the sample.

[40] It may be worth noting that a number of studies in social psychology

have produced comparable findings. Rosen and D'Andrade 1959 and Rosen 1962, for example, have suggested that homes where the mother has high expectations for her children, and the father, while concerned, does nothing to overshadow them, foster high achievement motivation.

References

BECKER, H., 1950, *Through Values to Social Interpretation.* New York: Duke University Press.

BEREDAY, G.Z.F. (ed.): 1969, *Essays on World Education.* Oxford, University Press.

BREER, P.E. and LOCKE, E.A., 1965, *Task Experience as a Source of Attitudes.* Illinois: The Dorsey Press.

BYNNER, J.M., 1972, *Parents' Attitudes to Education.* London: HMSO

CARNEY, M., 1970, 'Maladjustment and disadvantage'. Unpublished M.Psych.Sc. thesis, University College Dublin.

CAUDILL, W. and SCARR, H.A., 1962, 'Japanese value orientations and culture change'. *Ethnology,* 1, pp.53-91.

CHAMBERLAIN, J.P., 1970, 'Attainment and disadvantage'. Unpublished M.Psych.Sc. thesis, University College Dublin.

COOMBS, P.H., 1968, *The World Educational Crisis.* Oxford: University Press.

CRAFT, M., 1970, 'Economy, ideology and educational development in Ireland'. *Administration,* 18 (4), pp.363-74.

CRAFT, M., 1972, 'Social factors influencing participation in post-primary education in Ireland'. Unpublished Ph.D. thesis, University of Liverpool. (A summary of this research appears in the author's report to the Social Science Research Council, February 1972.)

CENTRAL STATISTICAL OFFICE, 1971, *Social Trends, No. 2 1971.* London, HMSO.

CULLEN, K., 1969, *School and Family.* Dublin: Gill and Macmillan.

DOOB, L.W., 1967, 'Scales for assaying psychological modernisation in Africa'. *Public Opinion Quarterly,* 31, pp. 414-21.

FRIIS, H., 1965, *Development of Social Research in Ireland.* Dublin: Institute of Public Administration.

GARVEY, C.P., 1970, 'Delinquency and disadvantage'. Unpublished M.Psych.Sc. thesis, University College Dublin.

GETZELS, J.W., 1958, 'The acquisition of values in school and society', in Chase, F.S. and Anderson, H.A. (eds.), *The High School in a New Era.* Chicago: University Press, pp. 146-61.

GOULDNER, A.W., 1970, *The Coming Crisis of Western Sociology.* Heinemann.

GUE, L.R., 1971, 'Value orientations in an Indian community'. *Alberta Journal of Educational Research,* 17 (1), pp. 19-31.

HALLIGAN, M.U., 1963, 'An investigation into ability, opportunity and environment in relation to certain schools in the Cork urban area'. Unpublished Ph.D. thesis, University College Cork.

HANNAN, D.F., 1966, 'Factors involved in the migration decisions of Irish rural youth'. Unpublished Ph.D. thesis, Michigan State University.

HOYLE, E., 1969, 'How does the curriculum change?' *Journal of Curriculum Studies,* 1(2), pp.132-41.

HUMPHREYS, A.J., 1966, *New Dubliners: Urbanisation and the Irish Family.* London: Routledge and Kegan Paul.

HUSÉN, T., 1969, 'School structure and the utilization of talent', in Bereday, G.Z.F., op. cit.

INKELES, A., 1969, 'Making men modern: on the values and consequences of individual change in six developing countries'. *American Journal of Sociology,* 75, pp. 208-25.

IRVINE, D.G., 1970, 'Participation in post-primary education in the Galway area'. Unpublished M.A. thesis, University College Galway.

JACKSON, J.A., 1967, *Report on the Skibbereen Social Survey.* Dublin: Human Sciences Committee.

JAYASURIYA, D.L., 1960, 'A study of adolescent ambition, level of aspiration, and achievement motivation'. Unpublished Ph.D. thesis, University of London.

KAHL, J.A., 1968, *The Measurement of Modernism: a Study of Values in Brazil and Mexico.* Austin: University of Texas Press.

KELLAGHAN, T. and GREANEY, V., 1970, 'Factors related to choice of post-primary school in Ireland'. *Irish Journal of Education,* 4(2), pp.69-83.

KELLAGHAN, T. and MACNAMARA, J., 1971, 'Family correlates of verbal reasoning ability'. Dublin: Educational Research Centre. (Unpublished paper.)

KELLAGHAN, T. and NEUMAN, E., 1971, 'Background characteristics of children of high verbal ability'. *Irish Journal of Education,* 5(1), pp. 5-14.

KELLY, S.G., 1970, *Teaching in the City.* Dublin: Gill and Macmillan.

KITCHEN, H.W., 1961, 'Differences in value orientations: a Newfoundland study'. *The Canadian Administrator* 5(3), pp. 9-13.

KLUCKHOHN, F.R. and STRODTBECK, F.L., 1961, *Variations in Value Orientations.* Illinois: Row, Peterson and Co.

KOHN, M.L., 1969, *Class and Conformity.* Illinois: The Dorsey Press.

McCLUSKEY, D., 1970, 'Factors in early school leaving: a sociological study'. Unpublished M.Sc.Sc. thesis, University College Dublin.

McGEE, P., 1970, 'Intelligence and disadvantage'. Unpublished M. Psych. Sc. thesis, University College Dublin.

MULLIGAN, M., 1967, 'Youth in a country town'. Unpublished M.Soc. Sc. thesis, University College Dublin.

NEVIN, M., 1968, 'A study of the social background of students in the Irish Universities'. *Journal of the Statistical and Social Inquiry Society of Ireland,* 21(6), pp.201-19.

NEVIN, M., 1970, *A Better Chance.* University College Dublin.

OECD, 1965, *Investment in Education.* Dublin: Stationery Office

OECD, 1966, *Investment in Education: Annexes and Appendices.* Dublin: Stationery Office.

OECD, 1969, *Reviews of National Policies for Education: Ireland.* Paris.

OECD, 1971, *Strategies of Compensation.* Paris.

O'NEILL, C., 1971, 'The Social function of physical violence in an

Irish urban area'. *The Economic and Social Review,* 2(4), pp.481-96.

O'SULLIVAN, S., 1969, 'The choice of post-primary education in rural areas'. Unpublished M.Sc.Sc. thesis, University College Dublin.

PEARLIN, L.I., 1972, *Class context and Family Relations.* Boston: Little, Brown and Co.

PEARLIN, L.I. and KOHN, M.L., 1966, 'Social class, occupation, and parental values: a cross-national study'. *American Sociological Review,* 31, p.466-79.

QUINN, P., 1971, 'The W.I.S.C. and disadvantage'. Unpublished M. Psych.Sc. thesis, University College Dublin.

ROSEN, B.C., 1956, 'The achievement syndrome: a psychocultural dimension of social stratification'. *American Sociological Review,* 21, pp.203-11.

ROSEN, B.C., 1959, 'Race, ethnicity, and the achievement syndrome'. *American Sociological Review,* 24, pp.47-60.

ROSEN, B.C. 1962, 'Socialisation and achievement motivation in Brazil'. *American Sociological Review,* 27, pp.612-24.

ROSEN, B.C. and D'ANDRADE, R.G., 1959, 'The psycho-social origins of achievement motivation'. *Sociometry,* 22(3), pp.185-218.

RUDD, J. 1972, 'A survey of National School terminal leavers'. *Social Studies,* 1(1), pp.61-72.

SUGARMAN, B., 1966, 'Social class and values as related to achievement and conduct in school'. *Sociological Review,* 14(3) pp. 287-301.

TRIANDIS, H.C., 1972, *The Analysis of Subjective Culture.* New York: Wiley.

VAIZEY, J., 1967, *Education in the Modern World.* London: Weidenfeld and Nicolson.

WARD, C.K., 1969, *New Homes for Old.* Dublin: Irish National Productivity Committee.

WATTS, B.H., 1969, 'Achievement-related values in two Australian ethnic groups', in Campbell, W.J. (ed.), *Scholars in Context.* New York: Wiley, pp. 110-28.

WILLIAMS, R.M., 1970, *American Society* New York: Knopf.

K M MARJORIBANKS

Home environment and mental abilities: an empirical analysis*

Much of the research that has investigated the relationship between the environmental background of children and intellectual test performance has concentrated on using global indicators of both the environment and intellectual ability. The environment has generally been defined in terms of social status characteristics such as the occupation of the father and the education of the parents, or family structure variables such as family size and crowding ratio of the home. The utilization of such gross measures of the environment has accounted for only a relatively small proportion of the variability in the intellectual performance of children. Furthermore, general indices of the environment have a limited functional or diagnostic value for the educator.

In an attempt to overcome the shortcoming of many of the existing environmental studies it was decided in this study to examine the relationship between a refined measure of the home environment and a set of mental ability test scores. It was proposed that the results of such a study would provide the educator with greater insight into the dynamics of the home environment and should help him to understand in more precise and operational terms the educational partnership between the home and the school.

Method

Mental abilities

In the study four mental abilities were examined: verbal, number, spatial and reasoning. These mental abilities were operationalized by the scores on the relevant SRA Primary Mental Abilities subtests (1962 revised edition).

Environment

The total environment was defined as being composed of a complex network of forces. It was assumed that a subset of the total network is related to each human characteristic.[1] Thus, for verbal, number, spatial, and reasoning ability it was proposed that subenvironments or subsets of environmental forces could be identified which would be related to each of the mental abilities.

*Reprinted from K.M. Marjoribanks, 'Home environment and mental abilities', Teacher Education (spring 1971), pp. 85-94, by kind permission of the author and publishers.

The union of the four sub-environments, which were postulated to be related to the mental abilities, was defined as the learning environment. This learning environment may be present in the home, school and community. Of these, the home produces the first and perhaps the most insistent and subtle influence on the mental ability development of the child. As a result, the home was chosen as the focus of the present study.

The forces operating in the home which were hypothesized to influence the mental ability test performance of the child were termed environmental forces. Eight such forces were identified from a review of relevant theoretical and empirical literature and were labelled as follows:

1. press for achievement; 2. press for activeness; 3. press for intellectuality; 4. press for independence; 5. press for English; 6. press for ethlanguage; 7. mother dominance; 8. father dominance.

Each environmental force was defined in terms of a set of environmental characteristics which were assumed to be the behavioural manifestations of the environmental forces.[2] These environmental characteristics facilitated the development of an instrument for the study which was used to gain a measure of the learning environment of the home. The instrument was in the form of a semi-structured home interview schedule. Thus the environmental forces were operationalized as the scores on the relevant environmental measures constructed for the study.

The sample

The sample for the study consisted of 185 fifth grade Ontario boys and their parents. The boys were assigned to two categories, one classified as middle class and the other as low class. The social class classification was based on an equally weighted combination of the occupation of the head of the household and a rating of his (or her) education.

The final sample consisted of 90 boys and parents classified as middle class and 95 as low class.

Hypotheses

In the development of the study it was postulated that subsets of environmental forces could be identified which would be related to the mental abilities. The following hypothesis was therefore investigated.

Hypothesis 1: the verbal, number, spatial and reasoning ability test scores will be significantly related to subsets of scores of environmental forces.

It was also proposed that the utilization of subsets of environmental forces was a means of moving beyond the use of gross classificatory variables such as social status indicators and family structure characteristics, as measures of the environment. The advantage of using the sub-environment approach was investigated by examining the following hypothesis:

Hypothesis 2: scores on the environmental forces will be more highly related to measures of verbal, number, spatial and reasoning ability than

TABLE I   Interrelationships between the mental ability test scores and
the scores of the environmental forces (N = 185)

	Abilities			
Environmental Force	Verbal	Number	Spatial	Reasoning
Press for achievement	.66*	.66*	.28*	.39*
Press for activeness	.52*	.41*	.22*	.26*
Press for intellectuality	.61*	.53*	.26*	.31*
Press for independence	.42*	.34*	.10	.23*
Press for English	.50*	.27*	.18*	.28*
Press for ethlanguage‡	.35*	.24*	.09	.04
Father dominance	.16†	.10	.09	.11
Mother dominance	.21*	.16†	.04	.04

*p < .01
†p < .05
‡Ethlanguage refers to any language other than English used in the home.

TABLE II   Unrotated factor loading matrix of the environmental forces

	Factors		
Environmental force	1	11	h^2
Press for achievement	.83	.06	.69
Press for activeness	.90	.08	.82
Press for intellectuality	.91	.01	.83
Press for independence	.64	−.25	.47
Press for English	.76	−.10	.58
Press for ethlanguage	.75	.10	.57
Mother dominance	.40	.84	.87
Father dominance	.41	−.84	.88
Eigenvalues	4.196	1.533	
Percentage of variance account for	52.4	19.2	
Cumulative percentage of total variance	52.4	71.6	

will other environmental measures such as social status indicators and family structure variables.

Results: Hypothesis one

The initial analysis of the first hypothesis involved an examination of the zero order correlations between the scores of the four mental ability tests and the scores of the environmental forces. These latter scores were computed from a simple summation of the scores on the environmental characteristics which were used to define the environmental forces.

The zero order correlations are presented in Table I.

The results in Table I indicate that the parental dominance dimensions had either low or negligible relationships with the mental abilities. To investigate the relationship between these two parental dimensions and the other environmental forces a principal component analysis of the eight environmental forces was conducted. The unrotated factor loading matrix of the interrelations among the forces is presented in Table II. Only those factors with an eigenvalue greater than unity have been included. The third factor had an eigenvalue of .65.

It can be observed from Table II that all of the environmental forces load strongly on the first factor. This general factor was labelled the learning environment of the home factor.

Because of (1) the exploratory nature of the study in identifying subenvironments for mental abilities, and (2) the presence of a general environment factor, it was decided to utilize the eight environmental forces as the subenvironment for each mental ability.

The relationship between the learning environment of the home and each mental ability was examined by computing the multiple correlation between the environmental forces and each mental ability. In this analysis the environmental forces formed a predictor set and the mental abilities formed the criterion vectors. The results of this analysis are presented in Table III.

TABLE III   Multiple correlations of each of the mental ability scores with the eight environment forces

Mental ability	Multiple correlation R	Corrected multiple correlation Rc	Percentage of total variance Rc^2
Verbal	.72*	.71*	50.4*
Number	.72*	.71*	50.4*
Spatial	.32†	.26	6.7
Reasoning	.43*	.40*	16.0*

*p < .001   †p < .01

‡Corrected to allow for cumulative errors in multiple R, and for small sample size

The results in Table III indicate that when the environmental forces are combined into a set of predictors they account for a large percentage of the variance in verbal and number ability test scores, and a moderate percentage of the variance in the reasoning ability test scores. For spatial ability, the corrected multiple correlation coefficient did not reach statistical significance.

Thus the analysis of the data supports the hypothesis that verbal, number and reasoning abilities are related to subsets of environmental forces. For spatial ability, the relationship with the environment, as measured in this study, was less definite.

Results: Hypothesis two

In Table IV the zero order interrelationships between a set of gross classificatory measures of the environment and each of the mental abilities have been presented.

A qualitative inspection of Table I and Table IV indicates that, in general, the environmental force scores are more highly related to the mental ability test scores than are the gross indicators of the environment.

A set of multiple correlations analyses were conducted in order to compare the effectiveness of the environmental force scores and the gross indicators as predictors of the mental ability test scores. In these analyses the amount of variance that could be attributed to the environmental forces was computed after accounting for the variance that could be attributed to the gross indicators of the environment.

The results of these analyses are presented in Table V.

The results in Table V indicated that the learning environment forces account for 25 per cent of the variance in verbal ability test, 34 per cent of the variance in number ability test scores, and 12 per cent of the variance in reasoning ability test scores after the variance due to

TABLE IV Interrelationships between gross indicators of the environment and mental ability test scores (N=185)

Gross indicators	Mental abilities			
	Verbal	Number	Spatial	Reasoning
Education of father	.29*	.27*	.26*	.22*
Education of mother	.39*	.33*	.21*	.16†
Occupation of father	.43*	.30*	.31*	.29*
Number of children in family	−.32*	−.33*	−.04	−.03
Crowding ratio	−.34*	−.34*	−.07	−.09
Ordinal position in family	−.26*	−.25*	−.04	−.04

*p < .01
†p < .05

TABLE V Relationship between mental abilities, environmental forces and gross indicators of the environment

Criterion	Predictor variables	Computed multiple correlation R	Corrected multiple correlation Rc	Percentage of total variance Rc²
Verbal ability	A = 6 status variables + 8 environmental forces	.74*	.71*	51.0*
	B = 6 status variables	.53*	.51*	26.0*
	C = A – B = environment			25.0*
Number ability	A = 6 status variables + 8 environmental forces	.72*	.71*	50.0*
	B = 6 status variables	.42*	.40*	16.0*
	C = A – B = environment			34.0*
Spatial ability	A = 6 status variables + 8 environmental forces	.38†	.36‡	13.0‡
	B = 6 status variables	.31*	.28*	8.0†
	C = A – B = environment			5.0
Reasoning ability	A = 6 status variables + 8 environmental forces	.47*	.42†	18.0†
	B = 6 status variables	.29†	.25	6.0
	C = A – B = environment			12.0†

*p<.001
†p<.01
‡p<.05

the combination of status characteristics (occupation of father, education of father, education of mother, number of children, ordinal position, and crowding ratio) has been allowed for. For the spatial ability test scores the corrected multiple correlation coefficient for 'environment' did not reach statistical significance. Thus the results provide support for the general acceptance of the second hypothesis.

Conclusion

If it is assumed that the mental ability test performance of children reflects educational achievement, then the results of this present study suggest that the development of education programmes would be facilitated by the identification of profiles of scores of malleable environmental forces. If the malleable aspects of the home environment can be isolated, then possibilities exist for the introduction of educational strategies to compensate for the major environmental deficiencies.

The strategies that might be developed, using a knowledge of environmental forces, may require intervention in the home and the use of large scale adult education programmes. The effectiveness of such strategies may depend upon a restructuring of the tasks of teachers, administrators and schools. It may be necessary for the school to adopt the responsibility for manipulating such environmental characteristics as parental expectations for the education of their children and for themselves, the language environment of the home, the use of books and other literature by the family, and the productive use of leisure time.

The fulfilment of this responsibility would require an active interrelationship between the learning environments of the school, the home and the community. The achievement of this relationship is likely to require a remodelling of the organizational structure of our schools and a reformulating of teacher education programmes. The present corporate bureaucracy model of education may need to be replaced by a model that reflects the 'missing community' or 'extended family' concept of human relationships. In this latter model, a commitment to community involvement would be a requirement of both teachers and administrators. It is only through continued research into the relationship between environmental forces and school outputs that we shall be able to determine what organizational structures will be the most beneficial for children.

APPENDIX A   The environmental forces and their related environmental characteristics used in the interview schedule

Environmental force	Environmental characteristic
1 Press for achievement	1a Parental expectations for the education of their child
	1b Social press
	1c Parents' own aspirations
	1d Preparing and planning for child's education
	1e Knowledge of child's educational progress
	1f Valuing education accomplishments
	1g Parental interest in schooling
2 Press for activeness	2a Extent and content of indoor activities
	2b Extent and content of outdoor activities
	2c Extent and purpose of the use of TV and other media
3 Press for intellectuality	3a Number of thought-provoking activities engaged in by children
	3b Opportunities made available for thought-provoking discussions and thinking
	3c Use of books, periodicals and other literature
4 Press for independence	4a Freedom and encouragement to explore environment
	4b Stress on early independence
5 Press for English	5a Language (English) usage and reinforcement
	5b Opportunities available for language (English) usage.
6 Press for ethlanguage*	6a Ethlanguage usage and reinforcement
	6b Opportunities available for the enlargement and use of the ethlanguage
7 Mother dominance	7a Mother's involvement in child's activities
	7b Mother's role in family decision-making
8 Father dominance	8a Father's involvement in child's activities
	8b Father's role in family decision-making

* Ethlanguage refers to any language that is spoken in the home other than English

II The ecology of educational provision

INTRODUCTION

Studies of demand are characteristically matched by studies of supply. If it is important to examine the distribution of opportunity then it is also important to investigate the distribution of resources that can provide opportunities. The uneven facilities for continued education after the normal leaving age, teacher capacity and many other variables, have been well documented, a practice springing from the political arithmetic traditions mentioned in earlier sections. A useful recent guide to the still widespread variations in the quality and quantity of educational provision is that of J. Pratt, T. Burgess, R. Allemano and M. Locke (1973) which follows usefully upon the earlier work of Taylor and Ayres (1969).

The abundance of well-documented records was probably one of the reasons for the somewhat surprising willingness of many sociologists to accept as given the uneven pattern of distribution while they were still probing the uneven patterns of effective demand. Yet the implications of differential resource provision were considerable. A notable one was the difference in the percentages of pupils entering higher education from the schools of different local education authorities. In 1960 the percentage ranged from 24.9 per cent in Cardiganshire to 5.1 per cent in the Isle of Ely for the counties, and from 17.9 per cent in Oxford to 1.7 per cent in West Ham for the county boroughs. A survey undertaken for the Robbins Committee showed that these variations were not a reflection of differences in student ability between the areas, as had often been supposed, but that they were related to differences in local authority provision and practice. In particular they were significantly related to the number of grammar school places provided by the local authority. In areas where more than 23 per cent of the pupils went to grammar schools, 11 per cent of the whole age group entered higher education. In areas where grammar school entry was low − 18 per cent of the age group or under − only 7.5 per cent entered higher education. The differences remained even though social class variables were held constant.

Even within local authority areas there are differences. The Robbins Committee reported that the West Riding of Yorkshire could be divided into three areas for selective purposes − areas of high, medium or low intake into the selective schools. The test requirements for entry into a selective school were highest where the selective entry was lowest. Yet a higher percentage went to higher education from the areas of high and medium intake, suggesting that an important variable is not only the ability of the students at eleven but also the local availability of places in schools which prepare students to enter higher education.

Acland (1973) assembles a range of research evidence to suggest that about one third of the variance in children's ability in English secondary schools is accounted for by differences between schools, that are at least in part accounted for by differences in provisions.[1]

A group of papers that go beyond descriptive analysis and attempt a causal explanation is presented here. These commence with the work of Lehtinen who examines the differentiation of the Finnish educational structure using a theoretical model of ecological differentiation through the formation of centre networks and 'cumulation'. (The exploration of sociological variables is a matter of considerable current interest in American sociological methodology (Borgatta 1969)).

This is followed by a paper by Eggleston which explores the links between supply and response to educational resources with reference to the incidence of 'staying on' after minimum leaving age.[2] The paper identifies a range of factors in administrative policies and executive strategies and relates these, through the experience of students, to decisions about staying on.

Differences in policies and their execution are manifest not only in the variations in resources such as buildings, teachers and equipment but also in the different values which are embodied in these variations. A good example of the fundamental value differences that may exist in apparently similar administrative strategies is to be seen between authorities devoting what appear to be roughly similar proportions of their resources to the provision of comprehensive schools. Yet there may be quite striking differences in administrative practice and ideology that lead to profound differences in the schools and the educational experience they provide. Examples such as these illuminate the importance of the administrative value context of education which can be seen to be significant in the same way as the value content of the home, community and peer group and of the school itself. As in the previous section, the exploration of values becomes central in the search for causality.

Commencing from this position Byrne and Williamson, in an examination of educational provision in north-east England, consider two policy models of local authorities. One is 'the elite oriented authority model in which resources are differentially concentrated on the sponsored elite with consequent high attainment of this elite'. The other is 'the egalitarian authority model where resources are more evenly spread throughout the school system with consequent "inferior" attainment of an elitist kind but where the evidence suggests that there is higher overall attainment of the total school system product'. Not surprisingly Byrne and Williamson find a close correlation between local social structure and the preferred local education authority policy.

But the study of educational provision, like that of demand, can also be enlightened by a conflict frame of reference and by an inter-actionist perspective. These were applied in a case study of development of local authority policy in a local context by Eggleston that indicates the complex patterns of interaction and value negotiations. This, the fourth paper in this section, examines the various stages in the long drawn-out transition to comprehensive secondary schooling in Corby New Town, Northamptonshire.

Following the publication of the Plowden Report the particular importance of local education authority policy in what the Plowden Committee labelled 'educational priority areas' became evident. Interestingly, it is in such areas that local authority provision shows some of its greatest variations. In the final paper of this section the differential characteristics of EPA provision, particularly the quantity and characteristics of teacher supply, are indicated and their relationship with the social characteristics of the areas is explored. The inclusion of the paper also provides a useful example of action research: research that is concerned primarily with discovering the most effective means of bringing about a desired social change, and in which the researchers are deeply involved in the policy implications of their research. The methodological issues àre fully discussed in Halsey (1972 chapter 9). Examination of the data presented is likely to indicate the attractiveness, even the compulsion, of such an involvement in at least some areas of sociological inquiry.

An important feature of this section and particularly of the final contribution is the use of interactionist and conflict frames of reference that begin to avoid some of the hazards of the functionalist/consensus frame of reference discussed in section I. Their capacity to illuminate, in new ways, some of the longstanding research areas of sociology of education is further considered in subsequent sections. But it is appropriate to notice here that it is only possible to talk of 'policy oriented research' when the researcher is able to recognize the existence of alternative policy implications in his field of study. In turn this may lead us to realize that many so-called 'consensus approaches' are often no more than latent policy oriented approaches. Yet again the capacity of new perspectives to throw new light on the concepts on which research is based is apparent.

Notes

[1] Workers at the Local Government Operational Research Unit (Myers 1966 and Robinson 1967) have explored the administrative variables leading to differential educational provision in greater detail. Using the techniques of operational research the Unit has attempted to provide a tool for the planning departments of local educational authorities in their determination of provision — its location, timing and eventual usage.

[2] The recent British Sociological Association study *Comparability in Social Research* concludes, 'the most significant educational variable is one which combines terminal educational age with 'staying-on' (Weinberg 1969).

References

ACLAND, H., 1973, *Social Determinants of Educational Achievement.* Oxford: unpublished D. Phil thesis.

BORGATTA, E.F. (ed.), 1969, *Sociological Methodology.* San Francisco: Jossey Bass.

EGGLESTON, J., 1969, 'The social context of administration' in Baron, G. and Taylor, W. (eds.), *Educational Administration and the Social Sciences.* London: Athlone Press, pp. 18-35.

HALSEY, A.H. (ed.), 1972, *Educational Priority.* London: HMSO.

MYERS, C.L., 1966, *The Scope for Operational Research in Local Educational Administration.* Reading: Local Government Operational Research Unit.

PRATT, J., BURGESS, T., ALLEMANO, R. and LOCKE, M., 1973, *Your Local Education.* Harmondsworth: Penguin.

ROBINSON, G.M., 1967, *Staying on at School.* Reading: Local Government Operational Research Unit.

TAYLOR, G. and AYRES, N., 1969, *Born and Bred Unequal.* London: Longmans.

WEINBERG, A., 1969, 'Education', in Stacey, M. (ed.), *Comparability in Social Research.* London: Heinemann.

JUKKA LEHTINEN

The differentiation of the educational structure: a location analysis on secondary education in Finland *

With the growing emphasis on education in society attention has been drawn also to the location and equality of distribution of educational services. The present study is a continuation of the author's previous report where it was established that great structural differences exist between different economic regions, with respect to secondary education. This study is an attempt to find causes for these regional differences in educational structure.

At the beginning of the study it was assumed that the dissimilarity in educational structure could be explained particularly by the regional differences of the network of centres, with their different factors of supply and demand of education in different combinations, in terms of quality and quantity. The distinct types of education partly depend in different ways on these factors of supply and demand.

The theoretical foundations of the differentiation of the network of centres used in this study were derived, on the one hand, from the explanations of the formation of the network of centres by regional scientists such as Christalier and Lösch; and, on the other hand, from the theories of differentiative cumulative development presented by Myrdal and applied to Finnish circumstances by O. Riihinen. Facts about population, the degree of centralization, ranking of centres, economic resources and industrial development were collected.

It was assumed that the factors of demand for educational services were the following: the number of potential students, the income level of the population, the possibility of using the knowledge gained by education to earn and to extend studies further, the supply of education and the attitudes of the population with regard to education. Correspondingly the factors of supply of education were considered to be the demand for education, the resources of the municipalities, the attitudes of political decision-makers and authorities, the egalitarian policy pursued by the state to equalize regional differences, and the information-giving by the regional level to the decision-making level.

Only some aspects of education itself could be studied, namely the satisfied demand for education, this demand being, by inference, already assumed to be in accordance with the theory of cumulation (growth generates growth, reduction causes new reduction).

---

*Reprinted from Jukka Lehtinen, Koulutusrakenteen Erilaistuminen. (Helsinki, National Planning Office, Series A:27, 1972) by kind permission of the author and publishers.

The factors of demand and supply were measured in a regression analysis, the results of which were interpreted by schemes and ways of inference borrowed from path analysis. The unit of observation was a municipality and the unit of analysis the whole region of the study. With the exception of the metropolitan region and a few municipalities in the archipelago, the investigation was directed at all municipalities in the country where there was a secondary level educational institute in operation in November 1967. Thus, there were 271 municipalities included in the observations.

The educational services were grouped in fifteen educational types according to the classification used in the preliminary study. In each educational type, the volume, i.e. the absolute number of students' places, intensity or volume in relation to the number of inhabitants in the municipality, and the percentage of the volume in the total educational volume in the observation municipality, were analysed. In addition, the diversity of education was measured by variables indicating the amount of the types of education and the heterogeneity of educational structure. All these variables indicating education were used, one by one, as the dependent variable in the regression analysis. Altogether sixty-eight independent variables had been obtained in the operationalizing of the factors of supply and demand. These were demographic numerical series on the cumulation of population, the amplitude of central place service, industrial activities and political and geographical factors.

Because there was a good reason to doubt that the heteroscedasticity and the abnormality of distributions would have an effect on the results of the measurement, the variables were transformed separately, either by logarithms or by extraction of the square root, whichever method most effectively promoted the homoscedastization.

Before this, smaller or larger integers had been added to many variables in order to make the values deviate positively from zero. The regression analysis of all the forty-nine dependent variables was then carried out, both on the original and transformed material.

Of all the sixty-eight explaining candidates available, the method used, the free regression analysis, which had an F value of 4.00 as the acception or refusal limit of the variables, chose less than half of the variables, i.e. thirty variables within different models, most commonly three to six in each.

On the basis of path schemes and causal assumptions based on them, and in comparing the standardized regression coefficients to correlation coefficients, the validity of each model was then considered.

The ability to explain in the models referring to volume was in many cases quite high, i.e. some 80-95 per cent. The ability to explain remained low only in educational types where the variance of volume was very little and which were not cumulative in their nature. The intensity was explained at best only in some 60 per cent, in the mean in some 30-40 per cent; and in many cases in under 10 per cent. The variables measuring the percentage ratio were the most weakly explained: in three cases not at all, and in general only by 20-30 per cent.

In the measurement it was found that the lower secondary level general education was usually located in municipalities characterized by a slight reduction in population, growth slower than the mean in the annual turnover per inhabitant in the retail trade, somewhat low rank of the main centre, and slightly larger political homogeneity than the mean. Lower level technical education, on the other hand, generally thrived in municipalities with high values of population potential, degree of centralization and ranking of centres, large size of industrial population and enlivened retail trade. The factors explaining variables indicating lower level commercial education were associated in the first place with centre formation and with trade. Centres with vigorous growth in population seemed to foster this education: the population and the degree of density of the populated area, as well as the plentifulness of youth, seemed also to promote this. The lower level education in the fields of health and welfare, on the other hand, presupposes a wide population basis, and it was an educational type that thrived in large centres or on the periphery of these. The volume and intensity of this type was increased by the development of the municipality as a retail trade centre. The absolute amount of lower level education in household economy was connected mainly with the population and growth of retail trade in localities where the distance from a neighbouring centre of at least the same rank was rather great. On the other hand, the relative frequency of this educational type was connected above all with municipalities where there were relatively more persons having completed the lower secondary school, middle school. Education in agriculture and forestry based on civic school turned out to have spread very equally in municipalities of different type, even though it favoured mainly rural municipalities. Its character turned out to be non-cumulative. The rest of lower level education was found to be thriving in the steadily growing centres of, so to say, industrial Finland. The amount of this type of education was connected with a slightly larger number of public figures in the locality.

The volume of upper level general education appeared to follow steadily the size of the population in the territorial area, even though additional service facilities in the centre further raised the numbers of pupils. The intensity was greatest in lively medium-sized centres, and the degree of centralization and the function as a trade centre raised the percentage of this educational type. Technical education on the upper level, on the other hand, was located in larger industrial centres. Commercial education on the corresponding level was found to a considerable degree to be located in a way similar to the previous type of education, but now function as a trade centre was more clearly emphasized as the characteristic feature of the localities. However, upper level education in the health and welfare fields, presupposes above all the solidity of the population basis in the sphere of influence, and the strength of the municipality as retail centre. The picture obtained from education in household economy at the same level referred to rural centres which had earlier been rather big but slow in their development. Upper level education in agriculture and forestry was promoted, above all, by the relative amplitude of forests owned by the state in the municipality and was decreased by the fact that the municipality was rather large or a large centre with its typical characteristics. Localities favouring teacher training were rather small municipalities judged by population but rather large, wage industrialized municipalities judged by the main centre, where a larger part of the population than normal was employed in service occupations. A populous and industry dominated centre was characteristic of the location of the rest of upper level education, but it included also wage industrialization of the sphere of influence. The municipalities concerned were situated mainly in industrial Finland and were not especially centres for trade or services.

The total volume of education was most essentially characterized by the current population of the main centre of the municipality, but the population living in the sphere of influence of the centre was almost as important. The population of the municipality did not prove to be an equal factor. Besides a large population the growth of the annual turnover of retail trade also served to a great extent to direct the satisfaction of the demand for education. The total intensity of education, on the other hand, was high in the municipalities with the high degree of centralization, where trade was relatively brisk and the economic resources of the municipality generally good. There were plenty of educational types, and the structure of education was thus diverse in municipalities with a high degree of centralization, where the population was slightly larger, and the structure of industries more heterogeneous than in other corresponding municipalities.

The hypothesis set at the beginning concerning the factors of demand and supply in education was found to be true to a large extent in the measurements. So it could be confirmed that the total population increased the volume of nearly all types of education, in most cases as the strongest factor. The effect of population on the intensity of education was, instead, very scarcely supported by the empiric findings. The assumption of the connections between upper level education and large population centres turned out to be justified to a large extent. Yet, population increased the relative profusion of only certain educational types, not of all types. The volume of education turned out to be in accord with the prevailing demand for education, so that the most recent totals of population were the best in general; only some less general types of education were associated with formed population figures in municipalities. The age structure of the population did not seem to have any effect on the determination of the education studied. The cumulation of population increased mainly the volume of lower education, the intensity of education at both levels and the diversity of education.

Its effect on the volume of upper level education turned out to be indifferent, The cumulation of activities and the increase of income level seemed generally to promote the amount of education, especially of lower level secondary education.

The possibilities for using knowledge in work promoted to some extent both the absolute and the relative amount of education, as well as its diversity, but correlations could not be observed in all educational types. The wealth of the municipality turned out to raise the total intensity of education but the hypothesis on its influence on the quality of education was not verified. The unifying pressure manifested as homogeneity in party support had a slight effect on education: it increased a little the relative amount of lower level education and decreased the respective amount of higher level education.

The activity of the people in the locality in the information-giving directed at the central administration turned out to have in some degree a promoting influence on education. The egalitarian policy of the state could be verified to have equalized the regional differences in the supply of educational services to some extent, although by no means totally.

The transformation of the variables was not found to have an effect on the substance of the results, because, although there were partly different independent variables in the alternative models, they were interpretationally close to each other.

Formally, the influence of the transformation was such that in models with high ability to explain it reduced, and in models with low ability to explain it raised the ability to explain. In many cases the number of independent variables increased simultaneously.

The arithmetical means of the independent variables thus selected were then computed by economic regions to indicate the regional differences in the distribution of the factors of demand and supply of educational services. When these regional means were put into the regression equations explaining the volume variables of education, computed values for each regional distribution of educational types were received. When comparing these to the real values it was found that in general the explanations corresponded quite well to the reality.

Finally, both the computed and the real structure of education in each economic region were analysed by comparing the percentual values. Except Ahvenanmaa, where the volume is little and the structure exceptional, the computed values were quite close to the real values. so that the hypothesis stated at the beginning of the study about the causes of the regional differences of educational structure could be considered to have been quite well verified.

JOHN EGGLESTON

Some environmental correlates of extended secondary education in England*

One of the major tasks of the English educational system since 1945 has been to supply increasing numbers of highly educated recruits to the labour force. As in other major industrial societies this has presented problems of expanding the provision of higher education. But a particular problem in England has been the pattern of state secondary schooling. In the selective 'tripartite' arrangement which has characterized the English state system since 1945, only the 20-30 per cent of students admitted to the selective grammar or technical schools have generally had the opportunity of an education which, in content or duration, could lead to entry to higher education. The majority of students who entered the secondary modern schools followed programmes which terminated at the minimum school leaving age and which were specifically precluded from leading to qualifications which could secure access to higher education.[1] For all but the minority the minimum school leaving age marked the maximum extent of full time education, and the ensuing limitation of life chances.

Both the Crowther Committee,[2] reporting in 1959 and the Robbins Committee,[3] reporting in 1963 were able to demonstrate that the expansion of higher education in England was being handicapped by twin shortcomings of the secondary school system. One was a failure to mobilize sufficient recruits, the other, seen as a consequence of the selective procedures employed at eleven plus and after, was a failure to mobilize all of the most able recruits.[4]

One beginning of current moves against the restrictive assumptions of ability implicit in selective secondary schooling arose during the 1950s in the secondary modern schools. A number of these schools contrived to run programmes after minimum leaving age leading to qualifications which were passports to pre-university and professional courses. They found that increasing numbers of their students were able to complete such programmes successfully.[5] In 1954 only 5.7 per cent of all secondary modern pupils remained after minimum leaving age, in 1963 20.7 per cent did so. A primary motivation of many teachers and administrators in these moves was to challenge, on behalf of their pupils, the class linked selective procedures of the tripartite system. In the late 1950s this was a challenge which could

---

*Reprinted from John Eggleston, 'Some environmental correlates of extended secondary education in England' Comparative Education, 3(2) (March, 1967), published by Carfax Publishing Company, by kind permission of the publishers.

be backed by the findings of the empirical studies of English sociologists.[6] The expansion of numbers eligible for higher education was only a by-product, though an important one, of such moves. More recent moves to replace tripartitism by non-selective comprehensive secondary schooling can still be seen to spring from similar motivations by teachers and administrators. Yet the prospect of expanding the numbers of eligible recruits for higher education presented by the comprehensive school is striking, for a common feature of all schemes of comprehensive reorganization is a more open access to extended secondary education by all students.

The expansion of opportunity for access to extended secondary education suggested the need for examination of the circumstances in which student decisions to stay on occurred.[7] The need for such study is underlined by the associated phenomenon — the relative decline of the selective grammar and technical schools. These schools have an 'institutionalized' holding power over their pupils until at least sixteen, for it is expected without question that all their pupils will complete a five-year course, and in fact nowadays virtually all of them conform. In the 'open' comprehensive situation decisions to stay on can be made at the minimum leaving age of fifteen, not at eleven. Moreover they tend to be made far more by the individual pupil and less by the school. In consequence the predictability of decision is lessened.

Opportunities for the writer to visit a number of comprehensive and modern schools in England brought an awareness of marked variations in decisions to stay on by students in different areas and in different types of school. This suggested that some predictive factors may be identified in the *external* environment of the schools, notably the socio-economic status of their catchment areas. But a further cluster of environmental variables seemed to lie in the local administration of education — the availability of places in comprehensive schools; the equipment and facilities of schools, and the post-leaving age programmes offered.

Accordingly a study was planned which would examine two areas of variables external to secondary schools; those associated with the administrative regimes in which the schools operated and those associated with their catchment areas. The hypotheses for the first area were that a high incidence of staying on at modern and comprehensive schools would be associated with high standards of buildings and equipment; well-developed programmes of extended courses and successful examination results therein; comprehensive rather than tripartite secondary schooling; low intakes to selective schools where they exist, and larger rather than smaller schools. The hypothesis for the second was that a high incidence of staying on would be associated with catchment areas where pupils came from homes of predominantly high socio-economic status.

The research was conducted in a representative group of eight English local education authority areas — the county boroughs of Burton-on-Trent, Coventry, Derby, Leicester and Nottingham and the county councils of Derbyshire (south and south-east division), Leicestershire and Staffordshire — over a five-year period, 1958-63. Though as befits its representative nature, this area was still predominantly served by tripartite secondary schools, it contained two of the longest-established areas of comprehensive school provision in England, the Coventry and Leicestershire comprehensive schools. Additionally it contained examples of two of the many variations of the tripartite system, the Nottingham bilateral schools and the special secondary school transfer.arrangements at Derby.[8]

Three indicators of staying on were established and applied to all 'non-selective' schools in the area (240 modern and bilateral secondary schools and 20 comprehensive schools). These indicators were as follows:

(a) Extent of staying on after fifteen (minimum leaving age) in the survey period, expressed as a percentage of the total 14 year old age cohort in the school in the previous year.

(b) Extent of staying on after sixteen (to enter a fifth year of schooling) in the survey period, expressed as a percentage of the total 14 year old age cohort in the school two years previously.

(c) Change in the rate of staying on in the school during the survey period.[9]

A list of administrative and socio-economic variables was subsequently drawn up for investigation in the schools. The final list of variables was as follows:

1 Sex of pupils.
2 Size of school.
3 Intake of pupils to selection schools from the non-selective school catchment areas.
4 The extent of staying on after sixteen in selective schools drawing pupils from the non-selective school catchment areas.
5 Material environment of the schools. This was a ranking of the specialist teaching facilities available in each school undertaken on similar lines to the survey reported in the 'Newsom Report'.[10] In each case the ranking was undertaken by two independent assessors, the few differences being resolved by investigation of the school by the writer.
6 Age of school building. Again following Newsom precedent, schools were asked to report the approximate date of the construction of the earliest part of the school buildings in current use.
7 Provision of extended courses. After preliminary investigation it was decided that the most useful inventory of courses was as follows:

  i Courses leading to GCE O level exams.
  ii Courses leading to other external examinations usually taken at the end of the fourth year of school, such as those of the College of Preceptors or the Royal Society of Arts.
  iii Courses leading to local education authority examinations held at the end of the fourth year, such as the Coventry Education Authority's Pre-Technical and Pre-Commercial Certificate. (Non-examination extended courses were almost non-existent.)

8   Success rates in GCE examinations taken in the fifth year of extended courses.
9   Success rates in examinations taken in the fourth year of extended courses.
10   Socio-economic status of the catchment area. This was established by applying the Juror Index[11] to the total population of the catchment area of each school.

Examination of these variables for each school was undertaken with the aid of school, local education authority and electoral records and the generous assistance of teachers, administrators and electoral officers is acknowledged. On completion, this data and that for the three indicators of staying on was coded and correlated and analysed along lines similar to those suggested by McKennell.[12,13]

The presentation of the results which follow is in two parts. The first reports the correlation matrix for the whole survey area and a separate matrix for 'conventional' areas of administration therein. The second part presents a more detailed examination of some of the local systems with emphasis on the schools constituting the Leicestershire Plan. These schools are of particular interest as they comprise one of the few local education authority areas wherein *all* state pupils have, over a period of five years, received a comprehensive type of secondary education. Moreover, it is a pattern of school provision which is now being adopted by many other local education authorities.

The survey area

Administrative variables

The correlations between the incidence of staying on and the administrative variables are presented in the following matrix:

TABLE I   Administrative variables and staying on. Bilateral and secondary modern schools. Product moment correlation coefficients *(r)*

Variable	Staying on after 15	Staying on after 16	Rate of change in staying on
School size*	0.2846	0.3571	0.2175
Intake of selective* schools in same area	0.0511	0.0021	0.0297
Staying on after 16 in selective schools in same area*	0.0720	0.0906	0.0783
School material environment*	0.3086	0.1507	0.1829
Age of school buildings*	0.2844	0.1244	0.1607
Extended course provision†	0.6525	0.6341	0.4180
GCE exam success†	0.5375	0.5409	0.3859
Non-GCE exam successes†	0.4495	0.2890	0.4495

*   Variables examined for 240 schools
†   Variables examined for 125 schools (all schools in Coventry, Derby, SE Derbyshire, Leicester, Leicestershire and Nottingham).

Not surprisingly the most highly significant correlations are those
between staying on and the provision of identified extended courses;
indeed this provision and the factors associated with it emerged as being
of overriding importance in the incidence of staying on.

What of the consequences of examination successes? Successes in
the GCE examinations, taken at the end of the fifth or sixth year, emerge
as having a highly significant correlation with both staying on after
fifteen and after sixteen. Though the non-GCE examinations usually
taken at the fourth year are also significant at both ages, they are of
a lower order of significance at both fifteen plus and sixteen plus. The
non-GCE examinations emerge, however, as the most significant factor
in changes in the rate of staying on in the survey period, probably by
virtue of their use by students as an intermediate goal which seems more
readily accessible when decisions to stay on are first made, even though
it is a goal which may be bypassed as its realization draws near. Abandonment of the fourth year examinations with the advent of courses
leading to the new Certificate of Secondary Education, taken at the
end of the fifth year, could have a handicapping effect on the growth
of staying on in non-selective schools. However, what appears to be a
growing confidence in the accessibility of GCE and CSE successes by
pupils from these schools, and the internalization of these five-year
courses into the programmes of schools, seems likely to overcome this.
Accordingly the recommendations of the Beloe Committee,[14] now
widely accepted, to discontinue fourth year examinations, seem
unlikely to restrict the growth of extended education in the non-
selective schools, except perhaps in the smaller numbers that have
made no beginning in examination work.

Also significant are the size, condition and age of the school
buildings. Of the three, school size is most closely correlated with
staying on, being significant at the 1 per cent level for all three
indicators. Large schools are closely identified with high rates of
staying on, particularly with staying on after sixteen.[15] The underlying
factors here seem to be the advantages in running examination courses
which large schools enjoy. These are particularly relevant in the modern
schools, where the generous staffing and facilities needed to launch an
examination course successfully have to be 'spared' initially from
elsewhere in the school. Only in a large school can this 'sparing' be done
without obvious sacrifice of the non-examination majority. Moreover,
the large school has advantages in attracting academically qualified
staff by virtue of its higher allowance of special responsibility posts.
The spiral of events, once established, continues. Academic staff can
be offered academic work and the higher points total which the
extended course pupils allow can still further facilitate staff recruitment.

The school material environment — an index of the quality of
specialist teaching facilities of the school — is also significantly correlated
with all three indicators at the 15 per cent level. The age of the school
buildings is also significant for all three indicators; the older the buildings the fewer pupils staying on and the lesser rate of increase. Both
factors are, interestingly, far more highly significant for staying on after
fifteen than for staying on after sixteen. The age and condition of the

school buildings seem to be more important factors in the initial decision to stay on than in subsequent decisions. At sixteen plus the pupils seem to have internalized the goals of the school and become relatively indifferent to the architecture.

The remaining correlations are those concerning the provision of selective secondary education in the catchment area of the non-selective schools, and the incidence of staying on in the selective schools after sixteen (staying on after fifteen to complete a fifth year in the selective schools is already the 'norm' and would not offer a useful variable). No significant correlations between either of these variables and staying on in the non-selective schools were established; indeed the relationship shown in Table I is close to random.

This evidence, though negative, none the less refuted the common suggestion that a high selective intake drained off the able pupils who would otherwise remain in the modern schools and take extended courses. However, the situation seemed to require further investigation, as the evidence obtained made no allowance for the way in which staying on in the modern schools might be affected by the overall approach of the local authorities to the provision of secondary education. As has been mentioned the group of eight local authorities under investigation contained some authorities which were unrepresentative in their secondary school provision (Coventry, Leicestershire, Nottingham and Derby).

Did these modifications to tripartite provision mask some of the relationship between the selective and modern schools' staying on figures which might occur in a 'conventional' local authority?

In an attempt to examine this secondary hypothesis some of the data for these 'conventional' authorities with almost entirely tripartite provision of secondary schooling was isolated and correlated with the three indicators of staying on (Burton-on-Trent, south Derbyshire and Staffordshire. Only three isolated comprehensive schools existed in these areas during the survey period). The correlation matrix for the 115 modern schools of these authorities is set out in Table II.

TABLE II   Administrative variables and staying on. 115 secondary modern schools in 'conventionally' organized areas. Product moment correlation coefficients (r)

Variable	Staying on after 15	Staying on after 16	Rate of change in staying on
School size	0.1485	0.2382	0.2284
Intake of selective schools in same area	0.1785	0.1976	0.1075
Staying on after 16 in selective schools in same area	0.3535	0.1806	0.0997
School material environment	0.3024	0.1628	0.1660
Age of school buildings	0.2916	0.0543	0.0858

In most respects the pattern of correlation is similar. School size is significantly correlated to staying on after sixteen and to change in the rate of staying on, though not to staying on after fifteen. As before, the condition of school buildings and the age of the school is significantly related to staying on after fifteen at the 1 per cent level but not significantly related to staying on after sixteen.

The most notable change is in the relationship of the variables associated with the selective secondary schools. In these conventionally organized authorities, staying on in the modern schools after sixteen emerged as being significantly and positively correlated to the selective school intake and, just, significantly and positively correlated with staying on after fifteen. Moreover the correlation between staying on after sixteen in selective schools and staying on after fifteen in modern schools is highly significant. These figures were substantiated by reciprocal correlations for the schools in the 'non-conventional' areas.

The evidence indicates that, in 'conventional' authorities, a high rate of entry to selective schools is associated with a high rate of staying on in the non-selective schools, and in turn suggests that the effective demand for extended education is not tied to a limited supply of pupils who can benefit from it, but rather is a demand which grows with the growth of educational opportunity. It may be that the situation was masked in 'reorganization' areas, not only by the provision of comprehensive schools, but also by location of such schools and the transfer arrangements associated with them — matters which are discussed subsequently.

It was not possible to subject the comprehensive schools to the same correlation analysis as the modern and bilateral, as they were not distinct in their administrative variables. All came into the largest categories of schools size; all had superior material environments and buildings; all had a full range of extended courses, and all shared a level of examination successes midway between those of the selective schools and the modern schools. Table III is presented, however, and indicates that staying on in the groups of comprehensive schools in Leicestershire and Coventry was of a higher order than the aggregate rate of staying on in the whole remaining tripartite area (grammar, technical and modern schools) of the same two authorities.

TABLE III   Percentage of pupils remaining after minimum leaving age in comprehensive and tripartite schools (Coventry and Leicestershire)

1964	Comprehensive schools*	Tripartite schools
Coventry	57.6	39.3
Leicestershire	49.2	33.4

*Only comprehensive schools established on or before September 1958 (Coventry) or September, 1960 (Leicestershire) are included

Socio-economic status

The Juror Index was applied to the 125 bilateral and modern schools in Coventry, Derby, Leicester, Nottingham, Leicestershire and south-east Derbyshire. The correlation between the Index and the three indicators of staying on is shown in Table IV.

TABLE IV Juror Index and staying on. 125 bilateral and secondary modern schools. Product moment correlation coefficients *(r)*

Variable	Staying on after 15	Staying on after 16	Rate of change in staying on
Juror Index	0.1964	0.2509	0.1414

The correlations are significant at the 1 per cent level for staying on after sixteen but only at the 5 per cent level for staying on to fifteen. The correlation with change in the rate of staying on just fails to reach the 5 per cent level of significance. The stronger direct relationship with the external environment of the pupil at sixteen plus would seem to be a corrolary of the diminished force of the school environment (buildings and facilities) noted previously at this age.[16]

The relationship between staying on and socio-economic status in the comprehensive and bilateral schools of Coventry, Leicestershire and Nottingham is of interest. Inspection of the Juror Indices of the catchment areas of these schools reveals not only a close relationship between socio-economic status and staying on, but also a relationship between the socio-economic status of the community and the provision of comprehensive or bilateral education. The relationship is shown in Table V. (For Coventry and Nottingham the catchment area assessed for socio-economic status is that from which both selected and non-selected pupils attend the school, not the extended catchment for selected entry.)

TABLE V Socio-economic status of school catchment area*

	Coventry	Leicestershire	Nottingham
Average JI of comprehensive, Leicestershire Plan or bilateral school catchment area	25.31	19.8	15.46
Average JI of modern school catchment area	20.25	13.17	9.22

*Averages are not weighted and are therefore approximate, particularly in Leicestershire where there is a wider variation in size of school. However, as the average size of comprehensive, Plan and bilateral schools is greater than that of the modern schools, the inaccuracy underestimates the difference in JI of the two sets of schools.

The table indicates that the reorganized secondary schools are characterized by catchment areas of superior socio-economic status in each regime.

In view of the relationship between socio-economic status and staying on shown in Table IV, the previously demonstrated success of these schools in holding their senior pupils seems less impressive. Does then the main advantage of the comprehensive type of secondary school lie not in its comprehensiveness but in its superior catchment area.

In an attempt to examine the situation more fully the Juror Indices for all the schools in Coventry and Nottingham were correlated for each area, with the indices of staying on. The results are shown in Table VI.

TABLE VI Juror Index and staying on in Coventry and Nottingham. Product moment correlation coefficients *(r)*

Variable	Staying on after 15	Staying on after 16	Rate of change in staying on
JI Coventry (N=22)	0.4293	0.2125	0.2993
JI Nottingham (N=32)	0.3018	0.2784	0.2178

The figures show that for both authorities the correlation between the JI and the three indicators of staying on for all schools is less than for the aggregate of schools shown in Table IV. (The actual number of *(r)* is of course higher in each position because of the far smaller number of cases.) The situation seems to be that though the majority of the schools are situated in areas of relatively superior socio-economic status, their influence is none the less to lessen the link between staying on and socio-economic status found in the secondary modern schools. This could in part result from the achievements in holding-power of the few comprehensive and bilateral schools in the lower socio-economic areas. But it also springs from the superior holding-power in the remaining modern schools in the area of reorganization, as compared with the modern schools in non-reorganized areas. The incidence of staying on in the modern schools of Coventry, Leicestershire and Nottingham was higher than that for all other authorities in the survey area (other variables held constant).

The link between high socio-economic areas and comprehensive versions of secondary education is an almost inescapable one for local education authorities. Clearly the authorities are under obligation to build new schools in response to rapid population growth — a particular problem in Coventry and Leicestershire. If the authority has adopted a policy of comprehensive education then it is logical that these new schools be comprehensive schools and equally logical to build them in the new housing areas where the demand exists. These new areas, whether of private or council housing, tend to be areas of high socio-economic status. Moreover they may contain the only large sites which are suitable for comprehensive schools in the authority's area. From the authority's viewpoint the building of comprehensive schools in these areas also avoids the difficulties of disturbance of other schools, especially if the new comprehensive schools are used as neighbourhood schools. And the policy of neighbourhood schools is often forced on the authority by the very rapidity of the growth of the child population in the new areas of the suburbs. In such circumstances the children from the old city centres are faced with multiple handicaps in their access to the comprehensive schools. Thus schools which may be designed to act as intruments of egalitarianism can, in many cases, only achieve it indirectly by the creation of a climate of educational expectation which spreads over from the comprehensive into the modern schools still serving the predominantly lower socio-economic areas.

Local Systems

The Leicestershire Plan[17]

The Leicestershire Plan is a 'two tier' comprehensive system wherein all pupils enter a 'high' school at the age of eleven plus. At fourteen plus they decide between continuing their education to sixteen or beyond at an 'upper' school or staying on at their high school and leaving at fifteen. Not surprisingly the incidence of transfer was found to be higher in the superior socio-economic areas and lower in the inferior ones. In the well-to-do Leicester suburb of Oadby, 50 per cent of the age group transferred in 1960 and 85 per cent in 1964. In the old industrial town of Hinckley the comparable figures were 30 and 39 per cent. In view of the interest in these schools it was decided to undertake more intensive examination of the pupils who made the transfer decision in 1964. An assessment of individual pupils' socio-economic status was made, occupations of parents being classified in accordance with the socio-economic groups of the General Register Office's Standard Classification of Occupations.[18] Of interest was the finding, presented in Table VII, that middle class children in superior areas have a higher transfer rate than middle class children in inferior areas; conversely that working class children in inferior areas have a lower transfer rate than working class children in superior areas.[19]

TABLE VII

1964 Percentage of children transferring from high to upper school	Superior suburb	Inferior suburb
Children of middle class parents	89.2	77.5
Children of working class parents	59.1	30.0

The community background was also linked with the career expectations of the pupils. In the superior suburb 73 per cent of the pupils who transferred expected middle class jobs. In the inferior suburb only 58 per cent of the transferees expected middle class jobs, even though they have elected to go to the kind of school which could lead them to the point of entry to such work.

The external social variables seemed to suffuse the working of the transfer arrangements. The upper schools tended to be predominantly middle class establishments, with up to 50 per cent of middle class pupils. Conversely the pupils electing to remain in the high schools after fourteen were predominantly of working class origin; the working class representation was as high as 94 per cent in one school and not less than 71 per cent in the others.

Within the schools a close relationship existed between membership of the three-track streaming arrangements and transfer decisions; 84 per cent of all 'A'-stream pupils transferred but only 26.6 per cent of 'C'-stream pupils transferred. The picture was completed when examination of the social backgrounds of the pupils from the various streams indicated that 'A'-stream pupils were predominantly from middle class homes, whilst 'C'-stream pupils were predominantly from working class homes.

On the face of it the social class differentiation is similar to the pattern of events in the tripartite system. But it must be noted that the figure of transfer to extended courses by 'C'-stream pupils is one which is seldom achieved in the corresponding area of the tripartite system — the lower half of a secondary modern school — in areas of similar socio-economic status. Indeed the figure compares favourably with the 17.5 per cent of all secondary modern pupils staying on after minimum leaving age in 1964.[20] Overall, children of all social backgrounds and from all neighbourhoods stayed on more in the Leicestershire Plan than in similar areas elsewhere. But the conditions of access to extended education brought a very high percentage of middle class children who were staying on (83 per cent) and a far smaller percentage of working class children (35.7 per cent). The result is a wider class difference in the incidence of staying on than that which occurs in tripartite school systems in similar socio-economic areas.

The transfer figure for the 'A'-(grammar-type)-stream pupils was one which called for further investigation. There is a contrast between the 84 per cent of 'A'-stream transferees and the overall staying on rate of 99.1 per cent of pupils over fifteen in all maintained grammar schools in 1964.[20] One possible explanation for the divergence seemed to be that some 'class' waste of ability, so far undetected, was occurring at the point of transfer over and above that which is normally associated with streaming. To explore this a fuller analysis was undertaken of the social backgrounds of 'A'-stream pupils. This indicated that 95 per cent of the middle class children transferred to the upper school, but that only 75 per cent of the working class children did so. This 'class' waste of ability was concentrated in the high schools serving inferior areas. The picture is reminiscent of the pattern of differential early leaving, once characteristic of the grammar schools. In most grammar schools the holding-power of the school organization has now overcome this problem. The open Leicestershire Plan schools, lacking such developed holding-power, appear to have to rely more fully on the holding-power which can be applied externally by the values of family and neighbourhood. In consequence they seem unable to hold all of even their most able pupils if they lack external support for continued education.

Transfer arrangements in Coventry, Nottingham and Derby

An interesting area of comparison between different arrangements for secondary education came to light in consideration of transfer arrangements. The situation in the Leicestershire Plan, where transfer is a central feature as an essential prelude to extended education, has already been discussed. The situation in three of the other authorities will be reported briefly.

In Coventry, with a range of comprehensive and modern secondary schools, staying on after minimum leaving age by the modern school pupils could be attained by optional transfer to a comprehensive school at thirteen plus or by staying on in their existing schools. Of the total age group in the modern schools 5.7 per cent transferred to comprehensive schools with the prospect of extended courses, and 11.3 per cent stayed on in the modern schools with generally inferior facilities.

In Nottingham, as has already been mentioned, a number of secondary modern schools were converted in 1957 into bilateral secondary schools with selective and non-selective intakes; these existed alongside continuing grammar and secondary modern schools. Although the bilateral schools received 'segregated' intakes, rigid divisions were not maintained within the schools, and transfer from non-selective to selective streams became common. In these schools the expectation of extended education for the selective intake soon became one of the norms of the school. But by 1962 the incidence of staying on of non-selective pupils in these schools had risen to 18.7 per cent as against 12.2 per cent for the non-selective pupils in the remaining secondary modern schools.

In a third area, Derby, with a 'conventional' pattern of grammar, technical and modern schools, there was also an opportunity for secondary modern pupils to stay on after minimum leaving age, but only through a process of selective transfer to the grammar and technical schools at age thirteen. Extended courses in modern schools were discouraged and there was virtually no provision for them. In this authority not only was the rate of staying on in the modern schools predictably the lowest in the whole of the survey area, but the staying on rate in the selective schools was too — a result in no small way brought about by the failure of these schools to hold their thirteen plus intakes.

When full account had been taken of all identified variables, the conclusion remained that the pupils were everywhere more willing to stay on if they were able to do so and still remain within their existing school community.

It is suggested that the evidence indicates the existence of a largely unreckoned force in the holding-power of the English comprehensive or modern school — that of the student community which may, under certain conditions, remain centred in the school after minimum leaving age. This seems to reinforce the previous suggestion that the socially selective aspects of the Leicestershire Plan are mediated by the adolescent population in both middle class and working class school areas; that pupils who are supported in decisions to extend their education by the home and the adult community are able, if need be, to dispense with the support of their peers, but that those who lack adult support need that of their fellows and are unlikely to remain at school without it. In Leicestershire the situation is intensified as the Upper Schools tend to become middle class institutions. The point was neatly put by a group of pupils from one of the 'inferior' area high schools who told the writer 'Don't expect us to transfer to that bunch of stuck-up snobs.'[21]

The evidence gives rise to further hypotheses. One such is that comprehensive systems require new relationships between schools and their adolescent pupils. Such relationships may involve the decline of the conventional strategies of English education, wherein the adolescent community is fragmented and differentiated in terms of future prospects and present behaviour, and wherein some of the leaders are absorbed into the official power structure of the school as prefects. Their place may be taken by the largely autonomous adolescent population already characteristic of much of tertiary education in England; a population with its own internally determined status hierarchy and with relationships of coexistence rather than subordination within educational organizations. Such a change would, moreover, seem to be a possible consequence of the egalitarianism on which so much of English comprehensive planning is based and a necessary basis of expansion. But the very innovation of comprehensive intakes can be seen as likely to speed such a change where, for the first time, the youth of a whole area is brought to a common school, and the policies of destreaming now being advocated in the comprehensive schools are further likely to accelerate it.[22]

The associated administrative changes may also be hypothesized, At the least they would seem to require the provision of extended course opportunity for all pupils, not only the most able, and of associated development of student counselling services. But a further change may be the elimination of situations where decisions to stay on have to be accompanied by decisions to transfer. This latter could be achieved by the establishment of a system of 'all-through' comprehensive schools, or by policies of obligatory transfer to common upper schools in two-tier systems, with transfer taking place at thirteen rather than fourteen to allow a greater chance of school community development and integration before leaving decisions arose. Indeed, such arrangements may offer the prospect of creating more homogeneous adolescent age groups than are possible in the 'all-through' school.

In the recognition of the potential strength of the adolescent community, and subsequent adoption of strategies of 'coexistence', the comprehensive schools may discover new resources in their task of matching the holding-power of the selective schools. Furthermore, they may be applicable not only to their able middle class pupils but also to increasing numbers of pupils from all social backgrounds. In so doing they may become more effective instruments of both extended secondary education and extended egalitarianism.

These further hypotheses may be explored by extended[23] correlational analysis of the kind employed in this study. But valuable examination of causal relationships may now be possible through the application of techniques of organizational analysis to the various forms of comprehensive secondary school now emerging in English education.

Summary

An examination of staying on beyond minimum leaving age in English non-selective secondary schools of eight representative English local education authorities was undertaken, to explore hypotheses that voluntary extension of schooling is associated with identifiable administrative and community variables in the school environment.

Optimum conditions for student decisions in favour of extended secondary schooling were, as hypothesized, the availability of successful examination courses (virtually no non-examination courses existed) in large schools with superior material environment and with catchment areas of superior socio-economic status. Student response was greater where provision was available in the school community where they received their initial secondary education; concentration of provision into a few schools by transfer arrangements inhibited response, though the inhibition was less in superior areas.

The hypothesis that low intakes to selective schools would be associated with high rates of staying on in the non-selective schools serving the same catchment areas was not substantiated. In the survey area as a whole there was no significant correlation. But in the 'conventional' areas of secondary provision the hypothesis was reversed — a high intake to selective schools was positively and significantly correlated with a high rate of staying on in the non-selective schools. Moreover high rates of staying on in both types of school were positively correlated.

Comprehensive systems emerged as being superior to tripartite systems in the provision and holding-power of their extended courses. (There was however, some evidence of less complete holding-power of the comprehensive schools over their most able pupils than would have been expected in a tripartite system.) The overall superior holding-power of these schools seemed largely to be accounted for by the superior socio-economic status of their catchment areas. But the opportunity for extended education within all schools seemed to be a feature of local authority areas where comprehensive provision existed; so that staying on even in their modern schools with inferior socio-economic catchment areas was of a higher order than in schools with similar areas elsewhere.

The examination of the hypotheses was followed by consideration of the prospect of extended education at a time of relative decline of the selective schools with their institutionalized holding power and their replacement by 'open' comprehensive systems with broader social and intellectual intakes. It was hypothesized that the school adolescent community could, in certain circumstances, act as a countervailing force to 'dropping-out' at minimum leaving age.

Notes

[1] *The New Secondary Education* (London: Ministry of Education, 1947). Continued education for secondary modern students was largely restricted to further education of a part-time nature, characterized by high wastage rates.

[2] The further education situation was outlined in the Crowther Report pp.318-68, volume 1 (London, Central Advisory Council for Education 1959). Ibid. volume 2 (1960).

[3] *Higher Education.* Appendix 1, *(The Demand for Places in Higher Education).*(London, Committee on Higher Education 1963).

[4] Little attention was paid to these problems in the years immediately following 1945. Thus the Central Advisory Council's report of 1954 concerned itself solely with student drop-out from the selective grammar schools and offered no consideration of that of the modern schools. *Early Leaving* (London, Central Advisory Council for Education, 1954).

[5] The sequence of events has been reviewed by W. Taylor, in *The Secondary Modern School* (London, 1963).

[6] See D.V. Glass, (ed.), *Social Mobility in Britain* (London, 1954), and J. Floud, *et al., Social Class and Educational Opportunity* (London, 1957).

[7] Previous research on English comprehensive schooling has been largely concerned with examination of the working-out of egalitarian policies rather than with extensions of schooling. For example, Miller has examined the degree of convergence of values amongst comprehensive school pupils. T.W.G. Miller, *Values in the Comprehensive School: an experimental study* (Birmingham, 1961). Both Dixon and Holly examined the relationship between social class and academic achievement and extracurricular activities, each working in a London comprehensive school; both noticed a persisting social class determination of educability in their schools. S. Dixon, *Some Aspects of School Life and Progress in a Comprehensive School in relation to Pupils' Social Background* (M.A., University of London, 1962), and D.N. Holly, *Social and Academic Selection in a London Comprehensive School* (M.A., University of London, 1963). Holly's thesis is summarized in an article in the *British Journal of Sociology,* p. 150, and is the subject of an interesting critique by A. Giddens and S.W. Holloway, in *British Journal of Sociology,* 16, p.351.

[8] *The Leicestershire Plan* is a 'two tier' comprehensive system. Pupils enter the lower tier (High Schools) at eleven and decide between transfer at fourteen to the Upper Schools with extended courses, or remaining at the High Schools and leaving at minimum age. The scheme was initiated in the Oadby, Wigston and Hinckley areas in 1957 and has since been introduced elsewhere.
The Coventry comprehensive schools are single tier schools opened since 1954, serving predominantly the new suburban areas of the city; the central areas still being served by secondary modern schools. In the survey period, selective schools still drew 10 per cent of the age cohort from *all* parts of the city; moreover the comprehensives

drew a 15 per cent 'second selective' entry from the school areas. Separate Catholic grammar and modern schools also exist.

The Nottingham bilateral schools are secondary modern schools which in the survey period drew a second selective entry of 15 per cent of the age cohort in all parts of the city, 10 per cent having already been offered grammar school places. All have, additionally, a non-selective 'secondary modern' entry. All have full extended course provision which is not closed to the 'modern' entry.

Derby transfer arrangements. In the survey period 27 per cent of age cohort entered selective schools at eleven, a further 7 per cent transferred at thirteen after tests. No extended courses existed in secondary modern schools. The official policy has been one of 'scraping the barrel for able pupils so that none shall be left in the modern schools'.

For an account of the *Leicestershire Plan* see:
S.C. Mason, *The Leicestershire Experiment and Plan* (3rd ed., London, 1964).

Information about the Leicestershire Schools is also to be found in:
S.C. Mason 'The Leicestershire Plan' in S. McClure (ed.) *Comprehensive Planning* (London, 1965) and in:
M. Armstrong and M. Young, *New Look at Comprehensive Schools* (London, 1964).

For an account of the Coventry comprehensive schools, see:
G.C. Firth, *Comprehensive Schools in Coventry and elsewhere* (Coventry, 1963).

For an account of the Nottingham bilateral schools, see *What about us?* (National Association of Labour Teachers, Nottingham Branch, Nottingham, 1959).

[9] Not surprisingly there was a highly significant degree of correlation between the three indicators. For the 240 modern and bilateral schools this was as follows:

n=240	Staying on after 16	Change in rate
Staying on after 15	r = 0.6877	r = 0.3508
Staying on after 16	–	r = 0.2176

[10] *Half our Future* (the Newsom Report), pp.250-9 (London, Central Advisory Council for Education, 1963).

[11] The Juror Index is described in P.G. Gray, *et al., The Proportion of Jurors as an index of the Economic Status of a District* (London, Central Office of Information, 1953). The Index is based on the existence of a property qualification for service as a juror, the occupation of a dwelling with a rateable value of £20 per annum or more, and it is therefore associated with social as well as economic status. It is readily calculable from electoral registers, the number of electors marked for juror service being counted and expressed as in relation to the total electorate. For the purposes of this study it offered

considerable advantage, in that the electoral registers on which jurors are indicated are expressed in a form which allows the allocation of jurors to school catchment areas, electors being listed by individual address. It should be noted, however, that further use of the JI at the present time (1967) would involve complications arising from rating revaluation of property. This problem did not arise in this study, however, as the major revaluations of 1957-8 and 1962-3 fell just outside the survey period, leaving a period of stable valuation practice. Since 1963 almost all occupiers of council (subsidized) housing are eligible for juror service, along with other occupiers of relatively low rateable property. In consequence the Index has become a much less sensitive instrument of socio-economic assessment.

[12] A.C. McKennell, Correlational analysis of social survey data, *Sociological Review*, 13, p.157.

[13] Further examination of these variables is now being undertaken by the Local Government Operational Research Unit in a research project on the raising of the school leaving age in Britain in consultation with the writer.

[14] *Secondary school examinations other than GCE* (London, Secondary Schools Examination Council, 1960).

[15] This would appear to be in conflict with the Robbins Committee finding of a significant correlation between staying on to seventeen and the percentage of pupils in small schools in local authority areas. This calculation is, however, based on primary and secondary schools in local authority areas. Moreover, the correlation is itself suspect. The report notes that 'the distribution of this variable is abnormal and a correlation coefficient has little meaning'. *Higher Education* (London, Committee on Higher Education, 1963), Appendix 1, p.67.

[16] The figures lend some apparent support to the 'community context thesis' which suggests that the socio-economic status of a catchment area has an effect on decisions to stay on over and above that of the influence of the socio-economic status of the pupils' home background. For a succinct account of this thesis see N. Rogoff, 'Local social structure and educational selection' in A. H. Halsey, J. Floud and C.A. Anderson (eds.), *Education, Economy and Society*, pp.242-3. (Glencoe Ill., 1961). An important critique of the thesis is to be found in W.H, Sewell and J.M. Armer, 'Neighbourhood context and college plans', *American Sociological Review*, 2, p.159. This thesis is neither supported nor rejected here, the evidence presented goes no further than to confirm that more pupils are likely to extend their secondary schooling in areas of superior socio-economic status.

[17] For further details of the area of the study see J. Eggleston, 'How comprehensive is the Leicestershire plan?', *New Society* (25 March 1965).

[18] The term 'middle class' is used to describe the socio-economic groups, 3, 4, 5, 6 and 7 of the Standard Classification: 'working class' is used to describe groups 2, 9, 10, 11 and 12.

[19] Again there is some apparent support for the 'community context thesis', but again the evidence presented neither supports nor refutes it. For example, it may be that the working class families in the

superior areas are different in fundamental ways from those in the inferior area and their different place of residence is but one indication of this. It *is* suggested however that the socio-economic community context offers a useful summary of a complex of background factors and a convenient predictor of the incidence of decisions to stay on in a catchment area.

[20] *Statistics of Education,* part I, p. 11 (London, Department of Education and Science, 1964)

[21] McDill and Coleman have suggested that in the 'open' American high school, decisions to enter college are more closely related to membership of the adolescent community than they are to home background. E.L. McDill and J.S. Coleman, 'Family and peer group influence in college plans of high school students', *Sociology of Education,* 38, p.112; see also previous work by Coleman in J.S. Coleman, *The Adolescent Society* (Glencoe Ill., 1961).

[22] See for example E. Blishen, 'Non-streaming in the secondary school', *Forum,* 8, p.21.

[23] The present stage of comprehensive reorganization of English education may be seen, to use Turner's conceptual framework, as a first stage in the replacement of a sponsorship system by a contest system of mobility, but a stage in which the organizing norms of sponsorship which have dominated the working of the system are not yet effectively challenged (see R.H. Turner, 'Sponsored and contest mobility and the school system', *American Sociological Review,* 25(5)).

D S BYRNE AND W WILLIAMSON

Some intra–regional variations in educational provision and their bearing upon educational attainment — the case of the north-east *

The purpose of this paper is to present some preliminary results of our research into the factors which influence the educational attainment of children in secondary schools and their patterns of uptake of further education. It seeks to demonstrate that the provision of educational resources by local education authorities, in so far as such provision is related to the wealth of each authority and the kinds of social policies pursued by each authority in the education field, is not only a neglected area of study but, more importantly, may be of equal significance in explaining variations in patterns of educational attainment than the better-documented factors associated with social class, school and family social structure.

The findings to be presented amount to no more than a research prospectus but they do lend support to our claim that whilst important advances have been made in such areas as the sociology of the family and social class, in so far as these bear upon educational attainment and the structure of educational opportunity, and whilst recent research efforts have concentrated on the sociology of the school, virtually nothing has been done on the sociology of the educational authority. This paper is an initial step into these hitherto uncharted waters.

Specifically the paper sets out to present a theoretical model of the way in which some variables of educational provision within a local authority area relate to educational attainment.

Educational attainment and the sociology of education

It is beyond the scope of this paper to summarize in any detail what achievements have been made by researchers into the problems of explaining why a significant proportion of children fail to extend their school careers beyond statutory age requirements. Twenty years of sustained educational research have pointed to the influence of family, class and community influences on patterns of educational attainment.[1] A series of official reports and Royal Commissions have lamented the failure of the schools to mobilize support for extended

*Reprinted from D.S. Byrne and W. Williamson, 'Some intra-regional variations in educational provision and their bearing upon educational attainment – the case of the north-east' Sociology, 6(1), (January 1972), pp. 71-87, by kind permission of the authors and publishers, the Clarendon Press.

school careers, thus depriving the nation of its needed supply of educated manpower and the individual of a fuller life.[2]

Sociologists have attempted to clarify precisely what it is in the socio-cultural environment of the child – and particularly the working class child – which limits educational aspirations and depresses learning ability.[3] Studies have been carried out on the relationship between the family and the school,[4] and on the effects of school organization on educational performance.[5] The effects of the peer group on a child's educational aspirations have also been examined in some detail.[6]

This research is cast in the mould of what we would like to call the 'stratification-education paradigm',[7] and whilst its policy implications have always been clear – in such fields as comprehensive reorganization and compensatory education – the extent to which educational attainment directly relates to the provision of educational resources in the local educational authority area has been scarcely examined. What we propose to show is that the provision of educational resources in an area may be a significant factor in explaining variations in school attainment of different social groups. Factors which can be associated with the socio-cultural learning environment of the child and the material situation of the family – social class factors – can be traced in their influence on educational policy and educational provision.

Educational ecology

Taylor and Ayres in their book, *Born and Bred Unequal,* differentiate between educational sociology and what they call 'educational ecology' in terms of the concern of the former with 'the effects of class – or social status – on parental attitudes to education', and of the latter with 'the effect of the material and social environment (in its widest sense) on the educational opportunity of the child'.[8] They go on to claim that:

> It is commonly assumed that the lack of enthusiasm for extended education among working class parents is mainly due to their values and order of priorities. It may well be, however, that the reasons for a shorter school life are to be found, not in the attitudes, *but in the material circumstances of the parent.*

They argue that differentials in the life provision of the social classes generate severe economic insecurity for the working class family and do 'nothing to encourage a far-seeing attitude towards education'.[10]

Their starting point is the view that 'The educational opportunity available to a child depends to a great extent on the variety and quality of education provided in the area in which he lives' and that 'whether th the child derives maximum benefit depends on a number of non-educational factors in the environment'.[11] These factors include the level of health of the family, the quality of available social services, the state of industrial dereliction, and the level of literacy of the family. Regional variations in these factors are carefully documented by Taylor and Ayres, but the strictly sociological connections between these

ecological variables are not carefully discussed. They say of the
northern region, for example:

> The majority of children leave school early. The region produces a
> large number of teachers (many of whom migrate on completion of
> training) though only a small number of graduates. The combined
> effects of migration, environmental deficiences and lack of education-
> al opportunities has resulted in a generation of parents whose level
> of education is low. Their understanding of the need for change and
> of the long term advantages of education is inevitably limited.[12]

What they are pointing to here is a complex interaction of the provision
of educational resources, the socio-economic environment of the family
and attitudes to education. The major limitation of their approach,
however, lies in the fact that they have made no attempt to measure in
any direct way the importance of any one factor against any other. The
present paper, dealing with a somewhat different and certainly limited
set of data, attempts to examine the differential importance of a number
of variables of educational provision on the extent of educational
attainment. We shall attempt also to state the influence of local authority
policy on educational attainment.

The approach we have adopted is similar in its methodological strategy
to that adopted by Eggleston in his paper on the variables which appear to
influence decisions to extend a school career.[13] The difference lies in
Eggleston's use of administrative variables and our use of provision variables.
The two sets of variables do, of course, relate to one another, but the
precise way in which this relationship holds is at the moment unclear.

TABLE I   Administrative variables and staying on: bilateral and
secondary modern schools. Product moment correlation
coefficients *(r)*

Variable	Staying on after 15	Staying on after 16	Rate of change in staying on
School size*	0.2846	0.3571	0.2175
Intake of selective* schools in same area	0.0511	0.00021	0.0297
Staying on after 16 in selective schools in same area*	0.0720	0.0906	0.0783
School material environment*	0.3086	0.1507	0.1829
Age of school buildings*	0.2844	0.1244	0.1607
Extended course provision†	0.6525	0.6341	0.4180
GCE exam successes†	0.5375	0.5409	0.3859
Non-GCE exam successes	0.4495	0.2890	0.4495

*Variables examined for 240 schools
†Variables examined for 125 schools (all schools in Coventry, Derby, SE
Derbyshire, Leicester, Leicestershire and Nottingham)

Eggleston's first hypothesis was that:

a high incidence of staying on at modern and comprehensive schools would be associated with high standards of building and equipment; well developed programmes of extended course and successful examination results therein: comprehensive rather than tripartite secondary schooling; low intakes to selective schools where they exist, and larger rather than smaller schools.[14]

A second hypothesis was that: 'a high incidence of staying on would be associated with catchment areas where pupils came from homes of predominantly high socio-economic status.'[15]

The first hypothesis clearly refers to the policies of local authorities as these are manifest in various types of educational provision; and in Eggleston's analysis 'the most highly significant correlations are those between staying on and the provision of identified extended courses'.[16] His results are as shown in Table I.

Further analysis reveals also a connection between staying on at school and the socio-economic status of the school's catchment area. This latter connection is of particular interest since it is not simply explained by reference to parental attitudes and values. Staying on also relates to the type of school available, its material environment and its provision of extended courses. Comprehensive schools in Eggleston's survey area were well endowed in all of these things and had a higher aggregate rate of staying on that the tripartite group of schools. This is shown by Eggleston's data for Coventry and Leicestershire, as presented in Table II. These results prompt the question: 'Does, then, the main advantage of the comprehensive type of secondary school lie not in its comprehensiveness, but in its superior catchment area?'[17] Once again, this is a question relating directly to local authority policy decisions, suggesting also that social class factors bear directly on educational policy as well as on the learning capacity and values of the child.

The work of Eggleston and of Taylor and Ayres points clearly to the importance of (a) describing carefully the way in which various indexes of educational provision interacting with social policy in education determine rates of staying at school; and (b) the need to organize these indexes, or variables, into a theoretical model which allows the precise influence of one variable against any other variable to be carefully assessed.

TABLE II   Percentage of pupils remaining after minimum leaving age in comprehensive and tripartite schools (Coventry and Leicestershire)

1964	Comprehensive schools*	Tripartite schools
Coventry	57.6	39.3
Leicestershire	49.2	33.4

*Only comprehensive schools established on or before September 1958 (Coventry) or September 1960 (Leicestershire) are included

Method

There are obvious difficulties in any attempt to evaluate the way in which the different policies of local education authorities influence the educational attainment of children and in separating policy influences from socio-cultural influences. However, potentially useful and published data are available which will sustain such a research objective. The data to be used in this paper come in three forms:

(a) The Northern Economic Planning Council has utilized census data from the 1966 sample census to relate social class to rates of staying on at school.[18] The value of these data is that they can be also used to assess the relationship between the social class composition of an educational authority area and the amount and nature of educational resources available.

(b) The Department of Education and Science publish annually statistics on the numbers of children staying on at school and the numbers of children who receive financial awards for various types of further and higher education.[19] These data are particularly useful since, by breaking the data down into local authority areas some indication can be gained of different patterns of uptake of further education. In short, these data give us a direct measurement of rates of educational attainment between different local authorities.

(c) The annual education statistics of the Institute of Municipal Treasurers and Accountants[20] can generate a number of measures of educational resources and provision within local authority areas. If we define 'resources' as factors beyond the control of LEAs and 'policies' as factors within their control, then the best measure of resources to be derived from the IMTA data is the product of the penny rate per pupil for whom the LEA is responsible. Variables which at least include an element of policy would seem to be:

  i   Rate equivalent based on actual penny rate product. This is a direct measure of how much of its income a local authority devotes to educational purposes and is is at least, in part, a measure of the policy being pursued.

  ii   Per capita expenditure; i.e. expenditure per pupil for whom LEA is responsible.

  iii Pooled primary expenditure; i.e. expenditure on teachers, books and equipment per primary school pupil.

  iv Pooled secondary expenditure.

  v   Percentage of pupils in oversize classes in primary schools.

  vi Percentage of pupils in oversize classes in secondary schools.

The precise way in which these variables interrelate with one another can be established with some confidence through the use of multiple regression statistical techniques. Whilst difficulties do still clearly exist in relating such data — particularly the difficulties involved in treating such data over time[21] — we can proceed on the assumption that educational policy as such is not so variable over time as might be, say, the percentage of pupils in oversize classes.

The final methodological point is that the data we are using do not allow us to make direct comments on what educational policies are being operated, nor does it allow us directly to take into account variables associated with particular schools or particular areas within a local authority. The data we have collected on resources and policy must clearly be related to the type of data collected, for instance, by Eggleston in the work referred to. Such data collection would represent the second stage of the research prospectus which this paper urges.

Models of the determination of attainment

It seems appropriate, before going on to discuss the results we obtained, to look at the basic 'theoretical' model which lends structure to this study. This is best done through an examination of other major sociological or socio-linguistic models of the determinants of attainment that have been developed in studies of the British educational system. Although certain elements in our model coincide with elements of earlier models, the explicit emphasis we place on the importance of policy, and on the operation of other factors through the intermediate variable of policy, represents a new conception of the processes under investigation.

Perhaps the most important basic element in sociological models of the determination of attainment has been the emphasis placed on social class. However, social class has never been considered to directly determine educational attainment but has been seen rather as operating through some intermediate variable. Douglas's work showed the high correlation between parental social class and the educational attainment of individual children. His subsequent analysis focused on socio-cultural aspects of the family, which he and others have related to class position. Bernstein's work on socio-linguistics has been used, however invalidly,[22] to reinforce a model of attainment determination which runs as follows:

$$\text{social class} \xrightarrow{+ve} \text{familial socio-cultural intermediate variables} \xrightarrow{+ve} \text{attainment}$$

This has been the most important model of the determinant factors of attainment current in British educational sociology. The only major variation upon it has been the divorcing of familial socio-cultural variables from class determination in the work of Wiseman, especially in his research done for the Plowden Committee and described by one commentator as 'getting us away from the unhelpful categories of social class'.[23] Wiseman's model can be diagrammatically expressed thus:

$$\text{familial socio-cultural variables} \xrightarrow{+ve} \text{attainment}$$

Taylor and Ayres with their 'educational ecology' radically departed from this concern with socio-cultural factors.[24] They saw material environment as a major determinant of attainment, although they totally neglect the question of relationship between social class and this environment. Their (implicit) model would run thus:

$$\text{material environment} \xrightarrow{+ve} \text{attainment}$$

Eggleston introduces the notion of variation in provision as a determinant of attainment.[25] While his labelling of variables as 'administrative' lays a stress of the determinant nature of patterns of provision, his concern with such variables as age of school buildings includes an element of 'resource' determination in his model. It must be stressed that Eggleston's was a dual model in that, running alongside his administrative/resource determination, is a conception of the determinant status of high socio-economic class, although the mode of operation of this determinant variable is not specified explicitly. Thus Eggleston's models can be expressed as follows:

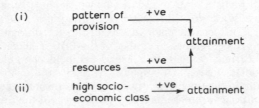

The hypothetical model we advance differs from all these discussed above in a number of important respects. The first relates to the determinant status of social class. Although we see social class as a major determinant of educational attainment, we consider that at least a major part of its influence is likely to operate through other, so far unexamined intermediate factors. In so far as high socio-economic class is a positive determinant of attainment, we see this as being a consequence of the interrelationship between high social class *and* availability of resources on the one hand, and high social class and élite orientated policy[26] (which will lead to high levels of attainment if attainment is defined in élitist terms) on the other. Élitist policy we see as being mediated through the political ethos of LEAs which is likely to be consequential on the social class background of the LEA. Thus *one* element in our model can be expressed as follows:

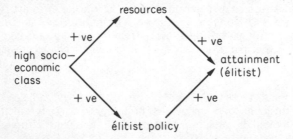

However, if we distinguish between 'resources', i.e. factors beyond the effective control of the LEA even over relatively long time periods, and policy and provisions, i.e. factors which are within LEA control, and if we consider what policy is mediated through local authority political control, then another element in our model relates to the positively determinant effects of *low* socio-economic class. Thus:

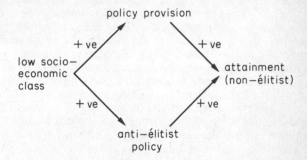

In other words, we might expect that low socio-economic class will be a determinant of a high level of 'provision' which will determine higher levels of attainment. At the same time, we might expect that low socio-economic class is likely to be related to anti-élitist policies on the part of the LEA, an ethos which will be negatively correlated with attainment if we define attainment in élitist terms; but it is likely to be positively related to alternative, non-élitist definitions of attainment.[27]

Now Eggleston related attainment to patterns of provision of secondary schooling, and it must be accepted that 'patterns of provision' are very much a consequence of local authority policy particularly as regards policies of comprehensive reorganization. But this is not a major problem for our exploratory study in that the north-east, in the period under an analysis, was not an area in which comprehensive reorganization had had any significant impact. Moreover, we would argue that it is perhaps generally possible to place too much emphasis on the determinant effect of administrative reorganization on attainment and too little on the 'policy' element inherent in such reorganization which has its origins we suspect in social and political pressures.

To justify this contention we must expand our hypothetical conception of the operation of 'policy' variables in determining attainment. We conceive of policy as being set by the power centres in the LEA (see the *Report* of the Maud Committee) in response to socio-political pressures that are primarily of social class origin, and that manifest themselves through political organization. We see the most important 'policy' dichotomy as being between those authorities who have an élitist orientation and those with an egalitarian bias. The policy orientation of the LEA manifests itself in practice through a variety of mechanisms, the most important of these very probably comprising the promotions procedure for head teachers and the allocation of resources between different schools.

To take the latter first, we consider it likely that authorities with an élitist orientation will tend to concentrate available resources on their 'sponsored élite'. On the other hand, authorities with an egalitarian policy will aim at territorial justice in the distribution of resources and even attempt 'positive discrimination'. Our research design incorporates at least an attempt to assess the validity of this contention. As regards the internal transmission of ideology within an LEA through promotions procedure and the like, these processes are beyond the immediate scope of this study but represent a logical development from it. It is extremely likely that 'policy' factors of this form will assume even greater importance in the wake of an 'administrative' comprehensive reorganization of an LEAs secondary school system, in that they are likely to be major determinants of the *internal* organizational form of the comprehensive schools. However, the best we can do within the framework of the present inquiry is to look at the resource distribution factors and their effects on attainment, bearing in mind that these represent underlying policy commitments which are likely also to be manifest through this class of variables left uninvestigated.

The findings given in Table III on the interrelationship between the resource and policy provision variables for LEAs in the north-east tend to confirm the model of the role of 'policy' as determinant of attainment. If we examine the correlations between low social class and resource variables we find that penny rate per pupil and the proportion in social class D/E are significantly and highly *negatively* correlated, $(r^2 = 0.62)$. However, the proportion in social class D/E is equally highly and significantly positively correlated with the policy provision variable, rate fund equivalent; i.e. with a measure of proportionate importance LEAs assign to their educational activities $(r^2 = 0.60)$. While, as one might expect, there is a negative relationship between available wealth of an LEA and the proportion of its constituents in the lowest social classes, there is a strong positive relationship between the proportion in the social classes D/E and the proportionate financial importance the LEA attaches to education. It is an importance which, on careful inspection, seems to be independent of LEA size and therefore *not due* to rich, large LEAs having responsibilities not possessed by small, poor ones. With regard to patterns of expenditure, low social class is positively correlated with pooled primary expenditure but *negatively* and highly correlated with pooled secondary expenditure $(r^2 = 0.40)$. However, high social class, i.e. proportion in social class A/B, is not significantly correlated with pooled primary expenditure but is significantly and positively correlated with pooled secondary expenditure $(r^2 = 0.26)$.

The policy provision variable, rate fund proportion, is significantly and positively correlated with pooled primary expenditure $(r^2 = 0.32)$ but negatively correlated with pooled secondary expenditure $(r^2 = 0.24)$. What these results indicate, then, is that LEAs which devote a larger proportion of their income to education, spend their money preferentially on primary education. As might be expected, pooled expenditure in primary schools is significantly and negatively correlated with primary overcrowding $(r^2 = 0.34)$. Thus the proportionate importance which an LEA attaches to its educational activities is negatively correlated with the resources of the LEA $(r^2 = 0.828)$.

TABLE III Resource variables and educational provision: north-eastern planning region: zero order, product moment correlation coefficients r^2

	Penny rate per pupil	Rate fund proportion	Per capita expenditure	Pooled primary	Pooled secondary	Proportion in social class A/B	Proportion in social class D/E	Primary overcrowding	Secondary overcrowding
Penny rate per pupil	x	0.8281	0.17	0.19	0.28	0.02	0.62	0.12	0.14
Rate fund proportion	0.83	x	0.003	0.33	0.25	0.01	0.60	0.12	0.01
Per capita expenditure	0.17	0.003	x	0.09	0.07	0.06	0.08	0.12	0.27
Pooled primary	0.19	0.33	0.09	x	0.02	0.07	0.16	0.33	0.08
Pooled secondary	0.25	0.24	0.07	0.02	x	0.26	0.40	0.006	0.01
Proportion in social class A/B	0.03	0.01	0.06	0.07	0.26	x	0.14	0.21	0.06
Proportion in social class D/E	0.62	0.60	0.08	0.16	0.40	0.14	x	0.09	0.04
Primary overcrowding	0.12	0.12	0.01	0.34	0.006	0.21	0.09	x	0.05
Secondary overcrowding	0.14	0.01	0.27	0.08	0.01	0.06	0.05	0.05	x

If we 'express' these findings in diagrammatic terms, then we have the following:

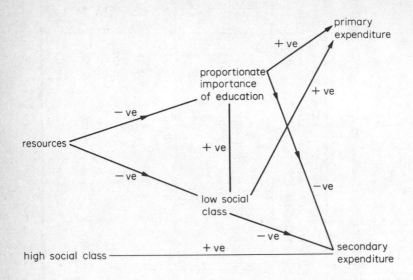

In other words those authorities with a high proportion in low social classes resident within their area both devote a higher proportion of their income to education than do authorities with higher social class constituencies, and spend their money on primary education rather than on secondary education, the reverse being true of the 'high social class' authorities.

These findings can certainly be interpreted as support for the idea of the determinant role of élitist and anti-élitist policies which we advanced in our model, since expenditure on universalist primary education is indubitably more egalitarian in its consequences than expenditure on secondary education, especially when there remains a strong selective element in the secondary sector.

If we now turn to look at our findings (Table IV) about the relationship between various indices of attainment and resources, provision and social class variables, we find a similar pattern. If we look first at staying-on indices; the proportion of students who stay on until their sixteenth birthday is positively correlated with the resource index, penny rate pupil ($r^2 = 0.22$), with per capita expenditure by the LEA on each pupil for which the LEA is responsible ($r^2 = 0.28$) and with the proportion in social class A/B ($r^2 = 0.56$). Staying on for the fifth form is negatively correlated with the proportion of social class D/E ($r^2 = 0.24$). It would seem that the major determinant of staying on is high social class but that higher rates of expenditure per pupil, stemming from higher resources, play a mediating role.

TABLE IV Measures of attainment and educational provision: north-eastern planning region: zero order, product moment correlation coefficients r^2

	University	Further education (I)	Further education (II)	Teacher training	5th form	6th form
Penny rate per pupil	0.06	0.33	0.11	0.18	0.22	0.25
Rate fund proportion	0.005	0.09	0.34	0.30	0.09	0.13
Per capita expenditure	0.12	0.54	0.23	0.005	0.28	0.08
Pooled primary	0.03	0.003	0.34	0.08	0.004	0.06
Pooled secondary	0.008	0.22	0.04	0.33	0.04	0.0001
Social class A/B	0.18	0.27	0.03	0.003	0.56	0.005
Social class D/E	0.007	0.19	0.01	0.02	0.24	0.29
Primary overcrowding	0.0003	0.001	0.05	0.01	0.02	0.30
Secondary overcrowding	0.48	0.36	0.10	0.03	0.17	0.29

Thus these findings suggest a model of the following form:

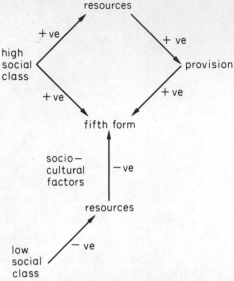

Although these models are here only suggested, rather than tested by partial correlation techniques, the very high positive correlation between high social class and fifth form staying on suggests that here the socio-cultural mode of effect of high social class is important. This is not the case with the findings relating to the correlation of staying on until seventeen with resource, provision and social class indices. Staying on until seventeen is positively correlated with primary overcrowding and secondary overcrowding and negatively correlated with proportion in social class D/E, this suggests a model of the following form:

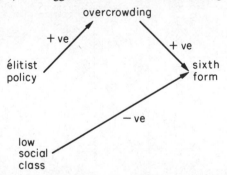

Or, in other words, it suggests that certain LEAs concentrate resources on secondary expenditure, in particular on 'élite' secondary expenditure, to the detriment of other sectors of the school system. This leads to high élite attainment, but is reflected in poor provision indices, such as overcrowding, elsewhere.

This pattern is strikingly confirmed by the correlates of different patterns of further education. Indeed, we can identify two significant patterns of further education which almost seem to be 'alternatives' in describing the further education attainment from different LEA areas. In one pattern the important forms of uptake are university awards and full value awards at other further education establishments, i.e. awards given for high level further education. The other pattern of uptake is characterized by the importance of lesser value further education awards, and even more significantly by the importance of awards granted for studies at colleges of education. Thus, in Table IV both lesser value further education — further education (II) — and teacher training awards are positively and significantly correlated with rate fund proportion, i.e. proportionate importance of educational expenditure for the LEA ($r^2 = 0.34$ and $r^2 = 0.30$ respectively). The only other significant correlation for these two variables are that further education (II) is significantly and positively 'correlated' with pooled primary expenditure ($r^2 = 0.34$) and teacher training is negatively correlated with pooled secondary expenditure ($r^2 = 0.33$). Thus, these two types of attainment are correlated with the variables which are of importance for the 'poor' egalitarian LEAs.

University awards per 1,000 age group and high grade further education follow a diametrically opposed pattern. High grade, further education (I) awards are positively and significantly correlated with penny rate per pupil, i.e. resources ($r^2 = 0.33$), with per capita expenditure per pupil, a variable including a considerable resource element ($r^2 = 0.84$), with proportion in social class A/B ($r^2 = 0.27$), and with secondary overcrowding ($r^2 = 0.36$). University awards are significantly and positively correlated with secondary overcrowing, ($r^2 = 0.48$).

This pattern of correlation is markedly similar to the two patterns established for correlation between resource variables. It would seem that poor local authorities, with high proportions of social class D/E, spending a larger proportion of their resources on education, 'produce' teachers and students who pursue low grade further education courses. Richer local authorities with greater resources and larger proportions in social class A/B seem to have an élitist policy, spending their money on a sponsored[29] élite of pupils who 'attain' in sixth form, university and high grade further education courses at the expense of scarcity of resources elsewhere, and, in particular, of high levels of overcrowding.

Thus, one is led to the following models:

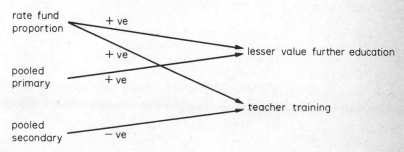

and

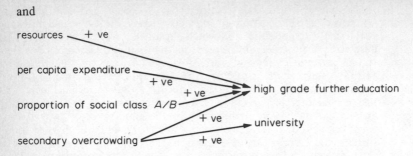

Thus the two 'policy' models of LEAs, i.e. those of the poor LEA with an egalitarian policy and the richer LEA with an élitist policy, seem to hold not only for patterns of resource distribution between school types, but for the type of further education attainment – with the élite authorities producing children who attain in élite terms, i.e. university and high grade further education, and the egalitarian authorities producing children attaining in lower grade further education training patterns.

Conclusion

This study has been specifically confined to LEAs within the north-east region, the only exception being the county borough of Carlisle, which, however, in many respects is a north-eastern town. The Cumberland and Westmorland LEAs, although lying within the NEPC area, have been excluded because of their overwhelmingly rural character. Results generated are therefore only applicable to the predominantly urban areas of the NEPC. This 'regionalism' is intentional. It would have been comparatively simple to extend the scope of the study to every LEA in England and Wales, since the analysis has been conducted with, in the main, readily available data. However this would have introduced socio-cultural and economic differences which might well have masked the policy variations which were our special concern. We think that regional analyses of this form have particular value for the explanation of educational variation, and hope to extend this study on a region-by-region basis.

The problem of confining our study to the north-east has introduced statistical problems in that there are only eleven LEAs and therefore only eleven cases. Despite this, a very high level of significance in results has been obtained. All results, i.e. r^2s, quoted in the body of the text are significant at the 90 per cent level and almost all are significant at the 95 per cent level. Scattergrams confirm these patterns. While we have somewhat stretched correlational techniques in our current application of them, we feel that this is justified in a study that does not claim to be more than exploratory.

Exploratory studies should lay out the guides for reconnaissance in depth. We consider that this study indicates several fruitful paths for those concerned with the influence of local policy in education in this country. One is the natural, region-by-region, extension of the current analysis which we have already suggested. Another is research in depth into the operations of particular LEAs, to explore policy and modes of policy enactment, transmission of policy conceptions etc. As we stated at the beginning of this article, the sociology of education in this country has fruitfully concerned itself with the influence of family, language, culture and national policy, but the crucial local level has been almost entirely neglected. We hope this present study does something to redress the balance.

Notes

[1] See, for example, P.W. Musgrave, *The Sociology of Education* (London, Methuen, 1965); J.W.B. Douglas, *The Home and the School: a study of ability and attainment in the primary school* (London, MacGibbon and Kee, 1964); O. Banks, *The Sociology of Education* (London, Batsford, 1968); D.F. Swift (ed.), *Basic Readings in the Sociology of Education* (London, Routledge and Kegan Paul, 1970).

[2] See, for example, Central Advisory Council, *Early Leaving* (London, HMSO, 1954); Central Advisory Council for Education, *15 to 18* (London, HMSO, 1960): Committee on Higher Education *Higher Education* Appendix I (London, HMSO, 1963).

[3] See for a review of some of the literature on this problem, D. Lawton *Social Class, Language and Education* (London, Routledge and Kegan Paul, 1968); S. Wiseman, *Education and Environment* (Manchester University Press, 1964).

[4] Douglas, op. cit.

[5] See, for example, B. Jackson, *Streaming: An Educational System in Miniature* (London, Routledge and Kegan Paul, 1964); D. Hargreaves, *Social Relations in a Secondary School* (London, Routledge and Kegan Paul, 1967).

[6] Unfortunately, on this problem, the literature is largely American. See, for example, J.S. Coleman, *The Adolescent Society* (Glencoe, Ill. The Free Press, 1961). For Britain, see J. Webb, 'The sociology of a school' *British Journal of Sociology*, 13(3) (1962) pp.264-72; B.N. Sugarman, 'Involvement in youth culture, academic achievement and conformity in school', *British Journal of Sociology*, 18(2) (1967) pp. 151-64.

[7] The concept of 'paradigm' derives from T.S. Kuhn, *The Structure of Scientific Revolutions* (1962).

[8] G. Taylor and N. Ayres, *Born and Bred Unequal* (London, Longman, 1969).

[9] Taylor and Ayres, op. cit. p. 15 (our emphasis).

[10] Taylor and Ayres, op. cit. p. 15.

[11] Taylor and Ayres, op. cit. p. 3.

[12] Taylor and Ayres, op. cit. p. 122.

[13] John S. Eggleston, 'Some environmental correlates of extended secondary education' in Swift, *Basic Readings in the Sociology of Education*.

[14] Eggleston, op. cit. p. 163.

[15] Eggleston, op. cit. p. 163.

[16] Eggleston, op. cit. p. 167.

[17] Eggleston, op. cit., p. 173.

[18] Northern Economic Planning Council, *Challenge of the Changing North − Education − Part I* (Newcastle, NEPC, 1970).

[19] Department of Education and Science, *Statistics of Education* (London, HMSO). Annual in several volumes. Data utilized in this study are from the 1968 series.

[20] Institute of Municipal Treasurers and Accountants, *Educational Statistics* (London, IMTA, annual). Data utilized in this study are from the 1968 volume.

[21] The model we are using postulates that attainment is at least in part the product of provision and it will be obvious that provision as a set of variables operates throughout the school life of children whose attainment is determined by it. Ideally one would like to relate provision data for a particular age-cohort to the attainment of that cohort, as Eggleston does for administrative variables. However, the model we are employing contains the assumption that provision itself is in large part the product of LEA policies, a variable set that will have considerable inertia over relatively long time periods. This reduces the time series problem but ideally one would like to employ a time-variate model.

[22] See B. Bernstein, 'A critique of the concept of compensatory education' in D. Rubinstein and C. Stoneman (eds.), *Education for Democracy* (London, Penguin, 1970).

[23] Howard Glennester, 'The Plowden research', *Journal of the Royal Statistical Society*, Series A, part 2, (1969).

[24] Taylor and Ayres, op. cit.

[25] Eggleston, op. cit.

[26] See, for example, R.H. Turner, 'Sponsored and contest mobility and the school system', *American Sociological Review* 25(5) (1960).

[27] Élitist definitions of attainment are rooted in culturally specific criteria concerning positions reached in the occupational educational hierarchy. This means they are concerned with only a minority of the products of the school system. A non-élitist definition would be concerned with the total output of the educational system − with *all* children rather than merely the academic minority. It can by hypothesized that élitist education policies, whilst promoting the attainment of the few, depress the potential attainment of the majority. Equally, non-élitist policies will improve the performance of all at the expense of the performance of a select few.

[28] See the Maud Committee Report, *The Management of Local Government* (London, HMSO, 1967).

[29] Turner, op. cit.

JOHN EGGLESTON

Going comprehensive — a case study of secondary reorganization *

Changes in the arrangements for secondary schooling present a challenge to many parts of the life of local communities. They can change the prospects of their children, parents and teachers. They may modify social structures and challenge the norms of political, industrial and religious life. It is hardly surprising that such proposals regularly evoke a lively response.

There is plenty of evidence to indicate the strength of these pressures. It is recognized in circular 10/65 of the Department of Education and Science; it is evident in the bewildering variety of local schemes reported by the Comprehensive Schools Committee. But so far there has been little evidence of the ways in which these local pressures influence the course of decisions on reorganization. The chance to undertake a preliminary inquiry into some of these occurred at Leicester University, where permission was generously given by the Northamptonshire Education Committee for a group of mature students to look at the development of plans for secondary reorganization in the Corby area of the county.

Corby, a small village in the north of the county which became a company town of Stewart and Lloyds steelworks in the 1930s, was designated as a new town after the war. Its secondary education was a straightforward pattern of secondary grammar and modern schools. Since the early fifties, population growth has been rapid and character-istic of much of south-east England and the suburbs of the conurbations elsewhere. Such areas are generally regarded as the easiest in which to reorganize secondary education. The fact that new schools have to be built seems to take much of the impact off existing schools, while the norms of a community receiving a heavy flow of immigrants are less set and so believed to be less disturbed by changes of this kind. Reasons such as these led the county education committee to select Corby as one of their first areas for secondary reorganization. Yet even in such an area the problems associated with change were large and complex.

Not surprisingly they began with the problem of what to do with the existing coeducational grammar school. The education committee in the late fifties was opposed to very large schools and decided to build a second school rather than extend the existing one. In March 1961 the committee announced that the two grammar schools would be single sex schools and all the boys from the existing one would be

---

*Reprinted from John Eggleston, New Society, No. 221 (22 December 1966) pp. 944-6, by kind permission of the publishers.

transferred to the new one. There is no clear record of whether the committee's decision was based on a preference for single sex education or on expediency, but there is a striking record of the local protest which followed. Parents, teachers, trade unions, churches, political parties and parish councils all made representations to the education committee and the county council, but both bodies were unyielding and ratified the decision in July. A year of intensive protest followed, with national press and television coverage, culminating in a deputation to Sir David Eccles, then Minister of Education. In June 1962 the minister decided that the grammar school should stay coeducational.

Before recounting the events in reorganization it is perhaps useful to identify the main groups concerned. Overall responsibility for education in the area is exercised by the Northamptonshire county council through its education committee, which in turn has a secondary education committee. There are local branches of the various associations for head and assistant teachers, all of which, initially, were represented on the ad hoc committee described subsequently. Local branches of the Communist, Conservative and Labour parties were involved in the events, as was the militant Association for Comprehensive Education. This seems to have been first discussed at the end of a Communist Party meeting in September 1963, and was formally constituted on 5 November 1963, with a committee of seven Labour and five Communist party members. Finally, the weekly *Corby Leader* provided a platform for many events.

Beginnings

Preliminary moves toward reorganization had begun in 1961. On 12 October of that year the Corby Labour party invited Fred Willey, then party spokesman on education, to talk on comprehensive schools. But at this time public interest was still focused on the coeducation issue and there was an audience of only fifteen people. In March 1962 the Corby communists asked the chief education officer what stage had been reached in discussions towards providing a comprehensive system of secondary education, but achieved only a negative reply. On 19 July 1963, after the minister's coeducation decision, one of the Labour county councillors for Corby asked the county council to consider the question of the abolition of the eleven plus and to institute a system that would give equal opportunity for higher education to all. There is no evidence that this was an official party resolution; indeed it was suggested that a number of Labour members on the council were unaware of it in advance. But it led to the first important public discussion of reorganization.

On 30 September 1963, the main cycle of events was set in motion. At the meeting of the secondary education committee it was agreed that the chief education officer should be asked to investigate, in consultation with governors and teachers, the possibility of establishing an organization of education similar to the Leicestershire Plan in Corby and report back to the committee. This followed a survey, by the chief education officer, which had suggested that the existing buildings in

Corby would make anything other than a two-tier arrangement impossible. After this decision the following chronicle of events occurred.

23 October. Governors and heads of secondary schools were invited to hear the Leicestershire director of education, Stewart Mason, talk on the Leicestershire Plan.

5 November. The inaugural meeting of the Association for Comprehensive Education was held at the Corby Trades and Labour Club, parents and teachers being called upon by the new association to begin a determined campaign aginst the eleven plus and to support comprehensive education; deep concern was expressed at the lack of a proper education plan for Corby.

15-22 November. Six separate meetings of various groups of secondary school governors, heads and teachers were held, including the meeting with Stewart Mason. The series culminated with a meeting at which the town's secondary school heads told the chief education officer of their misgivings about the Leicestershire Plan and indicated that they would be suggesting modifications. The important part which the head teachers were to play subsequently was made clear in the week's negotiations.

2 December. A National Union of Teachers meeting on the Leicestershire Plan was addressed by five teachers from existing plan schools in Leicestershire.

3 December. The Association for Comprehensive Education meeting at the Lutheran Church Hall was addressed by Brian Simon, already well known in Corby as an advocate of comprehensive education, who strongly supported the introduction of the Leicestershire Plan as a step towards a fully comprehensive system of education.

6 December. The *Corby Leader* gave extensive coverage to the various meetings and printed a leader attacking 'social pull and snobbery in the grammar school'.

9 December. A meeting of the secondary education committee was held at which consideration of the proposals was deferred to a special meeting in January. Meanwhile the teachers' organizations were invited to present their views to the committee.

3 January. The headmaster of the grammar school, John Kempe, contributed an article to the *Corby Leader,* following publication of a letter criticizing unfavourable references to the Leicestershire Plan at the school's speech day. Kempe drew attention to the brief existence of the plan, insufficient, in his opinion, for the advantages to be judged or the results assessed. This led to prolonged discussion in the correspondence columns of the *Corby Leader*, much of it between the grammar school staff and the members of the Association for Comprehensive Education. At this stage the secretary of the Corby Conservative Association was instructed, by his committee, to write to the clerk of the county council and to the chief education officer to ask that plans for reorganization be deferred so that full discussion could take place. Throughout the negotiations, however, the actions of the Corby Conservatives were somewhat constrained as the county council had a conservative and independent majority.

23 January. At the special meeting of the secondary education

committee the chief education officer reported on the results of his investigation of the possibility of introducing the Leicestershire Plan in Corby, and offered a detailed survey of local professional opinion, much of which had been submitted in response to the committee's invitation of 9 December. In general, opinion was incompletely formulated but tended to be in favour of delay or alternative proposals. The grammar school governors felt that insufficient evidence was available; the governors of the other secondary schools asked for a fact-finding committee. The head teachers were opposed and suggested an alternative plan. The Joint Four associations also opposed the scheme and suggested a retention of a modified form of selection.

The National Union of Teachers was undecided but generally in favour of a more detailed examination of the plan. The National Association of Schoolmasters regretted that their views had not been sought. Only the Catholic schools were not involved at this stage due to the fact that the church was already committed to translating their existing secondary modern school into a bilateral one to cater for all Catholic secondary schooling in Corby.

Notwithstanding the uncertainty of professional opinion the committee recommended that, as an experiment, the education committee should establish an organization of secondary education in the Corby area similar to the Leicestershire Plan from the beginning of the school year 1965-6, a decision which was followed by considerable professional and public opposition.

The local education authority was, by this time, in a situation of considerable difficulty. It was now committed to introduce reorganization by September 1965, but it had no detailed plan and was faced with a wide divergence of views, predominantly unfavourable. At this stage, the county NUT secretary, G.W. Elliott, a teacher representative on the education committee, offered to try to ascertain teachers' views. It was agreed that he should form an ad hoc committee which would produce a scheme for the consideration of the secondary education committee, provided that it was representative of all teachers in the county and so long as he could undertake to complete the job by early May to allow time for consultation before the decision which would have to be taken at the June meeting of the secondary education committee.

Teachers represented

Elliott acted with speed and was able to assemble a committee of twenty-four for a first meeting on 24 February. All teachers' organizations were represented in proportion to their membership which gave the NUT sixteen of the twenty-four places. The committee contained representatives of all types of school, both primary and secondary from all major centres of the county. But of particular interest was the proportion of head teachers — sixteen of the twenty-four members were heads. In the case of the primary representatives the proportion was even higher, six were heads and one was an assistant teacher. This aspect of the membership was subsequently claimed to have caused difficulties, particularly with the NAS delegates who withdrew after the first meeting as they declined to accept corporate responsibility for a report to be drawn up by a committee which was overloaded with heads. (Their request to remain as observers at the second meeting was rejected by the committee.)

Before the first meeting, members had received a memorandum of school populations and examination candidates in Corby for recent years, and a review of schemes of reorganization attempted or proposed in other parts of the country. The documents were discussed at the first meeting, and, in the two subsequent meetings, on 9 and 23 March, the committee after consultations in the schools was able to recommend a 'Northamptonshire Plan' which, in general outline, was similar to the arrangements proposed by Cardiff education committee. Though the plan retained the two-tier arrangement there were two important variations from the Leicestershire Plan. One was that optional transfer was to take place at thirteen plus instead of fourteen plus; the other was that extended courses after leaving age leading to external examinations could take place in schools in both tiers. The first change was attractive to the existing grammar school which would have its pupils for the longer period desired; the second change was particularly attractive to the present secondary modern schools who would still be able to retain their extended courses when they became lower tier schools.

The recommendations were followed by a further series of meetings to discuss details between heads and the chief education officer and his deputy and by renewed public discussion. The main focus of objection outside the profession was now, unquestionably, the Association for Comprehensive Education which argued strongly that the ad hoc committee's plan was not a comprehensive scheme but one in which parental selection would predominate and, as a result, there would be strong class differentiation in the rates of transfer. The association still recommended a 'pure' form of Leicestershire Plan in which, as soon as possible, obligatory transfer would replace optional transfer at fourteen plus. To this end a leaflet was published in May in which the Leicestershire Plan was shown as having only advantages and the new plan as having only disadvantages. This leaflet marked the beginning of a particularly intensive period of compaigning by the association, which included a strongly critical statement issued in June, claiming that in the ad hoc committee's plan the upper school would become 'a cloistered academic forcing house for the few', whereas under the Leicestershire Plan, 'all would receive the benefits of a broad, liberal education'. 'The final choice', it added, 'must be made by the people of Corby.'

Notwithstanding these objections, the secondary education committee approved the ad hoc committee's plan on 15 June, with only one exception, since rescinded, that GCE examinations could only be taken in the upper tier schools, though the lower tier candidates would still be able to take CSE. The decision was approved by the education committee on 29 June. At this meeting there was a split in the Labour membership of the committee. The Labour members from

Corby were 'distinctly unhappy' and voted against the proposals. They were, however, the only Labour members of the committee to do so.

Crucial factor

A crucial factor in the committee's decision, however, seems to have been the report by the chief education officer in which he was able to show that professional opinion, with the exception of the NAS, was now predominantly in favour of the new plan. Even the Catholic community now planned to modify their arrangements to harmonize with it. Support was confirmed by the fate of a petition against the new plan, organized immediately after the decision by a small group of Corby teachers in association with the Association for Comprehensive Education. Though the petition was circulated to every school, only sixty teachers signed and the organizers attracted a good deal of hostility from their colleagues. By this time it was also becoming clear that public opinion, despite the efforts of the association and the predictions of councillors, was tiring of the issue and the columns of the *Corby Leader* now tended to be more concerned with delinquency, housing and the other pressing social problems of the new town. Nonetheless, the Association for Comprehensive Education issued a further statement of 17 July calling for the education committee to have second thoughts on its proposals ' in view of the dissatisfaction felt in the town' — which brought slight response.

By the middle of July the way had become clear for the county council to finally approve the new plan and on 23 July a statement was issued to mark this approval. Later in the month the chief education officer issued a circular in which the arrangement for initiating the reorganization in September 1965 was outlined, and in which, at last, the new grammar school was able to feature, now as a mixed upper tier school. This time, considerable respect for parents' feelings was shown; all existing grammar school pupils of all ages were to be allowed to stay on and complete their secondary schooling in their present school, this was also to apply to those who were to enter the school in September 1964. Moreover, some pupils in the new grammar school catchment area would still be able to enter at eleven plus in 1965 and subsequent years as an interim measure. Explanatory letters were sent to all parents in January 1965 and the plan began to operate with only slight notice in September 1965, despite the continuance of the Association for Comprehensive Education campaign.

Influences

Throughout this chronicle there has been an important underlying feature; the pattern of county council government in Northampton-shire, which is one in which, in the past, sharp divisions over issues on political lines have seldom occurred. This pattern made it possible for the county's educational administrators to concentrate far more fully on opinions in the teaching profession, notably secondary school head teachers, than might otherwise have been the case. It is also notable that, both within the teaching profession and in the community at large, events were frequently influenced by a small minority of active workers, political as well as professional, in existing and new organizations. There was a great deal of evidence that many teachers and parents were indifferent to the issues, and we encountered many remarks such as, 'It's all being worked up by the CP but let them get on with it'; 'It'll make no difference to my child,' or even, 'I don't expect to stay long enough here for it to matter.' However, to attribute all the power to a minority ignores the great importance which all parties in the dispute attached to obtaining broadly based support through meetings, press reports and discussion. The power of the community at large can best be seen in the rapid collapse of the protest movement when it lost community support in the summer of 1964 despite massive attempts to retain it by the Association for Comprehensive Education. Similarly the wide teacher support for the new plan emerges as the chief reason for its success.

But whatever the debate about responsibility one unquestionable conclusion remains. Corby, though seemingly a highly suitable area for secondary reorganization, turned out to be a long headache for the administrative staff of the local education authority. Indeed, the sequence of events continues. There are signs that the Association for Comprehensive Education is still active, though in a less public manner than before. In other areas of the county the introduction of the new plan has been abandoned and the education committee is now committed to a policy of 'all through' comprehensive schools for all parts of the county – a policy which has been endorsed by the county council. It seems likely that in Corby, as in other parts of the country, secondary school reorganization is a continuing process.

A H HALSEY

The EPAs and their schools *[1]

Visits, visual impressions and documentary sources on the social and
demographic characteristics of possible areas helped in the choice of
our four experimental districts; but having chosen them we had to build
up a more comprehensive picture by systematic survey. This operation
served several purposes: it provided the action teams with information
to guide them in deciding which policies to pursue and how they should
be implemented; it allowed a systematic comparison to be made between
the four areas so that the effectiveness of differing strategies could be
assessed in the light of differing local conditions; it gave a measure of
the degree to which the selected areas satisfied the criteria proposed
in the Plowden Report for the identification of EPAs; and it also
suggested ways in which these criteria could be modified or supplemented.

During their first year in the field the project teams collected information, sometimes in considerable detail, on all but one of the Plowden
criteria (incomplete families), as well as on a variety of other matters
which were thought relevant to the problems of EPAs. Existing sources
were used where they were available, in particular the 1966 10 per cent
Sample Census and the schools' own records. To fill the gaps where
records did not exist three specially designed surveys were carried out.
These were firstly, a survey of all teachers in the project schools via a
postal questionnaire, which gathered information on their career
histories, their attitudes towards various aspects of teaching, and the
degree of their job satisfaction; secondly, a study of a random sample
of 800 mothers of children in the project schools conducted by means
of interviews in the home; and thirdly, a survey of the ability and
attainment of all the children in the project schools in which standardized tests of verbal ability and reading were administered.

The 1966 Census[2] was already nearly three years out of date when
the project began, a period which can bring considerable changes in
areas undergoing rapid population movements and redevelopment.
Nevertheless it provided the only source of information available to us
about overall conditions in the areas, and some of the facts it revealed
were striking.

The EPA with the smallest population was the West Riding, with

*Reprinted from A.H. Halsey (ed.), Educational Priority Volume 1:
E.P.A. Problems and Policies (London, HMSO, 1972), pp.60-79, by
kind permission of the editor and publishers, Her Majesty's Stationery
Office.

17,600 inhabitants. London and Birmingham had 49,500 and 56,000 respectively, while the Liverpool EPA covered a much larger district containing 85,000 people, though not working with all the schools in that district. The inner ring areas had all been receiving Irish and Commonwealth immigrants. This was especially true of the Birmingham EPA, where almost a third of residents had been born outside Great Britain, including over a fifth born outside the British Isles. In the London EPA at Deptford the proportion of residents born outside Great Britain approached 10 per cent, and in the Liverpool district 6 per cent. In contrast, 99 per cent of the population of the West Riding mining towns were indigenous. These differences were reflected in the fact that 16 per cent of Birmingham and 17 per cent of Deptford EPA residents had first come to live in the local authority area only within the previous five years, compared with 7 per cent in the West Riding EPA.

All four EPAs were overwhelmingly working class, with disproportionately large numbers of unskilled and semi-skilled workers. In the three inner ring areas, one in five of all economically active and retired males were unskilled manual workers, though relatively few in the West Riding fell into this category because of the dominance of coal mining in local employment. The concomitant of this dominance was, however, that only 4.5 per cent of males were in non-routine white collar jobs, a proportion which rose to only 8 per cent in Deptford and Birmingham, against 19 per cent in England as a whole.

Almost half the dwellings in England were owner occupied in 1966. In three of the EPAs this was true of fewer than one in five dwellings. In Birmingham the number was considerably higher, the difference being to some extent explained by the difficulty which Commonwealth immigrants have in obtaining any other form of accommodation.[3] Houses bought by immigrants are often given over to multi-occupation in order to meet mortgage repayments; thus while 37 per cent of dwellings in our Birmingham district were owner occupied, only 28 per cent of households lived in dwellings which they owned themselves. Housing stress in Birmingham was further indicated by the 7 per cent of dwellings which were rented furnished, compared with 1 per cent in England as a whole.

Overcrowding was a serious problem in all except the West Riding. In Liverpool 21 per cent of households were sharing a dwelling, while in Deptford and Birmingham the figure was as high as 35 per cent, five times as many as in England as a whole. While 1 per cent of households in England were living at a density of more than one and a half persons per room, 11 per cent in the Birmingham project area tolerated this degree of overcrowding. Not surprisingly, in these inner ring districts the large majority of households — from 64 per cent to 72 per cent — lacked exclusive use of at least one of the basic amenities of fixed bath, hot water tap and WC, and the situation for those households which were sharing a dwelling was considerably worse. Even in the West Riding, where there were virtually no shared dwellings, 45 per cent of households were in a similar position.

We were not able to obtain any direct information about income levels in the EPAs, but some indication was gleaned from two sources. Firstly, the census showed that while 46 per cent of households in England owned a car, only 33 per cent in our Deptford district and as low as 15 per cent in Liverpool possessed one. Secondly, we took from school records the number of children receiving free school dinners on one day in the summer term of 1969. At this time eligibility for free meals was based solely on income and not family size, and yet 28 per cent of the Liverpool children were in receipt of them. In Deptford and the West Riding the proportions were 24 per cent and 19 per cent respectively, and in Birmingham 14 per cent. It must be remembered that these figures represent families who have successfully claimed free meals and not the numbers entitled to them. Claim forms are very complex, and language difficulties might well lead to both ignorance of entitlement and failure to apply.

The contract between the Birmingham inner ring district in which Commonwealth immigrants had congregated and the two West Riding mining towns, which were not attracting new workers and had an ethnically homogeneous population, was demonstrated markedly by answers to a number of questions in the survey of parents. These findings are shown in Table I from which it is clear both that the West Riding had a much more stable population and that there were closer links among members of the community. The pattern in Deptford was similar to that in Birmingham, though not as extreme, while Liverpool approximated more nearly to the West Riding. It is noticeable in this table that questions about how long parents have lived in the same area differentiate the four EPAs to a much greater extent than do questions about the nearness of friends and relations. This probably reflects the natural tendency of immigrant families to move to areas where they already know people who can assist them, and shows how an area where the majority of residents are relative newcomers can nevertheless become a closely knit community.

The survey of parents gave much more information about the families of the children in the project primary schools. Perhaps the most startling fact which it revealed was the number of children who came from large families of five or more siblings. As may be seen from Table II in no district was this proportion smaller than 24 per cent, and in Birmingham the majority of children came from such large families. Practically all the mothers interviewed in the West Riding and Liverpool had left school at the age of fifteen or before, though in Birmingham and Deptford a few (13 per cent and 20 per cent respectively) stayed until they were sixteen. Despite the prevalence of large families at least a third of mothers in all the areas went out to work, and in Deptford almost one half did.

In Deptford and Birmingham there were sufficient numbers of immigrants to enable us to look separately at their characteristics: in Deptford forty-seven of the sampled children came from West Indian families, and in Birmingham forty-eight came from West Indian and fifty-two from Asian families.[4] In both Deptford and Birmingham the West Indian families were somewhat larger than the non-immigrant

TABLE I   Community links in four EPA project areas

Percentage of respondents in various categories

	Deptford EPA %	Birmingham EPA %	Liverpool EPA %	West Riding EPA %
Child's mother was brought up in same area	28	10	60	65
Child's father was brought up in same area	27	4	57	69
Mother or father attended child's present school	9	2	25	25
Many of mother's relatives live nearby	44	45	51	66
Many of father's relatives live nearby	33	46	45	62
Many of mother's and father's friends live nearby	50	56	58	86
Child plays with local children after school	77	76	90	95
Total No. of respondents	(204)	(181)	(191)	(195)

Source: EPA project parental survey (1969).

TABLE II   Size of families of primary school children, by EPA

	Deptford EPA %	Birmingham EPA %	Liverpool EPA %	West Riding EPA %
No information	0	0	1	0
1-2 children	31	9	19	36
3-4 children	39	36	43	41
5 or more children	30	55	37	24
Total No. of respondents	(204)	(181)	(191)	(195)

Source: EPA project parental survey (1969).

families in the same EPA, but there were more large families among
non-immigrants in Birmingham than among West Indians in Deptford.
The average size of Asian families was also larger than that of non-
immigrant families in Birmingham. It is difficult to compare standards
of education across different countries, for the age of starting school
may vary and school attendance may not be full time. However, on the
evidence of school leaving age the West Indian mothers in both Deptford
and Birmingham were somewhat better educated than their non-
immigrant counterparts, while over half of the Asian mothers had not
been to school at all. Roughly half of both West Indian and non-
immigrant mothers went out to work in Deptford; in Birmingham
rather more West Indian mothers and rather fewer non-immigrants
did so. In contrast, not one of the Asian mothers who were interviewed
had a job. Clearly the Asian mothers formed a very distinct group,
largely cut off from society outside their own family and friends.

We have given a picture of the districts and the families which the
project schools served; now, we shall describe the schools themselves.
Information was collected on forty-five separate primary schools or
departments,[5] comprising twelve in London, seven in Birmingham,
sixteen in Liverpool and ten in the West Riding. In this forty-five, infant,
junior and junior mixed with infants schools were represented in exactly
equal numbers. All of the Liverpool schools, and all but one of those
in Birmingham, were in receipt of the £75 EPA salary supplement,
though five project schools in Deptford and five in the West Riding
were not. In fact at the local level the allocation of the £75 supplement
can seem somewhat arbitrary, and the distinction is less important in
research terms than might first appear. The seven Birmingham schools
were on average rather larger than those in the other areas, the smallest
having 251 pupils on the roll in January 1969 and the largest 739. The
sixteen Liverpool schools and departments were rather smaller, ranging
from 114 to 266 pupils. The spread in London was between 137 and 468
pupils, and in the West Riding from 115 to 354. Though the majority
of the schools were maintained by the local authority, a handful were
denominational. Only two schools were not coeducational, and these
were both Roman Catholic junior schools in Liverpool. When the project
began all but five of the forty-five were housed in buildings which had
been put up before the First World War.

Within each EPA the number of pupils on the school roll fluctuated
considerably from year to year as demolition and redevelopment shifted
population across the district. One school had less than half the number
of pupils it had had five years previously; another had almost half as
many again. School buildings could not be adapted rapidly enough to
meet the changed demands on them, and some schools had empty
classrooms while in others desks were crowded into corridors and any
odd corner that could be found. Thus at one extreme there was a school
with 122 square feet of floor space (including non-teaching space) per
pupil, while in another in the same EPA each pupil had only 30 square
feet to himself. Pupil-teacher ratios, including full-time equivalents of
part-time teachers, similarly varied from the low twenties to the mid
thirties. Pupil-teacher ratio is not however a reliable indicator of the

size of teaching groups, as part-time teachers in subjects such as music may be used to relieve the class teacher entirely, while in some schools the ratio may be statistically improved by the existence of small remedial groups, without any general reduction in class size. It was often apparent from the number of pupils per purpose built classroom that teaching groups could be considerably larger than the pupil-teacher ratio would lead one to expect. It would be misleading, however to give an average figure for all the project schools because of the considerable variations in pressure on resources.

In the inner ring EPAs there were also wide variations in the proportions of immigrant pupils on the school roll. According to the DES definition of an immigrant, 4 per cent of children in Liverpool, 24 per cent in Deptford and 46 per cent in Birmingham were immigrants — there were none in the West Riding. In Deptford and Liverpool these children were by no means evenly distributed among the EPA schools: three of the Deptford schools had no more than one in ten immigrant pupils on their rolls, while four schools had more than 40 per cent, and in Liverpool eight schools had no immigrant pupils at all while two had almost one in five. In the Birmingham schools the proportions were more constant, ranging from 35 per cent to 57 per cent.

As might be expected from what has already been said about the instability of the population in the inner ring areas, pupil turnover presented a serious problem in all the EPAs except the West Riding. As a measure of this we took the number of pupils transferring to and from the schools during the course of the school year 1968-9, excluding, of course, those entering or leaving at the normal points, and expressed this as a percentage of the total number on the roll in January of that year. The result was startling: in Deptford 25 per cent, in Liverpool 29 per cent and in Birmingham 37 per cent of all pupils had moved during the school year, compared with only 11 per cent in the West Riding. In one school in Birmingham there had been almost 50 per cent turnover in the course of only one year.

Absenteeism was also high. Taking the total number of absences as a percentage of the total number of possible attendances during 1968-9 we found 11 per cent absenteeism in the West Riding and Birmingham, 13 per cent in Liverpool and 14 per cent in Deptford. These figures may be compared with a count for all ILEA primary schools, based on a survey taken on one day in September 1968, of 8.5 per cent.[6] Again, there were variations among schools, but in only five of them (four in the West Riding) was absenteeism as low as the ILEA average. In ten schools it was greater than 15 per cent.

From our survey of teachers[7] we learned something about the staff of these schools. The survey had a good response in all except the Liverpool district, where it was unacceptable to many teachers; hence we must leave Liverpool out of the present discussion. The most striking fact which emerged from the survey was the youth and inexperience of the Birmingham and, more particularly, the Deptford teachers, and the short time they stayed in the EPA schools. The West Riding schools had the opposite characteristics: Table III shows that while 32 per cent and 27 per cent of teachers in the Deptford and Birmingham EPAs respectively were not yet twenty-five years of age, only 10 per cent in the West Riding were as young as this. At the other end of the age scale, almost half of the West Riding teachers were over forty-five, compared with 28 per cent and 20 per cent of the teachers in the other two areas. Table III also shows that the Deptford and Birmingham EPA teachers were considerably younger than teachers in all maintained primary schools in England and Wales, while the West Riding teachers were rather older than the national average.

Table IV shows the number of years which the teachers had spent in the school in which they were teaching at the time of the survey. One half of the West Riding teachers had been there for five years or longer, but only a quarter of those in Deptford and Birmingham. For well over a third of teachers in the last two areas their present school was their first, and almost a half of the teachers in Deptford and a third in Birmingham were unmarried. It seems that the inner ring schools depended to a large extent on young newly qualified teachers without family ties, and that the departure of these teachers either on marriage, the arrival of a first baby, or promotion, lead to a constant turnover in staff.

This impression was confirmed by data which we gathered directly from the school records. In both Deptford and Birmingham there was only one school in which more than half of the staff had stayed for three years or more, whereas six of the ten West Riding schools were in this position.

It is sometimes remarked that teachers in EPA schools come from middle class families and live well outside the district in which they teach. This seemed true of the inner ring EPAs, and once more there was a contrast between them and the mining towns. The fathers of two third of the teachers in Deptford and Birmingham had white collar jobs, but in the West Riding 59 per cent were the children of manual workers. Only a handful of teachers in the inner ring schools lived within half a mile of their place of work, but 22 per cent of the West Riding teachers lived as close as this.

The teacher survey contained four attitude scales which had been used by the NFER in their study of streaming in primary schools[8] and on which the scores of two nationally representative samples of teachers in streamed and non-streamed primary schools were known. We were thus able to investigate how the attitudes of EPA teachers differed from those of their colleagues elsewhere. The scales were as follows:

Permissiveness: permissiveness of attitudes towards the child as a person;
Physical punishment: approval or disapproval of the use of physical punishment in schools;
Noise: tolerance or intolerance of noise in the classroom; and
Less able children: attitudes towards the worthwhileness and interest of teaching less able children.

On each scale junior teachers in the EPA sample were compared first with teachers in the NFER sample of streamed junior schools, secondly with teachers in the NFER sample of non-streamed junior schools, and

TABLE III Age of teachers in EPA project schools, compared with all teachers in maintained primary schools in England and Wales at March 1969

	Deptford EPA %	Birmingham EPA %	West Riding EPA %	Teachers in all maintained primary schools in England and Wales %
No information	1	0	0	0
Under 25 years	32	27	10	18
25-34 years	21	40	19	22
35-44 years	18	13	26	23
45 years and over	28	20	46	36
Total %	100	100	100	100
(N)	(145)	(70)	(59)	(153,259)

Source: EPA teacher survey (1969). Table 26, *Statistics of Education 1969*, volume IV, *Teachers*.

TABLE IV Number of years which teachers have stayed in project schools, by EPA

	Deptford EPA %	Birmingham EPA %	West Riding EPA %
No information	2	3	3
Less than 2 years	42	36	29
2 years to 4 years 11 months	32	37	19
5 years and over	24	25	50
Total %	100	100	100
(N)	(145)	(70)	(59)

Source: EPA teacher survey (1969).

thirdly with infant teachers in the EPA sample. Not unexpectedly it was
found that the scores of EPA infant teachers indicated a greater degree
of permissiveness and less approval of physical punishment than those
of the EPA junior teachers, though no statistically significant difference
was found between these two groups on the scales *Noise* and *Less able
children.* In turn the EPA junior teachers were more permissive, more
disapproving of physical punishment, and more tolerant of noise in the
classroom than were teachers in the NFER sample of streamed junior
schools, but, contrary to expectation, they were *less* interested in less
able children.

These findings should be interpreted cautiously. All schools in both
NFER samples had at least a two form entry, while several of the EPA
project schools had only one class in each year group. It might well be
the case that big schools create more problems of discipline than small
schools where each child is known personally to the head. Moreover, we
found that, within the EPA sample, the younger teachers were both
more permissive and more tolerant of noise than their older colleagues.
It has already been shown that in the inner ring EPA schools there was
a disproportionately large number of young and inexperienced teachers,
and it is more than likely that this provides part of the explanation why
the EPA teachers as a whole appeared more permissive than a national
sample.

The apparently lower interest of the EPA teachers in less able children
demands more attention, for, as we shall discuss below, the ability and
attainment tests which we administered showed that there were very
many more low attaining children in the EPA schools than in the population as a whole. It may be that the attitudes of the EPA teachers are
based on a more realistic assessment than teachers could have in schools
where very few children could properly be regarded as retarded; or they
may simply be overwhelmed by the enormity of the problem. Alternatively, because standards of attainment are generally much lower in
EPA schools, the less able child might be interpreted by the EPA teacher
as being someone who has much more serious learning difficulties than
teachers in other schools would conceive of as being shown by less able
children. In either case, it is clear that many EPA teachers do not enjoy
this important aspect of their job.

The final section of the teacher survey examined job satisfaction
directly. It fell into two parts: in the first teachers were invited to say
of each of fourteen features whether their job was better than, the same
as, or worse than the jobs of friends of approximately the same age and
with equivalent qualifications, and in the second they were asked to
compare thirteen aspects of their teaching situation with that of teachers
they knew in other schools. The responses of the teachers in all three
EPAs taken together are shown in Figures I and II.

When comparing their jobs with those of friends, more teachers
thought they were better off than thought they were worse off in
respect of security, intellectual stimulation, opportunities to improve
qualifications and general satisfaction. Among these aspects security
gave the most satisfaction. More teachers thought they were worse
off than thought they were better off in regard to social prestige, social

FIGURE I: EPA teachers' comparisons of their jobs with the jobs of friends of approximately the same age and with equivalent qualifications

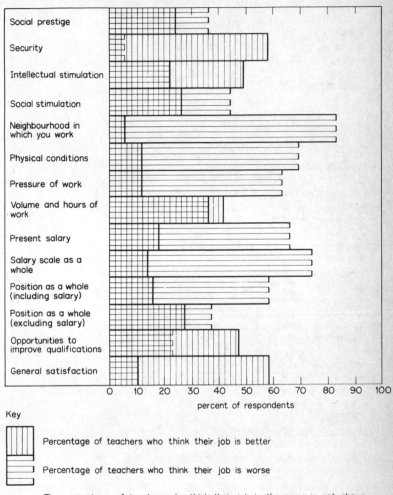

Key

Percentage of teachers who think their job is better

Percentage of teachers who think their job is worse

The percentage of teachers who think their job is the same is not shown

stimulation, the neighbourhood in which they worked, physical conditions, pressure of work, present salary, salary scale as a whole, position as a whole including salary and position as a whole excluding salary. The neighbourhood was the cause of the most dissatisfaction, but salary levels were also a major focus for discontent. Although the teachers tended to regard themselves as better off in regard to volume and hours of work, most of them thought that the pressure of work while they

FIGURE II   EPA teachers' comparisons of their jobs with the jobs of teachers they know in other schools

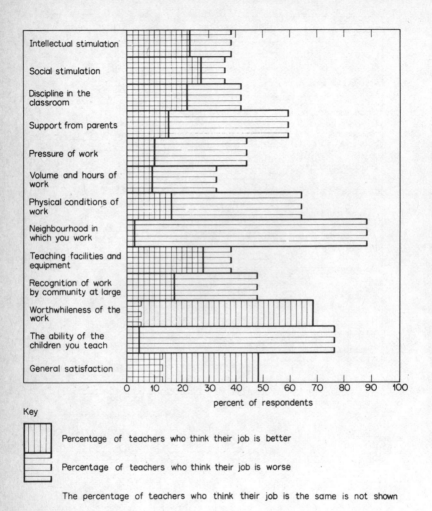

Key

Percentage of teachers who think their job is better

Percentage of teachers who think their job is worse

The percentage of teachers who think their job is the same is not shown

were actually on the job was worse than in other occupations. What is more remarkable however is the fact that nearly 60 per cent of respondents felt that their job yielded more general satisfaction than did the jobs which their friends held. This contrasts with only 16 per cent who thought that they were better off in terms of their position as a whole including salary. It seems that for EPA teachers psychological rewards are some compensation for low financial ones and poor working conditions.

The comparisons with teachers in other schools underlined this impression of a vocationally motivated teaching force. Only a small minority of EPA teachers thought that their situation was better than that of teachers they knew in other schools in eleven of the aspects specified: intellectual and social stimulation, discipline, support from parents, pressure of work, volume and hours of work, physical conditions, neighbourhood, teaching facilities and equipment, recognition of work by the community and ability of the children. On the other two items responses were totally reversed: these were the worthwhileness of the work and general satisfaction. As standards of attainment are generally lower in EPA schools, this apparently high level of general satisfaction seems to conflict with the finding reported above, that the EPA teachers were less interested in teaching less able children than were teachers in a national sample of schools. However we have found in conversation that they often mention the warmth and spontaneity of the children they teach, which certainly increases their satisfaction in their work. The features which EPA teachers compared most unfavourably with other schools were support from parents, physical conditions, neighbourhood and the ability of the children — in effect the four features which have typically been used to characterize EPA schools.

There are statistically significant differences between the three districts. The greatest discontent with salary was in Deptford, presumably because salaries were generally higher in London than in the other two regions and the difference was not fully compensated for by the London allowance. Teachers in both Deptford and Birmingham considered themselves worse off than teachers in the West Riding in respect both of the neighbourhood and physical conditions of work. The socially homogeneous and isolated small towns of the West Riding EPA probably provided a more pleasant environment and at the same time afforded less opportunity for contrast than either of the inner ring areas, and indeed the average age of the schools was rather less in the West Riding. West Riding teachers were also more content with the social prestige of their job, and indeed in an area where only 4 per cent of males held non-routine white collar jobs it seems likely that teachers would be accorded more status than in the diversified occupational structure of large towns. The stability of the West Riding community probably explains why teachers there felt happier about the support they received from parents and the recognition of their work by the community. Their greater satisfaction with the level of discipline in the classroom could be interpreted as another aspect of the same factor.

The questions about job satisfaction were originally used in a study of probationary teachers carried out at the Bristol University Institute of Education, and we were hence able to compare the responses of the EPA teachers with both a national sample[9] of teachers in their probationary year and two further samples in Southwark and Wolverhampton.[10] Our general finding was that EPA teachers were generally more dissatisfied with aspects of their work than the non-EPA teachers.

These then are our four Plowden educational priority areas. They certainly suffer from multiple economic and social deprivations and their schools labour under difficulties brought into them by the characteristics of the surrounding neighbourhood. But there is no unique description of either the EPA or the EPA school. The West Riding represents a distinctive type of economic misfortune and community stability. The city EPAs are variously complicated by urban redevelopment, migration and immigration and their schools by teacher and pupil turnover and by children from families with different cultural backgrounds. Even these children, however, are by no means identical copies of each other. The Liverpool EPA, and to a lesser extent Deptford, appear to have more of the residual character-istics of a settled working class community, with a considerable prop-ortion of parents brought up in the same area, than Birmingham, with its high influx of newcomers. No doubt too there is a wide range of conditions nationally which escapes the view presented in our four districts, for example in some rural areas and peripheral redevelopment housing estates. We therefore infer that the definition of EPA, the diagnosis of its ills and the prescriptions for its amelioration must always be based on detailed local study.

Notes

[1] This chapter is mainly the work of Joan Payne. Our description of the four English projects also applies in the main to the Scottish project in Dundee.

[2] Figures for the four EPAs in this and the subsequent paragraphs were calculated from the *1966 10 per cent Sample Census – Special Tabulation of Basic Statistics*, and national figures were derived from the *1966 10 per cent Sample Census Great Britain Summary Tables*.

[3] See J. Rex and R. Moore, *Race, Community and Conflict* (Institute of Race Relations, 1967).

[4] The term 'Asian' refers here and in the rest of the chapter to people from the Indian subcontinent. In the Parental Survey a family was classified as West Indian or Asian if at least one of the parents was brought up in those regions. Families of Irish origin were included in the non-immigrant group.

[5] An infant or junior department which had a separate head is counted in what follows as a separate school.

[6] ILEA Research Report No. 2A, p. 2 (mimeo), January 1972.

[7] Head teachers took part in the survey and are included in the figures in this account.

[8] J.C. Barker Lunn, *Streaming in the Primary School* (NFER, 1970).

[9] J.K. Taylor and I.R. Dale, with M.A. Brimer, *A Survey of Teachers in their First Year of Service* (University of Bristol, 1971).

[10] R. Bolam, 'Guidance for probationer teachers', *Trends in Education*, 21 (1970). Work on this second, regional survey is not yet complete.

III The organization of the school

INTRODUCTION

The previous section, with its contributions showing the importance of the values embodied in local education authority administrative policies, leads appropriately to studies that examine the values of the school itself and their relationship with its members, both staff and students. The potential importance of this area of inquiry was suggested early by Webb (1962) who portrayed the values of 'Black School' in this way:

> What sort of person would the boy become who accepted the standards the teacher tries to impose? In himself he would be neat, orderly, polite and servile. With the arithmetic and English he absorbed at school, and after further training, he might become a meticulous clerk, sustained by a routine laid down by someone else, and piously accepting his station in life. Or, if he got a trade, we can see him later in life clutching a well-scrubbed lunch-tin and resentful at having to pay union dues, because the boss, being a gentleman, knows best. To grow up like this a lad has to be really cut-off from the pull of social class and gang.

Subsequent writers considered more fully the structural forms of the school in which value orientations are embodied. Bernstein, Elvin and Peters (1966) suggested two models of the school with opposed strategies that echo the two local authority models explored by Byrne and Williamson in section II of this volume. One was characterized by stratified relationships with control exercised by strong inflexible ritualistic patterns. The other model was of a school in which behaviour was differentiated but not stratified; differentiation resting not on domination but co-operation. Here control was exercised through interpersonal, even therapeutic, relationships rather than through ritual.

It is only recently that attempts have been made to explore, through research, the ways in which the different value systems of the schools are transmitted through their administrative and teaching arrangements. Some of the first major studies of this genre to be published sprang from the research programmes of Manchester University. Hargreaves's study of Lumley Secondary School (1967) showed that the values of a school may be carried in its streaming system. Students with 'positive orientations' towards the values of the school tended over the four years to converge on the higher streams.

> For boys in high streams life at school will be a pleasant and rewarding experience, since the school system confers status upon them. This status is derived from membership of a high stream, where boys are considered to be academically successful, and are

granted privileges and responsibility in appointment as prefects and in their selection for school visits and holidays. The peer-group values reflect the status bestowed on such boys by the school in being consonant with teachers' values. Conformity to peer-group and school values is thus consistent and rewarding.

In the low streams boys are deprived of status, in that they are *double failures* by their lack of ability or motivation to obtain entry to a Grammar School or to a high stream in the Modern School. The school, as we have seen, accentuates this state of failure and deprivation. The boys have achieved virtually nothing. For boys in low streams conformity to teacher expectations gives little status. We can thus regard the low-stream boys as subject to status frustration, for not only are they unable to gain any sense of equality of worth in the eyes of the school, but their occupational aspirations for their future lives in society are seriously reduced in scope. ... Demotion to the delinquescent subculture is unlikely to encourage a boy to strive towards academic goals, since the pressures within the peer-group will confirm and reinforce the anti-academic attitudes which led to demotion, and the climate within the low streams will be far from conducive to academic striving. In order to obtain promotion from a low stream, a boy must deviate from the dominant anti-academic values.

Hargreaves shows not only that school organization brings about value consensus between the school and the high stream pupils and dissonance between the school and low stream pupils that did not exist in the earlier years of secondary school, but also that it brings about dissonance between pupils in the high streams and those in the lower streams.

Lacey in *Hightown Grammar* (1970), another important 'Manchester' study, presents a picture not of school induced cultural differentiation but of a closely linked process, status deprivation — another management strategy that may be used by the school to impose its values on its members. In exploring this process in a Manchester area grammar school he develops an important analysis not only of its consequences but also of the process using the twin concepts of polarization and differentiation to analyse classroom interaction.

In the papers presented in this section Lacey, in a previously unpublished study, develops his analysis of Hightown Grammar School to take account of the destreaming strategies introduced by a new headmaster in the early 1960s. Though it is quite clear that the values of the school are transmitted in other ways than through the streaming/non-streaming system, the administrative changes in streaming are shown to have led to important consequences in the experiences of the pupils, not least in their experience of the direct and indirect control strategies of the school. Yet the study, with the author's note of caution, reinforces the tentative conclusions reached by Barker Lunn (1970) and others, that the critical factor that appears to determine the outcome of moves from streaming to destreaming is the attitude and enthusiasms of the teachers concerned. Lacey's evidence suggests, however, that in Hightown

Grammar the attitudes of the teachers were, at least in part, influenced by the move to destreaming.

Bellaby's study, which builds upon the work of Lacey and Hargreaves, is based upon a study of three contrasting comprehensive schools. Using a range of perspectives he explores the incidence of deviant behaviour and its relationship to the control and organizational strategies employed in the different schools. Bellaby is able to bring out, in a manner that valuably complements Lacey's paper, the important ways in which the values of the school are manifest in the control arrangements. These include not only the more obvious disciplinary procedures but also the indirect but powerful control devices exercised through classroom interaction and the experience of the curriculum.

Consideration of the head teacher leads us to Shipman's paper where we turn directly to this largely unstudied area of the organization of schools: the determination of the curriculum. Again this is an area central to the phenomenologists' concern with the arrangements for the distribution of knowledge and social control. Here Shipman examines the responses of schools involved in a Schools Council curriculum development project and shows that their reception of the new curriculum and particularly its continued use was by no means that which was anticipated by the curriculum development project workers. Instead it appeared to be substantially determined by the structure and values of the school and by the perceptions of the school staff of their personal roles within it; in short by their definition of their situation.[1] Like the studies of Hargreaves and Lacey, Shipman's shows that the consequence of these perceptions and values can still take experienced teachers and administrators by surprise even though the perceptions and values are in fact their own.

Note

[1] The work of curriculum development projects set up by the Schools Council or other agencies is, like the curriculum itself, largely unexplored by sociologists even though it is central to the discussion on the control of knowledge. Some preliminary consideration is published by Young (1972).

References

BARKER LUNN, J.C., 1970, *Streaming in the Primary School*. Slough: NFER.

BERNSTEIN, B., ELVIN, H.L. and PETERS, R.S., 1966, 'Ritual in education'. *Philosophical Transactions of the Royal Society of London,* Series B, pp. 429-36.

HARGREAVES, D.H., 1967, *Social Relations in a Secondary School*. London: Routledge and Kegan Paul.

LACEY, C., 1970, *Hightown Grammar,* Manchester: University Press.

WEBB, J., 1962, 'The Sociology of a school'. *British Journal of Sociology,* 13(3).

YOUNG, M.F.D., 1972, 'On the politics of educational knowledge'. *Economy and Society,* 1(2), pp. 194-215.

C LACEY

Destreaming in a 'pressured' academic environment *

The connection between the form of an organization and its consequences for human behaviour is a complex and challenging aspect of
sociology. It has a broad and classical lineage extending through
grand theory[1] to small scale studies[2] and social anthropology.[3] It has
more recently crystallized out into a specialist area in sociology.[4] It
is very disappointing, therefore, that much of the empirical work
concerning the effects of organizational forms has degenerated to the
level of looking for simple 'one-to-one' relationships between a narrowly defined organizational arrangement and some desired characteristic
of human behaviour. This is particularly true of studies involving
school organization and levels of scholastic attainment. Studies have
all too frequently failed to spell out the assumption underlying the
investigation and failed, therefore, to fertilize the development of
theory. The time has long since passed when it was possible to review
the literature in the field without the aid of a tabulation summarizing
the *number of studies* that have found positive, negative or mixed
effects of, say, ability grouping on educational attainment.[5] The generally recognized outcome of a tremendous research effort culminating
in studies of whole school systems in the United States and Sweden[6] and
of many thousands of schoolchildren in other countries is that there is
no clearcut advantage in terms of academic achievement for either
homogeneous or heterogeneous ability grouping. Why this should be the
case has not been looked into with anything like the energy devoted to
the original research.

The argument has now moved on to centre around other aspects of
human behaviour, including creativity, self-concept, school interests
and attitudes and career aspirations. More recently still, attention has
moved towards finding out how streamed and unstreamed systems affect
teacher attitudes and behaviour. In all this research, the methodology has
been similar — to obtain as large a number of participating schools as possible and to compare gains in one system (say, streamed classes) with gains
in another (say, unstreamed classes). The research has been based on the
assumption that if only the 'n' is large enough, the results will be definitive.
The possibility that intervening variables might pose an even bigger problem
in a large sample[7] was never faced up to and, in some cases, recognized
and then ignored. For example, Goldberg, Passow and Justman[8] write
'No attempt was made to control or even investigate class (classroom)

---

*This paper is published for the first time in this collection.

differences in content or teaching method since the purpose of the study was to discover the effects of ability grouping per se and not of pre-determined special provisions' and 'No effort was made to examine the content or teaching style in any classroom or to gather information on what modifications — in substance or method — teachers believed they were making in the face of broader or narrower ability ranges. ...'

It was therefore left to Barker Lunn[9] to show in a much more broadly based survey that teacher attitudes are of immense importance to the outcome of destreaming exercised in primary schools.

The purpose of this paper is to take a different approach to the question. For, while I accept that it is true that destreaming does not, on a large scale, produce automatic gains in attainment,[10] it is also true that in some schools it does produce an improvement in attainment levels while in others it might well have a detrimental effect. I intend to examine a single case of an LEA grammar school where organizational change produced a definite improvement in GCE O level results. By examining the case in depth, I hope to suggest some of the intervening factors that it might be necessary to consider when examining the effects of an organizational form on behaviour.

More narrowly defined, the paper has three aims:

1 To demonstrate that the organizational change did have the effects attributed to it. In other words, to establish the case study.
2 To show that the pre-existing conditions characterized by the term 'pressured academic environment' were an important element, both in the generation of the particular organizational changes and their effectiveness.
3 To suggest that organizational changes of this sort can only be effective if they proceed on a broad front (i.e. are in themselves complex and contain a convincing ideological[11] component).

Before moving on to describe the case of destreaming at Hightown Grammar,[12] it is necessary to establish a definitional framework within which to locate the study.

A *set system* is an arrangement by which pupils are formed into groups specifically for each subject on the timetable. A *form system* is an arrangement by which a single group of pupils is formed and kept together for all subjects. Either of these systems can be streamed or non-streamed.

Streaming refers here to the formation of a hierarchy of academically differentiated, relatively homogeneous ability groups. The following paradigm exhausts the simple possibilities for combining these arrangements:

	Streamed	*Non-streamed*
Set systems	1	2
Form systems	3	4

It is important to notice that only non-streaming gives rise to teaching groups with relatively large ability ranges and that a streamed set system gives rise to homogeneous ability groups. While the non-streamed form system (4) is an arrangement which is growing in popularity in primary schools,[13] it is still very uncommon at the secondary level.[14] The trend at the secondary level is for any modification of the streamed form system (3) to move in the direction of combinations of either (4) and (1) or (2) and (1).[15]

The changes at Hightown Grammar described later refer to a move from a streamed form system (3) through a transitional stage to a combined (4) and (1) system.

An additional dimension to this characterization of the formal organization of secondary schools needs consideration. This dimension relates to the 'policy' or the aims underlying the introduction and continuation of the formal arrangement. While my characterization of this additional dimension rests heavily on an evaluation of the headmaster's formal policy, it also provides, at the operational level, ample opportunity for reclassification on the basis of 'objective' indicators concerned with the way the system[16] allocates its resources.[17]

The dimension can be characterized by the following three types:

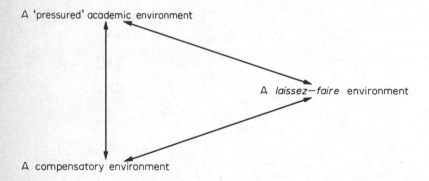

A 'pressured' academic environment

A *laissez—faire* environment

A compensatory environment

A 'pressured' academic environment is one in which great emphasis is placed on academic achievement in a traditional sense. Examination success is given great prominence and the school's resources are allocated to produce the highest possible achievement from the best pupils.

The *laissez-faire* environment is one in which a number of policies may be pursued (i.e. pressured academic and compensatory) but they have no discernible effect on the allocation of resources within the school.

The compensatory environment involves a policy which allocates resources in favour of the relatively low achiever.

The old regime – a pressured academic environment

When the study began in 1962, the school was run by a headmaster who had been at the school for eighteen years. His regime was characterized by a number of organizational arrangements that embodied his philosophy of education and, as he put it, the school reflected his personality.

Like many headmasters of his generation, he was a great admirer of the public school system and of the Oxford and Cambridge open scholarship system. This was reflected by his development of the house system to a degree not normally found in a grammar school and also by the emphasis he placed on the express stream, which linked the grammar school to the open scholarship system.

The express stream was the highest level of the streamed form system and came about in the following manner:

> Pupils entering the grammar school were randomly allocated to four first year classes and, at the end of the first year, were streamed on the basis of academic performance. The pupils in the top quarter of each first year class were promoted into the express stream (2E). This class of intelligent motivated pupils was expected to take the O level examination after four years instead of five. The rest of the first year pupils were streamed in a similar manner. The three other second year classes were expected to take the O level examination in the normal period of five years.

THE STREAMING PATTERN (old regime)

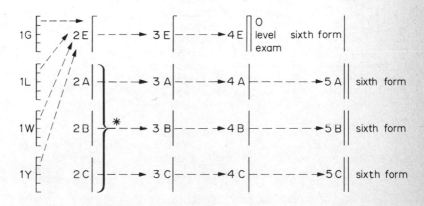

The existence of the express stream strengthened the third year sixth form[18] and linked the school into the Oxford and Cambridge open scholarship system in the following way:

> A pupil who entered the sixth form in September normally spent two academic years studying for the A level examination held in June. The Oxbridge open scholarship examinations usually took place around February. Non-express stream pupils wishing to leave school before their nineteenth birthday would therefore have to take the open scholarship paper after only one and a half years in the sixth form and before they had completed their sixth

form syllabus. The express stream boy, on the other hand, could enter the sixth form at fifteen years of age (instead of sixteen), study for two years to A level and then spend an additional six months on special preparation for the open scholarship examinations. In practice, only very few boys each year got open scholarships. Most express stream boys left at seventeen plus after taking their A levels and either went to university a year early or took a job for a year before going into university. The old headmaster strove to build up the third year sixth, gave prominence to its members and acclaimed the one, two or three boys per year who succeeded in getting to Oxford and Cambridge.[19]

In addition to the public support given to boys staying on into the third year of the sixth form (for instance, the head boy was usually chosen from among those staying on), the school supported the E-stream system at the moment it emerged in the second year by allocating to it the most trustworthy and experienced masters. This is borne out in the following table:

Percentage of classroom time (academic timetable) that each stream spent with the three categories of teacher, 1962-3

	E-stream	*Middle stream*	*Bottom stream*
Head of department	41	19	0
Deputy head of department	34	36	19
Others	25	45	81
Total	100	100	100

*A minor restreaming into science (S), modern language (M) and general (G) streams took place at the end of the third year. This does not affect the argument developed in this paper and is ignored in order to simplify presentation.

The new head

After the summer of 1963 the old headmaster retired. The new headmaster spent his first year of office learning about the school. He made no organizational changes and relied heavily on the advice of the senior master to discover how things had been in the past. Since the old head had delegated many of the essential day-to-day tasks to heads of house and the senior master, the school ran itself very much as it did before. This period can therefore be treated as an extension of the old regime.

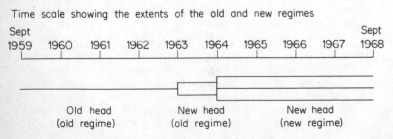

Time scale showing the extents of the old and new regimes

Sept 1959   1960   1961   1962   1963   1964   1965   1966   1967   Sept 1968

Old head (old regime)   New head (old regime)   New head (new regime)

The new regime

By the end of the first year, the new head had some firm ideas about the problems faced by the school:[20]

1 He was worried about the drop in the average IQ of the yearly intake (caused by the falling population and the social class selectiveness of the emigration from Hightown).

2 He was concerned about the strain imposed on the less able boys in the express stream. In an average year, one or two boys per intake dropped out of this stream while others left before entering the sixth form and some of those who remained were unable to cope satisfactorily with sixth form work. The new headmaster felt these boys suffered unnecessarily since they could have taken five years over the O level course. He was also worried by reports from experienced teachers that 2E (1962 intake) was the weakest express form the school had yet produced.

3 He was concerned about the low level of achievement in the bottom stream. The morale in this stream had declined and very few students usually achieved sufficient O level passes to get into the sixth form.

4 He was concerned about the number of pupils recruited into the sixth form. He felt that the grammar school course should be considered a seven year course and that nearly all of the intake should accomplish this.

It is important to note that these were the problems facing the school, as defined by the new head. The definition of the problems faced by an organization is part of the political argument about the solution. The previous headmaster would have defined the problems differently and different solutions would have appeared appropriate. For example, he saw the express stream as a success and quoted the names of boys who had successfully gained entry to Oxford and Cambridge colleges to illustrate this. He explained the failures in terms of the laziness of the individual pupils concerned and even, on one occasion, in terms of the poor quality of the staff, who did not push their pupils sufficiently. Before 1959, there had been two express streams and the old headmaster had been very proud of this arrangement. He was forced to give up one of these express classes because of pressure from the staff who, in his view, had not been willing to push the pupils hard enough.

The new head made organizational changes at the beginning of the academic year 1964-5 to meet the problems he had defined:

1 He destreamed classes 3A, B and C of the 1962 intake at the beginning of their third year. He did this to break up the demoralized group in 3C.

2 He kept class 3E intact but suggested that they would take five years instead of four years over the O level course.

3 He did not stream the 1963 intake and allowed them to maintain their house groups (forms) in the second year.

4 He instituted a more flexible sixth form organization in which O levels could be taken in conjunction with A levels. The arrangement made use of the November O level examinations and enabled the O level qualification for entry to the sixth form to be lowered.[21]

The overall effect of these changes was to move the school away from the pressured academic environment towards the compensatory end of the continuum described earlier. In the 1962 intake the E-stream no longer linked up with the third year sixth and in the 1963 intake it disappeared completely. There could no longer be a differential allocation of staff resources between unequal streams because they had ceased to exist. The allocation of resources within the classroom is more difficult to legislate about but it is important to note that many of the staff were in favour of the change and that some of the staff most likely to stream within the classroom[22] were not presented with the problem. Maths, for example, remained streamed set.

This analysis will measure the effect of destreaming classes 3A, B and C and the effect of not streaming the 1963 intake. The following diagram locates the position of the change, summarizing the experience of the 1959, 1960, 1962 and 1963 intakes.

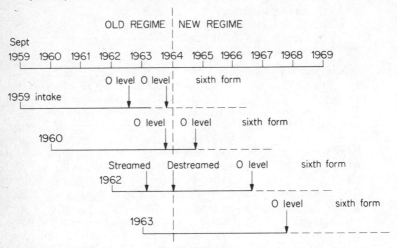

I originally collected data on four cohorts, the intakes of 1956, 1959, 1962 and 1965. In order to trace the effects of the changes described above, data on cohorts 1959 and 1962 were used and supplemented by data from the 1960 cohort (as a check on the 1959 results). The O level results of the 1963 cohort were later brought in to check on the results of the 1962 cohort.

1959 intake (old regime)

This cohort had the whole of its O level career under the old regime. In its last year (affecting streams A, B and C) the new head had taken over the school but, at that point, no organizational changes had been made.

1960 intake (old regime)

The express stream in this cohort took its O level examinations at the same time as the A, B and C streams of the 1959 cohort, i.e. under the old regime. By the time the ordinary streams took their O levels, the changes had been made. However, the change did not affect those streams directly (they remained streamed) and, although some of the ideology surrounding the change may have become known to them, its effect can be assumed to be slight. For example, a sociometric questionnaire revealed that only 5 boys out of 120 in this cohort had friends in the destreamed groups.

1962 intake (new regime – partial)

This cohort was the first one to be directly affected by the organizational changes. The A, B and C streams were destreamed in 1964 (September) and all the resulting classes 3E, 3P, 3Q and 3R took their O level examinations in 1967 (June). The non-streamed forms 3P, 3Q and 3R were regarded as a transition to the full non-streamed form system (4) in 1963. However, in both years some subjects were streamed set (1), for example, maths, and others were non-streamed set (2), for example options involving the sciences. The majority of subjects were taught in non-streamed form groups P, Q and R.

1963 intake (new regime in full)

This cohort was divided at random into four unstreamed groups IG, IL, IY and IW on their arrival at the school and they remained in them until the end of the fifth year. The majority of their subjects were taught in non-streamed form groups (4). It is in this cohort that the full effects of the organizational changes initiated by the new headmaster can be seen. They were the first cohort to spend all five years up to O level in non-streamed groups for most of their subjects.

The effects of the organizational changes – establishing the case study

The effects of the organizational change must be seen against the background of the slowly declining average IQ of the school population. In fact, in 1965 the intake was restricted to three forms in order to prevent a further decline in the 'quality' of the intake. If the usual intake had been admitted, the average IQ would have fallen an additional three or four points.

Year of intake	Average IQ measured before entry	Number of pupils admitted	'N' for average IQ
1956	122.3	125	125
1959	122.2	120	105
1962	118.4	120	116
1963	119.4	120	110
1965	118.7	90	87

The table shows that there can be no suggestion that beneficial trends in the quality of the intake affected the results recorded in Graph I.

The effects of the organizational change were measured in terms of the change produced in academic achievement of fifth year pupils and in the change in their subsequent careers. The O level examination results provide us with the main device for doing this. While the examination is not a standardized achievement test, it is a controlled examination. The syllabus examination paper and marking procedures are standardized by an examination board[23] on an area-wide basis.

The examination results are made public and have a direct effect on the reputation of the school and the individual teachers as well as the future career (academic or otherwise) of the pupil.

GRAPH I   Average number of O level passes achieved by the total fifth year — by year of examination

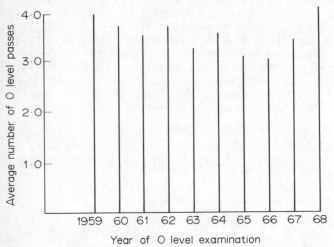

Graph I

The line of best fit 1959 to 1966 shows a steep decline in the average number of O level passes achieved. This downward trend was reversed in 1967 and the reversal confirmed by an even stronger set of results in 1968.[24]

The difference between the 1966 average, the last year of streaming, and the 1968 average, the first year of full non-streaming, is statistically significant. However, it is also important to determine how the *distribution* of O level passes has been changed by destreaming and non-streaming. It is, of course, impossible to ascertain how the streamed classes of the 1962 intake would have performed had they not been destreamed or the 1963 intake had they been streamed. It is only possible to gain an estimate of the effect by employing a device.

In graphs II and III, the O level results (means of the various fifth year classes) are plotted with the available IQ data for the 1959 and 1960 intakes. Since Graph III confirms the pattern of Graph II, it seems reasonable to assume that, had the 1962 and 1963 intakes

GRAPH II   1959 intake. Average IQ and average number of O level passes (taken in 1963 and 1964)

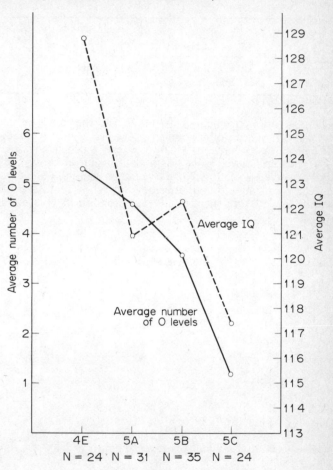

N = 24   N = 31   N = 35   N = 24

been treated similarly, they would have produced similar patterns. In order to test the effects of reorganization, the 1962 intake (5E, 5A, 5B, 5C) has been artificially restreamed (5-2A, 5-2B, 5-2C) and the 1963 intake artificially streamed (5E, 5A, 5B, 5C), using the same criteria[25] as was used in previous years. These groups did not, of course, exist as fifth year classes but, had the reorganization not taken place, they would have existed almost exactly as they have been used in this analysis.

Graph II

The mean number of O level passes obtained by boys in each class declines sharply between 4E and 5C. It is noticeable that the difference between 5C and the others is greater than the difference between 4E and the others.

		Difference in mean IQ	Difference in mean O levels
1	Comparing 4E and the rest	8.6	2.18
2	Comparing 5G and the rest	6.6	3.31

The large difference in IQ between 4E and the rest is associated with a small difference in the number of O levels gained while the smaller difference in IQ between 5C and the rest is associated with a larger difference in O levels gained. It is not possible to assess the cause of this negative association. While it could be caused by the depressing and demoralizing effect of streaming on 5C, it could also be caused by the fact that 4E spends only four years on its O level course.[26]

GRAPH III   1960 intake. Average number of O level passes (taken in 1964 and 1965)

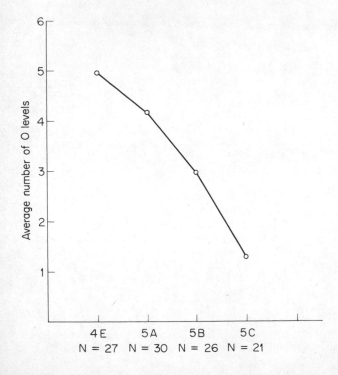

Graph III

The shape of the O level results curve for 1960 confirms the 1959 picture. Once again, the difference in average number of O level passes obtained between 5C and the rest is greater than between 4E and the rest (unfortunately, the IQ scores for these classes were not available).

Graphs IV and V

The graphs show that the streaming of the 1962 intake gave rise to a slightly higher differentiation in IQ than the 1959 intake and that this change is confirmed by the 1963 intake. However, despite the

GRAPH IV   1962 intake. Average IQ and average number of O level passes (taken in 1967)

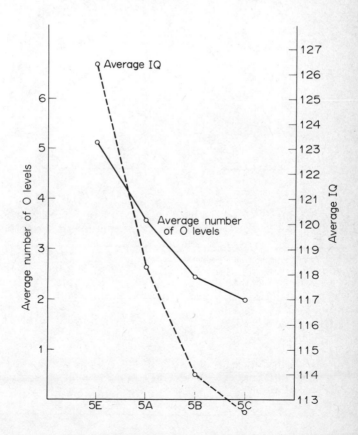

GRAPH V   1963 intake. Average IQ and average number of O level
passes (taken in 1968)

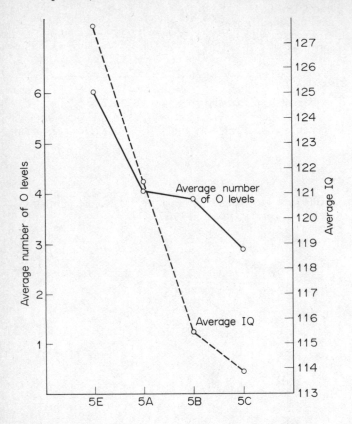

increased differentiation of IQ, the differentiation in performance
was far less marked. This is also made clear in the following table:

	1959	1960	1962 (reconstituted)	1963 (notional streaming)
Differences in average IQ top and bottom streams	11.4	Not available	13.9	13.8
Differences in average number of O levels, top and bottom streams	4.12	3.65	3.12	3.2

It is apparent that, while the effect of increasing the length of the E-stream course was to improve its expected performance (and increase differentiation), the effect of destreaming the other three forms has been to markedly improve the performance of the bottom stream and produce an overall decrease in differentiation and an overall improvement in the average number of O level passes achieved. This trend is also confirmed by the 1963 intake.

		Average IQ	Length of course	Average no. of O level passes
TOP STREAM:				
Old regime	1959	128.8	4 yrs	5.28
	1960	Not available	4 yrs	4.95
New regime	1962	126.4	5 yrs	5.12
	1963	127.7	5 yrs	6.1
BOTTOM STREAM:				
Old regime	1959	117.4	5 yrs	1.17
	1960	Not available	5 yrs	1.30
New regime	1962	112.5	5 yrs	2.00
	1963	113.9	5 yrs	2.90
MIDDLE STREAMS:				
Old regime	1959	121.6	5 yrs	4.06
	1960	Not available	5 yrs	3.56
New regime	1962	116.3	5 yrs	3.00
	1963	118.4	5 yrs	4.00

This concludes the presentation of evidence establishing the case study.

Discussion

An important indication of the causal mechanisms involved in the differentiation of pupils in the 1959 cohort is got by examining the differences between two classes, 5-2A in the 1962 cohort and 5C in the 1959 cohort. The average IQ of the two classes was similar (118.3 and 117.4 respectively). The difference between the classes in other respects was very great.

Students in 5C knew that they were the bottom stream and not highly regarded by teachers. They were frequently told how bad they were. When I administered a questionnaire to the class on one occasion, I was asked, 'Sir, are you asking us these questions because we're the throw-outs?'

Schoolmasters disliked the class because it was difficult to teach and because the children were not stimulating. Status in Hightown Grammar's pressured academic environment was clearly linked with teaching the sixth form and the more intelligent children in the E-stream (see table on p.151). Therefore 5C's reputation came largely from its *position* within the 1959 intake. Its pupils had lost out in competition with the rest of the cohort. It was being the *bottom* of the four fifth forms that caused it to have its particular reputation. If it had been compared to the 1962 intake in terms of IQ, the reputation of 5C for being 'thick' would not have been so easily established. The falling IQ level of the intake to Hightown Grammar School meant that 5C (1959) had a higher IQ than either 5-2C or 5-2B (1962) and the difference in IQ between 5C and 5-2A was only 0.9 of an IQ point. 5-2A's reputation was very different and the pupils in this form went on to obtain an average of three times as many O levels per person.

This analysis suggests that the organizational arrangement of classes has effects because it affects:

1 The students' view of themselves with respect to other students ('because we're the throw-outs').
2 The teachers' view of the students with respect to other students in the cohort (low intelligence - bottom stream).
3 The relationship between pupils and teachers (difficult to teach).

The importance of two of these intervening factors on the achievement of pupils is also suggested by the following data. In the fifth year, most of the teachers teaching 5C (1959) were asked to assess the 'academic performance' and 'behaviour' of each pupil.[27] In addition, they were given space to record remarks which they felt described any noticeable characteristics (relevant to 'academic performance' and/or ('behaviour') the pupils possessed. Only three teachers made use of the space and they did not make remarks against all the pupils.

The remarks were coded under the three headings:

1 *Condemning*   Remarks that include a subjective assessment of a derogatory nature, e.g. 'lout', 'congenitally idle', 'barrack-room lawyer'.

2 *Objective or*   Remarks that reveal a measured assessment of
conflicting   the individual. e.g. 'poor examinee', 'very nervous', 'recurrent absentee', and remarks that show a conflicting assessment, e.g. 'trying but thick' or 'trying but too late'.

3 *Praising*   Remarks that include a subjective assessment favourable to the pupil, e.g. 'working very hard', 'determined to pass' and 'generally good, could be faster'.

When the attitudes of these three masters are related to the examination success of 5C in their subject, a clear association is revealed:

	Condemning	Objective or conflicting	Praising	Passed	No. entered for exam	No. in form
Teacher A	9	2	0	1	12	24
Teacher B	5	7	3	8	19	24
Teacher C	2	8	14	13	19	24

Each teacher taught the total number in the form (24) but only entered those whom he thought would pass the exam. The numbers in the 'entered' column, therefore, reflect the teacher's own estimate of his success in teaching the form. Teacher C, in fact, obtained almost as many passes in his one subject as all the other teachers put together (i.e. in seven subjects) and this is reflected in his attitude towards the form as measured some months before the actual examination.

This result cannot be explained in terms of the normal success of the masters involved. By any other criteria used, Teacher B was usually more successful than Teacher C.

The teachers involved in teaching the form came to the conclusion that 5C had very limited ability and had simply put all their energies into C's subject and possible B's subject. This explanation of the results rests on the assumption that the ability level of the form determines the total number of passes obtained. It sometimes contained the insinuation that a form like 5C would go for those subjects that demanded the least intellectual effort. This explanation flies in the face of the evidence already discussed, in particular the performance of 5-2A which was at the same ability level (IQ) as 5C but obtained *three times* as many O level passes per boy.

Conclusion

The success of the organizational changes at Hightown Grammar has been shown to be linked closely with the destruction of the pre-existing system, characterized as a 'pressured' academic environment. Under the 'old regime' the school concentrated on the success of a relatively few talented pupils who could win external scholarships and bring high prestige to the school.[28] The pressured route via the E-stream to the sixth form and the allocation of the best teaching resources to the top and middle streams created a situation in which the bottom stream was neglected and demoralized. It is important to note that, in this situation, most teachers believed that the poor performance of the C stream was inevitably linked with their low ability (IQ) and their poor home backgrounds. When one master achieved a remarkable academic success with the class, he also displayed a completely different set of attitudes towards the pupils in the class. Far from seeing this as an example to be emulated, most masters explained this result in ways that did not interfere with their low expectations of the C stream.

The destreaming of the 1962 intake and the non-streaming of the 1963 intake inevitably broke up this system. A single group of pupils could not easily be labelled academically and even the streamed set aspect of the new system did not give rise to such a group. The resources of the school were no longer differentially applied to the groups within the system since they each had equal prestige.

In other words the changes can be seen as a move away from a pressured academic environment towards the compensatory end of the continuum.

A note of caution is necessary in the interpretation of these results: only one type of school was used in the study. The grammar school is a highly selective institution in itself. For example, the lowest single IQ recorded was well above 100. Had destreaming produced classes that teachers considered technically impossible to teach without streaming within the class,[29] the results might have been very different.

It could also be argued that the same improvement in the results could have been produced by reallocating resources and priorities within the streamed system. This case study can provide no answer to these questions and simply points to the necessity for more work of a detailed nature at the case study level to leaven the considerable effort already put in at the large scale survey level.

Notes

[1] Max Weber, *The Theory of Social and Economic Organisation* (New York, Free Press, 1947).

[2] L. Festinger, S. Schachter and K. Back, *Social Pressures in Informal Groups* (London, Tavistock, 1959).

[3] Max Gluckman, 'Succession and civil war among the Bemba: an exercise in anthropological theory', in *Order and Rebellion in Tribal Africa* (New York, Free Press, 1963).

[4] C.E. Bidwell, 'The school as a formal organisation' in J.G. March, *Handbook of Organisations* (Chicago, Rand, 1965).

[5] See National Education Association, *Ability Grouping* (Washington NEA, 1968), p.42.

[6] M.L. Goldberg, A.H. Passow and A.H. Justman, *The Effects of Ability Grouping* (New York, Teachers College, 1966).

[7] A large 'n', for example, has often meant that the data are thin and intervening variables cannot be controlled for.

[8] M.L. Goldberg, A.H. Passow and A.H. Justman, op. cit.

[9] Joan C. Barker Lunn, *Streaming in the Primary School* (Slough), NFER, 1970). This study is more broadly based in the sense that the researchers considered many more aspects of the education process that could have affected performance in a streamed or non-streamed set-up.

[10] In fact, I take the position that the question 'Why does a particular organizational change have a particular effect?' is prior to one which asks 'Will the same organizational change have the same effects in all superficially similar organizations?' The first approach leads to the development of understanding about social organizations; the second leads characteristically to the crudest form of social engineering.

[11] The term 'ideology' is used here in a specialist sense to mean, in this case, complex patterns of ideas justifying and explaining the organizational change.

[12] The research describes the effects of destreaming in a traditional LEA grammar school. The school, Hightown Grammar, served a mainly inner city area in a north-western conurbation in England. Pupils in Hightown who passed the eleven plus selection procedure (normally 15-20 per cent of the age cohort) could opt to go to the school. The school had a good academic reputation and so its students (approximately 5 per cent of the age cohort) were mainly selected from the

top half of the ranked 'pass' list. The eleven plus selection, was based on IQ tests (50 per cent weighting) and an assessment made by the junior school headmaster based on the pupil's past record of academic work (50 per cent weighting). See C. Lacey *Hightown Grammar: the school as a social system* (Manchester University Press, 1970).

[13] J.C. Barker Lunn, op. cit.

[14] T.G. Monks, *Comprehensive Education in England and Wales* (Slough NFER, 1968).

[15] Characteristically the non-streamed (2) or (4) variant in these combinations is applied to 'non-academic' subjects — art, music and sometimes English, while the streamed area includes maths, foreign languages and sometimes the sciences.

[16] I am not suggesting that the system actually allocates resources but that the way resources are allocated may differ from the headmaster's formal policy.

[17] Resources are meant here in the broadest sense to include social and psychological rewards as well as the more material resources like the allocation of the 'best' teachers.

[18] The sixth form was split into years as follows: first year sixth, second year sixth, third year sixth.

[19] These famous individuals headed all honours lists and were frequent subjects of notices and progress reports in assembly after they had left the school.

[20] This list of problems was compiled from conversations with the new headmaster. It is not an exhaustive list nor is it in any order of importance.

[21] In previous years, the November O level examination had not been used because of the difficulty involved in teaching a fifth year repeat class in which some boys would take the examination in November and the rest in June of the following year. The new sixth form organization avoided this dilemma.

[22] Barker Lunn has shown that teachers who favour streaming but who work in a non-streamed environment produce detrimental effects in many of the areas she investigated.

[23] The candidate is given an examination number and his papers are graded by examiners appointed by the board, who have no connection with the school. Each of the academic subjects is graded separately and awarded a grade (1-9). Grades 1-6 designate a pass, grades 7-9 designate a fail.

[24] This figure (4.1) represents the highest average number of O level passes ever achieved by the school.

[25] The criteria altered slightly from year to year. In fact, several variations of these criteria were tried out and, although they did make some difference to the composition of the classes, particularly in marginal cases, the size of the variation of the class averages was not enough to affect the argument developed here.

[26] There is, in fact, no reason to expect a linear relationship between average IQ and average number of O level passes. The association is merely pointed out as a feature of the 1963-4 results. It disappears in 1967 and 1968.

[27] A full discussion of this procedure is given in C. Lacey, *Hightown Grammar: the school as a social system* (Manchester University Press, 1970).

[28] I should stress that I am not suggesting the existence of an 'élitism for its own sake'. The success of these boys was always seen in terms of a contribution to the school.

[29] See J.C. Barker Lunn, op. cit. chapter 9.

PAUL BELLABY

The distribution of deviance among 13-14 year old students *

'How to control a class' is a familiar problem to beginners in teaching, but not only to them. For an experienced teacher, to admit to difficulties with whole classes amounts to an admission of failure. The head is usually unsympathetic, and educational researches may seem so, because they tend to stress that order depends on the teacher's effective role performance in the lesson.[1] It is safe to single out an individual from a class and comment upon his behaviour, since this may be attributed to his background and emotional adjustment alone. Nevertheless, in sympathetic company — a clique of colleagues for example — many teachers will say that whole classes are problems to control, and in secondary school no group is mentioned more frequently than third year boys and girls, especially of low ability. It is the aim of this paper to explain the frequent hostility and intransigence of some of these students.

No definitive explanation can be given here. There are various ways of approaching this problem, as any other, and each may uncover some aspect of an eventual solution. This perspective is sociological. It does not give an account of disorder and hostility in terms of teachers' role performances in class, nor in terms of the case histories and emotional problems of students. Such an account might be valid in its own limits, but it leaves out some facts, some possibilities. It may also perpetuate distortions of an ideological kind, since it draws attention from the fact that hostility to staff may result from a structural conflict between teachers and students, which cannot be eliminated by psychotherapy or adjustment in interpersonal relations. It is this other possibility which is explored here.

There are several precedents for the approach. This paper owes something to each of a handful of sociologists who have studied (often indirectly) discipline and compliance in schools.[2] It is also based on a field study of third year boys and girls and their teachers in three English comprehensive schools.[3]

A review of earlier theses and their predictions

The bare bones of the argument are simple. They are that hostility to school arises where the third year student's concept of his or her future status makes schooling seem irrelevant, and where the staff of the school impose what is on the whole a strict as opposed to a lax

---

*This paper is published for the first time in this collection.

disciplinary regime. Other sociologists have adopted three, or perhaps four, theses about order in class that are relevant here.

A Culture clash

Disaffection towards school is an outcome of a conflict between the student's upbringing and the norms and values imposed by teachers. In an English context this has most often been seen as a clash of class subcultures.[4]

B Status frustration

The secondary school distributes rewards chiefly on a narrow scale of academic attainment. Those who become hostile to school are of low status on this scale and their hostility implies rejection of this judgement.[5]

A variant on the status frustration thesis incorporates elements of the culture clash view, and should perhaps be regarded as a separate thesis. It suggests that school exposes children of working class upbringing to middle class aspirations. However various features of working class upbringing make it much more difficult for a working class child to realize his ambitions than for a middle class child to achieve his. Failure results in status frustration.[6]

C Discrepant statuses

In this view the critical factor is not whether an individual student finds himself in a low status position at school, but whether he can adjust his expectations about *future status* (as an adult) to fit immediate realities. If his present performance implies that his aspirations are unrealistically high, and yet he is under great pressure internally or from others such as parents to achieve his goals, he is likely to develop a reaction-formation and reject the career through school and the goals as irrelevant to the present.

This brief account of the three or four different theories in the literature necessarily oversimplifies the writings of those who put them forward. However, the object is less to review the literature than to examine the main distinctive predictions that are suggested by the theories. Subsequently the predictions will be matched with data from the comprehensive schools study.

The culture clash thesis anticipates the more hostility, the greater the difference between the values and norms of the teachers and those of the students. Thus middle class teachers in a working class slum should encounter widespread and deep hostility from their pupils. This is borne out by Webb's observations upon 'Black School', but not by those of Mays in a similar setting. Webb finds a vicious circle of violence and counterviolence between staff and pupils, sustained by the delinquent subculture of the area. Mays, on the other hand, remarks upon the submissive acquiescence of children at school in his slum.[7]

The 'discrepant statuses' thesis gives rise to quite different predictions. Stinchcombe, in his study of a California high school, successfully predicts hostility to school ('expressive alienation') among middle class boys who find themselves in a non-academic track. He argues that middle class boys are more ambitious than working class boys and than girls. They have most difficulty in adjusting themselves to a situation where the path before them seems blocked. Unable to change the situation or their aspirations, they 'rebel' against conventional ambition and become, at least for the moment, hedonistic and negative. Adults, like teachers, who impose discipline that now seems irrelevant are rejected.[8]

It is hard to find support for this thesis in studies of English schools. Those by Lacey and by Hargreaves are confined to one boys' school apiece, the first a grammar school and the second a modern school. In them they find that working class boys, especially of the third year and fourth year, are overrepresented among rebels. It is not middle class boys who predominate.[9]

Both English studies find hostility concentrated in lower streams and treat it as a function of low attainment. Their explanations are in terms of 'status frustration'. Lacey's is focused on minute description of the process by which individuals are differentiated academically and concomitantly develop attitudes 'pro' or 'anti' school. The aggregation of students possessing similar commitments or hostility to school in the same streams may give rise to subcultures, the one supportive of staff and sanctioning educational attainment, the other hostile to staff and antithetic to academic ideology.[10] Hargreaves takes this process as given, showing that the processes of differentiation and polarization have the same consequences for upper and lower streams in a modern school as for streams in a grammar school. He also seeks to show that the school exposes all its boys to middle class aspirations, but that working class boys are disadvantaged by their upbringing in the competition for academic rewards and fall to the bottom of the scale. Here because of their exposure to middle class aspirations they experience status frustration, and reject the invidious standards they are judged by with hostility, overt misbehaviour and truancy. Thus Hargreaves adopts some elements of the culture clash thesis in his own status frustration perspective.[11] Webb's thesis in his paper on 'Black School' contains similar elements.[12]

The three or four theses each account for their proponents' findings. Yet at some points they contradict each other.

This is manifest in the clash of views put forward by Stinchcombe and Hargreaves. Their predictions oppose each other. Is this because there are real differences between the schools they study? If so what might emerge if schools are compared systematically? Or is it rather because the investigators have not put other theses to the test in their own studies? In any event some other perspective might be developed that would encompass the various findings of different investigators, and modify some or all of the theses in order to subsume them under a more general theory. The thesis that will now be propounded accounts for the findings of the comprehensive schools study, but it was developed after some consideration of alternative theses by earlier writers and, tentatively, one is able to extend it to provide an umbrella for other points of view.

The study represents a comparison of social structures at a similar

TABLE I   Examples of the association between stream and
conformity with or hostility to school in the third
year

	Stream		
	Top	*Middle*	*Bottom*
Teachers are 'squares' Average scores on a scale of five items measuring the view that teachers were sympathetic (+) or hostile (-) to adolescent interests	+1.29 (167)	+.28 (155)	-.45 (164) Max +3 Min -3
Attendance Average absenteeism, in number of half days summed over autumn and spring in the third year			
BOYS	14.9 (85)	15.7 (100)	28.0 (88)
GIRLS	15.0 (93)	30.8 (75)	31.6 (96)
Disobedience Students' own reports of their disobeying a teacher in class, by degree of seriousness	1.38 (158)	1.76 (152)	2.11 (148) Max 4 (offences of increasing boldness and rarity) Min 0

Note: There were six streams in the sample in each school: each also had
a remedial class but this was excluded from the survey. Here the streams
are grouped by putting the top two from each school together into the
'Top' category, and so forth.

point in time. Three schools are compared. Students are categorized by,
for example, sex, class, stream, ambition, and compared with each
other. The English studies that have been cited are designed differently.
Each focuses on a single school. Each of the schools is an element in a
selective system, and so does not include a cross section of the children
in a catchment area. Stinchcombe's study is of an American comprehensive school. Yet in his, as in the English studies, the probability that
schools might have different disciplinary regimes, and that these regimes
might have varied consequences for pupils' attitudes and conduct, is
unexplored. It is of course possible to make some retrospective
comparison between one case study and another on the basis of
information supplied about the regimes of the schools. However it is
difficult to determine whether variations in the intake of the schools
or variations in the regimes adopted by teachers (or some interplay of
these two) might account for findings that differ between the cases

studied. The three schools in the comprehensive study are of similar intake, since they serve in new town neighbourhoods which are quite similar in their social composition and since the town is sufficiently small to provide the same range of employment opportunities for its inhabitants.[13] These schools were also similar in their size and their physical amenities — all had about 1,000 pupils including a fully developed sixth form, and all were in new purpose built accommodation. They were chosen from among seven similar schools in the town both for the length of time that they had been established, and for differences in their official disciplinary policies.[14] In so far as 'controlled comparisons' between social units are ever possible in sociology, the conditions in the town gave some opportunities to vary 'disciplinary regime' independently of 'intake'.[15]

Unlike this study, several of the earlier ones — particularly that of Lacey — cover a time span great enough to enable the investigators to establish a 'natural history' of the development of commitment and hostility to school. Some are also intensive enough, because confined to one school apiece, to enable the authors to make a refined micro analysis, for example of peer group structure and norms and of classroom interaction. While the comprehensive study includes some material of this kind, it is less detailed and a proportionately greater part of the data was collected by self-administered questionnaires. Thus in many ways the earlier studies and this one complement each other.

The comprehensive school findings lend support to the thesis of Hargreaves and Lacey to this extent. First, in all schools low stream students and poor attainers in any given stream are more hostile and on the whole more deviant in conduct than others (Tables I and II).

TABLE II   Examples of the association between attainment within the student's own form and commitment or hostility to school

	Attainment		
	In top 25%	Middle range	In bottom 25%
Attendance Proportion absent 10 half days or more in two terms	43% (103)	57% (220)	75% (93)
Disobedience Proportion who score 2 or more on the scale of seriousness of disobedience in class	37% (86)	53% (216)	60% (87)

Note: Attainment could not be measured in the same way for all schools. In one school it is based on overall form position; in the other two on a system devised by the writer to standardize grades in all subjects. Two forms had to be left out, because their school reports could not be traced.

Secondly a disproportionate number of middle class students fall in the top streams and of working class students in the bottom streams, thus bearing out Hargreaves's general prediction. The disparity between top and bottom streams is more marked than the table below suggests since in stream 1 fifty out of eighty-one students in the three schools are middle class, whereas in stream 6, fifty-four out of sixty-four pupils are working class (Table III).

TABLE III The association between class and stream

	Stream		
	Top	Middle	Bottom
Middle class	50.5%	36.2%	25%
Working class	49.5%	63.8%	75%
N.	160	141	128

Note: Class is obtained by locating students' reports of their fathers' occupations in the Registrar General's Occupational Classification for 1966, and deriving his five 'social classes'. 'Middle class' consists of classes I and II plus non-manual workers in class III; the rest are 'working class'. About 15 per cent of students gave too little information to permit classification.

There is little support for the contradictory predictions of Stinchcombe that middle class boys will be the chief rebels. Not only is hostility to school a predominantly working class affair, but it also occurs about as frequently among girls as boys. The same proportion of girls as boys (34.6 per cent) thought that teachers were unsympathetic to their interests; the average 'seriousness' of their acts of disobedience was only marginally less than that of boys (0.22); but more of them reported having stayed out of a lesson than boys (53 per cent as opposed to 39 per cent).

A thesis that accounts for the comprehensive school findings

A more adequate account of the comprehensive school findings can be given by bringing to the fore two 'novel' concepts and reordering some of the ideas of the earlier writers in relation to them. These 'novel' concepts are that whether the student sees his schooling as relevant to the status he can realistically expect to achieve as an adult is critical to his attitudes and conduct, and secondly that the nature of the disciplinary regime imposed by most staff in a school determines whether those who see school as irrelevant also feel hostile to it.[16]

The first of these concepts is different from the 'discrepant statuses' idea, because it is not the subjective strain of being unable to adjust high aspirations to poor prospects that accounts for alienation from school, but whether schooling can be reconciled with realistic expectations for the future, or instead seems to be 'time serving' until the pupil can 'get out into the world'.

The orientation of students to their schooling were identified by cross-classifying their own expectations as to occupation at age twenty-four and staying at school beyond the legal leaving age, with what they thought were their parents' aspirations. The boys and girls were separated into three main categories: 'the ambitious' who with their parents anticipated a professional or managerial career and wished to stay at school; the 'leavers' who like their parents expected something short of this career and wished to leave school at fifteen; and the 'failures' who — rather like Stinchcombe's rebels — experienced status conflict here between the parents' high *aspirations* and their own lower *expectations.*

The concept of variable disciplinary regimes proved hard to delineate. In order to establish some variations in disciplinary regime, schools were chosen, otherwise quite comparable, which had different official policies and different institutions of social control. Thus the head and many staff in one school favoured positive control. They tried to ensure this by requiring that each teacher award ten 'positive' points (rewards) a week, and no more than two 'negatives' (his only official punitive sanctions). The general policy was that encouragement be given rather than criticism and inhibition. The policy was supposed to be furthered by tutor groups, coextensive with the normal taught forms (streams), who competed with each other to acquire as many positives and as few offsetting negatives as possible each week. This school I shall call 'Cross Street'. In another school, 'Hinsley Mill', there were no similar official facilities for encouragement, and the use of 'negative' controls, such as regimented progress about the school and detention after school for rule breaking, were more conspicuous. The third school, 'Castle Town' had a reputation, both outside and with many of its staff, for being 'easy going', not in a way that was thought deliberate, but rather by default. Otherwise its discipline was similarly organized to that of Hinsley Mill.

While, on the face of it, these regimes might fall into some such classification as 'democratic', 'authoritarian' and *'laissez-faire'* (Lewin et al),[17] further investigation showed that the 'positive' control school (Cross Street) did not have the consequences for individual teachers' conduct that were intended. Rather the positive points system was a means of imposing uniform standards of conduct and attainment, and singling out individuals for invidious comparison with others. In short it was an instrument of 'authoritarianism'. Further, the official policies of the schools may have affected discipline indirectly rather than directly through recruiting staff with similar experience and outlooks on discipline and attainment. Important here is the fact that Castle Town — the 'lax' school — had, until its reorganization as a comprehensive five years before the fieldwork, been the most important grammar school for the town, albeit a grammar-modern bilateral. It had attracted a far higher proportion of staff with degrees and previous grammar school experience than the other schools, both of them so-called technical-modern bilaterals before 1962. The predominantly 'grammar-type' teachers in Castle Town appeared to be no less committed to the academic standards than the mainly 'modern-type' teachers in Cross

Street and Hinsley Mill. What did distinguish the Castle Town teachers was their tendency to treat all classes as if the students' interests in lessons were sufficient to secure order by themselves, rather than to differentiate between top streams and the others by giving the latter more set work in class, more question-answer drills and few opportunities for classroom discussion, as was the pattern in the other schools.[18]

What grounds are there in the data for treating hostility as a result of the two key factors, orientation to schooling and the regime of the school? Leavers were on balance more hostile to staff, less well behaved in class than other groups. They also took least part in extracurricular activities and absented themselves from school most often (Table IV).

TABLE IV   Examples of the associations between orientations to schooling and attitudes and conduct

	Orientation to schooling		
	Ambitious	Failures	Leavers
Find teachers sympathetic to adolescent interests (see Table I)	70.0%	44.7%	25.2%
mean scale scores:	+1.39 (147)	+.24 (85)	-.46 (115)
Seriousness of acts of disobedience (see Table 1)			
report no act or one only	70.9%	46.9%	28.9%
mean scale scores	1.34 (134)	1.83 (80)	2.20 (106)
Participation in school societies and clubs after hours			
attended at least one	57.4% (149)	42.8% (84)	25.2% (119)
Absences over two terms: the number of periods of one week or less, on average	3.95 (147)	5.48 (85)	7.05 (114)

Hostile attitudes to staff were, however, far more marked among leavers in the two strictest schools, Hinsley Mill and Cross Street, than they were in the relatively lax school, Castle Town (Table V).
Furthermore there is justification for singling out these two factors and placing them at the centre of a reconstructed theory since, when stream is controlled, the pattern of differences between leavers and others remains (Table VI).

TABLE V Willingness to accept the restrictions conventionally applied by teachers to conduct in class (+), or tendency to reject them (-) Max +10, Min -10

	School		
	Strict		Lax
	Cross Street	Hinsley Mill	Castle Town
Ambitious	-.48	+.87	+.69
	(46)	(50)	(50)
Failures	-1.49	-1.58	+2.38
	(37)	(26)	(21)
Leavers	-2.29	-2.58	-.59
	(41)	(39)	(37)
Overall	-1.20	-.94	+.34
	(168)	(170)	(152)

TABLE VI The association between orientation to schooling and attitudes and conduct, holding stream constant

	Stream			
	Top	Middle	Bottom	All
Willingness to accept restrictions in class (see Table 5)				
Ambitious	-.02	+2.18	-.13	+.39
	(102)	(28)	(15)	(145)
Failures	-.13	-1.05	-.40	-.56
	(27)	(32)	(25)	(84)
Leavers	-1.40	-.37	-3.00	-1.83
	(10)	(35)	(72)	(117)
Overall	-.25	+.40	-2.80	
	(171)	(157)	(164)	
Seriousness of disobedience in class (see Table I)				
Ambitious	1.25	1.44	1.58	1.34
	(93)	(30)	(12)	(134)
Failures	1.46	1.94	2.28	1.83
	(24)	(31)	(25)	(80)
Leavers	2.11	2.18	2.41	2.20
	(9)	(33)	(64)	(106)
Overall	1.38	1.76	2.11	
	(158)	(152)	(148)	

This suggests, at least, that orientation to schooling and the disciplinary regime of the school are important 'intervening variables' in the correlations between class, stream and attitudes and conduct at school.

It may also be that 'status frustration' is not the immediate source of disaffection towards school. All three schools in this study were streamed: every student could locate himself on a standard scale of past attainment and future potential. As the numbers in brackets in Table VI show, orientation to schooling was associated with stream. Leavers were concentrated in the bottom streams, the ambitious in the top, and failures, though more dispersed, were relatively numerous in the middle. Yet there were leavers in higher streams, and ambitious students in lower streams. Their attitudes were more like those of students with similar orientations to schooling than they were like those of form mates. This suggests that orientation to schooling as distinct from high or low status may be the *immediate* source of conformity with or hostility to school.

It is also worth noting that each school placed emphasis on academic attainment and rewarded it, certainly none more so than Castle Town, which was the only one to have an express stream, taking some O level examinations in four years rather than five, and which had a reputation with teachers in other schools for 'separating the sheep and the goats'. Yet it was in Castle Town that there was *less* hostility to school than elsewhere, especially among leavers. The key factor would appear to be not a degree of academic pressure which makes those at the bottom of the heap feel aggrieved at their status, but instead whether the disciplinary regime of the school is 'strict' or 'lax'.

Something else that corroborates the impression that status frustration is not the immediate source of hostility to school is the attitudes of lower streams to the form at the top of the hierarchy. If status frustration were the immediate source one would expect that the lower the stream, the greater the degree of rejection of the 'successful' on grounds of their academic success.

Table VII shows that the top stream *is* rejected more emphatically by bottom streams than by those above them. However, the difference between streams is far less marked when the grounds are the *academic success* of those at the top, than it is where their *social attitudes* are considered. In other words low stream students do not express 'sour grapes' about those who are officially cleverer than they so much as they consider them 'standoffish'. This may reflect the fact that the top stream was predominantly 'ambitious', and that as a general rule those with similar orientations to schooling befriended each other: the students were thus divided 'socially' by the same factor that differentiated their attitudes to and conduct at school.

What alternative to the status frustration thesis does all this suggest? Certainly not the 'culture clash' perspective. For class background, like stream, is a less good predictor of attitudes and conduct than is orientation to schooling.

Table VIII shows that class *is* correlated with orientation to schooling: there are more leavers among working class than middle class children, and more ambitious students who are middle class than working class. Yet workers' children who are ambitious behave and seemingly feel

TABLE VII   The attitudes of children in lower streams to those in the top stream of the third year

		Accept/reject them on social grounds * Max 4, Min 0	Accept/resent their academic success** Max 4, Min 0
Stream 2		2.40 (85)	2.42 (85)
Streams 3-4		1.77 (159)	2.35 (159)
Streams 5-6		1.34 (160)	1.83 (159)
		difference -1.06	difference -0.59
Ambitious		2.45 (89)	2.65 (89)
Failures		1.66 (73)	2.25 (73)
Leavers		1.46 (100)	2.07 (99)
		difference -0.99	difference -0.58
Strict	Cross Street	1.43 (135)	1.98 (136)
	Hinsley Mill	1.88 (143)	2.11 (142)
Lax	Castle Town	1.89 (126)	2.50 (125)

*The maximum score resulted from agreeing that 'They are nice and friendly' and disagreeing that 'They are nothing but snobs'.
**The maximum score resulted from agreeing that 'They are the cleverest people in the third year' and disagreeing that 'They are just lucky to be there. They do not deserve it.'

TABLE VIII   Examples of the association to be found between orientations to schooling and attitudes and conduct when social class is held constant

		Class	
		Middle class	Working class
Finding teachers sympathetic to adolescent interests (see Table I)			
	Ambitious	+1.65 (74)	+1.13 (61)
	Failures	+.19 (26)	+.64 (44)
	Leavers	-.22 (18)	-.28 (79)
Staying out of lessons when at school: proportion who have NEVER done so by their own reports			
	Ambitious	67% (72)	67% (63)
	Failures	35% (26)	55% (44)
	Leavers	22% (18)	46% (81)

much as do other ambitious students, and the same applies to middle class children who are *not* ambitious. Thus an account of hostility to teachers must be given in different terms from 'status frustration' or 'culture clash'.

Perhaps the relevance of schooling to his future may be critical to the conduct of the 13-14 year old, because this period of 'decision' heightens a dilemma in which adolescence already places him. For present purposes the important aspect of this dilemma is that the pupil is expected to accept the way teachers frame his activity while at school, and at the same time to assert an increasing measure of control over his own destiny. All adults, even teachers, give support to certain expressions of independence. Yet what, for the adolescent, constitutes repudiating 'childish' styles of life may, for some adults, be quite unacceptable — for example long hair, nylon stockings. The reverse may be the case — for example, that adults expect a 'mature' attitude to the spending of money, while the adolescent regards this as his own affair and acts 'hedonistically'. The ambiguity is furthered by the fact that the adolescent lacks the material bases for independence — a job and income, a marriage partner, a house. Materially he depends for his very independence on the adults against whom he is fighting to gain it.[19]

For some adolescents, the school, more specifically the relation with teachers, supplies a way of resolving this dilemma quite as much as it contributes to it. These are ambitious students who see school as not only the legitmate but also the feasible path to their high aspirations. Much of their struggle for independence is realized *through* an accommodation to teachers, who are seen as a means for bringing them to adult status in the long run. School does not altogether resolve the dilemma even for them. Not only may there remain struggles with parents, but their relations with teachers may be abrasive from time to time, since within the terms of their accommodation to teachers there is scope for differences about what is 'childish', what is 'old-fashioned' and, further, about what is technically adequate and relevant as preparation for their careers.

As for leavers, not only does the school deprive them of any chance to resolve this dilemma, except by leaving school and establishing the material basis for adult status, but it also *worsens* the dilemma. For in school they face restricted opportunities to realize culturally appropriate ways of expressing independence — in dress, for they must wear uniform; in speech, for street corner and 'teenage' argot and topics of conversation are proscribed in lessons. The dilemma will be worsened to a greater extent the more 'strict' the regime of the school. Hence the greater resistance to teachers' demands by leavers in the strict schools, Cross Street and Hinsley Mill, than in Castle Town (see Table V above).

In general an account of attitudes to staff that takes as its starting point the adolescent role dilemma, recognizes the potential for conflict between students of this age and teachers and then proceeds to identify the bases for differential responses, antagonism or accommodation, appears to satisfy the findings in the three comprehensives better than previous theses taken as they stand.

The new perspective as an umbrella for the others

There is also a way in which this perspective can be extended to assimilate other writers' thinking. It must first be accepted that the process by which orientation to schooling is formed is a *labelling process.*[20] In this process home and school will — over a considerable span of time — each give definition to the child's concept of his future, often amplifying each other, occasionally contradicting each other. On the school's side, it may well be true, as Hargreaves and Lacey point out, that English schools reward a narrow range of achievement. On the other hand, teachers not only single out the academically successful for praise, they also quite consistently reject the unsuccessful, and often segregate them in their own forms. In being so consistently rejecting of some and rewarding of others over a long period of time they furnish the bases for identification by the student with 'realistic' ambitions for either a professional or managerial career or for the prospect of routine clerical or manual work.[21] In English schools this process of labelling may stretch back to the age of seven. By the age of thirteen to fourteen those in low streams — especially in modern and comprehensive schools — will often find themselves alongside boys and girls with similar expectations for the future that they may well have known for a long time. It is likely that they will have all but accepted the school's academic judgement of them. Indeed they may well reflect the teachers' opinion in their belief that schooling is largely irrelevant to their future. There is no basis here for status *frustration*. All the same their school careers will have helped form their attitudes to schooling. The careers will differentiate between the ambitious and those we may call 'fatalists' (the leavers).

Similarly class background and family variations will be factors in this history. They will not be altogether independent of school career since clearly how the child adjusts at school, how successful he is in convincing the teachers of his ability, depends a great deal on his family. Also it is likely that family attitudes to his education will be to some extent responsive to his progress at school. The more home and school amplify each other, and the longer the period of time over which academic differentiation takes place, the less likely is the student to feel that his status, high or low, is in any way inappropriate for him.

How useful a labelling approach can be may be seen again if we note that the ambiguity of labelling may have consequences for actors as well as any specific label that is attached to them. Ambiguity might apply to those students who have been called here 'failures', whose parents aspire higher for them than they expect to achieve. On the whole students' own expectations corresponded throughout the sample to what their present position in school, their prospects of doing O level or CSE, suggested they might actually achieve in the way of a job by the age of twenty-four. For failures, however, home did not entirely amplify school. The students appeared more realistic than their parents. Failures in the middle streams seemed to experience a greater strain than failures elsewhere in the school, since they were more hostile to teachers than failures elsewhere, in many respects approaching leavers in their attitudes. A glance at Table VI above (the top half) will show that 'failures' in the middle streams were less willing to accept the teachers' demands than anyone but leavers in the top and bottom streams. It is also the case that 64 per cent reported having stayed out of one or more lessons in their careers: this is nearly twice as high as the proportion of ambitious students who said they had done so, and similar to the level for leavers. Yet their conduct in class was less intransigent than that of leavers, as may be seen from the lower half of Table VI. Perhaps the conflict with staff is less clearly drawn for failures than for leavers, and so overt confrontations are avoided. It may be that in the middle stream failures are not sure whether their aspirations ought to be lowered and yet feel that a professional or managerial career is uncertain. This might be because in the middle streams there is a prospect for some students of being examined in a few O level and several CSE subjects. Perhaps these failures have a parallel in Lacey's C-stream grammar school boys. These boys entered as 'best pupils' from their primary schools, with high aspirations which presumably became less realistic as their attainment failed to match their ambitions, and they fell into streams of boys similarly disappointed. And yet the C-stream offers some prospect of advance into middle class occupations through external qualifications. Such pupils might experience ambiguous identification, and it may be ambivalence that accounts for their veiled hostility to school. The fact that these boys had been exposed to middle class aspirations at entry to the school does not receive prominence in Lacey's account of his own findings, but it is a possible way of viewing them.

Even Stinchcombe's apparently aberrant findings might be assimilated under this rubric. In his California high school the experience of being placed in a non-academic track is more sudden than the slow differentiation in the English school system. As a result there are more likely to be middle class boys with ambitions who experience an unexpected reversal of fortune. There is not time to adjust to this change and build up fresh realistic expectations, and so the students develop a reaction formation to school. If there is not opposition to school among American *working class* students to be compared with that found by Hargreaves, for example, it may be a reflection of the more permissive regime of that school compared with the two strict comprehensive schools and Webb's 'Black School' and Hargreaves's modern school.

Though there is not room to elaborate it here the perspective that has been adopted allows one to account for variations in conduct and inconsistencies in attitude by the same pupils. For example Lacey and Hargreaves both note that neither pro nor anti school subculture is exclusive to any group of pupils, and that some students vacillate between the different attitudes and in their conduct appear compliant in some situations and deviant in others.[22] Observations during lessons and talks with students in the comprehensives obliged one to take a similar view. Nevertheless the perspective in this paper implies *latent conflict* between teachers and all their adolescent students. The ambitious merely *accommodate* their interests to staff. They may accept the need for a teacher's guidance, yet be critical of his attitudes to their dress and even, more specifically, be 'supercilious' as one teacher put it about the content of the lesson and the method of teaching. Further, the regimes sustained by staff in a school will produce different responses from leavers, or 'fatalists' as they have been characterized here. Students may in one context (for example Castle Town school) be relatively favourable to staff but absentee and uncommitted, in another context (Hinsley Mill) hostile but acquiescent and in a third (Cross Street) hostile and intractable.[23] Variation in regime might account for findings as diverse as these in schools other than the three comprehensives, for example in Mays' Crown Street School as opposed to Webb's Black School, or among the various schools in Hammersmith whose delinquency records were compared. Further, even within a single school, conduct of the same, frequently 'difficult' students might vary from teacher to teacher or with lessons, and this can be explained if it is recognized that behind it are many ambiguities and misunderstandings in adult and adolescent expectations of each other.

Notes

[1] Studies of interaction in class and the teacher's performance in particular are by no means consistent in their findings. This has not deterred some from advocating uniform solutions to all problems of order and learning. Yet the inconsistent findings are bound to suggest that the researchers have been looking for uniformity at the wrong level of abstraction.

[2] See the select list of references at the end of the paper.

[3] The fieldwork covered a total period of some four months, spread intermittently from May 1966 to July 1967. Two similar forms in each school were observed for a week each at all their lessons. Various questionnaires were completed by all the third year forms in each school, except the remedial classes. The staff who taught third year classes filled in a questionnaire. Observations were also drawn from records, from perambulations of the buildings and grounds and the neighbourhoods, and from many conversations with teachers, administrators and students. I am very grateful to the heads, teachers and pupils of these three schools, and to their education officer. In the long course of this study — before, during and after the fieldwork — I was advised at various times by Dr. Royston Lambert, Dr Marten Shipman, Professor Ronald Frankenberg, Dr Colin Lacey and Mr Ray Jobling. To all these I am grateful. None of the weaknesses in this paper is their responsibility.

[4] American writers have sometimes referred instead to the clash between *local* cultures (whatever their description) and *the cosmopolitan* culture of the teachers. See, for example, W. Waller, *The Sociology of Teaching* (1932), especially chapters 4-6.

[5] The theoretical basis of 'status frustration' might be blockage of the legitimate route to highly desired goals (e.g. a prestigious style of life) by some social-structural inhibition on opportunity (e.g.

poor income prospects). Where no other route may be substituted for the legitimate one (such as stealing), the victims of the situation are likely to 'rebel', that is to develop a 'reaction formation' to the goals and the legitimate means to them. See R.K. Merton, *Social Theory and Social Structure* (1957), pp. 131-94 for a cogent statement of this theory.

6 The classic statement of this view is to be found in A.K. Cohen, *Delinquent Boys* (1955).

7 J. Webb 'The sociology of the school', *British Journal of Sociology*, 13 (1962), pp.264-70, and J.B. Mays, *Education and the Urban Child* (1962). For discussion of these and several other approaches in the context of *juvenile delinquency*, and a specific attempt to evaluate their claims against data from Britain, see D.M. Downes, *The Delinquent Solution* (1966).

8 A.L. Stinchcombe, *Rebellion in a High School* (1964) especially the introduction.

9 C.Lacey *Hightown Grammar* (1970).
D. Hargreaves, *Social Relations in a Secondary School* (1967).

10 Lacey, op cit, chapter 4.

11 Hargreaves, op cit, chapter 8.

12 Webb, op cit.

13 This was a 'new town' in the south-east of England. By the time of the study it had been developing for nearly twenty years and was approaching its projected size (it was then of 70,000 inhabitants). Average housing standards were high compared with the country as a whole: they were also relatively homogeneous. The range of employment opportunities was representative of the SE region, as was the occupational distribution of employed men living there. The age structure was atypical, because it was skewed towards young couples and their children. The then recent Sample Census (Registrar General, 1966) was a reliable source for these kind of data.

14 All schools in the town were mixed and comprehensive in intake. Only a score of the 1,300 children in the age group studied were attending schools outside the town. The eight secondary schools took, or planned to take students from eleven to eighteen, but one was a very new Catholic school, drawing from all the town, while the others took about 85 per cent of their intake from their particular catchment areas. The three schools selected had been established between eight and ten years before, initially as 'bilateral' schools, housing two grades — one selective and the other non-selective — in the same building, and eventually, in 1962, as full comprehensives.

15 Needless to say, the controls were not perfect. In particular the class composition of the schools varied. Some implications of this for the kinds of regimes staff were able to sustain are discussed below (n.18).

16 'Novel' must be taken figuratively. The general idea of relating variations in disciplinary regime to different orientations to schooling and examining the resultants came from Etzioni, *A Comparative Study of Complex Organisations* (1961).

[17] This classification was used in the well-known experiments upon the impact of different leadership styles upon small groups of 10 year old boys, reported by White and Lippitt, 'Leader behaviour and member reaction in three "social climates" ' in Cartwright and Zander (eds.), *Group Dynamics* (first ed., 1953) or Lippitt and White, *Autocracy and Democracy* (1960). The different official policies (or failings) of the three schools might have favoured the adoption of one or other of these leadership styles in the classroom. 'Democratic' leadership involved encouraging the boys to follow out inclinations the leader approved. 'Authoritarian' leadership consisted of imposing courses of action upon the boys, praising individuals who succeeded and criticizing those who failed. *'Laissez-faire'* leadership was 'non-interventionist'.

[18] These patterns were discovered by observing lessons and checked with questionnaire responses by teachers. In n.15 above it was observed that matching of schools on all but disciplinary regime was *not* complete. They differed not only in the characteristic careers of teachers, but also in the class composition of their intakes. About 85 per cent of students could be classified by their own reports of their fathers' occupations as either 'middle class' or 'working class'. Of these, 28 per cent at Cross Street, 46 per cent at Hinsley Mill and 40 per cent at Castle Town, the lax school, were middle class. Now it is arguable that the 'positive' regime at Cross Street was undermined less by the attitudes teachers brought with them from their past careers than by their confrontation with a predominantly working class student body. This view would be the more plausible if teachers conducted their lessons differently when they had a mainly working class form to teach. But comparison of only the two 'strict' schools shows no consistent relation between teacher behaviour and the class composition of the form — for example the top stream at Cross Street was mainly working class, but teachers there taught it much as did their counterparts at Hinsley Mill where the same form was mainly middle class; also predominantly working class lower stream forms were treated very differently by teachers in the lax school, Castle Town, than by teachers at the strict schools.

[19] For a similar approach to adolescence, see E. Friedenberg, 'Adolescence as a social problem' in H.S. Becker (ed.), *Social Problems* (1966).

[20] The concept of 'labelling process' has many adherents. For a critical but also sympathetic discussion of the literature, see D. Matza, *Becoming Deviant* (1969), chapter 7, 'Signification'.

[21] The 'realistic' character of occupational choice at this age has often been remarked upon, see for example J. Maizels, *Adolescent Needs and the Transition from School to Work* (1970). Incidentally in this sample girls rarely chose manual work, boys rarely chose clerical work.

[22] Lacey, op cit, pp. 85-92
Hargreaves, op cit., pp. 180-1.

[23] Apart from their more favourable attitudes which have already been reviewed, 64 per cent of students at Castle Town had never attended a school society after hours, as opposed to 57 per cent at Cross Street

and 56 per cent at Hinsley Mill; and 83 per cent of students as opposed
to 73 per cent at Cross Street and at Hinsley Mill had been absent at
least six times over the two terms. That Hinsley Mill students were
less intractable than those at Cross Street is suggested by observations
and by teachers' reports of how often they had to use punishments
in class: against individuals for misbehaviour Cross Street teachers
said they used them 41 per cent more often; against whole classes for
their intractability they used them 45 per cent more often. Two factors
may have contributed to what appears to be more effective discipline
at Hinsley Mill — the teachers there were more experienced than at
Cross Street, and the head of Hinsley Mill was exceptionally stringent
in keeping order out of class (for example detentions for breaking
school rules, usually out of class, were given three times as often in
that third year as in the other schools).

References

HARGREAVES, D., 1967, *Social Relations in a Secondary School.*
London: Routledge and Kegan Paul.

LACEY, C., 1970, *Hightown Grammar: the school as a social system.*
Manchester University Press. 'Some sociological concomitants of
academic streaming in a grammar school'. *British Journal of
Sociology,* 17 (1966), pp.245-62.

MAYS, J.B., 1962, *Education and the Urban Child.* Liverpool:University
Press.

STINCHCOMBE, A.L., 1964, *Rebellion in a High School.* Chicago:
Quadrangle.

WEBB, J.,1962, 'The sociology of a school'. *British Journal of Sociology,*
13, pp.264-70.

M D SHIPMAN

The impact of a curriculum project *

This paper has been extracted from a follow-through study of thirty-eight secondary schools involved in the trial of a Schools Council curriculum materials or new teaching methods. It is focused only on the relation between the organization of the schools and the persistence of curriculum innovation.

The evaluation of current curriculum projects will provide evidence in this crucial but rather neglected area. The evaluation of the Schools Council Humanities project includes both intensive and extensive studies of the experiences of schools during innovation.[1] Already MacDonald and Rudduck have shown some of the difficulties in communication between schools and project team, even when this has been singled out for attention.[2] This confirms the findings of Gross *et al.*, that even where research and development support for an innovation has been intensive, the teachers concerned may still be confused about their new role.[3] Shipman has argued that this arises out of the contrasting and changing definitions of the curriculum situation, not only among curriculum developers and teachers, but heads and local authority advisers.[4]

The object of the research into the Schools Council Integrated Studies project based at Keele was to find how different aspects of school organization influence the success or failure of the trial of curriculum materials and new teaching methods. It was hypothesized that investment by teachers in innovation would be the crucial factor in deciding the impact of a curriculum project. No precise measures of input or output could be made. Often the important factors were not detected in advance, not adequately defined, or too elusive for the techniques used in measuring. In retrospect, trying to detect the factors in schools that determine the success of curriculum innovation is like trying to repair a watch while wearing mittens.

Definitions of inputs, outputs and organizational factors

1 Output
   a) Contractual success was defined as the fulfilment by the school of the 'contract' to try out integrated studies. Of thirty-eight schools, twenty-two were, in this contractual sense, successes, seven were

Reprinted from M.D. Shipman, 'The impact of a curriculum project', Journal of Curriculum Studies, 6 (1) (May 1973), by kind permission *of the author and publishers.*

failures and five only entered in the second year of the trial. Another four schools did not complete the trial period but left to continue with their version of integrated studies independent of the project. These were contractual failures, although they were continuing with the innovation.

b) *Curriculum impact* was defined as the extent to which curriculum change had resulted from the trial experience. Each school was rated on one of four three-point scales. These measured the amount of trial material in use after the end of the trial period, developments arising from the trial in integrated studies, developments in the related fields of the humanities and the persistence of forms of team teaching.

2 Input

a) *Time and energy* invested by teachers was measured on three three-point scales. These covered attendance at meetings, accumulation of supplementary materials and the provision of feedback to the project.

b) *Investment by the school* was measured on another three three-point scales covering the provision of a special team leader, adjustments to the timetable and the provision of special planning time for the integrated studies team.

c) *High level manpower* was measured by the extent to which head, deputy head or heads and heads of departments were involved in teaching integrated studies.

d) *Material resources* were measured by the provision and suitability of rooms and the availability of money and special facilities for the trial within the schools.

3 The context of investment

a) *The support of non-involved staff* was measured through their attitudes towards the trial in their schools.

b) *The basis for integrated studies* was assessed by the existence in the school curriculum of ongoing work before the trial in this or similar areas of the humanities.

c) *The climate of innovation* was a subjective assessment by the central project team of the esprit of the schools, on a scale derived from the Organizational Climate Description Questionnaire, Form IV part III, developed by Halpin.[5]

The collection of data started in 1969 and was completed in the spring of 1972 after the trial period had finished in August 1971. Information on the organization of the schools was collected by direct observation, through the routine returns of the project team and the feedback from the schools. Further information was provided by an interview programme. This was based on a schedule prepared on the basis of taped interviews with groups of teachers. The final interview programme involved thirty-five teachers, fourteen head teachers and seven local authority advisers. Another twenty-five teachers returned the schedule by post. No attempt was made to select at random. The object was to contact those who had played an important part in the project. Data was compressed into 2 by

2 tables and hypotheses tested by χ^2. The reliability of these methods was probably low, particularly as variables contaminated each other as the author and project team collected new data in the light of old collected across a period of over two years. Wherever possible different methods were triangulated and independent evidence, such as that collected by an observers' panel of advisers and College of Education lecturers as part of the evaluation, used as a check. Nevertheless, the results need to be interpreted with caution.

Results

The table shows the results of testing for association by χ^2.[6] Null hypotheses were confirmed (x) or rejected (beyond the 5 per cent level) as follows.

Outputs	Inputs						
	2a	2b	2c	2d	3a	3b	3c
Contractual success	.01 > .001	.01 > .001	x	x	x	x	.01-.001
Curriculum success	.05 > .02	.01 > .001	x	x	x	x	x

The most predictive indices for the persistence of curriculum change within 2a and 2b were the feedback of information to the project, the accumulation of supplementary material by teachers and the provision of planning time by the school. The message of this table overall is that the net impact of this curriculum project seemed to depend on the commitment of the teachers involved. This confirms the now common finding that any innovation, means of organization or teaching method depends for success on the attitudes of the teachers, regardless of the intrinsic merits of the scheme.

Behind these superficially impressive significance levels lie measures of interest and effort that reflect the strains on teachers involved in innovations. At one extreme there were schools where the commitment to trial involved little disturbance to routine. At the other extreme were schools where teachers planned their team work in the vacations or in the evenings, integrated across a variety of subject boundaries, attended meetings at Keele and in teachers centres, fed back new ideas, materials and evaluations and built up supplementary resources. In the latter the persistence of innovation seem to be ensured through the effort that had been put in.

There were also indications of a threshold beyond which schools seemed to break through into self-sustained innovation. They had not only invested enough to ensure sufficient momentum for further development, but had begun to experience the limelight of the innovator. Instead of feeling that it was a bore, not worth the effort, teachers in these schools were appreciating the public recognition that innovation can bring. Observers, visitors, researchers, inspectors, advisers, students and journalists, often seen as inconvenient or hostile witnesses, were now welcomed. Nine of the thirty-eight schools seemed to be in this category. All were building on the trial experience in the year after the project had finished in the schools.

The significance of 3c, the measure of organizational climate is probably only another reflection of the commitment of teachers as the crucial factor. It consisted of measures of enthusiasm and drive. Indeed, it is misleading to suggest that indices can be separated into teacher and school investments. Thus the provision of timetabled time for team meetings had to be accompanied by effort by the teachers to be effective. Similarly timetables could be blocked to facilitate team teaching and inquiry methods, but teachers could still use blocked time in traditional ways. It is therefore probably safer to concentrate on what teachers actually do than to rely on the concept of school organization as if this can operate apart from the teachers who put it into practice.

The failure of the remaining investment indices may have been due to the blunt measuring instruments or their irrelevance to the organization of innovation. In one case, the effect of involvement of high level manpower on curriculum, there were conflicting influences. Probability level was $0.30 > 0.20$, but in a negative direction. Breaking down this manpower showed that involvement of heads of departments increased the chance of successful curriculum innovation, but involvement of head teachers reduced the chance of success. Involvement of deputy heads seemed to make little difference.

The retrospective analysis based on information gathered after the trial project had ended, uncovered three important influences not taken into account in designing this investigation.

1 *Turnover among staff.* Two of the seven schools that dropped out before completing the contracted trial and five of the twenty-two schools which completed, lost over half their integrated studies staff during the trial period. But this was not all loss. Seven teachers moved to other schools to take over or start integrated studies. But staff turnover, while not significantly related to failure to complete the trial, was significant (probability between 0.05 and 0.02) in determining the extent and persistence of curriculum change. Loss of staff on any scale stopped innovation. Three of the six schools with high investment by teachers and low curriculum impact had lost over 50 per cent of their original integrated studies team.

2 *School reorganization.* Both actual and planned, or even anticipated, reorganization turned out to be important in determining whether the experiment with integrated studies survived beyond the trial period. Thus three of the five schools in one local authority area that had completed two years of trial gave up integrated studies in junior forms because reorganization meant that they received a 12 year old entry instead of an 11 year old one. In another area one school has successfully finished the trial, but reorganization finished off the innovation. However, the staff involved were moving to two other local schools to start up integrated studies for the first time.

3 *Pressganging.* It had been anticipated that the level of commitment would vary widely between schools. This was no doubt reflected in the investment indices. Some staff, interviewed after the end of the trial, firmly maintained that they had really not been part of the trial. They were 'helping out' or 'just interested'. But the interviews in the

schools and with the local advisers revealed another anomaly. In three of the six schools that failed to complete the trial there was an enthusiastic head and unenthusiastic staff. These teachers claimed to have been pressed into service. Local advisers confirmed this. Curiously however in the remaining three schools where teachers seemed to have been pressganged there was one with high teacher/high school investment and high curriculum impact, one with high teacher/high school investment and low curriculum impact, and another with low teacher/school investment and high curriculum impact.

Discussion.

Gross *et al* have detailed four barriers to change encountered by teachers.[7] One of these, the lack of the necessary materials, did not seem important in implementing the Keele project. The remaining three barriers, lack of clarity in the new teaching role, lack of skills and knowledge to implement the innovation, and the existence of school organization incompatible with change may have been present. To Gross *et al* these barriers resulted in a failure to implement the innovation. Hoyle has described this as tissue rejection.[8] The evidence collected here suggests both an elaboration of this problem and a possible way through the barriers.

The secondary changes in schools seem as likely to be beneficial as malignant, and change in one school can be beneficially infectious for others. In Britain at least, innovation has involved grassroots efforts by teachers. Thus Brown has shown how innovation in primary schools often comes through the head teacher adopting ideas that have been found to work by other teachers.[9] Where there has been planned innovation this local enterprise can lead to unpredictable results. It may be that these unintentional side effects are as important as the planned change itself. The interview programme after the end of the Keele project revealed some aspects of this ripple effect of innovation. The teachers and head teachers saw innovation from their own viewpoint, as part of their school's future. The trial was of limited duration. Had all schools given up integrated studies it would have been no reflection on the success of the project which was concerned with the whole school system. But the experience of team teaching, of organizing inquiry based methods and of working in an integrated way, added another set of ideas and experiences to the planning of new curriculum, particularly to ensure a smoother transition from junior school and to design courses for school leavers. In only ten of the thirty-eight schools entering the trial (four of the twenty-two who completed two years) was there a negligible impact. In all other schools there had been innovation, both at the curriculum level and in the attitudes of staff through the experience of involvement in planned curriculum change.

The impact of the project was not however confined to trial schools. The turnover of teachers in the project teams was a major disturbance, but it was not only those who moved to take up posts elsewhere who were spreading the ideas. There was also lateral movement of ideas between neighbouring trial schools, voluntarily sharing ideas. The teachers involved saw this exchange of information as the most important form of communication. Informal contacts and teacher centre meetings were appreciated more than meetings at Keele. But alongside the organized and informal groupings of trial schools was a spread of ideas to neighbouring schools not involved. Again this had occurred partly through informal contacts and local curriculum groups organized for ROSLA preparation.

The extent of this persisting influence on the teachers involved and on their schools was primarily determined by their own input. The final impact reflected early efforts. Where the project was accepted as a marginal activity and worked with minimum disturbance to established organization, or where staff had been reluctant to join, the failure rate was high and net impact low. It did not seem to matter whether schools accepted the philosophy of integration or not. The critical but involved teachers were often those who produced a lasting effect on their schools. The direction may not have always been identical with that recommended by the project team, but the resulting tension did not weaken the impact of the investment made. The failures were those schools where innovation was welcomed or just accepted but not as an opportunity to work at creating change.

The practical implication for overcoming resistance to change is that innovation must not be presented on a plate to schools. The successful organization of planned curriculum change may depend more on mobilizing teachers into planning and implementation than on getting schools to accept packaged materials. Given the way teachers plan their courses this will not be easy.[10] This was a dilemma for the project organizers at Keele. The schools had volunteered to enter the trial. The object was to test new materials and methods, not primarily to initiate changes in just these thirty-eight schools. The project could have been a success if nothing had changed in these trial schools. As it was, twenty-eight out of the thirty-eight involved had been affected. Curriculum projects may be important as initiators, stimulating and accelerating change, but not necessarily in the anticipated direction. The alien tissue may be transmuted not rejected.

So far the strategy has usually been to try out materials in trial schools and then hope that the published materials will be diffused under the stimulus of in-service courses and conferences. It might be better to concentrate on mobilizing teachers into the continuous development of these materials from the start. For curriculum projects this means local organization. Centralized projects may not be able to influence or even detect the actual extent of innovation. The strength of the Keele project was its local nature and the appointment of local co-ordinators to link project and schools. Without this close support the level of investment would have been lower, the trial could not have been monitored by the project and this research would have been impossible. But even more important, with one co-ordinator to some eight schools, the teachers seem to have felt that they were involved in the innovation. They felt that they were contributing. Significantly they wanted even more visits and were unanimous in their praise for the efforts of the co-ordinators.

It would be rash to generalize about the nature of the innovatory school from the evidence on the thirty-eight investigated here. The salient points are that the school which is likely to successfully introduce and implement a planned innovation would:

- have teachers who would feed back information to the project
- have teachers who would accumulate supplementary material
- have teachers who had volunteered knowing that they would be involved in a lot of work
- reorganize its timetable to provide planning time for teachers involved in innovation
- have a head teacher who supported the innovation but did not insist on being personally involved
- have a low staff turnover among key personnel
- be free of any immediate need to reorganize as part of a changing local school structure.

It could be argued however that if you could find such a school there would be no point in trying to get it to change.

Notes

1 B. MacDonald, 'The evaluation of the humanities curriculum project: a holistic approach', *Theory into Practice,* 10(3) (June, 1971), pp.163-7.
2 B. MacDonald and J. Rudduck, 'Curriculum research and development projects: barriers to success', *British Journal of Educational Psychology,* 41(2) (June, 1971), pp.148-54.
3 N. Gross, J.B. Giacquinta and M. Bernstein, *Implementing Organizational Innovations* (Harper and Row, 1971).
4 M.D. Shipman, 'Views of a curriculum project', *Journal of Curriculum Studies,* 4 (2), (1973).
5 A. Halpin, *Theory and Research in Administration* (Macmillan, 1966), pp. 131-249.
6 H. Selvin, 'A critique of tests of significance in survey research', *American Sociological Review,* (1957), pp.519-27. See also D. Gold, 'Statistical tests and substantive significance', *American Sociologist* (1969), pp.42-6.
7 Gross *et al,* op. cit. pp. 196-8.
8 E. Hoyle, 'Planned organizational change in education', *Research in Education* (May, 1970), pp. 1-22.
9 M.R. Brown, 'Some strategies used in primary schools for initiating and implementing change', unpub. M.Ed. thesis (University of Manchester, 1971).
10 P.H. Taylor, *How Teachers Plan their Courses* (NFER, 1970).

Appendix

The collection of the data.

The collection of data started in 1969 and was completed in the spring of 1972 after the trial period had finished in August 1971. The basis of this collection was a combination of information collected by the project team and of observations, interviews and questionnaires to obtain more precise measures. Extreme caution is necessary in interpreting this evidence. Wherever possible at least two sources were used. Where documentary evidence was not available to check evidence from observation, interviews or questionnaires, the project team were asked for their assessment.

One major weakness remained. A follow-through study, designed to check predictions, suffers from the difficulty of collecting the data quickly. Here information on schools was accumulated over a period of time. The variables inevitably got contaminated. Thus schools which were investing heavily at the start were already visible as innovatory. It was not only that the variables were not clearly distinguished through precise definition, but that assessments of final results were made in the knowledge of the predictions made a year or more before. The triangulation of methods, using data from the teachers and the project team, was some check on that collected by the author, but reliability must have been low.

A final warning is necessary over the statistical methods employed. Hypotheses were expressed in null form and tested by χ^2. But there are a number of objections to the use of significance levels in so loosely controlled an investigaton.[6] Secondly, there were only twenty-nine schools (twenty-two 'successes', seven 'failures') used in calculating contractual success and thirty-three (adding in the four 'independent successes') in calculating curriculum impact. The data was grouped into 2 x 2 tables to ensure expected values of 5 or more, but the numbers were still small. Thirdly, while all schools were tracked over two years, some had lost contact with the project before then. Lastly, while every effort was made in interviews to isolate the impact of involvement in the project from other simultaneous developments, this was impossible for the teachers, head teachers and advisers concerned.

Data was collected in the following ways. Numbers in brackets refer to the indices being assembled in each stage in this collection of information.

September 1969 to January 1972

Accumulation of documentary material from the project team and feedback from schools.
(1a, 1b; 2a, 2b, 2c; 3a, 3c)

Spring 1970 to autumn 1970

Direct observation in schools. Completion of schedules on investment within schools by project team. Taped interviews with groups of teachers in nine schools.
(2a, 2b, 2c, 2d; 3b, 3c)

Autumn 1971

Interviews with head teachers, teachers, local authority advisers and Schools Council field officers. Questionnaires from teachers. Interviews with teachers in all twenty-two contractually successful schools, in five of the seven schools that had dropped out, three of the four schools that dropped out to carry on independently and four of the five that joined in the second year. Only one school refused to co-operate. Of the remaining three of the thirty-eight schools in the trial, one had lost all the staff who had been involved and the other two had never been involved in any real sense in the project.

Interviews were carried out with seven local advisers in the five authorities involved, with thirty-five teachers and fourteen head teachers. Selection for interview was not random but to ensure that key figures in the trial as nominated by the project team were included. Questionnaires identical to the schedule used in the interviews were left for those key teachers who could not be contacted. Twenty-three of these were returned. The final sample of views was not necessarily representative, being made up of those most involved in the project. The interview schedule and questionnaire were partially structured on the basis of the taped interviews. The schedule went through two pilot runs between October 1970 and April 1971.

(1b; 2a, 2b)

Spring and summer 1971

During this period an independent evaluation panel of local authority advisers and college of education staff carried out an evaluation of the trial in the schools. Simultaneously the project team were involved in their own evaluation exercise. These sources were used to check the bespoke data.

(1b; 2a, 2b; 3a)

IV Roles and interaction
in the school

INTRODUCTION

For sociologists the study of interaction in the school probably begins with Waller's monumental study (1932), a work that has now been rediscovered and reprinted so many times that it has become almost legendary. But the early impetus given by Waller failed to lead to a sound tradition of sociological research of interaction or even of the roles of the classroom. Hoyle (1969) in a study of research on the role of the teacher showed that, even in this limited area, little work had been done and that much of this was concerned with general discussions of professionalism and marginal areas such as the social origins of teachers.

The study of interaction in the classroom was, surprisingly, left to be explored by approaches that were predominantly psychological. A pioneer in this field was Flanders who developed, from the analytical work of Bales and others, sophisticated strategies for the recording of classroom behaviour of teachers and pupils. Work of this nature has been undertaken widely and many detailed records of verbal and non-verbal behaviour in a variety of classrooms are now available.

There are particular problems in the categorization of behaviour in these researches to which sociologists have become particularly alert. One previously mentioned is the imposition of arbitrary statistical aggregates which have no relationship with the realities of individual behaviour. But another, that is an even greater danger in the study of classroom behaviour, is the set of expectations that may be built into and around categories offered to a teacher and that may lead not only to an inaccurate set of observations but also to a research induced distortion of the situation. Of course teachers and pupils are constantly establishing and using categories to structure their experiences, and a developing interest of sociologists is in labelling theory — study of the ways in which labelled categories are constructed and used. (A useful introductory discussion of labelling theory is to be found in Berger and Berger (1972).) Discussions of labelling have in the past centred largely around the labelling of delinquency and on this topic in particular Cicourel has argued that research should be on the labelling and categorizing process rather than on the statistics of delinquency (1967). But the school implications of labelling are increasingly seen to be of importance and the hypotheses of Becker, Geer, Hughes and Strauss (1969) concerning the processes whereby labels come to be ascribed or achieved have particular relevance for future research.

An example of the abundant 'observational category' literature that has the advantage of being sociologically sensitive is included because it is of a kind that can provide a basis for future sociological work. This is a study by Lundgren of classroom behaviour in Sweden which formed part of the Compass project of Gothenburg University. Like similar studies it is concerned to establish and relate categories of behaviour. Lundgren's paper largely avoids the hazards characteristic of this kind of work and goes further than most similar studies in an exploration of the social structure of the pupil group — a social structure that can be seen to be, in part, a consequence of the teacher's perceptions of the classroom situation and the organizational strategies to which they give rise.

The remaining studies have a more sharply defined sociological identity. Grace undertakes a straightforward but valuable examination of the role conflicts experienced by the teacher in the school and in the classroom. He bases his investigation on the early analyses by Wilson (1962) of teacher role conflict which, until Grace's initiative, have been untested by empirical research. Grace shows that experiences such as 'role vulnerability' are a consequence not only of the specific classroom situation, but also of the teacher's response to the organizational characteristics and value connotations of the school itself. The inclusion of Grace's contribution is also important because it serves as a reminder of the considerable time lag that exists between the setting up of speculative hypotheses and the publication of empirical research to examine them, a time lag of some ten years in this case. Yet this time lag has in no way precluded the widespread use and even acceptance of the Wilson hypotheses as a set of satisfactory definitive statements.

Bernbaum, in a first report of the findings of a SSRC inquiry into the role of the school head, explores an issue that is at the heart of a number of themes raised in papers in this and the previous section — the values and perceptions of the head and how these are internalized through his previous professional and other experience. The head is still a key figure in the determination of all that happens in school and, as Bernbaum reminds us, not least of all in the determination of the value orientations and their structural embodiments within the school. Indeed, earlier discussions on the 'values of the school' are, for many schools, largely discussions on the values of the head.

Nash's brief account of the study of classroom behaviour explores further the ways in which teachers' perceptions may be transmitted through the pattern of classroom interaction. His identification of the labelling strategies used by teachers in non-streamed schools suggests again that the teacher's perception of the differences or similarities between children is of far more fundamental importance than any labelling brought about by the streaming system (a point that was suggested in a previous section when the continuity between the results of Lacey and of Barker Lunn was noted). But of particular interest in Nash's account are the ways in which children responded to this differential labelling even when the labelling was latent rather than manifest.

The final contribution by Robinson takes the form of a review of classroom studies that indicates the importance of the emergent field of research that is springing from the application of ethnographic approaches to the sociology of education. Here investigators are concerned with the identification and labelling of such things as knowledge, behaviour and ability in the classroom and the part played by the consciousness of the teachers and the children in these processes. They draw our attention to the 'given' nature of the labels commonly used in the classroom and their potency in influencing behaviour. One has only to recall the motive and emotive force of labels such as 'clever', 'bright', 'dull', 'dim', 'high status subject', 'O level syllabus' and the like to accept the point.

A particular problem of work in this area has been the paucity and inaccessibility of published research. In part this is due to the newness of the field but an important reason arises from the sensitivity of the data and the ways in which its illumination of professional and pupil behaviour may be interpreted. Apart from a single paper by Keddie (1971), most existing studies remain in research dissertations and reports. Robinson's paper presents a valuable review of a number of these relatively inaccessible initiatives in the ethnographic field, making particular reference not only to Keddie but also to important studies by Beck and Green. Like Keddie, Beck and Green use field study data to explore the ways in which teachers define and evaluate classroom behaviour in terms of normality and deviance and how they use this categorization to organize and structure the experience of schooling. This enables them to 'construct' both their knowledge about pupils and their anticipations of their activity. It is closely linked with Keddie's illustration of the distinctions teachers make between school knowledge (subjects) and non-school knowledge (commonsense) and the resulting hierarchical relationship between them that they use to differentiate children.

Using the dichotomy of Bruyn, mentioned in the introduction, it can be seen that the participant strategies that Robinson describes are considerably removed from the pure scientific approaches on which earlier researches were modelled. Nonetheless, it is clear that work of this nature will be a model on which many future inquiries will be made. Certainly the interest and quality of the findings of these studies is likely to be greater than that derivable from many of the more 'statistically reputable' inquiries that have characterized classroom observation in the past.

References

BECKER, H.S., GEER, B., HUGHES, E. and STRAUSS, A., 1969, *Making the Grade*. New York: Wiley.

BERGER, P.L. and BERGER, B., 1972, *Sociology, a Biographical Approach*. New York: Basic Books.

CICOUREL, A.V., 1967, *The Social Organisation of Juvenile Justice*. New York: Wiley.

HOYLE, E., 1969, *The Role of the Teacher*. London: Routledge and Kegan Paul.

KEDDIE, N., 1971, 'Classroom knowledge' in Young, M.F.D. (ed.), *Knowledge and Control*. London: Collier-Macmillan.

WALLER, W., 1932, *The Sociology of Teaching*. New York: Wiley (reprinted as a paperback, 1965, New York: Science Editions).

WILSON, B.R., 1962, 'The teacher's role, a sociological analysis'. *British Journal of Sociology*, 13(1).

ULF P LUNDGREN

Pedagogical roles in the classroom *

The purpose of this article is to present a social-psychological aspect of a comprehensive educational model (Dahllöf 1971, Lundgren 1972). The main idea is to explain the teaching process in terms of rules governed by frames. The frames can be classified on various levels. I will here just allude to two groups of frames; the organizational frames (class size, composition of class according to ability etc.) and the time frame (time at disposal). The main assumptions of relevance for the discussion to come are:

A The teaching process is defined as a system of transformations following a set of rules.
B The rules are functional expressions of the organizational frames and the time frame.
C The relevance or meaning of the actions that constitute the transformations are understandable in relation to the intentions of the actors and thereby in relation to the goals set up for the teaching.

The frames govern the process and make a specific process possible to exist or not exist, but from a set of frames we can possibly predict the rules, not the actual process in terms of specific actions. Using an analogy with a game, we can see the frames as giving rise to some general rules. How the actual game develops is another question; a question that has to be answered through an analysis of the players' intention with the game.

The notion of rules and the analogy with a game are basically taken from Wittgenstein (1958) and the study of classroom language by Bellack et al (1966). One way of analysing the consequences of the rules to look upon its pragmatical dimensions. (Watzlawich et al 1967), in the sense of pupils' pedagogical roles. Some important studies have been carried out (Waller 1932, Good and Brophy 1969, Adams and Biddle 1970), but most work in which classroom behaviour patterns have been studied has been concerned with the teachers' behaviour toward the class as a whole and has thereby neglected the behaviour of the single pupil. These studies have primarily aimed to find a relation between the teachers' behaviour and the pupils' achievement or attitudes. The purpose has been to answer the question of teacher effectiveness from a level where effectiveness is seen as a result of personality variables.

---

*This paper is published for the first time in this collection.

By pedagogical roles I mean the specific type of actions that each student in a class is performing.

A The roles are defined in relation to the teachers' and the students' perceptions of the goals and the frames limiting the process.
B The limitations will govern the interaction in various ways, but the more the frames limit the process the fewer groups of students will be established that interact in a similar way.

The concept of the steering group

In order to test these basic notions we have to identify the specific actions that constitute a pedagogical role. We will do that not from the actions of the single pupil, but from common actions for groups of pupils within the class (Lundgren 1972).

In a re-analysis of research on ability grouping Dahllöf (1971) found a similarity in result patterns. The time spent on elementary curriculum units covariated with the absolute value of the students between percentile 10-25 in relation to general ability in each class. This pattern was interpreted in terms of role behaviour. The students in this group seemed to function as a criterion group for the teacher — a check-up group when learning a curriculum unit and going over to a new one.

This can be theoretically interpreted on two levels. On one hand we can see the forming of this group as an effect of the actual frames and goals. This means that, when studying different classes, the actual steering group will change. On the other hand we can interpret this as a fixed group. This means that the teacher relates the goal level to the frames and interprets his educational role in a way that the process always will be steered by the group at about percentiles 10-25 (P_S). These two interpretations are not contrary but complementary. The explanation of the phenomena must be interpreted in two respects. The actual steering group is varied, but according to the teacher's interpretation of his role there are limits.

In its turn this interpretation can be hypothetically formulated. The students between percentile 10-25 according to ability in each class will act in a way different from other pupils in the class. In starting with this hypothesis the concept of pedagogical roles is defined in relation to the content and goals of the teaching.

Methodology

Eight classes were followed during one semester in the teaching of mathematics. The lessons were sampled. Neither the teachers nor the pupils knew when the observer was coming. In all, fifty-seven observations were undertaken. The classes studied were in the academic high school grade 11, which means that the students were about seventeen to eighteen years of age. (Lundgren 1972). The analytical unit is the single utterance. All lessons were taped and then typescripted. Every utterance (even non-verbal utterances of relevance noted by the observer) were coded into five main categories. We have used a category system developed by Bellack *et al* (1966) but extended and somewhat modified. In the analogy we will use the term pedagogical moves for the categories.

The five basic pedagogical moves are:

Structuring (STR), which serves the function of setting the context for subsequent behaviour by (1) launching or calling — excluding interactions between teachers and pupils, and (2) indicating the nature of the interaction in terms of the dimension of time, agent, activity, topic and cognitive process, regulations, reasons and instructional aids.

Soliciting (SOL) which is intended to elicit (a) an active verbal response on the part of the person addressed, (b) a cognitive response e.g. encouraging persons addressed to attend something or (c) a physical response.

Structuring and soliciting are initiating moves. The responding moves are reciprocated in relation to soliciting.

Responding (RES) and

Reacting (REA). The latter is related directly to the other three moves, but need not in itself be initiated by any of them (Bellack *et al* 1966, pp. 16-18, Lundgren 1972, pp. 71-2, 232).

In addition to these moves we have a fifth move — *Individual help* (HEP), which is classified when the teacher talks to just one student and no others can hear the conversation, when, for example, leaning over the desk giving individual guidance.

The first four moves are classified on the basis of complete statements. 'One or more pedagogical moves may occur within an utterance, which is defined as a complete statement by a teacher or a pupil at any one time in the discourse.' (Bellack *et al* 1966, p.16). A move is an utterance having a certain intention, which means that the one who does the classifying determines when the content changes intention.

The moves have temporal and content relations — cycles. A cycle is a message in which a certain sequence of pedagogical moves follow each other. A teaching cycle is then a series of pedagogical moves, that begins with either a soliciting or a structuring move. Over 70 per cent of all cycles can be classified in seven types (Lundgren 1972, p. 276). The moves are classified according to the type of cognitive process and in addition the structural moves are classified according to the type of rating.

	Analytic process	*Empirical process*	*Evaluative process*
Information treating process	Interpreting (INT)	Explaining (XPL)	Justifying (JUS)
Information giving process	Defining (DEF)	Fact stating (FAC)	Opining (OPN)
Rating is divided into:			
Positive (POS)	*Positively toned:* Admitting (ADM)	Repeating (RPT)	
Qualifying (QAL)	*Negatively toned:* Not admitting (NAD)	Negative (NEG)	

The demarcation of categories and definitions are given in Lundgren 1972, p.227).

Teachers' and students' roles

The teacher dominates the teaching, and the roles teacher and students play are relatively fixed. The teacher explains and asks questions, the student answers. Students very seldom communicate with each other. 'Pedagogically speaking, the teacher and the pupil play different but complementary roles in the classroom game. The roles of the teacher and the pupil may be defined in terms of frequency of behaviour in each category of pedagogical moves . . . . ' (Bellack *et al* 1966, p. 46).

The role of the teacher is to structure, solicit and react. As receiver he consequently gets responses and to a certain extent is a target for reactions. The pupil asks and reacts. The distribution of the HEP moves shows that the teacher is the sender and the pupil the receiver, which means that the pupils seldom initiate requests for help.

Bellack *et al* (1966) carried out a study in the beginning of the sixties. The study included civics in corresponding grade to our study The study was done in New York. Our study and Bellack's agree almost completely (Table I). Totally, the teacher is the sender in 63 per cent of all moves in Bellack's study; in ours the figure is 62 per cent. The differences are mainly concentrated in structuring and reacting, which could be explained by the differences in subject under study.

The interesting question arising when comparing these two studies is the question of why the pattern is so stable. When comparing studies carried out in various countries (Bellack 1973) the same pattern appears. Hoetker and Ahlbrandt (1969) have compared studies during fifty years and find similar stability in interaction patterns. The recitation pattern seems to be the same in spite of the fact that each generation of educational thinkers have condemned this patter. Our basic theory suggests one answer.

Going one step further and comparing the distribution of categories for cognitive process and rating for the teacher and pupils, the roles become still more marked. The teacher has a wider repertoire. This is not surprizing as the classifications refer to the way in which he supplies the content of the course to the students. The teacher uses somewhat fewer statements of fact and offers more opinions.

There are marked differences in participation rates within each class. The relative distribution of participation has a form of a J. There is also a covariation between the value of P_S in each class and the number of pupils that participate less than the others. The lower the values for the P_S group the more the pupils are passive. The communication is spread evenly more often from the teacher to pupils, while there are more marked variations between pupils as senders. In comparing active and passive pupils we find that:

There are no differences in general ability between active and passive pupils.
There are no differences in home background (social grouping) between the active ones and the passive ones.
There are significant differences in relation to sex. Boys are more active than girls.

TABLE I Relative distribution between teacher and pupils in moves, classified as to sender and receiver and compared with Bellack's study (1966)

	Bellack				Sender				Receiver			
	Teacher	Pupil	Total	N	Teacher	Pupil	Total	N	Teacher	Pupil	Total	N
STR*	86	12	100	854	96	4	100	1 193	4	96	100	1 187
SOL	86	14	100	5 135	84	16	100	3 300	13	87	100	3 287
RES	12	88	100	4 385	12	88	100	2 943	88	12	100	2 955
REA	81	19	100	4 649	67	33	100	3 579	30	70	100	3 591
HEP	-	-	-	-	99	1	100	314	4	96	100	355
Total	63	37	100	15 023	62	38	100	11 329	37	63	100	11 375

*2 per cent AV-aids

The amount of participation is about the same for the students as receivers of moves in relation to passive and active role.
The more active pupils have more structuring moves.
The active students have more information-treatment processes.
There is a significant correlation between degree of activity and interest in mathematics.
The teacher seems not to activate the more passive students.

The pedagogical role of the steering group

What role does the steering group (P_S) play in the communication? From the standpoint of the theoretical model we have set up, this role is especially prominent in the transition from one unit to the next. We cannot divide the communication into phases, since we are working within a given time frame for one unit. However, we should be able to proceed from the fact that, in taking up different parts of the unit under study, the teacher uses the steering group as a criterion. There is also a clear pattern of significant correlations between the value of the steering group and the relative distribution of different categories within each class. In these correlational studies the pedagogical moves have been classified in a much more extended way than here presented (Lundgren 1972). The next question is, does the steering group differ from other pupils in frequency of participation, and what role does P_S play in the communication? Table II shows for the eight classes the average value of frequency for these pupils versus the class as a whole. In this comparison, the pupils constituting the steering group are included in the class. We therefore minimize the differences.

TABLE II   Average value of number of moves for the pupils in the steering group and for the class as a whole

	Sender		Receiver	
Class	P_S	Class	P_S	Class
1	1.7	3.4	7.7	6.9
2	8.3	15.5	12.8	23.9
4	32.0	27.2	42.0	35.7
5	10.0	30.4	12.0	36.2
6	25.8	22.0	35.0	29.7
7	7.3	7.9	13.0	12.2
8	15.5	10.6	18.0	15.1
9	10.3	12.1	18.3	14.7

There are no differences for senders. In half of the classes, the pupils in the steering group have on an average more moves than the class as a whole, and in the rest of them the pupils in the steering group have fewer moves than the class itself. For receivers, however, there is a difference, even though it is small. In six classes, the pupils in the steering group are more often receivers than those in the average class, and in two classes we get the opposite proportions.

It is above all as receivers that the steering group differs from the rest of the class. Table III shows the differences in pedagogical moves between the steering group and the whole class. Here we have used x^2 and used the distribution for the class as a whole as the expected value. As the observed value we have used the distribution of moves for the pupils in the steering group. In this way, we reduced the possibilities of differences, as the pupils in the steering group also became part of the class as a whole.

TABLE III   Distribution of significant x^2 when testing distribution of pedagogical moves between the steering group and the class as a whole. Level of significance 5 per cent.

Class	Sender	Receiver
1		sig.
2		
4	sig.	sig.
5		
6		sig.
7	sig.	sig.
8	sig.	sig.
9		sig.
Total	sig.	sig.

We get the same result here as for frequency of participation. Totally, we get a significant variation for both senders and receivers. Within classes, there is a variation for receivers. The same two classes that differed in frequency of participation earlier show no significant difference in the distribution of pedagogical moves between the steering group and the class as a whole. What then distinguishes the steering group from other pupils in the class as to pedagogical moves?

TABLE IV   Distribution of pedagogical moves for pupils in the steering group and for all pupils

	Sender		Receiver	
	P_S	All	P_S	All
STR	1	1	3	16
SOL	5	10	39	39
RES	75	61	4	5
REA	18	28	46	35
HEP	1	(-)	9	5
Total	100	100	100	100
N	376	4278	561	7218

As senders, the steering group pupils differ from other pupils in that they make fewer soliciting and reacting and more responding moves. As receivers, the steering group pupils get the same amount of questions, but more reacting and fewer structuring moves from the teacher. This pattern is somewhat bewildering. The structuring moves ought to increase more than the others, but it is quite in line with our theoretical model that these pupils make relatively more responding and HEP moves. They also get more reaction.

Before we analyse reacting moves, we shall take up the distribution of cognitive process for the pupils in the steering group versus all pupils. We report only the difference in distribution within each group. Minus value means that relatively all pupils have more moves in the category than the pupils in the steering group. Consequently, for each category, the steering group is subtracted from all pupils when the values are distributed relatively within each group.

TABLE V   Difference in relative distribution in cognitive process between the steering group and all pupils

	Analytic		Empirical		Evaluative	
	DEF	INT	FAC	XPL	OPN	JUS
Sender	0.6	0.8	-0.4	0.2	-1.3	0.0
Receiver	-0.1	-0.3	2.9	-0.8	-1.1	-.07

The greatest difference concerns FAC moves by receivers, where the steering group receives more fact-stating than all pupils totally. There is not the same difference for the senders. The greatest difference between the groups as regards responding is thereby tied to the stating of fact.

TABLE VI   Difference in relative distribution in rating between the steering group and all pupils.

	Positively toned			Negatively toned		
	POS	ADM	RPT	QAL	NAD	NEG
Sender	-20.5	26.2	12.0	-0.8	-0.7	(-16.2)
Receiver	-13.8	-2.1	20.6	-3.1	-0.7	-1.1

Here we get an interesting picture (Table VI). From a relative point of view, the pupils in the steering group receive fewer negative ratings, but also fewer clearly positive ratings. Instead, the steering group pupils as senders make considerably more moves of type repeating, and especially as receivers. As these pupils steer the pace, and the teacher by questioning them knows when he can go on, it seems logical that, for the sake of control, the relative share of repeating statements should increase. This also explains why the number of responding moves increases, without an increase in initiating moves. Negative statements are in parentheses, as no pupil in the steering group was sender for any moves that can be classified as negative ratings. For senders, these figures must be interpreted with caution. The pupils in the steering group have too few moves classified as rating. Our interpretation is that the steering group pupils get direct praise, and are more often asked to repeat an earlier statement. As senders, the steering group pupils more often ask for rating than the other pupils.

The role we have here described for the steering group is consistent with the pattern of correlations obtained for the steering group and various classifications of verbal behaviour (relative, that is, in each class).

Pedagogical roles extended

The constellation of frame factors and their importance is a question of how the teachers perceive and internalize the frames. It concerns how the teacher perceives the goal and the pattern of the teaching, how well he can diagnose the students' learning pace and how well he plans the teaching in accordance with these factors and the total time available. A functional way to handle the situation, in order to save the teacher's energy, is for him to group the students within the class and give these groups different roles. If the steering group can be described in terms of the teacher's cognitive groupings of students, we get another approach for explaining the pragmatical dimension in the teaching process. These groups may constantly be changing, but each time he perceives the class, he makes such a grouping of the pupils. When time is limited and goal fixed, these groups may be functional for the teaching and then govern the teaching process. When the time available and the goals are changed, these groups may be irrelevant to the teaching, and even if the teacher cognitively still groups the students it may be on the basis of characteristics having no direct importance for their learning.

The idea we present in this discussion comes from Miller's (1967) theories of human information processing. Briefly, we assume that the teachers group the pupils in 'chunks' with about seven students in each 'chunk'. The great problem lies in determining how these 'chunks' form and become a cognitive 'structure'. Marton (1970) has developed a method for analysing how complex information is reduced to cognitive structure. His method is based on measuring the temporal relations between units in recalling. We have used Marton's methodology on this problem.

In an interview at the end of the spring term, each teacher was asked to name the pupils in the class. The following instruction was given 'This question may seem strange. Later I shall explain why I asked it. Who are the pupils in the class? Will you please name them in the order you remember them, but not in alphabetical order, and not according to how they are seated in the classroom?' The teachers' answers were recorded, and the pause time in seconds between names was measured with an oscillograph. From the list of pause lengths, a cumulative graph was plotted. From this graph, the cognitive groups were reconstructed. As Table VII shows, the teacher named about six students with a short pause between each name, and then came a longer pause, followed by about six more names with a short pause in between each name. A small group of students was always forgotten.

TABLE VII The average pause length in seconds between names within each group and between groups

Groups

Class	1 Within N	M	Between	2 Within N	M	Between	3 Within N	M	Between	4 Within N	M	Between	5 Within N	M	Forgotten
1	8	3.9	42.8	7	9.2	31.8	9	26.9	-	-	-	-	-	-	4
2	4	2.2	7.3	4	2.4	8.3	5	2.4	7.9	3	4.2	10.9	6	1.9	4
4	8	2.9	11.9	3	1.1	17.2	3	10.8	89.4	2	3.2	37.0	2	6.7	8
5	5	1.3	10.2	3	1.0	12.4	3	4.8	38.0	7	4.1	-	-	-	4
6	5	1.4	24.4	6	4.7	17.2	13	2.6	15.8	3	4.5	-	-	-	2
7	13	4.3	17.4	3	5.6	39.1	4	12.9	-	-	-	-	-	-	10
8	5	0.6	8.8	8	1.1	4.5	4	0.5	4.1	9	2.8	-	-	-	4
9	5	0.8	3.2	13	1.3	26.5	8	1.2	22.6	2	0.3	-	-	-	2

The grouping of pupils made by the teacher in each class consists of three to five groups, each group having two to thirteen pupils. The average number of pupils in each group is 5.7, and the average number of forgotten pupils is 5.6. These analyses are very rough. Classifying the names that the teachers recalled into specific groups is to some extent a subjective act as, for instance, in deciding when a pause length may be said to belong within a group or between groups. However, in nearly all cases, the classifications were rather easy to determine on the basis of the accumulative distribution of the pause length. After the teacher had recalled the names of the pupils, we asked what principle he had followed in naming them in that order and why he associated certain pupils with others.

Probably the teachers find it impossible to recall the names of the pupils without following some kind of principle. One teacher maintained that his enumeration was made at random. Two teachers very vaguely stated a principle, and four teachers clearly stated a functional principle.

In the two classes achievement was given as the reason for the ranking; the average test value for the groups also, from a relative point of view, had about the same rank order. It seems that the first group named by the teacher often has a higher proportion of boys. One teacher distinguished a clearly marked grouping as regards sex. For the average value on the test, we find a significant ranking according to the pupils' intellectual ability. One of the groups contains about three of the four pupils that fall between percentile 10-25 according to ability, which means that we here find a better way of determining the steering group.

According to the teachers' communication to and from these pupils, we definitely find differences between groups as regards the teaching given to the pupils. The cognitive groupings of pupils made by the teacher reflect the roles different groups of pupils play in the teaching process. We look first at the differences in frequency of participation in the communication. In this connection, we tested the distribution of moves between the teachers' cognitive groupings, i.e., we worked out an average value for each pupil. This average value, multiplied by the number of pupils in each group, represents the expected value in a χ^2 calculation.

TABLE VIII   Test of differences (value of significance 5 per cent) in distribution of pedagogical moves between teachers' cognitive groupings in the class

Class	1	2	4	5	6	7	8	9
Sender	Sig.	Sig.	Sig.		Sig.	Sig.	Sig.	Sig.
Receiver	Sig.	Sig.	Sig.	Sig.	Sig.	Sig.	Sig.	Sig.

For frequency of different moves as sender and receiver, the cognitive groupings we defined from the descriptions of the teachers differ significantly from the distribution in the class seen totally. There is one exception in one class, where the pupils as senders do not differ between the different groupings. The values we get on χ^2 are also high, and with a few exceptions the same could apply to the .001 per cent level. The cognitive grouping the teacher has of the class is functional, in the sense that he behaves toward these pupils in a specific way, and these pupils in turn respond in a specific way.

Next, we look at the way the teachers' cognitive groupings differ as to pedagogical moves. In this connection, we tested differences in distributions of each move for these groupings. We then used the distributions showing significant differences to describe which differences exist between the groups, relatively speaking, in the distribution of pedagogical moves. The distribution differs for three moves especially — soliciting, responding and reacting.

For senders, it is not surprisingly the RES move that separates the classes. One class shows no differences at all as senders. In another class, the move that distinguishes it from others is soliciting, and in two classes it is reacting and responding.

TABLE IX   Test of differences (value of significance 5 per cent) in distribution of pedagogical moves between teachers' cognitive groupings in the class

Class		1	2	4	5	6	7	8	9
	SOL						Sig.		
Sender	RES		Sig.	Sig.	Sig.	Sig.		Sig.	Sig.
	REA					Sig.		Sig.	
	SOL	Sig.	Sig.	Sig.	Sig.	Sig.		Sig.	
Receiver	RES						Sig.		
	REA	Sig.	Sig.	Sig.		Sig.	Sig.	Sig.	Sig.

For receivers, the soliciting and reacting moves separate the teachers' cognitive groupings. In one class, it is the responding move instead of soliciting. So far, the differences between the groupings show only that they exist in the characteristics of the pupil's role. If we consider the existing data on how the teachers' cognitive groups differ, we find almost without exception the same thing occurring for receivers, but in soliciting and reacting moves. Although the lines are not strictly drawn, we can see one group as especially important for soliciting, one for reacting and one for responding. Furthermore, we find that one group of pupils to some extent plays the same role as the steering groups have been shown to play. Although some teachers said they followed no principles in their grouping, we still find differences between these teachers' cognitive groupings as to their participation in the communication. In passing, we may mention that the greatest difference in the distribution between the groupings is found in the class whose teacher denied having any principle.

To a certain extent, we can explain the variation in the distribution of the communication as an effect of the teacher's perception of the class and his conception of the pupils. This perception is at first not linked to each specific pupil, but the teacher groups the pupils according to the different functions they take on and does this in order to adapt them to the aim and content of the teaching.

These analyses extend our possibilities for interpreting beyond the first tested hypothesis about a steering group. Returning to our theoretical model the data here given verify our theory on some critical and principal points (Lundgren 1972).

Some concluding remarks

The behaviour of the pupils seems to be explainable in terms of role governed behaviour in three dimensions or levels, in one we see the whole group of pupils and their role in relation to the teacher's role. The pupil role is simply to elicit response. In the second dimension or level we see groups of pupils within the class as an expression of the frame factors, and how these factors govern the teacher's perception of the pupils. Here, the pupils' roles are different. In this dimension we have the steering group, whose responses are used as a 'feedback' by the teacher when he decides to leave one topic and go on to the next. Consequently, these pupils play a greater role in responding and repeating moves than the other pupils. Other groups play the roles of structuring and initiating discussions. Still others have the passive role of merely listening to the class discourse. Since these groups will have different characteristics in different classes, the groups may also be changed during the teaching period, both as a consequence of changed behaviour and different content studied. In some respect, we may assume that the teaching process itself stabilizes these groups. The teachers' expectations of the pupils' achievement will form the communication, and the pupils will act in accordance with these expectations (Rosenthal and Jackson 1968). In the third dimension or level, we see the role of each pupil as formed by his participation in the communication, with the other pupils in the class.

References

ADAMS, R.S. and BIDDLE B.J., 1970, *Realities of Teaching, Explorations with Video Tape.* New York: Holt, Rinehart and Winston
BELLACK, A.A., KLIEBARD, H.M., HYMAN, R.T. and SMITH, F.L., 1966, *The Language of the Classroom.* New York: Teachers College Press, Columbia University.
BELLACK, A.A. (ed.), 1973, *Studies in the Classroom Language.* New York: Teachers College Press, Columbia University.
DAHLLÖF, U., 1971, *Ability Grouping, Content Validity and Curriculum Process Analysis.* New York: Teachers College Press, Columbia University.

GOOD, T.L., and BROPHY, J.E., 1969, *Analyzing Classroom Interaction: a more powerful alternative.* Austin, Texas: The R and D Center for Teacher Education, Report Series No. 26. Mimeo.

HOETKER, J., and AHLBRAND, P.A.Jr., 1969, 'The persistence of recitation'. *American Educational Research Journal,* 6(2), March, pp. 145-67.

LUNDGREN, U.P., 1972, *Frame Factors and the Teaching Process. A contribution to curriculum theory and theory on teaching.* Stockholm: Almqvist and Wiksell.

MARTON, F., 1970, *Structural Dynamics of Learning.* Stockholm: Almqvist and Wiksell.

MILLER, G.A., 1967, *The Psychology of Communication.* New York: Basic Books Inc.

ROSENTHAL, R. and JACOBSON, L., 1968, *Pygmalion in the Classroom. Teacher Expectations and Pupils' Intellectual Development.* New York: Holt, Rinehart and Winston Inc.

WALLER, W., 1932, *The Sociology of Teaching.* New York: Russell and Russell (new ed. 1965, New York: John Wiley).

WATZLAWICH, P., BEAVIN, J.H. and JACKSON, D.D., 1967, *Pragmatics of Human Communication.* New York: W.W. Norton and Company.

WITTGENSTEIN, L., 1958, *Philosophical Investigations.* Oxford: Basil Blackwell.

GERALD R GRACE

Vulnerability and conflict in the teacher's role*

The following chapters report the results of an investigation undertaken in the period 1967-70 into the intra-role conflicts of 150 secondary school teachers. The primary stimulus behind this work was the fact that Wilson's (1962) analysis of teacher role conflicts, which had suggested so many valuable lines of inquiry, remained virtually untested by empirical research, although the analysis itself was widely quoted in sociological studies in education.

The investigation had three major objectives. The first was to establish whether certain categories of role conflict suggested by Wilson were in fact seen as problem situations by a sample of serving teachers and, if so, how important these conflicts were thought to be in the teaching situation. An important related question was the extent to which the teachers as a whole had personally experienced such role conflicts as problems and had been to some degree troubled by them. A second objective was to investigate relationships between particular categories of teacher (classified by years of experience, professional qualification, sex, type of school, social composition of school and main subject specialism) and overall levels of perceived and experienced role conflict. The final major objective was to examine relationships between particular categories of teacher and particular categories of role conflict in order to reveal more precise 'role conflict profiles' than the initial measures would show.

The role conflict schedules (first stage of inquiry)

To investigate both the perception and personal experience of role conflict by the sample, two schedules were devised, following a model outlined by Getzels and Guba (1955). Schedule I was designed to measure role conflict perception (RCP) and schedule II to measure role conflict experience (RCE). The operational definition of role conflict used in the schedules was 'problems for the occupant which arise as the result of role incompatibilities'. The role conflict areas were therefore presented to the respondents as problems which teachers might meet with during the course of their work. Each area

*Reprinted from Gerald R. Grace, Role Conflict and the Teacher, (London; Routledge and Kegan Paul, 1972), pp.29-35 and pp. 60-71 by kind permission of the author and publishers.

of role conflict was represented by two items which suggested role incompatibilities within the area. Four potential role conflict areas were presented: area I: problems arising from role diffuseness; area II: problems arising from role vulnerability; area III: problems arising from tension between role commitment and career orientation; area IV: problems arising from value conflicts.

A central problem arising from the diffuseness of the teacher's role (area I) was taken to be the difficulty of knowing what had been accomplished as the result of role performance. Thus the items in this area were concerned with knowledge or lack of knowledge of goal achievement as a factor in role conflict. This was expressed as follows, e.g. (item i) 'Whereas many occupations give clear "knowledge of results" to practitioners, teaching, by its very nature, can do this only to a limited extent.' The assumption in area I was that conflict could arise from this role ambiguity – from the incompatibility between the normal desire of role occupants to know what they were accomplishing and the relative invisibility of many of the teacher's achievements.

In area II the concept of role vulnerability was introduced. The teacher's role was taken to be vulnerable and exposed to conflict in two senses. First, because the role, lacking the defences of mystique, jargon or narrowly defined technical expertise, could frequently be exposed to incompatible expectations from various external agencies, all of whom felt confident of their ability and right to define the teacher's role. This was expressed in (item iii) – 'The teacher, unlike many professional practitioners, is subject to a variety of conflicting opinions as to how he should carry out his professional work.' Second, vulnerability and hence conflict was seen to arise from the uncertain status of the teacher as a professional. This was expressed in (item iv) – 'The teacher is a professional practitioner but despite this is generally treated as if he were not.' In this way, area II was designed to present role conflict arising from exposure to conflicting expectation and to conflicting perceptions of the professional role, seen as two related aspects of role vulnerability.

Area III represented conflict between role commitment and career orientation. This was presented to the respondent in the following way, e.g. (item v) – 'To obtain promotion, the teacher must be mobile and "gain experience", yet the nature of the work ideally requires a sustained relationship with particular groups of pupils.' The conflict suggested in this area was that between the widely held belief that promotion went to the 'movers' and the widely held belief that teachers should show loyalty to a school and its pupils.

The final area of role conflict focused upon incompatibility between the values which teachers were expected to uphold to the pupils and those which were generally current in society. This was expressed in, e.g. (item vii) – 'The teacher is expected to maintain traditional[1] values and standards yet at the same time society in general largely ignores these values and standards.'

On schedule I, which was designed to measure role conflict perception, the teachers were asked to respond to each item on the following scale:

This seems to me to be
    0 Not a problem at all
    1 A problem of little importance
    2 A problem of moderate importance
    3 A problem of great importance
    4 A problem of very great importance

On schedule II, concerned with role conflict experience, the items of the first schedule were repeated but the teachers were asked to respond on a different scale:

I have personally felt this as a problem
    0 Not at all
    1 To a small extent
    3 To a moderate extent
    3 To a great extent
    4 To a very great extent

Each respondent completed, in addition to the two schedules, a short personal questionnaire to elicit characteristics (years of experience, etc.) to be related to role conflict perception and experience.

It was felt that the best method of distributing the schedules was in group meetings with the teachers. The purpose here was threefold. In the first place, it gave an opportunity to the researcher to stress the distinction which was being made between perceived and experienced problems. Second, it gave an opportunity for the teachers to raise any queries regarding the schedules and to ask for any clarification. Finally, it made possible discussion in general terms of the value and purpose of the research. The schedules were distributed at meetings in morning, mid-day or afternoon break periods, which were attended by most of the full-time staff of the schools approached. At these meetings, the teachers were asked to complete the schedules individually and not to discuss the issues arising until they had all made their responses. This they agreed to do. Completed schedules were handed in to the school secretaries (with the head teacher's permission) and collected at the school after one week.

In analysing the schedules, the distribution of scores over the whole range was first examined for each area of role conflict, with particular reference to the percentage of teachers scoring 0 to indicate rejection of the area as an actual problem (schedule 1) or to indicate total lack of personal experience of the conflict (schedule II). The basic question of whether the suggested conflicts were meaningful in the teaching situation was involved in this analysis. Thereafter, for the purposes of comparison and evaluation between various groups of teachers and various areas of role conflict, scores were dichotomized on a low-high classification and the χ^2 test applied to determine the significance of differences.

In addition to analysis of scores in each role conflict area, the sum of scores on each schedule was taken as a measure of overall role conflict perception and overall role conflict experience for each respondent. Overall RCP and RCE scores were also dichotomized and compared by χ^2. Comparison groups were formed using the variables of years of teaching experience, professional qualification, sex, type of school, main subject specialism and social class composition of the schools. For the latter, the following classification was used (see Taylor 1968) — schools where over 50 per cent of the pupils' fathers were in white collar employment were regarded as 'middle class'. Schools where the proportion of pupils from white collar and manual working class backgrounds were approximately equal were regarded as 'mixed'. Schools where the majority of the pupils' fathers were in manual employment were regarded as 'working class'.

The interviews (second stage of inquiry)

Merton has suggested that the impersonal and limited nature of questionnaires as instruments of social research makes it necessary to use, where possible, interviews in order to explore the thinking, nuances and qualifications which lie behind the objective responses. This procedure was followed. The schedules, even though they provided considerable space for additional comment, could not be regarded as sufficient in themselves. While they revealed the broad outline of teacher reaction to suggested role conflict and indicated some valuable pointers towards explaining such reaction, they remained essentially surface instruments. To attempt to probe more deeply, a series of one-hour 'focused interviews' was subsequently undertaken with 80 of the original 150 teachers.

It was considered important also to interview the head teachers of ten secondary schools which were involved, in order to obtain more information about the schools as organizations. Information regarding school 'climate', internal organization and clientele was already available, partly from the researcher's own local knowledge of the schools, and partly from the comments volunteered by the teachers during the interviews. The teachers had also, during the course of interviews, frequently made reference to the role of the head teacher as they perceived it in their various schools. One-hour focused interviews with the ten head teachers provided further useful information on how the heads conceived of their role in relation to the problem areas under investigation.

The sample and the sample area

The social context of the investigation was a prosperous midland borough of approximately 60,000 inhabitants. The town had developed particularly in the nineteenth century as the result of railway development and today it possesses important mechanical and electrical engineering industries. An above average proportion of the male working population is composed of white collar and skilled manual workers employed in industrial, technical and scientific activities. A considerable number of men are also employed outside the town in the car factories of a large midland city. The standard of housing is generally good and there are few areas in the town which could be described as industrial slums. Some of the Victorian terraces in the central railway area of the town are occupied by West Indian and Indian families which together represent about 5 per cent of the total population.

The town has a public school and ten secondary schools, including two grammar schools, two bilateral schools and six non-selective schools. The boys' grammar school (voluntary aided) was founded in the late nineteenth century and provides places for about 600 pupils. It enjoys high status locally, arising partly from its association and scholarship connections with the public school. The girls' grammar school, which was founded in the early part of this century, provides places for a similar number of pupils. The two bilateral schools are also single sex and occupy modern buildings in a pleasant residential part of the town. Each school accommodates about 700 pupils. Of the six non-selective schools, one is a Roman Catholic foundation of 450 pupils (coeducational) and one a Church of England foundation of about 600 pupils (coeducational). The remaining schools vary between 300 and 400 pupils, two being coeducational and two single sex. The majority of the schools are in modern buildings and pleasant surroundings.

The total number of full-time secondary school teachers (excluding head teachers and deputy head teachers) at the time of the inquiry was 223. Schedules were distributed to each one and 158 were returned, of which 150 were usable. The sample of 150 teachers consisted of 87 men and 63 women. 43 were grammar school teachers (23 men and 20 women); 38 were bilateral school teachers (25 men and 13 women); and 69 were secondary modern teachers (39 men and 30 women). The characteristics of the sample were compared with the characteristics of the total secondary school teaching population in maintained schools in England and Wales as at March 1967. This showed that the sample was very representative of the total secondary teaching population in respect of age structure and type of school, although it contained a somewhat higher proportion of younger teachers than was the case nationally. The sample was most atypical in the area of professional qualification, where graduate teachers were overrepresented and certificated teachers underrepresented in terms of their proportion in the national population.

The possibility of generalizing the results of the inquiry beyond its immediate social context must be approached with some caution. While the sample of teachers studied was quite representative of the larger teaching population, the context within which they perform their roles was essentially 'small town' and 'small school'. Investigations in a metropolitan area, with more social problems and with larger secondary schools, would be likely to produce a different picture of role conflict in the teaching situation. . . .

Frequently exposed to incompatible expectations about how and what they should teach, and struggling for professional status, teachers in America are generally seen to be in a vulnerable position, beset with conflict. This sample of British secondary school teachers felt more secure in their professional status and less vulnerable to external pressures than is characteristically the case with American teachers.

Less than half (47.3 per cent) saw conflicts of role vulnerability as of high importance in the teaching situation and less than one quarter (22 per cent) had been personally troubled to any extent by such conflicts. Comparison of the scores of various categories of teacher, however, modified this general picture in important respects.

Teachers in secondary modern schools were once more differentiated from their colleagues by significantly higher scores. For the secondary modern teacher, conflicts of role vulnerability had a reality in terms of personal experience which hardly existed in grammar and bilateral schools. Grammar school teachers in particular were hardly touched at all by personal experience of role vulnerability and the differences between the scores of these two categories of teacher were statistically very significant.

Role vulnerability on the conflict schedules was a composite area of exposure to conflicting expectations for the teaching role and exposure to conflicting evaluations of the teacher's professional status. Item (iii) had suggested that the teacher was vulnerable because he 'is subject to a variety of conflicting opinions as to how he should carry out his professional work'.

TABLE I RCP and RCE: percentage of high scores in the role vulnerability area[1]

		RCP	RCE
(87)	Men	45.9	25.3
(63)	Women	49.2	17.5
(83)	Teachers[2]	44.6	16.9
(67)	Teachers[3]	50.7	28.3
(69)	Secondary modern	63.7[5]	36.2[5]
(43)	Grammar	25.6	4.7
(69)	Secondary modern	63.7[4]	36.2[4]
(38)	Bilateral	42.1	15.8
(39)	Men secondary modern	64.1[5]	41.0[5]
(48)	Other men	31.2	12.5
(30)	Women secondary modern	63.3[4]	30.0[4]
(33)	Other women	36.4	6.1

[1] No significant differences were found between the scores of grammar and bilateral school teachers
[2] Less than ten years' experience
[3] More than ten years' experience
[4] Significant differences in χ^2 test beyond the 5 per cent level
[5] Significant differences in χ^2 test beyond the 1 per cent level

Item (iv) had suggested vulnerability in relation to professional status — 'The teacher is a professional practitioner but despite this is generally treated as if he were not.' Although inter-item correlation of scores was at an acceptable level, important qualitative differences in teacher reaction to these two suggested aspects of vulnerability were revealed during the interviews. For this reason, interview material for each item is presented separately.

Incompatible expectation

It can be argued that exposure to incompatible expectations for a role will not of itself create serious personal conflict for the role occupant, unless these expectations are accompanied by pressures to comply and by sanctions for non-compliance. Here an important distinction exists between the situations of the British and American teacher. While both may be subject to a variety of conflicting expectations for their role, the teacher in Britain, unlike his American counterpart, experiences very little pressure associated with these expectations. Consequently, he feels free to determine his own role concept and his own role behaviour in a situation of virtual autonomy.

This sense of freedom and autonomy emerged as the characteristic response of almost all the teachers interviewed:

Opinions there may well be, of differing complexities, but the teacher is the sole arbiter of how he decides to do his job in the classroom. (Man graduate: age forty-one: secondary modern)

We are very free of pressure — they leave us alone — we are really gorgeously free. (man graduate: age sixty-two: grammar)

I've done what I wanted to do — I've always had a completely free hand. (woman certificated: age forty-eight: bilateral)

References to 'complete independence' and being left to do the job as they thought it should be done, were frequent. Of the eighty teachers interviewed, only three complained of having been seriously troubled by pressure. These three cases involved clashes in expectations concerning how a subject should be taught and occurred between young teachers and older members of the profession. One involved conflict with a head teacher — the other two with heads of department.

Teachers with high scores on this item tended to regard conflict of incompatible expectations as affecting particularly the young teacher, who was seen to be in an especially vulnerable position:

This depends on the stage in one's career. The young teacher has a great problem here, bombarded in early days by all sorts of opinions. (man certificated: age forty-six: secondary modern)

For the young teacher, it can be hell. (man certificated:age fifty: secondary modern)

Despite these comments, a comparison of the scores of teachers in the twenty to twenty-nine age group with those of teachers in other age groups revealed no significant differences in role conflict experience. This raises the interesting possibility that older teachers who claimed this as a serious problem for the young teacher were reflecting their own early experience of more restrictive and authoritarian conditions.

Out of 150 teachers, only 28 scored high on personal experience of this conflict and of these, 23 taught in secondary modern schools. The basic reaction of these secondary modern teachers was one of irritation over the unwelcome flow of advice to teachers from various quarters and some took the view that head teachers and teachers were too amenable to the influence of these external agencies:

> Almost any magazine will tell parents how their children should be taught. The gutter press is keen on educating parents about their rights. Waves of fashionable thought are mediated through the HMIS. (woman graduate: age thirty: secondary modern)

> Everybody thinks they can teach. What annoys me is that some parents are full of advice — they think that they are the experts in teaching. (man certificated: age forty-one: secondary modern)

> Too much in education is decided by outside influences. Many heads want a good ordered school for the governors and a free activity school for the inspectors. Head teachers are at fault here — they are swept along by external forces. (man certificated: age fifty: second modern)

Despite these comments, there were hardly any examples of the classic conflicts of American teachers. One of the few examples occurred in the very specialized context of religion teaching in a Catholic School:

> There is more conflict in teaching religion than in any other subject. There are the views of the parents, the priests and the college lecturers. You try to do many things which conflict. You try to please the parents — to give the idea of religion which they want — but this clashes with the new ideas in religion. In using new approaches you may come into conflict with the priests or with other teachers of religion.

The role of the teacher of religion in Catholic schools in a time of rapid change in religious thinking seems likely to be exposed to the type of conflict mentioned here but it represents an exceptional case in the present inquiry.

Because conflicting expectations for the teacher's role exist in Britain without associated pressure, it was possible for some teachers to regard this situation as a stimulus rather than a problem. As one teacher put it: 'this is an aspect of the job which adds to its interest.'

It was clear therefore that exposure to incompatible expectations was not a serious problem or role conflict situation for the teachers. While incompatible expectations for the role were *seen* to exist, virtually no pressure to comply with these expectations was felt. The teachers gloried in their freedom of action and this sense of autonomy gave them considerable satisfaction. Those who had high scores were in nearly every case expressing generalized irritation about the unwelcome number of opinions, rather than concern over pressure. There was no evidence that young teachers felt significantly more vulnerable than other teachers, although older teachers 'recollected' that it had been a problem. Some teachers, far from being irritated or troubled by a variety of expectations, saw this as a positive stimulus to discussion and to clarification of their own ideas about the teacher's role.

Professional status

Item (iv) had suggested conflict between the teacher's professional self-concept and the way in which he was actually treated. Seventy-one of the 150 teachers in the sample saw this conflict as a problem of high importance, but schedule II revealed that of these only thirty-one had personally experienced such conflict to any degree. Twenty of these taught in secondary modern schools.

The great majority of teachers had not been personally troubled by feelings of conflict and vulnerability over their professional status. This 'non-vulnerable' group were composed of many heterogeneous elements and of many different orientations.

Professional confidence

Grammar school teachers felt confident of their professional position and they had virtually no experience of having been regarded or treated in other than a professional way. Some of them, who felt that there was a problem in other sectors of the education system, suggested that lack of confidence among teachers was the basic reason for it:

Professionalism is about confidence — it's up to the teachers. (man graduate: age sixty-two: grammar)

If you are unsure of yourself — you are likely to feel that you are not treated as other professional classes. If you are confident you don't notice it. It may depend on a person's background and training. (man graduate: age thirty-six: grammar)

The importance of professional confidence in this area was reiterated by teachers in other types of school. Some felt confident because their own professional preparation was longer than the usual period and for some, professional confidence was related to teaching a particular subject:

Teachers do not behave as if they felt professional — they lack a really professional confidence in their own judgement — perhaps this is because of a lack of a sufficient level of education. (man certificated: age fifty-six: secondary modern)

A longer Scottish professional training has given me a sense of confidence. (woman certificated: age forty-nine: secondary modern)

The maths teacher is in a stronger position. In other subjects which are less precise — the teacher may be regarded with less status — but not in maths. Maths has helped my professional status. This position has been improved by modern maths — the parents find it a mystery! (man certificated: age thirty-six: secondary modern)

The non-aspirant

A frequent theme during the interviews was that there was too much concern about 'professionalism' in teaching, that individuals got the due they were worth and that the really important thing was the satisfaction to be obtained from the work. Such replies were however more characteristic of women than of men:

> People get what they ask for — some teachers are responsible for their own bad image. I've never expected much in the professional field — teachers expect too much. (woman certificated: age forty-eight: bilateral)

> The important thing is self-satisfaction — whether I've done a good job in the class. I'm unconcerned about whether I'm regarded as equivalent to a shop keeper or a doctor by outsiders. (woman graduate: age thirty-seven: bilateral)

> I've no highfalutin' ideas of my own importance. (woman certificated: age twenty-four: secondary modern)

> I never look upon teaching as a profession — I'm just a worker. Many teachers feel they are on a higher level than anyone else — the idea of a profession is too high flown. (man certificated: age fifty-six: secondary modern)

It can be seen then that the factors of type of school, type and length of training, teaching subject and orientation to professionalism were important in explaining the responses of those teachers who felt little vulnerability on this issue.

Aspects of vulnerability

Among those who saw an important conflict related to professional status, or who had personally experienced such conflict, there was a tendency to answer in general rather than specific terms.

There were relatively few references to teachers having been treated unprofessionally by head teachers, inspectors or the local education authority. The remark by one teacher, that 'we are the last ones consulted in educational change — the system is run by laymen', did *not* represent a generally expressed sense of grievance. Similarly, although there were some pungent references to the role of the head teacher — 'Heads too often treat staff as children' — these again were not representative of the majority.

It was clear from the interviews that the majority of teachers felt that they were both regarded and treated by their head teachers as professional persons, particularly in connection with their expertise in various subject fields. Problems and conflicts of professional status were attributed in the main to attitudes of the general public, particularly in the Midlands, and to a general decline in the status of the teacher as a result of social and economic change.

The local context and social change

Graham Turner in *The Car Makers* noted the effect which midland affluence was having on some class attitudes - 'We feel sorry for school teachers,' remarked a leading official of one of Coventry's largest trade unions. 'Our people have been earning their £30 a week for a long time.'

As he pointed out, 'The old professional pillars of the community are regarded with pity, not awe.' This attitude had been encountered and resented by some teachers, particularly those who had experience of other areas where they believed teachers were regarded with greater respect:

> A lot depends on the area. In the Midlands, teachers are regarded as of little significance - 'the people who look after the kids' - whereas in Wales, teachers are looked up to as important in the community. The teacher there is a really telling force in the school and town. There is so much money here that education is not important. (woman graduate: age thirty: secondary modern)

In general, teachers in Wales, Scotland, Ireland, the home counties and the west country were seen as enjoying higher status and respect than the teacher in the English Midlands!

In addition to specifically local factors, the view was frequently expressed that the status of the teacher was declining as the result of increased numbers in the profession and the growth in the size of communities. Teachers were seen to be 'so to speak, two a penny' and there were nostalgic references to the position of respect thought to have been enjoyed in the past by village and small town schoolmasters.

Subject specialism

Mathematics teachers felt that their main subject specialism helped their professional status — others felt that their subject and their teaching role was undervalued and marginal. Teachers of woodwork, commercial and technical studies, domestic science, physical education and art mentioned problems and conflicts arising from marginality. For some, these were role conflicts of immediate experience and as such they resulted in spirited comment. For others, the conflicts were in the main of past experience and they took the view that the situation was improving:

> A very sore point is the lack of professional regard from colleagues. The practical teachers are regarded as practical helpers, not teachers. We are used as a service department. The caretaking staff look on us as an adjunct to their function.

> The attitude to craft teachers is changing for the better. There are better standards now — less drawing on industry and the use of more college trained men. Many staff remember being taught by the local carpenter — it will still take a generation to change attitudes completely.

> Sometimes I'm made to feel that my particular subject is less 'professional' than others. This was particularly true in the past — the attitude of *only* commercial subjects. The position is much better now — commerce is accepted — but the position can still be styled 'instructor' rather than teacher.

> I get the feeling that heads are not sympathetic to PE — a bit of a time filler — get rid of some surplus energy to concentrate

on the real work. This is more so for girls than for boys. It is very irritating to have one's subject regarded in this way.

In the sample as a whole, there were forty-two teachers of what may be called 'practical and creative arts'.[2] The fact that twenty-two scored high on perceived role conflict related to professional status, while twenty scored low, suggests a good deal of inter-school variation in this area. The attitude of colleagues was obviously important as was also the attitude of the head teacher. Clearly some head teachers were careful to make all their staff feel that their role activities were significant, while in other schools, a particular academic or examination orientation caused certain teachers to feel that their activity was less significant. Reaction to this situation was expressed particularly forcefully by two art teachers:

> The teacher of the fine arts in this country is at a disadvantage. Culturally, we are a literary oriented society rather than a visual one.
> The head should be aware of the role of art in the curriculum but nevertheless heads are wholly ignorant of the role of art. They have no understanding of its function educationally. Generally we are always regarded as the odd men out — regarded as eccentric. No claims made by us are taken seriously.

> Art in schools is treated as a 'C' stream lesson — it is treated as a Cinderella. The heads says 'I'll give you the "C" streams because they can do art.'
> I'm very keen on freedom in the art room but since the caretaker is the power this causes conflict. One spot of clay on the floor and there's trouble.

Musgrove and Taylor (1969, p.70) have suggested that subjects 'have become highly organized social systems with heavily defended boundaries'. They have suggested also that a secondary school teacher's self-concept is very much bound up with his subject. Such an identification with the main teaching subject was generally apparent throughout this study and while in some cases this provided a sense of security for the teacher, in other cases it resulted in a sense of vulnerability and conflict.

Bureaucracy

A good deal of attention in sociology has focused upon the role conflicts of professionals in bureaucratic organizations. Within the school situation, the professional orientation of a teacher may conflict with bureaucratic requirements in two main areas — in the specialized activity of teaching within the classroom (or resource area) and in the formulation and execution of general school policy. It has already been shown that the teachers experienced hardly any conflict in the first area — their professional autonomy was virtually complete. Boyan (1969, p. 203) has argued that schools exhibit much more 'structural looseness' than is usual in bureaucratic organizations and this serves to preserve the teacher's autonomy. This was the case here.

Very little conflict was apparent also in matters relating to general school policy. A few teachers had strong feelings on this: 'In schools there is a hierarchy — decisions are made without consultation with all the professionals. The hierarchy in education as a whole ignores the teacher in the classroom,' but for the majority there was no evidence of serious conflict between professional expectations and bureaucratic procedures. Most teachers seemed satisfied with the degree of professional consultation and shared decision making in their schools. There was an impression (it can only be stated tentatively) that many staff were prepared to accept quite readily the head teacher's policy in general matters provided their autonomy in the classroom was untouched. Where a policy, such as non-streaming, had direct implications for the classroom, attitudes changed.

Some of the teachers showed explicitly an approach which Corwin (1965) has distinguished as characteristic of an 'employee' role rather than a professional role:

> I feel that I am employed by the head and I do feel that he has the ultimate say, although as a good employer he has a responsibility to ask the opinions of those who have to carry out the policy.
> I am not angry about lack of participation because I have the feeling of an employee — I tend to accept things without too much fuss.
> I've always tried, if it was possible, to carry out the wishes of authority — probably because I'm a member of the older generation.

The absence of serious conflict over general school policies and bureaucratic procedures was clear. The reasons for this absence included the relatively small size of the schools, the amount of participation practised in some of them and the orientation of the teachers to questions of wider professional involvement.

Summary

In general, conflict arising from a sense of role vulnerability was to be found in its clearest form among secondary modern teachers. Basically, this conflict reflected marked differences in the teacher's evaluation of his role and profession and those of the general public with whom he interacted. Graduate teachers within such schools felt themselves to be less vulnerable in this respect and the indications are that the certificate in education as a professional qualification exposes its holders to a feeling of role vulnerability.

The importance of a secondary school teacher's main specialism was also apparent as a factor in vulnerability and there was evidence that in some schools marginal status was still a reality for teachers of certain subjects.

There was virtually no evidence however that teachers in any type of school felt vulnerable or in conflict about pressure exerted upon them, lack of professional treatment or bureaucratic constraints. Above all, a sense of autonomy emerged as being the most prized possession of the British school teacher, the enjoyment of which prevented serious experience of role conflict in this area.

Notes

[1] These were defined as: honesty, truthfulness, Christian morality, respect for persons and property, thrift and the 'work ethic'.

[2] Practical and creative arts: art, music, woodwork/metalwork, technical/commercial studies, domestic science/needlework, physical education.

References

BOYAN, N.J., 1969, 'The emergent role of the teacher in the authority structure of the school' in Carver, F. and Sergiovanni, T. (eds), *Organizations and Human Behaviour*. New York: McGraw-Hill.

GETZELS, J. and GUBA, E., 1955, 'The structure of roles and role conflict in the teaching situation', *Journal of Educational Sociology*, 29(1).

MUSGROVE, F. and TAYLOR, P.H., 1969, *Society and the Teacher's Role*. London: Routledge and Kegan Paul.

TAYLOR, P.H., 1968, 'Teachers' role conflicts - II: English infant and junior schools'. *International Journal of Educational Sciences*, 2(3).

WILSON, B.R., 1962, 'The teacher's role: a sociological analysis', *British Journal of Sociology*, 13(1).

G BERNBAUM

Headmasters and schools: some preliminary findings * [1]

The recent development of educational administration as a distinct field of study associated with the sociology of education has been accompanied by a growing concern with the nature of leadership in educational settings and particularly with the role of the headmaster. Frequently, however, observations on the nature of the headmaster's task are characterized by general statements relating to the increased complexity of educational organizations associated with their increase in size, and also by diffuse references to changes occurring in the wider society which, according to the observers, make certain designated traditional leadership styles inappropriate. Thus, Taylor has argued recently that

> It is no longer so easy for the head to be in close personal contact with his staff and pupils, to be able to claim that he knows everyone in the school. . . . The skills involved in co-ordinating the work of several department and house units, in interpreting the school to the community in which it serves, in initiating innovation and encouraging others to innovate, all become of greater importance; the head must add managerial skills to his existing commitment to educational objectives and the needs of children.[2]

In a similar fashion a correspondent to *The Times Educational Supplement*[3] has suggested that

> The traditional view of his [the headmaster's] job needs reconsideration. It has been assumed in the past that a teacher with academic qualifications and the right sort of personality could become a head, and that he picked up the administrative side of his work as he went along. The assumption was reasonably correct while the management function of a head was reasonably straightforward and could be undertaken by a well-educated man who had no special training for his role as a manager. The reasons why we can no longer take this view are
>
> 1 The increasing size of schools and their complexity of organization
> 2 The expectations we have for big schools have increased

---

*Reprinted from Bernbaum, G., 'Headmasters and schools: some preliminary findings', The Sociological Review, *21(3), (August 1973)*, by kind permission of the author and publishers.*

3 The world is changing
4 Management techniques can be applied to many sorts of organizations other than business firms
5 The realization that a newly appointed head is moving from one kind of job to a new and different one.

The managerial function of a head is becoming more important. Management by objectives and a conscious style of management are essential in any school.

The point about such statements is that they are at least as much pre-scriptive as descriptive and consequently do not contribute to a socio-logical analysis of the headmaster's role. The purpose of this article, therefore, is to present some preliminary findings relating to the social origins, educational experience and work experience of headmasters in the three major categories of secondary schools, grammar, comprehen-sive and secondary modern. Later publications will consider the relation-ships between the variables to be outlined here and self-perceptions of role in respect of the different categories of headmasters.

The inquiry was conducted by means of a small sample of depth interviews, and a mailed questionnaire sent to a large sample of secondary school headmasters. Forty depth interviews were conducted. Each interview lasted between one and a half and two hours, was taperecorded and then typed in full. The material collected through the interviews has served, in the first instance, as qualitative data. Quotations from the interviews have been used in the analysis to provide a sense of richness and detail impossible to obtain in any other way. Secondly, the interpretation of the interviews served, along with perspectives developed from other similar studies, as a foundation upon which the questionnaire was designed.

The interviews were conducted amongst headmasters in the East Midlands, and all the interviews took place in the respective offices of the headmasters. Not one of the headmasters objected to the interview being taperecorded, though a few made 'off the record' comments during interview.[4] The sample for interview was drawn from the East Midlands at the convenience of the researcher. Following the completion of the interviews the questionnaire was designed and then piloted amongst those headmasters who had been interviewed. After modifications had been made the questionnaire was distributed to a large national sample of the members of the Headmasters' Association.

The choice of the sample highlighted certain problems associated with this kind of research. Headmasters are, in general, reluctant to become exposed to the research methods of the social sciences. More-over, they tend to define themselves as overworked and especially overburdened by requests from investigators and the returns made necessary by the demands of the local authorities and the Department of Education and Science. From many sources the view was expressed that a low response rate would be likely if the mailed distribution of the lengthy questionnaire was not supported by other approaches. It was decided, therefore, to seek the co-operation of the Headmasters' Association, one of the leading professional associations for headmasters of maintained secondary schools. Two significant consequences, however, followed from this decision. Firstly, the investigation was conducted only amongst members of that association and therefore does not include headmasters who belong to the National Association of Head Teachers, nor does it include headmasters who do not belong to an organization exclusively for headmasters. There is a sense, however, in which this is not a major problem, as the Headmasters' Association includes amongst its members the headmasters of almost all the maintained grammar schools in the country, and over half the heads of comprehensive schools. Its membership is only seriously deficient amongst the headmasters of secondary modern schools, and it must be allowed, therefore, that those secondary modern school heads who are members and who are included in this survey are possibly 'special'.

In order that the nature of the project could be explained to the potential respondents it was further decided not to work with the full list of members but to concentrate attention on five geographical regions corresponding to five out of the eighteen administrative divisions of the Headmasters' Association. In this way it was possible to publicize the research project rather than relying on an unannounced mailed questionnaire. The members of each of the five divisions had the project explained to them at one of their termly meetings and each division agreed, by a majority vote, to receive the questionnaire. It should be emphasized that this approach did not mean that only 'tame' headmasters were being investigated, for there was no guarantee of co-operation from individual members. The final response rate however was good; 415 questionnaires were sent to all the headmasters in the five selected divisions[5] and 315 usable replies were received, representing a response rate of 75.9 per cent. Three of the replies were from headmasters of technical schools and for the purposes of the major analysis these responses have been omitted.

Leaving aside the difficulties already described of the sample coming only from amongst members of the Headmasters' Association, the main question remains about the degree of representativeness of the sample in relation to the association as a whole. The geographical regions represented were — Division I, London; Division VII, Dorset, Hampshire, Isle of Wight, Channel Islands and Wiltshire; Division XIII, Cheshire, Lancashire and Isle of Man; Division XIV, Durham, Northumberland and the West Riding of Yorkshire; Division XVI, Lincolnshire. There is, therefore, a full range of urban and rural regions in England as Divisions XIII and XIV include the schools in the conurbations of Lancashire and the north-east. Table 1 shows the type of schools in the sample in relation to their overall membership of the Headmasters' Association.

TABLE I

	Sample	Membership
Technical	3	37
* Grammar	190	968
** Comprehensive	77	350
Modern	45	283

*includes direct grant and bilateral schools
**includes all types of comprehensive schools

The responses, therefore, can be said to be reasonably representative of the membership of the Headmasters' Association, and the high response rate seems to have justified the slightly unusual way of drawing the sample.

One of the main purposes of the inquiry was to examine the origins and previous experiences of the headmasters. Thus information has been gathered relating to the occupations of the headmasters' fathers, to the school and university experience of the headmasters and their formal and informal professional preparation. In the following discussion the data is presented in relation to the whole sample and then, where appropriate, differences between the different categories of headmasters are considered.

In the first instance it is useful to examine the headmasters in terms of their fathers' occupations. Though difficulties arise[6] in making a comparative study involving occupational classifications, it was decided to use the Registrar-General's Occupational Classification and to deal individually with the occasional difficulties of categorization and to ignore the more permanent problem arising from the fact that the occupations being classified relate to some time past. Table II shows the social class origins of the 315 headmasters in the sample as indicated by the major lifetime occupations of their fathers.

TABLE II   Headmasters and social class

		%	
Social Class I	16	6	Professional and Administrative
II	109	35 ⎱	Intermediate
III	95	30 ⎰	
IV	73	22 ⎱	Manual
V	22	7 ⎰	

These figures do not seem especially remarkable in relation to other data available on graduates and the teaching profession. Though strict comparisons are extremely difficult to make, Floud and Scott[7] found that the social origins of male teachers in different types of school in the period in which the respondents in the present study would have entered the profession, to be those shown in Table III.

TABLE III   Social origins of male teachers in three types of schools, entering the profession at various times

%	Elementary			Technical			Grammar		
Period of entry	Prof.& Admin.	Inter.	Man-ual	Prof.& Admin.	Inter.	Man-ual	Prof.& Admin.	Inter.	Man-ual
1930-9	3.9	45.9	50.2	5.8	49.8	44.5	14.8	50.6	34.6
1940-4	8.7	38.5	52.9	32.4	35.1	32.4	9.0	72.4	18.5
1945-55	7.9	48.7	43.3	4.6	50.5	45.0	9.1	59.1	31.7

Floud and Scott also showed the distribution of teachers by social origin, in different types of school in 1955, and a summary of these results is presented in Table IV.

TABLE IV   Social origins of male teachers in grant-earning schools England and Wales 1955.

% Father's occupation when teacher left school	Primary	Modern	Technical	Grammar	Direct grant
Professional and Administrative	6.0	7.5	6.0	12.5	19.8
Intermediate	48.3	45.9	51.0	55.1	61.5
Manual	45.7	46.6	43.0	32.4	18.6

The comparison (Tables II, III, IV) of the social origins of headmasters with the data available on the origins of schoolmasters entering the profession at relevant times in the past and occupying positions in schools in 1955 does not suggest that headmasters are more likely to originate in the higher social classes than the male teaching profession as a whole. Allowing for the difficulties of making comparisons over time, there is the clear suggestion that the distribution of the social origins of headmasters in the sample is remarkably similar to that amongst the part of the male teaching profession from which the head-masters in the present sample will have come — the secondary sector.

The most notable feature of the comparison of data is the apparent under-representation amongst the headmasters of men originating in the administrative and professional groups, in relation to their numbers in grammar school teaching particularly.   One explanation for this might be, as some American evidence[8] suggests, that high status entrants into the teaching profession have lower aspirations than those who enter from the working class. Alternatively, the explanation for the under-representation of social class I amongst the sample of headmasters might be seen in terms of the structure of the English educational system and the ideologies which surround it. Accepting Turner's[9] concept of 'sponsorship' as characterizing the English educational system, particularly in that period when the headmasters in the present sample would have been receiving their education, then it could be argued that men, originating from the working class, who graduate at a British university and then become secondary school teachers, represent the ideal products of a 'sponsorship' system. It should be noted that throughout the period during which the headmasters in the study would have been at university the proportion of graduates of working class origins emerging from the universities has been around 25 per cent.[10] If, furthermore, the argument[11] is accepted that able working class graduates are likely to choose schoolteaching as a career then it is, perhaps, not remarkable that 29 per cent of the present sample of heads should have originated in the working class.

There are, however, some slight but interesting differences in the social origins of headmasters of different types of schools, these are shown in Table V.

TABLE V   Schools and social origins of headmasters

School/social class	I	II	III	IV	V
Grammar	13	66	59	43	9
Comprehensive	2	23	23	20	9
Secondary modern	1	20	12	9	3
					N=312

The figures show that 41 per cent of grammar school headmasters originate in social classes I and II compared with 32 per cent of the comprehensive school headmasters. Similarly, only 5 per cent of the grammar school heads had fathers who were unskilled manual workers, but 12 per cent of the comprehensive school heads have social class V origins, as do 26 per cent of the secondary modern school heads. These differences do not reach statistical significance, and can be explained not so much by any determination on the part of local authority officials to appoint heads of upper middle class origins to their grammar schools, as by the existence in secondary modern schools of a larger proportion of male teachers who originated in the working class than is the case in other types of secondary school (see Tables III and IV). As headmasters tend to have had experience of teaching in the type of school to which they later become appointed then it is to be expected that a higher proportion of secondary modern headmasters will originate in social class V. It should also be noted that some comprehensive schools have been formed by merging secondary modern schools, and by appointing one of the existing headmasters to the headship of the new school; such policies are likely to increase the number of headmasters of working class origins who are now represented amongst the comprehensive school heads.

The overall data suggests, therefore, that the social origins of headmasters generally reflects the distribution of social origins amongst the relevant sectors of the teaching profession as a whole. Thus, close examination of the present sample reveals that of the twenty-seven direct grant school headmasters in the sample, five originate in social class I, but the forty-five secondary modern school heads include only one whose origins are in the highest social class. Similarly, in contrast with only three of the twenty-seven direct grant school headmasters, twelve out of the forty-five secondary modern school heads come from the working class. These figures are as might be expected from the evidence of Floud and Scott, which is set out in Tables III and IV; the teachers in direct grant schools are more likely to come from social class I than those in secondary modern schools, and, in the main, the teachers in the particular types of schools can be regarded as the 'pool' from which the headmasters will be drawn.

Thus, whilst the data relating to the social origins of headmasters provides much that is worthy of comment it is nevertheless clear that social class origins is not an especially powerful variable with which to differentiate headmasters of different types of school. Despite the extremes, as illustrated in the comparison between secondary modern and direct grant school headmasters, the differences do not reach statistical significance, and this is the position in respect of the differences between the headmasters of grammar schools and those of comprehensive schools which are the two largest categories in the sample. If, therefore, social class is an inadequate variable with which to distinguish headmasters from the teaching profession as a whole, or to distinguish headmasters of different types of schools, then attention is focused upon other factors, notably the educational experience and the professional socialization of the headmasters in the study.

Table VI shows clearly that the largest single group of headmasters of all types of schools were educated at grammar schools. Nevertheless, amongst the grammar school headmasters 42 out of 190 (22 per cent) had been educated at direct grant schools, and a further 34 (18 per cent) at independent schools. Thus 40 per cent of the grammar school headmasters have been educated at the relatively few independent and direct grant schools.

TABLE VI   Schools and types of school attended

Headmaster of/school attended	Direct grant	Independent	Grammar
Grammar	42	34	114
Comprehensive	11	7	59
Secondary modern	3	1	41
			N=312

In comparison, the school background of the comprehensive and secondary modern school headmaster is very different. Of the seventy-seven comprehensive school headmasters in the sample only eleven (14 per cent had been educated at a direct grant school, and just seven (9 per cent) at an independent school. Only one of the forty-five secondary modern school headmasters had been to an independent school.

Table VII shows that the differences between the headmasters of grammar and comprehensive schools in respect of their own schooling are statistically significant.

TABLE VII   Schools and type of school attended

Headmaster of/school attended	Direct grant	Independent	Grammar
Grammar	42	34	114
Comprehensive	11	7	59

$$x^2 = 6.689, \text{d.f. } 2, p<.05$$

It is, of course, difficult to be certain why the headmasters of grammar schools are much more likely to have been educated at the high status direct grant and independent schools than their comprehensive school counterparts. It is possible, however, that attendance at a certain type of school is the beginning of a process of professional socialization which becomes defined as important as the person concerned enters a career in schoolteaching. The process will lead, on the one hand, to those who experience it developing orientations and self-perceptions which eventually lead to a headship, and, on the other hand, becoming regarded by those who select heads as potential headmasters. In the context of this argument it should be noted that the independent and direct grant schools which such a large proportion of the heads, and grammar school heads had attended might be said to represent most powerfully the values traditionally associated with the headmaster's role.[12] Such associations will be of especial importance as they are part of the visible qualities which the potential headmaster takes to his first appointment. Visible qualities of this kind are likely to be seen as being of great significance since the characteristics of personality normally said to be required for the job are, in fact, extremely difficult to inspect and assess prior to the actual performance of the task. Under these circumstances, therefore, the generalized educational experience of teachers is likely to be a strong determinant of the self-concepts which they hold, and also, of the judgements formed by others.

The argument can be developed further by an inspection of Tables VIII and IX which show the sample in terms of the type of university attended. As can be seen 129 (38 per cent) went to university at either Oxford or Cambridge. For the grammar school heads, however, the proportion rises to 52 per cent. By comparison, only 26 (34 per cent) of the comprehensive school headmasters had been to an ancient university, and as few as 9 per cent of the secondary modern school headmasters.

TABLE VIII   Headmasters and university attended

Oxford or Cambridge	129
London	68
Large civic*	47
Other	68
	N=312

*Birmingham, Sheffield, Manchester, Leeds, Liverpool, Bristol

TABLE IX   School headship and university attended

Headmaster of/ university attended	Oxbridge	London	Large civic	Other
Grammar	99	31	23	37
Comprehensive	26	22	12	17
Secondary modern	4	15	12	14

$$x^2 = 30.618, \text{d.f.} = 6, p<.001$$

Table IX shows that the different university experiences of the headmasters of different types of school are statistically significant. It is possible, of course, that the high rate of Oxbridge experience is associated with earlier attendance at a direct grant or independent school, as the opportunity to enter Oxford or Cambridge from these schools has been much greater than from other types of schools, especially at the time when the present sample would have been making the transfer from school to university. Equally, however, it is likely that attendance at an ancient university is an important factor in the process by which headmasters are both selected and self-selected. Undergraduate experience at Oxford and Cambridge is, like attendance at a certain type of school, an objective measure which can readily be taken as an index of immeasurable personal qualities, particularly of those which are linked to the historical development of the headmaster's role through the fact that virtually all the late nineteenth and early twentieth century headmasters were graduates of Oxford or Cambridge.

The force of the influence of university attended and the associated self-concepts on the possibility of self-rejection was evocatively recalled at interview by one grammar school headmaster:

When I was at school or just after school at university and coming out of university, I'd never in my wildest dreams envisaged being a head because a headmaster to me at school seemed to be a being so remote that it was absolutely unthinkable that I would be able to contemplate getting well enough qualified or having qualified. I mean I was at the University of Exeter and I thought all heads came from Oxford and Cambridge, and I thought if you didn't talk with a fancy accent you knew you would stand no chance. I'm a Cornishman and I'm conscious of my Cornish accent, I would have thought they didn't take anybody.

A further category by which the headmasters can be distinguished is the subject which they read for their first degree. Tables X and XI give details of the main subjects which headmasters studied at university.

TABLE X   Headmasters and subject of first degree

	Arts	225
*	Science	87
	Social science	0

*including Mathematics

TABLE XI   School headship and subject of first degree

	Arts	Science
Grammar	139	51
Comprehensive	52	25
Secondary modern	34	11
$x^2 = 1.582$ d.f. 2 not significant		

The figures show the dominance of the arts graduates amongst headmasters. Two hundred and twenty-five (71 per cent) of the headmasters are arts graduates, whereas only 87 (29 per cent) have science degrees. Since there is no evidence that heads who have arts degrees have significantly better classes of degree than those with science qualifications, the preponderance of arts graduates requires some explanation. It is possible, of course, that there are more arts graduates to choose from than science graduates. Such evidence as is available, however, does not suggest that arts graduates dominate the teaching profession as a whole to the extent that they do the ranks of the headmaster. Thus, in 1950, when most of the headmasters in the present sample would have already entered the teaching profession, the number of male science graduates teaching in all maintained schools was 7,828, and the number of arts graduates was 9,559. The figures for grammar schools only were 4,151 science graduates and 5,479 arts graduates.[13] Even recognizing the fact that both sets of figures do not allow for a large group of teachers where the degree subject is 'not known' in the official statistics, there is nothing to suggest that, at a relevant (1950) point of time, there were two and a half times as many arts graduates as science graduates teaching in schools, which now turns out to be the ratio of arts trained headmasters to science trained headmasters.

The explanation for the greater number of arts graduates who become headmasters is best offered in terms of the characteristics possessed by arts graduates, as compared with those who graduate in science, and the different tasks which they come to take up in the school organization. It is likely that in studying and teaching the subjects which represent and explore human values the arts graduates will have more opportunity to display, or even acquire, those personal qualities which are seen to be so important to becoming a headmaster. Science teachers, on the other hand, might be less 'people oriented' and conceive of the job essentially in terms of their subject.[14] Consequently, they may not display characteristics associated with leadership roles, or even personal manipulation, in relation to the school as a whole. Moreover, such differences between arts and science graduates have been reinforced over the last twenty years by the shortage of science teachers. The inadequate supply of science teachers has meant that science graduates have found it relatively easier to obtain special responsibility allowances and headships of departments without being called upon to accept pastoral, extracurricular or administrative responsibilities within the school. Conversely, arts graduates in schools are likely to be expected to involve themselves with such work in order that extra allowances can be paid to them. In the long run, however, the careers of arts graduates might benefit, as experience and commitment above and beyond the formal teaching role is usually looked for in potential headmasters. Thus, at interview, the headmasters were asked what advice they would give to a young man currently on their staff who had expressed the desire to become a headmaster. The reply from one grammar school head typifies the general quality of the answers:

> Well obviously he's got to take an interest in more than just his own subject, and it certainly doesn't do any harm to volunteer for lots of activities around the school. Obviously he ought to take a fair interest in house matters and I always think the best way to get to know the boys, of course, is to go off with them on Saturday — cricket team or rowing — this tends to help one to become a headmaster.

Tables X and XI offer a slight suggestion that the proportion of comprehensive school headmasters who are science graduates is greater than the proportion of science trained grammar school headmasters. Nevertheless, the differences do not reach statistical significance. It can be presumed, finally, that the complete absence of social science graduates from the headmaster's study can be explained by the very small number of such graduates at a time when the present generation of headmasters would have left university.

The headmasters' degrees can also be examined in terms of the class awarded. Tables XII and XIII show the headmasters in terms of their first degrees.

TABLE XII   Headmasters and class of degree

I	61
II i	155
II ii	54
III	24
IV	0
Pass	18

TABLE XIII   Headship of school and class of first degree

	I	IIi	IIii	III, IV, Pass
Grammar	53	100	22	15
Comprehensive	6	38	20	13
Secondary modern	2	17	12	14

$$x^2 = 47.072 \quad \text{d.f. } 6 \quad p < .001$$

Altogether it is clear that, measured in terms of first degree, the head-masters have better academic qualifications than the graduate teaching profession as a whole, and also, that their class of degrees is significantly better than the distribution of awards from British universities as shown by the Robbins[15] inquiry. Thus, Robbins showed that the highest proportion of first class honours degrees was in the field of applied science and technology, where 10 per cent of the candidates were awarded firsts. In the arts subjects, in which most of the headmasters have graduated, the proportion of firsts was 2.5 per cent. Table XII shows however, that of the present sample almost 20 per cent have first class honours degrees. Moreover, in the early 1960s when reliable figures first made available, just over 7 per cent of male graduates teaching in maintained secondary and direct grant schools had first class honours degrees.

It should be noted, however, that amongst grammar school head-masters possession of a first class honours degree is especially important. Fifty-three (36 per cent) out of 190 grammar school heads in the sample have such degrees, which compares with 9 per cent of the comprehensive school heads, and 4 per cent of those in secondary modern schools. The differences in class of degree between the heads of the different types of schools are statistically significant. Similarly, the data shows that failure to obtain a good honours degree, as conventionally defined, is likely to be a barrier to promotion to a headship. Only forty-two (13 per cent) of the heads in the sample did not have a good honours degree, whereas in the early 1960s, 47 per cent of graduate males teaching in maintained secondary and direct grant schools did not have good honours degrees.

Class of degree, therefore, is an important factor in a teacher obtaining a headship, and is especially significant for those aiming to become heads of grammar schools. As with school and university attended it can be looked upon as a measure of qualities which apparently defy direct assessment. A first class honours degree, therefore, can come to be regarded, especially by appointing committees to grammar school headships, as a mark of those values, a certain excellence and industry which the men who have general responsibility for the school believe to be its main purpose. In this way the first class honours degree can come to be regarded as a mark of the general personality and character of the applicants for headships.

In this context, the statistically patterned differences between the academic qualifications of the heads of different types of schools require further comment. The evidence shows clearly that, measured in terms of first degree, the grammar school headmasters are significantly better qualified than the heads of comprehensive schools. Partly this can be explained by the fact that some comprehensive schools have been formed by the merging of secondary modern schools, and the appointment of one of the existing headmasters to the newly established school. As has been shown in Table XIII the heads of secondary modern schools are less well qualified than other categories of secondary school heads, and this will account for at least some of the comprehensive school headmasters being less well qualified than their grammar school counterparts. Equally, however, it is possible that attainment of high academic qualifications leads teachers to be placed in working situations which provide the opportunities to attain the indices seen to be relevant to promotion to a headship. Thus, the academic qualifications of teachers in direct grant and independent schools are superior to those in maintained schools. A further factor explaining the relatively poorer class of degrees of the heads of comprehensive schools could be the ideologies relating to comprehensive education which may encourage those who appoint to headships to place more emphasis on other qualities of the candidates and less on academic excellence.[16] Further evidence which supports this argument can be gained by examining the position with respect to the headmasters' higher degrees. Eighty-three of the 312 have been awarded higher degrees but those who are heads of grammar schools have fifty-nine of these. Table XIV sets out the details in full.

TABLE XIV   Headship of school and possession of higher degree

	Higher degree	No higher degree
Grammar	59	131
Comprehensive	15	62
Secondary modern	9	36

$x^2 = 4.995$ d.f. 2   p lies between .05 and .10

Before leaving the area of the professional education of headmasters it is interesting to examine the extent to which they have been specifically trained as teachers. Of the 312 in the sample 102 do not possess the graduate certificate of education or any historical equivalent. However, whereas only 25 per cent of the secondary modern school heads, and 22 per cent of the comprehensive school heads are not trained teachers, the proportion rises to 39 per cent for the grammar school headmasters. Table XV sets out the details of these statistically significant figures.

TABLE XV   Headship of school and experience of teacher training

	Trained	Not trained
Grammar	116	74
Comprehensive	60	17
Secondary modern	34	11

$x^2 = 8.831$ d.f. 2 $p < .02$

Thus, grammar school headmasters are much less likely to be trained teachers than their equivalents in comprehensive and secondary modern schools. Indeed, this is true of the teaching profession as a whole; of maintained schools, the grammar schools have the smallest proportion of trained teachers. Also, altogether the independent schools have the fewest trained teachers. It is not surprising that, of the present sample, the grammar school heads should include the smallest proportion of trained teachers. The evidence already suggests that they are more likely to possess what can come to be regarded as objective measures of prestige and high status — attendance at direct grant or independent schools, university education at Oxford or Cambridge, first class honours degree, a higher degree. It is not surprising, therefore, that professional teacher training with its low status elementary school origins and with its marginal position in universities should not be deemed as so essential in the grammar schools.

The argument that comprehensive heads and secondary modern school heads are more likely to have reached their position by climbing a professional career ladder during their work in the schools rather than by entering the profession with certain presumed marks of excellence can be developed further by examining the differences between the heads of the different types of schools in their work experience.

The differences in career lines are likely to relate to the point of arrival at the first headship. Tables XVI and XVII show the experience of schoolteaching which the headmasters had had before receiving their first headship.

TABLE XVI   Teaching experience before first headship

Less than 5 years	2	13-16 years	110
5-8 years	36	17-19 years	36
9-12 years	84	20+ years	44

The differences are especially clear when comparing the grammar and comprehensive school headmasters. Fifteen per cent of the grammar school heads had achieved their headship within nine years of beginning teaching, and 43 per cent by the end of twelve years. In contrast, the comprehensive school heads had to wait longer. Only 6 per cent had headships within nine years, and only 30 per cent by twelve years. At the other end of the time scale 35 per cent of the comprehensive school heads had to wait seventeen or more years for their first appointment, but only 24 per cent of the grammar school headmasters had such a lengthy experience.

TABLE XVII   Type of headship and years of teaching experience

	<9	9-12	13-16	17+
Grammar	28	53	64	45
Comprehensive	5	18	27	27
$x^2 = 6.279$	d.f. 3		p lies between .05 and .10	

Again, the data suggest that the comprehensive school heads are more likely to have lengthy teaching experience before being appointed to a headship than their grammar school counterparts. It is not unreasonable to emphasize how these two major categories of headmasters can be distinguished by the way in which, on the one hand, professional experience in schools, and, on the other, certain apparently independent measures of prestige within the educational system, seem to carry different weight in the career patterns.

Similarly, support for this view can be gained by seeing the differing proportions of the major types of headmasters who have also been deputy heads. Forty-seven per cent of the secondary modern school headmasters had previously worked as deputy heads, 40 per cent of the comprehensive school heads had had similar experience, but only 30 per cent of the grammar school heads had held this position.

TABLE XVIII   Headship and previous experience of deputy headships

	Deputy head	Not deputy head
Grammar	57	133
Comprehensive	31	46
Secondary modern	21	24

$x^2 = 5.2174$ d.f. 2   p lies between .05 and .10

Finally, when considering the experience of the headmasters it is helpful to examine the schools in which they taught as assistant masters before attaining a headship. The overall figures for this are shown in Table XIX. It should be noted that most headmasters have taught in more than one school.

TABLE XIX   Type of headship and school teaching experience

Headship/ experience	Independent	DG	Grammar	Sec. Mod.	Comp.	Others
Grammar	67	52	154	11	12	14
Comprehensive	21	17	68	33	38	25
Secondary modern	6	6	31	33	10	8

It is interesting to note that ninety-four of the heads had spent at least part of their teaching careers in independent schools. Of the 190 grammar school heads as many as 67 (31 per cent) had taught for some time in independent school, while even 28 per cent of the comprehensive school heads had had such experience. Recent figures show, however, that only 16 per cent of the male graduate teaching profession work in independent schools.[17] Though, over time, these figures are not strictly comparable there is, nevertheless, a suggestion that experience of teaching in an independent school is a relevant factor in obtaining a headship in the maintained sector.

It has been argued, therefore, that the social origins of headmasters are not a significant variable with which to distinguish heads from the teaching profession as a whole, nor to distinguish the heads of different types of schools. As with other studies of teachers it appears that the educational and professional socialization undergone by the headmasters is the important process which leads to differentiation. Overall, the data shows significant differences between the heads of the grammar and the other maintained secondary schools, the differences between the grammar and comprehensive school heads perhaps being of most contemporary interest. There are differences in relation to type of school attended, university attended, class of degree attained, possession of a higher degree, experience of teacher training, length of teaching experience, experience of deputy headship. The evidence supports the view that the grammar schools, which historically have embodied the nineteenth-century independent school traditions within the public sector of education, have headmasters who are more likely than their counterparts in other secondary schools to possess certain marks of high educational status which will lead them to be seen, and to see themselves, as having those generalized qualities which traditionally have come to be regarded as relevant to the task of being a headmaster. In contrast, though in no sense divorced from this tradition, comprehensive school headmasters are more likely to have worked their way to a headship over a longer period and had more of what might be termed a professional career.

It is important, however, to note that none of these descriptions necessarily tells anything of the performance, values and self-concepts of the heads. It remains, in later publications, to explore these kinds of differences in relation to a full range of variables.

Notes

[1] This work was undertaken with the help of a grant from the Social Science Research Council. I am pleased to acknowledge help and encouragement, also, from my colleagues at Leicester, especially Paul Croll and Tom Whiteside. Needless to say I accept full responsibility for the formulation of the paper.

[2] W. Taylor, *Heading for Change* (Harlech Television, 1970).

[3] *The Times Educational Supplement* (12 February 1971).

[4] It was notable that those who did this were also likely to offer information of a private kind which was not 'off the record'.

[5] The researcher selected the five Divisions from a list of ten in which it was known the regional officers would be approachable.

[6] For a full discussion of problems in this area see F. Bechhofer, 'Occupations' in M. Stacey (ed.), *Comparability in Social Research* (London, Heinemann, 1969).

[7] J. Floud and W. Scott, 'Recruitment to teaching in England and Wales', in A.H. Halsey, J. Floud and C.A. Anderson (eds.), *Education Economy and Society,* (Glencoe, Ill., The Free Press, 1961).

[8] J.L. Colombotos, *Sources of Professionalism: a study of high school*

teachers (US Office of Educational Co-operative Research, Project No. 3301, Ann Arbor, Department of Sociology, University of Michigan).

9 R.H. Turner, 'Modes of social ascent through education: sponsored and contest mobility', in A.H. Halsey, J. Floud and C.A. Anderson, (eds.), *Education, Economy and Society*. (Glencoe, Ill., The Free Press, 1961).

10 *Higher Education,* Report of the Robbins Committee (London, HMSO, 1963).

11 B. Jackson and D. Marsden, *Education and the Working Class* (London, Routledge and Kegan Paul, 1962).

12 For a fuller discussion see, G. Baron, 'Some aspects of the "headmaster tradition" ', in P.W. Musgrave (ed.), *Sociology, History and Education,* (London, Methuen, 1970), and G. Bernbaum, *The Headmasters,* forthcoming.

13 *Education 1900-50,* Ministry of Education (London, HMSO 1950).

14 F. Musgrove and P.H. Taylor, *Society and the Teacher's Role,* (London, Routledge and Kegan Paul, 1969).
G. Grace, *Role Conflict in the Teaching Situation,* unpublished M. Ed. thesis. (University of Leicester, 1970).

15 *Higher Education,* Report of the Robbins Committee (London, HMSO, 1963).

16 Consideration of the self-rated qualities of the headmasters of the different types of schools provides tangential support for this argument.

17 An estimated figure calculated from the data provided in the official *Statistics of Education* and G Kalton, *The Public Schools* (London, Longman, 1966).

ROY NASH

Camouflage in the classroom *

Group teaching in the non-streamed primary school is the normal and approved method in Britain. A recent study showed that almost 50 per cent of small junior schools grouped children for arithmetic and over a quarter for reading and English. The Plowden report, *Children and their Primary Schools,* advised that, in particular, teaching groups should be formed for 'children who have reached the same stages in reading and computation'. But the Plowden committee saw one major danger in this form of organization: 'Clear-cut streaming within a class can be more damaging to children than streaming within a school. Even from the infant school there still come too many stories of children streamed by the table they sit at, of "top tables" and "backward reader" tables.'

One can see the basis of the committee's concern. The fear is that the child whose achievements are poor will intuitively feel from this form of grouping that he is backward. And from this it may be that a self-fulfilling prophecy will begin to operate. Children who know they are *thought* poor at school *will be* poor at school.

The point was brought out again by *Streaming in the Primary School,* published last year. The National Foundation for Educational Research report said:

> The image a child has of himself appears to be based on his teacher's attitude, how well he can do his school work, and how he compares with his classmates in terms of his work standard, marks and even class position. *More* boys of below average ability in streamed schools had a good 'self-image' compared with a comparable group of boys in non-streamed schools, presumably because although they were likely to be in the lower ability stream, some of them could still be top or do the best work in their class: this being a much more unlikely feat for children in non-streamed classes.

Research here seems to have confirmed the obvious.

If children are taught in rather tightly streamed groups *within the classroom,* the effects on their feelings of self-worth are likely to be

*Reprinted from Roy Nash, New Society, 128 Long Acre, WC2, No. 447 (22 April 1971), pp.667-9, by kind permission of the author and publishers.

worse than the effects of streaming *between classes*. One of the devices by which teachers have tried to prevent children making this sort of self-identification has been to designate teaching groups with labels that don't imply rank — groups that are colours or animals rather than A, B, or C.

During a year spent observing teacher/pupil interactions in a non-streamed school, I became aware that children were not fooled by this camouflage. Teachers invariably referred to teaching groups by their nominal description. They rarely, if ever, gave class tests from which children could gain direct information about their position. And they marked only the first three places on the twice-yearly school reports. The children, though, still had a good knowledge of the relative abilities within their class.

I suspected, also, that the degree of 'within-class streaming' would influence the children's perceptions. Clearly, the greater the 'streaming' the more accurate the children's knowledge could be expected to be. I decided to test these loose hypotheses: (a) that children know very well what their position in the class is, and (b) the greater the degree of 'within-class streaming' the more accurate their perception of their positions will be.

Following the Plowden model, most teachers in this school (six of the eight studied) seated their pupils in groups of more or less mixed ability. All of them had separate groups for teaching reading, number and writing. Often there were other groups formed for whatever activities the teacher thought fit. It is important to realize that these were not seating groups. The only formal 'meetings' of these groups took place when a teacher gathered a particular group around her table for special instruction.

It is most interesting to compare the class in which a 'top' and a 'bottom' table were most obviously apparent, with the class in which they were least apparent. Class three (pupils aged eight) was clearly 'streamed by table'. Pupils were grouped for number, reading, English and writing. The degree of overlap between these groups is shown by Figure I (right).

The highest English and reading groups are composed of the same children. They all sit together at what may be fairly called the 'top' table. Three of them form the highest group for learning number. The situation is similar in the lowest ability groups. Of the seven children who sit together at the 'bottom' table, six are members of the lowest reading group. Furthermore, ten of the eleven pupils in the lowest reading group form the whole of the lowest English group.

Class eight (pupils aged eleven to eleven and a half) was very differently arranged (see Figure II). This teacher formed only two teaching groups (number and English) and ensured that these groups were not reflected in the teaching pattern. Figure II shows that although half of the eight children in the highest English group form half of the highest number group, they did not sit at the 'top' table. In fact, only half of the six children at this table are members of either the highest number group or the highest English group. In the lowest ability groups, a similar dispersion exists. Here the 'bottom'

Venn diagrams showing the degree of overlap between the teaching groups.

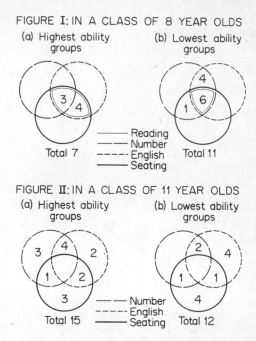

FIGURE I: IN A CLASS OF 8 YEAR OLDS

(a) Highest ability groups

(b) Lowest ability groups

3 / 4

4
1 6

——— Reading
— — Number
- - - - English
——— Seating

Total 7   Total 11

FIGURE II: IN A CLASS OF 11 YEAR OLDS

(a) Highest ability groups

(b) Lowest ability groups

3 4 2
1 2
3

2 4
1 1
4

— — Number
- - - - English
——— Seating

Total 15   Total 12

table contains only one pupil from each of the lowest number and English groups. Note also that two of the three children in the lowest number group are also members of the lowest English group.

As practised by this teacher, the group teaching method could hardly have been bettered. In spite of this, however, her pupils were still able to tell exactly which group was higher than another and which children were better or worse than they.

An extract from a taperecorded interview with four of the children helps to illustrate this:

RN: What groups are you in Jane?
J: The purple group, the red group and the yellow group.
RN: Take the purple group. What's that for?
J: Sitting.
RN: Ah, just by seats. What's the next one?
J: The red group's for sums.
RN: The red group's for sums. Now are any of you others in the same group as Jane?
J: Christine and Carole are in the red group and in the purple reading group.
RN: Carole and Christine are in the same group as you. And what group are you in then?

S: The purple group for sitting.
RN: And what sum group?
S: The green sum group.
RN: Is that a higher one or a lower one?
S: It's another one. She's . . . the red group's the top group.
RN: I see, you do easier sums do you?
S: Yes.
RN: Now what English group are you in?
S: The yellow.
RN: You're in the yellow English group. Who else here is in the yellow English group with you?
S: No one.
RN: So you're mainly in groups for sitting, for sums and. . . [all the children] for reading.
RN: What are the reading groups then?
S: Yellow, pink, green and blue.
RN: Now you can tell me about that Christine. Who's in the same group as you?
C: Jane and Carole.
RN: Again? So you're the same . . .
C: Us three are always in the same groups.
S: Except they're not in the same sitting.

It looks most confusing. But these girls knew just what groups there were, knew which were the higher and which the lower, and knew who was in each group. One of the implications of this struck me particularly strongly when a 6 year old remarked boastfully to me of a classmate: 'She's not so clever as me. I'm on book six.' Her friend was on book five and in a lower teaching group. It's a very simple piece of reasoning.

If book two is higher than book one, and it's true that children who read better are the cleverer — then when Joan is on book two and Susan is on book one, the conclusion must be that Joan is cleverer than Susan. Once children know which group is higher than another, the same is true of groups.

Joan knows she is cleverer than Susan — and so does Susan. Whatever else children may learn or fail to learn at school, they learn this — to measure themselves against their classmates. It is just possible for a child to leave school unable to read. But it is inconceivable that he should be unaware that this puts him at the bottom of the list. There is a sense, therefore, in which it can be said that schools teach hierarchical levels of personal worth more successfully than anything else. The child in school is in a position where the teacher and the other children all, by their relationships with him, place him in certain positions with respect to themselves and oblige him to take up certain roles. From these positions and roles he must build up his ideas of what he is. In such a manner is the schoolchild's self-image fashioned.

To establish precisely how accurate children's perceptions of their class positions were, I first of all got from each teacher the position of each child in her class on various abilities. I then took each child individually and asked him or her to point to the names written on cards arranged randomly on the desk before him — of the 'people who were a wee bit better than you at [say] reading'. From the number of children he placed before himself I was able to see what he saw as his class position. Finally, I then related this position with that given him by his teacher. The complete figures are given in the table below. The results corresponded more closely to my prediction than I had expected. Children as young as eight gave themselves positions which correlated most highly with those given them by their teacher.

Correlations between teachers' ranks on school subjects and pupils' own estimates of their positions

Age in years	Reading	Writing	Arithmetic	Totals	No.
8	0.69	0.44	0.64	0.85	28
10	0.31	0.20	0.45	0.46	30
11-11½	not applicable	0.47	0:80	0.82	33

Let us be quite clear about what was happening. The teacher's rankings were made at my request and were not communicated to her pupils. In theory, children should have had no idea of their position, and indeed had I asked children directly to tell me their positions I may have got very strange answers. But, in my roundabout way, I tested three classes, asking each child to indicate which of his classmates were better than he at reading, at writing and at arithmetic.

As a result of this it is reasonable to ask if the attempt to disguise from children their class positions is worthwhile. It seems a pointless mystification to call teaching groups by colours or animals when children are, in fact, aware of their real status. Certainly, the technique is not enough to prevent children gaining knowledge about the relative abilities within the class. It is more than interesting to see that, although pupils from all classes were good at this exercise, the 'streamed' 8 year olds were generally better than the two older 'non-streamed' classes. Perhaps one should not make too much of this. The ages of the children are not comparable and three classes is a small sample, Nevertheless, these results seem worth following up.

Robert Rosenthal reported, in *Pygmalion in the Classroom,* the findings of a study in which it was shown that people want to have their expectancies fulfilled, so much so that they will prefer bad news to good, if it is bad news that they expect, Perhaps children, even those with low positions, expect these positions to be confirmed and so may even learn to *prefer* these positions?

If so, then my research results have some interesting implications. The assumption that children strive to maintain their relative status within the class for the sake of personal consistency makes some sense. Can it be that the position you know is better than the position you don't? Once children have firmly accepted their positions, with respect to their classmates, perhaps they not only do not attempt to alter it but adapt their learning responses to keep it constant. Experiments by the psychologist, S.E. Asch, have demonstrated the power of group pressure to alter considerably even the perception of visual stimuli.

These experiments in which people were shown lines, the lengths of which they had to guess — in company with stooges who *all* lied about their guesses, may have some relevance to the classroom problem I am concerned with. Most of Asch's subjects went along with the stooges' (highly inaccurate) guesses.

Certainly, a child who believes he is somewhere in the middle of the class, but not as clever as Tommy, Sarah, Johnny and the rest of their group, will probably not strive to outshine them. Similarly, if he also believes that he is not as slow as Freddy, Joan, Billy and their group he will probably try hard to keep above them. Sociologists have described a similar mechanism operating between the 'respectable' and the 'rough' sections within working class society. The 'respectables' do all that they can *not* to be associated with the 'roughs' who, in their turn, are not keen to be associated with their 'respectable' neighbours whom they typically regard as 'stuck-up'.

Each group maintains its position by investing divergent cultural habits with a ritual significance to denote its separateness from the other group. So children in the classroom may use their knowledge of their relative abilities in ways which maintain their status.

References

BOURI, J., and BARKER LUNN, J., 1969, *Too small to stream.* NFER.
BARKER LUNN, J., 1970, *Streaming in the Primary School.* NFER.
'PLOWDEN REPORT', 1967, Central Advisory Council for Education, *Children and their Primary Schools.*HMSO.
ROSENTHAL, R. and JACOBSON, L., 1968, *Pygmalion in the Classroom.* Holt, Rinehart and Winston.

PHILIP E D ROBINSON

An ethnography of classrooms *

The problem for sociology addressed in this essay is the problem of 'knowing' school classrooms. Even to state the problem thus is to beg the question, what is it to know? It is not my intention to pursue the task of repeated definition which can only end in a tautology, therefore the problem faced is to reach an understanding of classrooms which is relevant both to the teachers and pupils who work there and relevant to sociologists trying to get some purchase on the process at work within classrooms. This essay has both plot and subplot. The main intent is to examine some of the various activities which count as research in classrooms. The research discussed falls into four groups; interaction analysis as developed by Flanders and Amidon; the attempt of Smith to follow Glaser and Strauss's prescription to discover grounded theory; the descriptive anthropologies of King and Wolcott; and finally that research inspired to different degrees by the phenomenological philosophy of Alfred Schutz. The subplot is a concern with the level of understanding possible in sociological inquiry. To what extent is an objective sociology possible without incurring the charges of reification, or reductionism? Clearly any statement made about classrooms has an objectivity; the task facing the social scientist, the point where his work goes beyond the 'objectivity' of the novelist or journalist, is that he must make explicit the grounds upon which his objectivity is based, must point out the inferential chain leading to his 'account'. The weakness of much of the research discussed in this essay is that the grounds of interpretation are not given, or if given have a spurious objectivity based on the correspondence between evidence and the appropriate number system being used, the validity of the number system, its isomorphism to the 'real world', remaining unquestioned.

This essay then is a discussion of the methodology of classroom research; throughout is the counsel that the researcher enter a public debate with himself in an attempt to elicit the basis of his own perception. Similarly in presenting this account the bias of the writer should be made apparent. The statements made, critical or not, are the product of my own training as a social scientist. Briefly this

*This paper is published for the first time in this collection. The author wishes to thank John Eggleston, University of Keele, Brian Davies, University of London, and Derek Blease, Loughborough College of Technology, for their comments on an earlier draft of this paper.

bias is towards a scepticism with quantitative methods, a belief that the constant search after the methodology of the natural sciences has produced some sophisticated and elegant statistical techniques but has done little to enhance man's understanding of man. This is not to say that numerical techniques haven't a use; the frequency of an event, the magnitude of a category may help in understanding the complexity of human existence, but this is secondary to the patient observation of the sympathetic observer rigorously analysing his own presuppositions, his 'findings', his interpretations, and constantly rechecking his account of the world with that of its members.

Discussion of research in classrooms has tended to be within a psychometric paradigm[1] − that is, the data of interaction, whether this be teacher talk, gesture or movement, or more rarely pupil talk, gesture or movement, are taken as fundamentally non-problematically open to measurement by existing instruments. Simon and Boyer (1968 and 1970) list seventy-nine such instruments[2] in their fourteen-volume review of the field, and the NFER's recent contribution in this country (Chanan 1973) shows the strong influence this approach has had. Reviews of classroom studies, by Biddle 1967, Sindell 1969 and Bealing 1973 reflect the strength of the tradition of 'interaction analysis' while sounding the caution that unless some linking under-pinning theoretical structure is articulated we are in danger of sinking under the vast accumulation of coding grids.

While work in this tradition is not uncritical about the assumptions of its methodology, too often the criticism is given as an aside, or expressed in the form of an insuperable problem beyond the scope of present research. For instance, in noting the tendency of research into student teaching to be 'based on scores obtained from attitude or personality tests, or subjective assessment by supervisors'[3] Wragg implies doubt as to the isomorphism between marks on paper and the human behaviour that the marks are alleged to represent. Deutscher (1966) illustrates the tenuous nature of the inferences made from written responses to attitude scales and similar instruments to actual beha-viour. He quotes LaPiere who suggests, 'Quantitative measure-ments are quantitatively accurate; qualitative evaluations are always subject to the errors of human judgement. Yet it would seem far more worthwhile to make a shrewd guess regarding that which is essential than to accurately measure that which is likely to prove quite irrelevant.'[4] Wragg seems to feel unease in his position but in the end appears to prefer the 'certainty' of number systems rather than face the conse-quences which his doubts suggest.

Criticism of the psychometric paradigm can be levelled at both a fundamental and at a substantive level. The former questions the basis upon which knowledge is generated while the latter questions the cover which the various techniques adopted give to the field. At the fundamental level there is a tendency for the research to be self-validating in terms of the categories used, that is, any procedure for coding the 'real world' into particular boxes reveals as much information about the boxes used as it does about the phenomenon so coded; one sees what the measuring instrument allows one to see. The pre-existence of coding categories results in closure rather than openness to the field. Rather than being open to alternative explanations, in recognition of the tentative nature of all accounts, energy is invested in improving the 'fit' between the data and the categories which have been developed. In the type of interaction grid proposed by Flanders[5] there is a disregard for the situation in which the interaction is placed; Walker (1972) provides an apt illustration. He says 'If the teacher asks one child, "What are you doing?" when all the other children are playing an audience role, and it is clear that what the child should be doing is listening, it has quite different meaning from the same question, asked of the same child during a science experiment when each child is engaged in his own task.'[6] Flanders could argue that the observer would code the first '7' (Teacher talk direct influence) while the second would be coded '4' (Teacher talk indirect influence). The point is that the reader has no evidence to educe the procedures the observer is using, to elicit the coding rules which are operational in placing the same talk in different categories. Walker's own work on classroom observation using stop-frame cinematography with synchronized sound goes a long way towards capturing the data from which inferences can be drawn and which can be continually rechecked against the 'raw data.'[7] While interaction schedules are not sensitive to the spatial setting neither are they sensitive to the temporal setting of the interaction. Each point in each contact is a part of the unique biographical experience of the members. As such the meaning of the act to the participants may not be immediately apparent to the observer, who has more to do with the members' project at hand or the particular face which is being negotiated. Any research in classrooms is in danger of committing the 'mechanistic fallacy',[8] that is of ignoring man's subjectivity, of creating an artificial framework of action which is neither related to man's intent nor gives any indication of the gap between researched and researcher's accounts.

While the above criticism questions the dominant approach to classrooms at a fundamental level, that is, questions the basis upon which knowledge is generated, the various coding systems can be criticized at a substantive level. Even if one accepted the validity of constructing tight observation schedules, one is still faced with a problem of reliability, for what does the schedule cover? The focus tends to be on teacher talk rather than on pupil talk, and where the latter is admissible it tends to be only in terms of teacher talk. Too often pupil/pupil talk is reduced to a residual category of 'everything else the observer can't place on the existing schedule'. There is also an insensitivity to the fact that a teacher is still on public display even when having a 'private' conversation with a pupil. In commenting on teacher failure to adopt the learning theory developed by behaviourist psychologists Philip Jackson writes, 'Like the researcher, the teacher also works with individual subjects from time to time but even during such moments (and they are much less frequent than the educator's talk of individualized instruction would have us believe) he is usually mindful of the

presence of others and adapts his behaviour accordingly.'[9] The stage
whisper of 'private conversation' can influence the behaviour of many
without appearing on an interaction schedule. The schedules seem
biased towards a particular whole-class pedagogy: 'As far as we could
tell very few of the major research studies had made extensive observations in informal classroom contexts.'[10]

The advantages of such approaches to classrooms seem to lie in the
ease with which research is facilitated. An instrument is constructed
but the process of its construction tends only to be examined in terms
of its validity to existing numerical systems, the ease with which it can
be adapted to a computer programme. The efficiency of the instrument
is seen in the economy of its exclusive categories which tend to increase
inter-coder reliability rather than reflect the complex reality constantly
negotiated in classrooms.

While building up criticism of much existing interaction analysis one
is also creating standards against which any alternative approach may be
judged. I intend to develop the arguments used so far to discuss alternative approaches to classrooms which are labelled micro-ethnographic,
anthropological, sociographic and ethnographic. I shall use the last as
the generic title for these approaches. The common theme of ethnographic studies is the stance taken to theory. Rather than developing
a priori theoretical statements for which empirical validation is sought
in the 'real world', this approach adopts an appositional relationship
to the world so that 'facts' are seen as the product of the interrelationship between the researcher and the researched. Denzin suggests that
'The act of observation must be seen interactionally . . . until investigators realize this and begin systematically to study the social features
of their own conduct few methodological advances will be forthcoming'.[11]
In Argyris's terms[12] the research act needs to be seen as a system of
negotiation between the researcher and the subject. The discussion of
grounded theory by Glaser and Strauss (1968) illuminates some of the
problems and characteristics of the ethnographic approach. They
advocate the comparative analysis of data (by which is meant simply
the observation of the phenomena under question in more than one
setting) as the appropriate methodology for 'generation'. Their aim is
to generate categories, and explanations of the relationship between
categories, from the field rather than entering the research situation
with a clearly defined set of categories for which validation is sought.
This approach has been adopted with effect by Smith and his colleagues
(with Geoffrey 1968, with Pohland 1969 and with J.A. Brock). Basically Smith attempts to overcome the limitations of 'observer-as-
participant' and 'participant-as-observer' research positions by using
both in an open, ongoing relationship with emergent data. In his study
of Geoffrey's classroom in 1968 Smith entered into a research partnership with him which was novel at the time. Geoffrey was the teacher/
researcher, Smith being the observer/researcher. This approach is
beginning to be further explored. For instance Shipman[13] sees the
changing role of the professional researcher in the Inner London
Educational Authority to be that of consultant to teacher-based
research. Bartholomew[14] argues for 'research' to be taken back to the

'researched' instead of being used as the currency of the academic market. However, the dual research role has been criticized by Radin.[15] A student of Boas, Radin was critical of the way Boas dominated research styles in ethnography, and he consciously tried to separate his own thinking from the master rather than fall into the consensus of Boas's school. Geoffrey was one of Smith's exceptionally able students and though there is a refreshingly self-critical look at methodology in the book there is no attempt to try and explicate the effects of membership of the same 'epistemic community'.[16] How much does Geoffrey reflect the research spectacles of his teacher and share a predilection for similar theory? In the last analysis the categories which they generated are researcher categories not teacher categories. Their substantive theory is at the level of professional psychology. The achievement of Smith and Geoffrey lies in the extent to which they make their interpretation of data explicit and present substantial extracts from their field notes to facilitate discussion of their argument. The authors discuss the different 'realities' in research. The observer in the field is facing one reality. The field notes on which he operates are another, often becoming paramount. The unwritten recollections of the investigator represent a third. As Schutz has argued,[17] often in social interaction the 'meaning' of an event at a point in time only becomes clear when it is reinterpreted in the light of subsequent events. The recollections are not of the past as it was but of the past seen through the filter of the present which is itself changing in terms of projects for the future. Thus no research account is ever final but always the 'present' frozen at the point of writing.

By 'substantive theory' Glazer and Strauss mean theory developed for an empirical area of inquiry such as teacher/pupil relationships or organizational constraints, and by 'formal theory' that developed for a conceptual area of sociological inquiry such as social control, or socialization. Two major problems seem unresolved in their discussion. Firstly, the word 'for' raises a major difficulty. Theory is conceived as emerging, as arising *from* the data of everyday life, therefore it may not be *for* social control or organizational constraints, notions which themselves presuppose a theoretical model in existence prior to the data. Secondly the concept of 'data' itself is not without problems. What in classroom research are to count as data, at what level is the analysis to operate? Glaser and Strauss make the assumption that data exist independently of their perception. They write, 'to be sure one goes out and studies an area with a particular sociological perspective, and with a focus, a general question or problem in mind.' Again Smith and Geoffrey meet the problem, they make explicit their organizing perspective: Smith (1970) notes, 'In some broad ultimate sense we find that we are still behaviourists.'[18]

When Glaser and Strauss face their own problem they enter into circumlocution. Relevance to the researcher's area of concern is seen as the major guideline to the generation of categories, but what is not explicated is the basis of relevance and the process whereby this is to be linked to generation. The maxim which is recommended is that emergent theory should guide conceptualization, a maxim which could be labelled the serendipity principle without any designation as to the basis of choice. Glaser and Strauss ignore the basic assumptions which underpin their generation of theory, the role of the guiding perspective , the relationship between this and previously developed theoretical categories, and the fitting in of data to emergent theory.

The stance adopted in this essay is that the processes by which members organize their activities of everyday life are the basic phenomena. The sociologist as 'researcher' is included in this so that 'doing research' is equally part of the analysis. 'The observer is very likely to draw upon his own past experiences as a common-sense actor *and* scientific research-er to decide the character of the observed action scene. The context of our interpretations will thus be based upon 'logic-in-use' and 'recon-structed logic' and therefore include elements of common-sense typifi-cations and theorizing.'[19]

The task facing this sort of ethnographic approach is to try and get at how members develop 'interpretative procedures' for the evaluation of the surface rules of action; in other words, how do members — teachers, pupils, researcher — come to formulate their particular social structure of the classroom.

> The interpretative procedures provide for a common scheme of interpretation that enables members to assign contextual relevance; norms and values are invoked to justify a course of action, 'find' the relevance of a course of action, enable the members to choose among particulars for constructing an interpretation others can agree to or an interpretation designed to satisfy the imputed interests or demands of others.[20]

The sociologist is also in the process of developing interpretative proce-dures, a process which is as yet still at the level of initial strategies rather than in the form of explicit theory.

A search through the literature suggests what essentially seem to be two related strategies for 'getting at' members' interpretative procedures. The first argues that the sociologist learn the vocabulary, the dictionary, of the members in recognition of the situational specificity in which the meaning of words is both formed and sustained.

> The interests of ethnomethodological research are directed to provide, through detailed analysis, that accountable phenomena are through and through practical accomplishments. We shall speak of 'the work' of that accomplishment in order to gain the emphasis for it of an ongoing course of action. The work is done as assemblages of practices whereby speakers in the situated particulars of speech mean something different from what they say in just so many words, that is, of glossing practices.[22]

In classroom terms, what is the meaning of phrases which are in common use like 'work hard', 'normal child', 'child-centred', 'good teacher'? What are the shared meanings necessary to normal behaviour whch are implicit in the use of these words? At a surface level 'work hard' may mean a child completing a piece of work which the teacher has decided is appropriate to a child of his type. Reality is managed on the assumption of a reciprocity of perspective — that you will see the situation as I do for all practical purposes should you be in my position. This management implies that the definition of working hard used by the teacher is in fact shared by the child. What is in fact assumed may be highlighted by the use of the second strategy, that of 'anthropological strangeness' in order to tease out the principles whereby members make 'accounts' to each other. Quoting Garfinkel again, this strategy provides 'that interpretation be conducted whilst holding a position of "official neutrality" towards the *belief* that the objects of the world are as they appear'.

Throughout his lifelong study of the Winnebago Indians of Wisconsin, Radin maintained a healthy scepticism towards the methodological procedures he adopted. His prescription was for long-term observation grounded in the lives of specific individuals. He argued that only after this could one begin to reach an understanding of the member's world view from his position. Radin was conscious that each interaction takes place both within the micro context of individual biography and the macro context of the historical setting of the location of action, understanding being born in perceiving the relationship between each. The weakness of many ethnographic accounts is that they tend to focus at only one level. Work influenced by the perspective of phenomenological philosophy focuses on the level of member's procedures. Much descriptive anthropology for instance, such as that of Wylie, Singleton and King, focuses at the level of the location of action. Radin adds an important third level, that of the researcher himself: 'Our ideal may very well be to secure all the possible facts, but every investigator soon realizes that the facts he is likely to secure depend, to a marked degree, not merely upon his competences, his knowledge, and his interests but to a factor frequently overlooked, his personality.'[23] In developing 'anthropological strangeness' Radin recommends a historical attitude to unique individuals, to the unique setting of action and, possibly most important, to the researcher's own history. Research accounts can never be more than provisional, a temporally dependent presentation of findings constantly open to reinterpretation in the face of new information and new understanding. Horton summarizes the relevance of anthropological studies in general to sociology by arguing that it is the potential of pre-literate belief systems to provide insights into the categories used in Western society. 'Because it prevents one from taking anything for granted, an unfamiliar idea can help to show up all sorts of puzzles and problems inherent in an intellectual process which normally seems puzzle free.[24] This is to suggest that a major problem facing the sociologist looking at any aspect of his own society is that he inevitably shares part of the perspective of those he studies, a sharing which might desensitize him to the necessity of accounts and impede the stance of anthropological strangeness. This realization prompted Becker to write:

We may have understated a little the difficulty of observing contemporary classrooms. It is not just the survey method of educational testing or any of those things that keeps people from seeing what is going on. I think instead, that it is first and

foremost a matter of it all being so familiar that it becomes
almost impossible to single out events that occur in the classrooms as things that have occurred, even when they happen
right in front of you. I have not had the experience of observing
in elementary and high school classrooms myself, but I have
in college classrooms and it takes a tremendous effort of will
and imagination to stop seeing only the things that are conventionally 'there' to be seen.[25]

Increasingly sociologists are beginning to see language not as a common
backdrop to interaction but as an integral part of the world to be
explained. Language both structures the world and allows for the world
to be structured. In using language a member is both acceding to his
cultural setting and exercising some control over that setting. How the
social structure of the classroom is produced, maintained and transformed through language becomes a central research problem. The
socially situated meaning of words becomes a topic of inquiry. The
meaning of the words used by the teacher resides not so much in any
universal dictionary as in the particular dictionary operant in the inter-
actional setting. Walker and Adelman provide several examples from
their own research of the embeddedness of talk, for example a joking
situation:

Green is giggling and whispering to another boy.

T. Come on Green. Get on with it — or we'll have to see what
you're wearing won't we? (laughter)

Walker and Adelman fill in the background to the joke as follows:

Joke 6 has a longer history — when we asked the teacher about it
he said that when he first taught the class, when they were in their
first year, some of them used to giggle a lot. To control this he
would say, 'I know what your trouble is — you've still got your
woolly pants on, haven't you?' Over the course of four years this
phrase had become restricted and incorporated into the shared
private culture of the class.[26]

The indexicality of this particular classroom talk is related to its classroom setting. Other talk is indexical to the school, yet other to the
local community, and at each level its exploration is part of the
researcher's task.

Given the requirements of constructing a dictionary of everyday
terms and of remaining 'anthropologically strange' towards the world
of the classroom, some form of participant observation would seem
to be the most appropriate research procedure.

In other words the researcher needs to participate as fully as possible
in the world of the classroom, learning its language and attempting to
understand the negotiations taking place. Bruyn[27] provides a critical
account of the requirements and implications of the role of participant
observer. Sharing the life, action and sentiments of people in face-to-
face relationships presents problems of negotiation for the researcher.
How does he define himself in relation to the ongoing activity in which

he will participate and how does this identity reciprocate back on his own self-definition? How does he avoid the danger of over-involvement with certain groups with the possible consequence of overrepresenting their perspective in his eventual report? An even more subtle problem highlighted by Schwartz and Schwartz[28] is that of 'reinterpretation'. This occurs when the account is written up and the meaning given to an event as it occurred is subsumed in the wider perspective of subsequent events. Schutz argues[29] that often in social interaction the meaning of an event at a point in time only becomes clear when it is reinterpreted in the light of subsequent events. The impossibility of writing up everything the moment it occurs means that to counteract a potentially distorting reinterpretation of an event the sociologist constantly checks his account with those of the actors involved. The advantage of the photographic/sound techniques being developed by Walker and Adelman would seem to be in preserving a larger 'bit of action' to which the researcher can return in later explications of his thesis. A further problem, as Becker points out,[30] in the role of the participant observer lies in the tension between the requirements of the initial problem, the orientating perspective, and its reformulation during the actual period of observation. 'The first thing we note about participant observation research is that analysis is carried out sequentially, important parts of the analysis being made whilst the researcher is still gathering his data.' The concepts which are initially conceived can be no more than sensitizing concepts suggestive of the hypothesized relationships between the data; as such they can be discarded should more powerful concepts emerge as the researcher's understanding of the world in which he is a participant member increases. Interpretative frameworks are always tentative, are always at the stage of being preliminary rather than final statements of the field, but will grow in strength as the researcher's reflexive involvement with the group increases. Becker writes, 'Any social group, to the extent that it is a distinctive unit, will have to some degree a culture differing from that of other groups, a somewhat different set of common understandings around which action is organized; and these differences will find expression in a language whose nuances are peculiar to that group and fully understood only by its members.' Participant observation itself involves several techniques some of which may anticipate the symbols which are possibly important in reaching an understanding of the world of classrooms. Denzin[31] suggests that participant observation involves the collection and analysis of documents, interviewing people with different perspectives, particularly those with 'key' information, as well as direct participation in the activities of the group.

Having discussed some of the methodological issues related to an ethnographic approach to classrooms I want to conclude this essay by discussing some of the existing research which loosely falls within the 'ethnographic' tradition. The purpose of this discussion is to highlight some of the points already under consideration by placing them within the context of specific research situations. I shall first consider some studies which present an account of school life but which give little indication as to how that account was presented (an example of uncritical case study techniques), and then look at some research which does try to present the material from which inference is made.

King in *The School at Mopass* describes a residential school for ındian children in the Yukon Territory of north-west Canada. Though this is essentially a descriptive study King does try to explain the low commitment of children to the 'school game' by introducing a theory of 'marginality'. Basically the school is seen as marginal to the life world of its pupils, and as making little concession to the idigenous culture. The teachers are also marginal men on the periphery of the educational system, seen as not being 'normally' preoccupied with the career pattern of the public school teacher. King argues that insecurity stemming from the marginal position results in the teachers adopting a rigid pedagogy and curriculum involving, in Bernstein's terms, strong classification and strong framing. King's theoretical speculation is interesting but seems to have been arrived at while the book was in the process of being written — in other words there is no way of validating his ideas through the account which he presents. Singleton's study of the Nichu Middle School in Japan has a similar weakness. Singleton's focus is not so much on the classroom but on the school seen as an arena of negotiation for several pressure groups. Again one has to take the picture on trust. His description is a still rather than a moving photograph. The transference from one to the other, the interpretation of dynamics, is not possible from the data which is provided. Wolcott is particularly sensitive to the 'rough handling' by anthropologists of the data of schools,[32] an insensitivity which he sees as the result of a lack of fieldwork, unitary conceptions of the school, and ideological bias either against schools or against groups within the school — be these parents, teachers, pupils or administrative staff. His own study of Blackfish School, a local school for the Kwakiutl Indians of British Columbia, tries to overcome some of these problems. He tries to capture the different 'Blackfish Schools' by using a variety of research techniques; as well as being a participant observer (he taught in the school for a year) he does a content analysis of children's writing. 'The older pupils were asked to write their recollections of previous teachers. I had hoped to identify prevailing attitudes towards all teachers in their accounts. Instead recollections tended to be of specific incidents, usually of especially pleasant occasions or of occasions of particular strife between pupils and the teacher.'(p.97)   It is not possible from Wolcott's account to examine the situation in which the children presented their essays. Here is a need to adopt Radin's historical humanism and ground the research in the life world of particular individuals. On p.99 Wolcott writes, 'The actual behaviour accorded me by the pupils is another source of data on pupil attitudes towards the teacher, albeit a more subjective source than their written comments.' However, we are given no indication of the rationale underpinning his selection of comments. Wolcott is presenting an account of himself as a teacher in the comments he uses, but what audience has he in mind? His study goes further than King and Singleton in allowing the process of interpretation to be examined,

yet doubts centre on the amount of information that it was possible
for him to attain in a year and his failure to state the preliminary nature
of his research.

A consequence of the 'new directions in sociology of education'[33] is
a shift in research strategy of many away from the explorations of the
input/output of the educational system characteristic of the research
of the late fifties and early sixties towards the case study approach
discussed in this essay. The phenomenological philosophy of Alfred
Schutz has infused much of the research in this field, research which
is still too often in the form of higher degree dissertations and therefore not widely known. Most easily accessible is Keddie's 'Classroom
knowledge',[34] an exploration into the process of categorization in a
comprehensive school through a consideration of 'two aspects of
classroom knowledge: what knowledge teachers have of pupils, and
what counts as knowledge to be made available and evaluated in the
classroom'. (p.133) The substantive study is too well known to require
repeating though one or two comments need to be made on the study in
relation to the discussion in this essay. Keddie has presented an account
of the differentiation process as it works in a school. As she writes in
her original study,[35] 'The crucial problem is the question of the frame
that I, as observer, used to select from ongoing events what I would
record, and having recorded how I have made further selections from
that material.' The responsibility to the methodology selected is that
the researcher tells much more about herself than Keddie succeeds in
doing. What model of the child does she hold, what pedagogy, what
counts as 'ability' for her? In other words there is the necessity for
making explicit the interpretative framework the researcher holds as
he enters the research situation. If, as has been argued, research accounts
are the product of the interrelationship between the researcher and
the researched, then the account must contain information about the
intellectual stance of the former. While going much further than
Wolcott in presenting evidence on which interpretation is based, Keddie
still doesn't give enough information about the *process* of selecting
the evidence used.

Keddie makes an early attempt to get at the interpretative procedures
used by members in their everyday world, an attempt which later
studies have built on. Beck[36] conducted a non-participant observation
study of the techniques of transference into a secondary school.

> My procedure involved initially basing myself in a single tutor group
> (a group of thirty children and 'a complete mixture of ability')
> observing these children coming together with their tutor for
> registration at the beginning and end of each day, and following
> pupils from this group into school and home assemblies and into
> their various lessons. . . . During classroom observation, I normally
> made use of at least one tape recorder to supplement my own
> observation, and field notes.[37]

From the various recordings made during lessons he prepared an edited
tape which was played back to pupils in an interview situation as the

basis for discussion, an attempt to get members' responses to his initial data. However Beck sees as a general deficiency of his study the lack, overall, of such an 'interpretative check'; of getting members' responses to his analysis. There are other problems; he wants to invoke structural factors without generating a theory of social structure. In discussing 'anxiety' he analytically differentiates between anxiety resulting from children's experience of uncertainty, strangeness and anonymity resulting from exposure in the new school to what are seen as its less stable qualities — for example bells, movement, different teachers etc. — and that stemming from the different expectations of different teachers. Nowhere in the study is an indication given of the magnitude of the problem. We are not clearly told whether none, few, many or all of the children fall into one or other of these categories. It would be interesting even to compare different teacher assessments of the magnitude of the 'anxiety' problem as well as getting their interpretations of 'anxiety'. Not only is there doubt as to the size of the problem but discussion is presented with the school seen in isolation. What are the effects of parental pressures, expectations; community pressures; an anticipatory socialization within the primary school? Sindell notes the frustration in Smith and Geoffrey's work in that they rarely relate the behaviour in school to anything outside the school or classroom, while Beck's study breeds a similar frustration.

In a study of an infant classroom Green[37] attempts the methodological self-criticism, the provision of an interpretative framework for his own explanation, and an account of social structure which it has been argued are variously absent from the studies already discussed. Green spells out the dimensions of his report as '(a) to present a description of the teacher's consciousness of her own actions as a teacher in the classroom context, (b) to situate these perspectives within the immediate structural problematics encountered by her in the classroom, and (c) to partially situate her consciousness and actions in the classroom within the wider context of the structure of staff relations and school ideology'. In looking at members' negotiation of everyday life he is cognizant of both the material and political setting in which the negotiation takes place; immediately the model of man as a freewheeling creator of his world is tempered somewhat in recognition of the constraints, the lack of manoeuvrability in any negotiation. Thus Green is critical of many phenomenologically inspired explanations in that they 'stress the shared nature, or commonality of meanings and underplay the explanation of actions in terms of power and control, with the social structuring of the opportunities to act. . . . They therefore underplay the need to explain and invoke features of social situations external to and impinging upon the actors, of which they may or may not be falsely conscious.' (page 13) He extends Keddie's distinction between 'educationist' and 'teacher contexts' and offers a threefold model — of theoretical practice, substantive practice and the interpretation of the situation in which the first two interact — in which analysis of the teacher is presented. In exploration of this relationship he remains conscious that the 'work is exploratory, having the aim of generating interesting, and possibly useful, sociological constructs, particularly with regard to offering more sophisticated situating of social action than is usual in hermeneutic researches.' (p.24)

In research of this kind – that of Green, Beck and Keddie, as well as that of Smith and Wolcott – to talk of 'findings' is to misconstrue the nature of the research. It is not the intention at this stage to develop propositions which have been verified – C.W. Mills[38] has warned of the sociologist 'who would love to wear white coats with an I.B.M. symbol of some sort on the breast pocket', who would only succeed in building an impressive edifice of trivia. The call in this essay is for an understanding of classrooms as they are to the children, teachers and parents for whom they are a very pressing reality. This understanding is not tapped by a questionnaire, elicited by an hour's interview or captured on a sociometric chart, but may be reached through the persistent observation and shared analysis of the 'events' as they happen. This is not to say that the questionnaire, interview schedule or sociometric test have no uses; they have, but should be supplementary to observation. Observation is not a simple journey armed with the most sophisticated tape recorder, or even video tape, into the back of the nation's classrooms. There is a danger in fact that this 'journey' could become 'educational research', with the proliferation of as many 'glib' findings as are 'discovered' by the ubiquitous questionnaire. The challenge to sociologists is to build up case studies of classrooms, where the stance of 'anthropological strangeness' has sensitized one to the taken-for-granted assumptions which sustain members' views of the world; where the analysis of language has been used to illustrate the embeddedness of language, the situational specificity of its meaning; and where the researcher's own self-analysis has illuminated the particular bias which his account has reflected. It is not the intention at this stage to develop propositions which have been verified, but it is the intent to build self-critical case studies of the classroom and related worlds. Given the existence of such studies, it may be possible in the future to generate theoretical statements which have a wider application than to the study in which they were born. Too much research in education has been characterized as being in pursuit of researcher rather than teacher problems (that research might even focus on children's problems is something hardly to be mentioned!). Cane and Schroeder's study, *The Teacher and Research*, indicates an official awareness from the NFER of the irrelevance of much research in education, but then the study falls into its own trap by asking teachers to comment on a list of research areas which has itself been drawn up by researchers. The first plea then is to bring research back to the researched. The second is for more ethnographic research, more long-term case studies of classrooms and schools. If these are met then possibly we will be in a position to generate theoretical statements having a wider applicability than the local classroom. As well as being 'irrelevant', too much research in education is conceptually empty, taking the form of a series of predictions built from a mathematical framework. In Leacock's terms, 'A great many "field trips" are needed in a wide variety of schools, and with a variety of focuses, to yield the descriptive data necessary for posing generalizations about formal schooling and its results.'[39]

Notes

[1] See G.M. Esland in Young (1971), p.88
[2] It depends on how you count; Wragg (1973), p.90 finds ninety-two instruments!
[3] Wragg (1973), p.88
[4] Lapiere (1934), p.237
[5] Flanders 1970.
[6] Walker (1972), p.33
[7] See Walker and Adelman 1972.
[8] Douglas (1970), p. 196
[9] Jackson (1968), p.161
[10] Walker and Adelman note that the only possible exception is J.S. Kounin, *Discipline and Group Management in Classrooms* (New York, Holt, Rinehart and Winston 1970). Also see B. Simon, *The Nature of Classroom Learning in Primary Schools, Final Report of SSRC Project*, HR 291 (1972).
[11] Denzin (1970), p. 369
[12] Argyris 1968.
[13] M.D. Shipman, quoted in the *Guardian* (3 July 1973).
[14] *Hard Cheese*, 1973 (available from T. Bowden, 95A Shooters Hill Road, London SE3 8RL).
[15] Radin 1933.
[16] For a discussion of 'epistemic community' see B. Holzner, *Reality Construction in Society* (Cambridge, Mass., Schenkman, 1968) p.60.
[17] Schutz 1967.
[18] Smith 1970
[18] Cicourel (1973), p.32. The reference to 'logics-in-use' and 'reconstructed logics' is to A. Kaplan, *The Conduct of Inquiry* (San Francisco, Chandler, 1964).
[20] Cicourel (1973), p. 72.
[21] Garfinkel 1967, Cicourel 1973, Douglas 1971, C.Wright Mills 1963.
[22] Garfinkel and Sacks (1970), p. 342
[23] Radin (1933), p.113.
[24] Horton (1967), p.52.
[25] Becker quoted in Wax, Diamond and Gearing (1971), p.10.
[26] Walker and Adelman (1972), p.60. Adelman (1973) has developed some of these ideas in *Cambridge Journal of Education*, 3(1) pp.52-7. See also C.M. Coulthard, 'The analysis of classroom language', *SSRS Newsletter* (19 June 1973).
[27] Bruyn 1963.
[28] Schwartz and Schwartz 1955.
[29] Schutz 1967.
[30] Becker 1958.
[31] Denzin (1970), p.365.
[32] Wolcott 1971.
[33] See Young 1971; R. Brown (ed.), *Knowledge, Education and Cultural Change* (London, Tavistock, 1973); Gorbutt 1972; and Eggleston 1973.
[34] Keddie 1971.
[35] Keddie, 'The Social Basis of Classroom Knowledge' (unpublished MA thesis, University of London, 1970).

[36] Beck 1972.
[37] A.G. Green, 'Theory and practice in infant education', (unpublished MSc dissertation, University of London, 1972).
[38] C. Wright Mills (1963), p. 569.
[39] Leacock (1971), p. 173.

References

AMIDON, E.J. and HOUGH, J.B., 1967, *Interaction Analysis — Theory, Research and Application.* Reading, Mass: Addison-Wesley.

ARGYRIS, C., 1968, 'The unintended consequences of rigorous research'. *Psychological Bulletin,* 70(3).

BARTHOLOMEW, J., 1973, 'The teacher as researcher'. *Hard Cheese,* No. 1.

BEALING, D., 1973, 'Issues in classroom observational research'. *Research in Education,* 9, pp. 70-82.

BECK, J., 1972, 'Transition and continuity: a study of educational status passage'. University of London: unpublished MA thesis.

BECKER, H.S., 1958, 'Problems of inference and proof in participant observation'. *American Sociological Review,* 23, pp.652-60.

BIDDLE, B.J., 1967, 'Methods and concepts in classroom research'. *Review of Educational Research,* 37(3).

BRUYN, S., 1963, 'The methodology of participant observation'. *Human Organisation,* 22(3), pp.224-35.

CANE, B. and SCHROEDER, C., 1970, *The Teacher and Research.* Windsor: NFER.

CHANAN, G., 1973, *Towards a Science of Teaching.* Windsor: NFER.

CICOUREL, A.V., 1973, *Cognitive Sociology.* Harmondsworth: Penguin.

DENZIN, N.K., 1970, *Sociological Methods: A Sourcebook.* Chicago: Aldine.

DEUTCHER, I., 1966, 'Words and Deeds: Social science and social policy'. *Social Policy,* 13(3), pp. 235-54.

DOUGLAS, J.D., 1971, *Understanding Everyday Life.* London: Routledge and Kegan Paul.

EGGLESTON, J., 1973, 'Knowledge and the school curriculum'. *Education for Teaching,* summer 1973.

FLANDERS, N.A., 1970, *Analysing Classroom Behaviour,* New York: Addison-Wesley.

GARFINKEL, H., 1967, *Studies in Ethnomethodology.* Englewood Cliffs: Prentice-Hall.

GARFINKEL, H. and SACKS, H., 1970, 'On formal structures of practical actions', in J.C. McKinney and E.A. Tiryakian (eds.), *Theoretical Sociology: Perspectives and Development.* New York: Appleton-Century-Crofts.

GLASER, B. and STRAUSS, A.L., 1968, *The Discovery of Grounded Theory.* London: Weidenfeld and Nicolson.

GORBUTT, D., 1972, 'The new sociology of education'. *Education for Teaching,* autumn 1972.

GREEN, A.G., 1972, 'Theory and practice in infant education: a sociological approach and case study'. University of London: unpublished MSc dissertation.

HENRY, J., 1971, *Essays on Education.* Harmondsworth: Penguin.

HORTON, R., 1967, 'African traditional thought and western science'. *Africa*, 37, 1 and 2.

JACKSON, P.W., 1968, *Life in Classrooms.* New York: Holt, Rinehart and Winston.

KEDDIE, N., 1971, 'Classroom knowledge' in M.F.D. Young (ed.), 1971.

KING, A.R., 1967, *The School at Mopass.* New York: Holt, Rinehart and Winston.

LAPIERE, R.T., 1934, 'Attitudes vs. actions'. *Social Forces,* 13(2), pp.230-7.

LEACOCK, E.B., 1971, 'Theoretical and methodological problems in the study of schools' in M.L. Wax *et al.,* 1971.

MILLS, C. Wright., 1963, 'Language, logic, culture' and 'IBM plus reality plus humanism = sociology', in I.H. Horowitz (ed.), *Power, Politics and People.* Oxford University Press.

RADIN, P., 1933, *The Method and Theory of Ethnology.* New York: Basic Books.

SCHUTZ, A., 1967, *Collected Papers Volume One.* The Hague: Martinus Nijhoff.

SCHWARTZ, M.S., and SCHWARTZ, G.C., 1955, 'Problems in participant observation'. *American Journal of Sociology,* 60(4), pp.343-53.

SIMON, A. and BOYER, E.G., (eds.), 1970, *Mirrors for Behaviour,* Philadelphia: Research for Better Schools.

SINDELL, P., 1969, 'Anthropological approaches to the study of education'. *Review of Educational Research,* 39(5), pp.593-605.

SMITH, L.M. and GEOFFREY, W., 1968, *The Complexities of an Urban Classroom.* New York: Holt, Rinehart and Winston.

SMITH, L.M. and BROCK, J.A.M., 1970, *'Go, bug, go!' Methodological issues in classroom observational research.* Central Midwestern Regional Educational Laboratory.

WAX, M.L., DIAMOND, S. and GEARING, F.O. (eds.), 1971, *Anthropological Perspectives on Education.* New York: Basic Books.

WALKER, R., 1972, 'The sociology of education and life in school Classrooms'. *International Review of Education,* 18(1), pp.32-41.

WALKER, R., and ADELMAN, C., 1972, *Towards a Sociography of classrooms.* London: Centre for Science Education.

WOLCOTT, H.F., 1967, *A Kwakiutl Village and School.* New York: Holt, Rinehart and Winston.
1971, 'Handle with care; necessary precautions in the anthropology of schools' in Wax *et al.,* 1971.

YOUNG, M.F.D., (ed.), 1971, *Knowledge and Control; new directions for the sociology of education.* London: Collier-Macmillan.

V Values and learning

INTRODUCTION

In this final section of papers we return to an aspect of research in the sociology of education that has recurred throughout the volume — the significance of values, attitudes and perceptions as a key area of causality, underlying not only observable behaviour but also the patterns of interaction that lead to observable behaviour. Each of the papers included in this section could have found a place in at least one of the preceding sections: they are grouped here because they also bear a wider range of implications that form an appropriate conclusion to this volume.

At this stage in the collection it is proper that the papers should speak for themselves. The first, by Bernstein and Henderson, is a highly regarded, influential paper indicating the importance of differential parental value systems as expressed in the use of language in child socialization in middle class and working class families. This is part of the work of an overall research programme that has been executed with notable skill and effectiveness in the major studies of the Sociological Research Unit of the London Institute of Education directed by Bernstein (Bernstein 1971, 1973). (The same theme appears in its different research context, in the work of the educational priority areas research project (Halsey 1972) and in a number of other researches represented in this collection.)

The paper by Ford is an excerpt from her well-known *Social Class and the Comprehensive School* (1969). Again it is concerned with the interaction of value systems, in this case the interaction of parental and teacher values in Cherry Dale Comprehensive School. Together these are shown to be a more powerful influence on achievement than the more manifest and seemingly widely endorsed objectives of the school. In short, the school, even though comprehensive, appears to have had unexpectedly little influence on the social distribution of opportunity of its pupils. This excerpt has been chosen because of its considerable relevance to earlier research papers in this volume, though an important feature of Ford's work is her analysis, in subsequent chapters, of the 'social arguments' as well as the academic arguments used in favour of comprehensive schools.

As the various studies have shown, the analysis of values is complex and is regularly in danger of oversimplification. Witkin's paper on social class influences on the evaluation of school lessons demonstrates this complexity in a highly effective way and offers a cautionary example of the dangers of an over enthusiastic acceptance of 'self-evident truths'. A similar example arises from Patrick's work on the study of Glasgow gangs, anticipated in the introduction to the first section, which provides one of the most dramatic and informative contributions to the volume. His participant observation study offers an illuminating account of the values of a small but highly significant part of the Glasgow adolescent population and the ways in which these influence their perception of and interaction with the community and the schools — ways that have previously been largely unknown to those outside the gang. Patrick offers us a salutory reminder of the merits of pioneer studies such as those of Thrasher (1927) and Whyte (1940) that have at times been overlooked in a search for scientific purity.

A final paper by Bourdieu in collaboration with Saint-Martin leads us, almost in culmination, to the complex central matrix of values and perceptions that constitute the educational system and its schools. In particular it explores the link between the thinking and intellectual activity of teachers and the nature of schools, their structural and behavioural patterns and their values.

The consideration of these papers brings us to a point where we can see a close connection between what conflict theorists have labelled as values and phenomenologists have labelled constructions of reality. Indeed, in many of the analyses the terms are in principle, if not in practice, interchangeable. Certainly the two are complementary. Conflict analysts are able to emphasize the recurring and regular nature of values and the ways in which they are expressed in action. Phenomenologists, by viewing them as 'definitions of a situation' or 'constructions of reality' have helped sociologists to come to terms with their subjective, illusive, shifting, often irrational but undeniably motivating nature.

This dual perception of values must in turn alert us to the elusiveness of certainty and predictability in the field of sociological research. A built-in caution in the appraisal of all the research reported in this volume may have been noted; certainly it was one of the criteria of selection applied. Shipman (1972) in a review of research on socialization comments:

> At one extreme there are investigations into natural situations in family and school. These may have produced valuable insights but there are too many factors in natural situations for the research to be completely reliable. At the other extreme there are experimental studies where all but a single factor have been controlled. Here the method may be reliable, but the results come from such a synthetic situation that generalization is impossible.

But if even sensitive and skilful research cannot guarantee to lead us to certainty what can it offer? Here Taylor (1972) offers part of the answer:

> Only exceptionally will the daily discussion of a problem or difficulty include the citation of a particular piece of research that contributed significantly to resolution or decision. Yet even when there is no explicit reference to particular studies, it is unlikely that such discussion will be unaffected by research. It exerts its influence by helping to determine the agenda of problems and difficulties, and in providing some of the elements that shape

individual and group orientations towards particular issues. Just as anyone who talks and writes about man and society today is likely to have been influenced by, even if they never refer to, have never read or have never even heard of, the work of Darwin, Marx or Freud — so discussions about education are likely to be influenced by research on such topics as, for example, social class and educational opportunity and stages in children's learning as have been reported during the past twenty-five years. This, and earlier research, arose from the problems of its time, and produced findings which have helped to suggest and define new problems and issues. Research on mental functioning has had the effect of removing certain concepts from our vocabulary, such as faculties, and of downgrading the importance of others, such as attention and memory. Equally, it has pointed up the existence of problems which now feature as important items in the agenda of our concerns, such as the effects of early maternal deprivation, or of impoverished linguistic environments, or the task of delimiting more accurately the stages of growth.

Taylor is saying that the most fundamental consequence of research is the development of awareness and sensitivity. He is also reminding researchers of their indirect but heavy burden of responsibility to a very wide public. To use the highly appropriate language of phenomenologists, research leads the individual to redefine the situation; to develop and to adjust his constructions of social reality. Here appears to lie the only way forward both for research as an activity and for sociology as a discipline.

References

BERNSTEIN, B.B., 1971, 1973, *Class, Codes and Control, Volume 1: Theoretical Studies towards a Sociology of Language, Volume 2: Applied Studies towards a Sociology of Language.* London: Routledge and Kegan Paul.

FORD, J., 1969, *Social Class and the Comprehensive School.* London: Routledge and Kegan Paul.

HALSEY, A.H. (ed.), 1972, *Educational Priority.* London: HMSO.

SHIPMAN, M.D., 1972, *Childhood, a sociological perspective.* Slough: NFER.

TAYLOR, W., 1972, 'Retrospect and prospect in educational research'. *Educational Research,* 15(1).

THRASHER, F.M., 1927, *The Gang.* Chicago: University Press.

WHYTE, W.F., 1940, *Street Corner Society.* Chicago: University Press.

BASIL BERNSTEIN AND DOROTHY HENDERSON

Social class differences in the relevance of language to socialization *

Introduction

One of the most important movements in behavioural science since the war is the convergence of interest upon the study of basic processes of communication and their regulative functions. The one discipline which appears so far least affected is sociology. However, from different quarters there are now signs of growing interest (Grimshaw 1967, Fishman 1966, Circourel 1964, Garfinkel 1967, Hymes 1968). The study of the educationally disadvantaged has also led to a concentration of research into the process of language acquisition, into the relationships between language and cognition and into the social antecedents and regulative consequences of forms of language use.

The Sociological Research Unit at the University of London is engaged upon an exploratory study of forms of familial socialization which affect orientations towards the use of language. We shall present here the results of a closed schedule designed to reveal the relative emphasis which members of social class groups place upon the use of language in different areas of the socialization of the pre-school child. Although this report is confined to a study only of the mothers' *orientation* towards the relevance of language, as this group of mothers have been interviewed twice within a three-year period and because two speech samples have been collected from their children when aged five years and seven years, it should prove to be possible to obtain some measure of both the reliability and validity of the mothers' reports.[1]

This report is the first step in the analysis of the section of the second questionnaire given to the mothers which inquired into the orientation of the mother towards various uses of language. As the other sections were concerned with the decision making within the family, its kinship and community relationships, the procedures of control and role definition, the relationships between home and school, we can relate the orientation towards various uses of language to a range of variables.

In the discussion section of the paper we present a model which gives a sociological explanation of social learning in terms of the mediation of the linguistic process in socialization.

*Reprinted from Basil Bernstein and Dorothy Henderson, 'Social class differences in the relevance of language to socialization', Sociology, 3(1) (January 1969), pp.1-20, by kind permission of the authors and publishers, the Clarendon Press.

Hypotheses

The following hypotheses (derived from Bernstein 1966 and 1968) are to be tested:

1 Both middle class and working class would place greater emphasis upon the use of language in inter-personal aspects of socialization than the emphasis placed upon language in the socialization into basic skills.
2 The shift in emphasis in the use of language from the skill to the person area would be much greater for the middle class group.
3 Within the skill area the middle class group would place a greater emphasis upon language in the transmission of principles.

Description of the sample

The total sample consists of 311 mothers drawn from two areas: one a working class area and the other a middles class area. The r between area and social class of the parents is 0.74. The index of social class was constructed by W. Brandis of the Sociological Research Unit and is based upon the terminal education and occupation of husband and wife. A full description of the index will be found in Brandis, W. and Henderson, D. (1968). Social class is measured on a ten-point scale 0-9. The sample used in this papers consists of fifty mothers randomly selected from the middle class area and fifty mothers randomly selected from the working class area. It was necessary to limit the sample of this study in order that a detailed analysis could be carried out, and to examine possible social class differences in response to the schedule. In terms of the ten-point scale, the mean social class position of the middle class group is 2.8 and the mean social class position of the working class group is 6.9.

The closed schedule[2]

The closed schedule consisted of a list of eleven statements which covered the major aspects of socialization. As the schedule was presented, the interviewer put to each mother the question which was printed above the list of statements: 'If parents could not speak, how much *more* difficult do you think it would be for them to do the following things with young children who had not yet started school?' The mother's attention was then directed to the statements and she was asked to asses the difficulty she thought dumb parents would experience in dealing with each situation. A six-point scale was provided: very much more difficult, much more difficult, more difficult, not too difficult, fairly easy, easy. The statements are listed below in the order in which they were presented on the schedule:

1 Teaching them everyday tasks like dressing, and using a knife and fork (Motor skill)
2 Helping them to make things (Constructional skill)
3 Drawing their attention to different shapes (Perceptual skill)
4 Playing games with them (Dummy)

5 Showing them what is right and wrong	(Moral principles)
6 Letting them know what you are feeling	(Mother oriented affective)
7 Showing them how things work	(Cognitive)
8 Helping them to work things out for themselves	(Independent cognitive)
9 Disciplining them	(Control)
10 Showing them how pleased you are with their progress	(Dummy)
11 Dealing with them when they are unhappy.	(Child oriented affective)

Statements 4 and 10 were deliberately inserted as dummy statements designed to move the mother's responses across to 'fairly easy' and 'easy' and thus mitigate the emphasis placed on 'difficulty' in the initial question. In fact, these statements elicited the responses 'fairly easy' from 72 per cent of the middle class mothers and from 76 per cent of the working class mothers. No other statements shifted both groups to the 'easy' points of the scale to this extent. Four of the statements – 1, 2, 3 and 7 – were concerned with the transmission of skills. Five of the statements – 5, 6, 8, 9 and 11 – were concerned with aspects of social control. Statements 1, 2, 3 and 7 will be referred to as the *skill* area of statements, and statements 5, 6, 8, 9 and 11 will be referred to as the *person* area of statements. The points of the scale 'very much more difficult', 'much more difficult' and 'more difficult' will be referred to as the 'difficult' points of the scale, whilst 'fairly easy' and 'easy' will be referred to as the 'easy' points of the scale. 'Not too difficult' will be referred to as the mid-point of the scale.

It will be remembered that the aim of the schedule was to examine the effect of the social class position of the mothers on their perception of the role of language as a socializing process. In order to obtain such information it was necessary to focus the mother's attention upon the relevance of language across a number of different areas. It was thought that mothers would experience great difficulty if they were simply asked to what extent they relied upon language when dealing with their children. We constructed a general situation such that each mother was faced with a problem of comparison. She also had to assess the difficulty of transmitting skills and dealing with inter-personal processes without language. This focused her attention upon the relevance of the linguistic component of the interaction. At the same time, it was necessary to ensure, as far as possible, that the mother should not feel that the problem was a challenge to her own extra-verbal ingenuity with her child, and so the problem was presented with the general referents *parents* and *young children*. It was equally necessary to preclude the possible use of other linguistic alternatives and therefore we stated the problem in terms of young children who had *not yet started school* and were thus unlikely to be able to read written instructions or explanations.

Method

The analysis was carried out in three stages. In the first stage we examined the population scores, in the second stage we examined the responses of individual mothers within each social class to each statement, and in the third stage analyses of variance were carried out in order to examine the interaction between the social class position of the mothers and their responses within and between the *skill* and *person* areas of statements.

First stage

The population scores enabled us:

a   to examine the distribution of maternal responses across the scale for each statement
b   to examine the total number of responses across the scale within each area of statements
c   to compare the total population scores within each area of statements in terms of 'difficult' and 'easy' responses.

We were then in a position to compare differences in patterns of response in relation to the statements.

Second stage

The difference between the number of 'difficult' responses and the number of 'easy' responses to each statement was examined in terms of the social class of the mothers. This procedure also enabled us to compare the 'difficult' to 'easy' responses for each statement with reference to social class.

Third stage

(a)   A 2 x 2 analysis of variance on repeated measures was carried out. This type of analysis enabled us to control for within-person variance as well as for between-people variance and residual variance. Each point on the scale was assigned a score as follows:

Very much more difficult	+3
Much more difficult	+2
More difficult	+1
Not too difficult	0
Fairly easy	−1
Easy	−2

The basic unit of the analysis here was the individual mother's mean response score to the four *skill* statements. This was compared to the mother's mean response score to the five *person* statements. The analysis enabled us to test for significance the differential emphasis upon difficulty in response to each area of statements and its relationship with social class.

(b)   A 2 x 5 analysis of variance on repeated measures was carried out on the maternal responses to each of the statements within the *person* area, in order to find out whether there was a significant interaction effect between the social class of the mothers and the individual statements.

(c)   For the same reason a 2 x 4 analysis was carried out on the maternal responses to the individual statements within the *skill* area.

Results

First, we will deal briefly with the results which were found when the population scores were examined. It must be emphasized that the main justification for this stage of the analysis was to discover whether differences between the responses to the statements, as well as differences between the social class groups, were sufficiently large to justify carrying out a more sensitive analysis on the data. We will then deal at greater length with the results of the second and third stages of the analysis.

1 The population responses

The distribution of the population responses across the scale show that the patterns of distributions differ markedly between the *person* statements and the *skill* statements (Table I). The responses cluster at the 'difficult' points of the scale in response to the *person* statements, whereas the distribution is normal, with 'not too difficult' operating as the midpoint, in response to the *skill* statements. Since the two areas of statements were clearly eliciting quite different patterns of response, we decided to compare the summed scores across all the statements within each area for each point of the scale. We then found that although both middle class and working class mothers showed a marked move to 'difficult' responses within the *person* area in comparison with their responses within the *skill* area, the relative shift was greater in the case of the middle class responses (Table I). In order to make a more stringent comparison the responses 'very much more difficult' and 'much more difficult' were summed within each social class and compared with the summed responses 'fairly easy' and 'easy'. We found that the social class differences in response within each area of statements were very great. In particular, the shift of middle class responses from the *skill* area to the *person* area in terms of the emphasis upon difficulty was just over 5 to 1, whereas the shift of working class responses from the *skill* area to the *person* area was just under 2 to 1 (Table II).

2 Individual responses to statements

In the next stage of the analysis we examined the *individual* responses within each social class to each statement, in terms of the ratios of 'difficult' to 'easy' responses. Again we found that both middle class and working class mothers had shifted to the 'difficult' points of the scale in response to the *person* statements. But *within* the *person* area, middle class mothers placed greater emphasis upon difficulty than did working class mothers (Table I). Within the *skill* area we found a reversal in the pattern of response on the part of middle class mothers. Middle class mothers were less likely to give an 'easy' response to the statement 'Showing them how things work' than the working class mothers. Table I also shows that more working class mothers than middle class mothers gave a 'difficult' response to the statement 'Teaching them everyday tasks like dressing, and using a knife and fork'.

TABLE I Distributions of population responses to statements

		Skill statements				Person statements				
	The scale*	1	2	3	7	5	6	8	9	11
Middle class responses	0	0	1	1	3	12	12	13	19	11
	1	0	4	5	9	12	12	12	8	11
	2	7	12	11	13	19	12	18	14	15
	3	20	21	16	17	5	11	4	8	9
	4	15	7	12	7	2	2	3	0	2
	5	8	5	5	1	0	1	0	1	2
Working class responses	0	9	4	4	4	4	10	11	11	10
	1	5	5	5	6	13	4	9	7	4
	2	3	7	6	8	11	12	14	13	11
	3	23	23	27	20	14	10	11	8	10
	4	5	7	6	10	4	8	4	9	8
	5	5	4	2	2	4	6	1	2	7

*Note:
0 – Very much more difficult
1 – Much more difficult
2 – More difficult
3 – Not too difficult.
4 – Fairly easy
5 – Easy

TABLE II   Percentages of summed difficult/easy responses in each area

		% Difficult (0, 1)	% Easy (4, 5)	Total No. responses
Middle class	{ Person statements	48.8	5.2	250
	Skill statements	11.5	30.0	200
Working class	{ Person statements	33.2	21.2	250
	Skill statements	21.0	20.4	200

3 The analysis of variance

(a)   The results of the 2 x 2 analysis of variance on repeated measures show that the differential emphasis on difficulty between the two areas is highly significant ($F_{1,98} = 294 \cdot 53$, $p > \cdot 001$). Very much greater emphasis was placed upon difficulty within the *person* area of statements than within the *skill* area of statements. However, the analysis also showed that, although greater emphasis was placed on the difficulty of dealing with the situations described in the *person* area by *all* the mothers, the difference between the responses of the middle class mothers in relation to the two areas of statements was significantly greater than the difference between the responses of the working class mothers ($F_{1,98} = 73.60$, $p > \cdot 001$). Middle class mothers placed much *greater* emphasis upon the difficulty of doing the things described in the *person* area than the working class mothers, but they placed much *less* emphasis upon the difficulty of doing the things described in the *skill* area than the working class mothers. This highly significant inter-action effect illustrates the polarization of the responses of middle class mothers in relation to the two areas of statements.

We will now turn to the results of the analyses of maternal responses *within* each area.

(b)   Within the *skill* area the results show that middle class mothers placed very much less emphasis on language than working class mothers on the difficulty of doing the things described in these statements, and that this difference in response was highly significant ($F_{1,98} = 228 \cdot 78$, $p > \cdot 001$). This finding replicates the result found by the previous analysis. However, a highly significant interaction effect between the social class

TABLE III   Summary table of mean scores

	Statements		
	Skill area	Person area	Total $\bar{x}$
$\bar{x}$ middle class:	·07	1·49	·78
$\bar{x}$ working class:	·33	·80	·56
Sample $\bar{x}$	·20	1·04	

TABLE IV   Summary table of mean scores

	Skill statements				
	1	2	3	7	Total $\bar{x}$
$\bar{x}$ middle class:	−.48	·12	·04	·62	·30
$\bar{x}$ working class:	·48	·28	·36	·36	1·50
Sample $\bar{x}$	·01	·20	·20	·49	

of the mothers and responses to individual *skill* statements was revealed by this analysis. Working class mothers placed significantly greater emphasis on difficulty in response to the statement 'Teaching them everyday tasks like dressing and using a knife and fork', than did middle class mothers; middle class mothers, on the other hand, placed significantly greater emphasis on difficulty in response to the statement 'Showing them how things work' than did working class mothers ($F_{3,294} = 74\cdot88, p > \cdot001$).

(c)   The 2 x 5 analysis of maternal responses to the five *person* statements shows that middle class mothers considered that these situations would be more difficult to deal with without language than did working class mothers. This differential emphasis on difficulty in relation to the *person* statements is highly significant ($F_{1,98} = 14.25, p > \cdot001$). A highly significant main order effect, *irrespective* of the social class position of the mothers, arose out of differences in response to individual statements ($F_{4,392} = 6\cdot49, p > \cdot001$).

This result shows that individual statements within the *person* area had elicited very different responses from both middle class and working class mothers. We were therefore interested to know how the responses differed *between* the *person* statements. In other words, how were the *person* statements *ranked* in difficulty? The mean scores are presented below as they were ranked in order of difficulty by *all* the mothers in the sample.

	Person statements	Mean scores
8	Helping them to work things out for themselves	1.37
9	Disciplining them	1.32
5	Showing them what is right and wrong	1.14
6	Letting them know what you are feeling	.98
11	Dealing with them when they are unhappy	.91

Summary of results

Differences in response were shown to be due to (a) the statements within each area, (b) the social class of the mothers and (c) the interaction between social class and individual statements. We find that middle class mothers consider language less relevant to the situations

TABLE V   Summary table of mean scores

		Person statements				
	5	6	8	9	11	Total $\bar{x}$
$\bar{x}$ middle class:	1·54	1·36	1·56	1·70	1·28	7·44
$\bar{x}$ working class:	·74	·60	1·18	·94	·54	4·00
Sample $\bar{x}$	1·14	·98	1·37	1·32	·91	

described by the *skill* statements than do working class mothers.
There is one exception. Middle class mothers considered that
'Showing them how things work' would be *more* difficult to deal with
without language than working class mothers. Conversely, middle class
mothers place greater emphasis upon language than working class
mothers in response to the *person* statements. However, *all* the mothers
considered the *person* situations more difficult to cope with than the
skill situations.

Methodological criticisms of the schedule[3]

The rationale for the construction of the schedule has been given
earlier in this paper, nevertheless, a number of methodological issues
are raised by the design.

Let us examine the points one by one, and see to what extent
each issue is resolved in the light of the analysis.

1 The definition of the problem is lengthy and contains three
items of information which the mother has to bear in mind throughout
her responses to *all* the statements if the results are to be a reliable
measure of her orientation to language in relation to major aspects of
socialization.

Very great differences in response were found between the statements
which described skills and the statements which described aspects of
inter-personal processes, irrespective of the social class of the mothers
in the sample. It can reasonably be argued that such differences in the
emphasis upon difficulty would not have been found if the mothers had
merely assessed each statement without reference to the role of speech
and its absence. We can assume then that the question, despite its
complexity, was borne in mind by the mothers throughout their
responses. It focused their attention on the linguistic aspect of their
own behaviour with their children.

2 In order to assess the difficulty for dumb parents when doing a
number of things with young children, the mother can only refer to her
own experience in each situation and try to imagine how difficult she
herself would find each situation if *she* could not speak. Such an assessment involves an internal three stage experiment, and this may have
been quite difficult for some mothers. However, this point is clearly
related to the first point, since it can reasonably be assumed that if the
mother bears the problem in mind *throughout* her responses then she
is forced to focus upon her *own* reliance upon language.

3 The mother is asked to discriminate *between* degrees of difficulty on a six-point scale, two points of which do not refer to difficulty but to ease. It may be that some mothers found it difficult to use the six-point scale. They had either to keep all the points in mind in response to each statement, or they had frequently to refer back to the scale. If they failed to do this then their responses would be unreliable.

The 2 x 5 analysis of the mother's responses to the five *person* statements has shown that, although all mothers emphasized difficulty in response to these statements rather than to the *skill* statements, there were significant differences in the emphasis upon difficulty *between* the statements. The fact that the problem emphasized difficulty — 'how much *more* difficult do you think it would be?' — may have given rise to greater discrimination between degrees of difficulty. This result strongly suggested that the mothers, irrespective of social class, were indeed discriminating between the 'difficult' points of the scale. We decided to examine the data in order to find out whether the percentage of mothers within each social class using *more than one 'difficult' point* in response to the control statements and *more than one 'easy' point* in response to the *skill* statements differed. We found that there was no difference in the percentage of mothers within each social class using *all three* 'difficult' points in response to the *person* statements, and that *all* the percentage differences were minimal in response to the *skill* statements. The major differences between the social class groups occurs in the relative use of only *one* 'difficult' point in response to the *person* statements. Eighteen per cent of the middle class mothers used only one 'difficult' point in response to these statements whereas 40 per cent of the working class mothers used only one 'difficult' point. This could well argue a lack of discrimination between degrees of difficulty as set out in the scale on the part of nearly half the working class subsample. One final point should be made in regard to discrimination. Discrimination between the 'difficult' points did not relate to the *number* of *person* statements which elicited a 'difficult' response, nor to the *number* of *skill* statements which elicited an 'easy' response. It is important to stress this point since we suspected that there may have been a greater likelihood of discrimination if a mother was confining herself to the 'difficult' part of the scale across all five *person* statements.

We were also interested in the extent of movement *across* the scale. We considered that this, together with the discrimination *within* the scale might justify a six-point scale, since this would reveal the extent to which mothers limited their responses to adjacent points. Seventy-eight per cent of the middle class mothers and 62 per cent of the working class mothers distributed their responses across at least four points of the scale. Examination of the data showed that mothers who moved across four or more points of the scale when responding to the statements were much more likely to use one of the extreme points 'very much more difficult' and 'easy' than were mothers who moved across less than four points.

We then examined the number of mothers who moved across five or six points of the scale, since this clearly involved the use of one or both extreme points. We found that 48 per cent of the middle class mothers, but only 28 per cent of the working class mothers, moved across five or six points. This may be an indication that the middle class mothers in our sample were better able to use a six-point scale, either because of their ability to bear the six points in mind, or because of their greater readiness to refer back to the scale frequently.

4   There was inadequate randomization of the statements. This is particularly relevant to the close proximity of the statements 'Helping them to work things out for themselves' and 'Showing them how things work'. It was thought that the lexical similarity of these two statements might have prevented the mothers from discriminating between them, despite the fact that they describe rather different activities and orientations. Surprisingly, the analysis of the mothers' responses showed that more working class mothers than middle class mothers discriminated between these two statements. The implication of this finding will be taken up later in the discussion. At present it is sufficient to point out that the social class group which one may have least expected to discriminate between two very similar statements did, in fact, do so. Finally, the fact that the mothers did discriminate between the statements — that they did not exhibit response sets — is shown by the pattern of their responses across the scale. Statements 1, 2, 3 and 4 elicited 'easy' responses; statements 5 and 6 elicited 'difficult' responses; statement 7 elicited 'easy' responses; statements 8 and 9 elicited 'difficult' responses; statement 10 elicited 'easy' responses; and statement 11 elicited 'difficult' responses. This pattern was consistent for both middle class and working class mothers.

Summary of criticisms

It is clear that movement from 'difficult' responses to 'easy' responses was triggered by the two main areas. Discrimination between degrees of difficulty was dependent upon individual statements: there were significant differences in the ranking of the *person* statements in order of difficulty, and the order was the same for both social class groups. Movement across four points of the scale was found to involve the use of one of the extreme points, and there was very little difference in the number of middle class and working class mothers who used the scale in this way. However, more of the middle class mothers moved across five or six points of the scale than did the working class mothers. This raises the substantive question as to the orientation of the working class group; they may not have required such a sensitive scale. We might add that few researchers have carried out such a close examination of their results in terms of their scaling procedures. Our experience suggests that, although on balance our scaling procedure was justified, the following recommendation might provide a more reliable measure. We suggest that in order to overcome some of the scaling difficulties for the mother it is recommended first to ask the general question and then, for each statement, ask the mother whether she thought it on the whole difficult or on the whole easy. We could then present the mother with a three-point scale for degrees of difficulty or a three-point scale for relative ease, depending upon her general response.

Discussion

The results show that the middle class, relative to the working class, place a greater emphasis upon the use of language in dealing with situations within the person area. The working class, relative to the middle class, place a greater emphasis upon the use of language in the transmission of various skills. However, within the skill area the middle class place a greater emphasis upon the use of language in their response to the statement, 'Showing them how things work', whereas within the same area the working class place a greater emphasis upon the use of language in response to the statement, 'Teaching them every day tasks like dressing, and using a knife and fork'.

Can these differences in emphasis be accounted for in terms of differences in the relevance of these two *areas* for the social classes? In other words, does the move to language simply reflect the relevance of the area? Or is it the case that both areas respectively have equal relevance to the social classes but their verbal realization is different? It is unlikely that the middle class relative to the working class value basic skills less and yet it is this group which places a reduced emphasis upon language in the skill area. It would be just as difficult to maintain that socialization into relationships between persons is not of *equal* relevance to every subcultural group, although the *form* of that socialization may well vary. On the other hand the very marked shift by *both* groups towards language in the person area and away from language in the skill area may well reflect the greater importance of control over persons rather than control over the development of skills in the socialization of the very young child. It is therefore unlikely that the shifts in emphasis placed upon the use of language in each of the two areas respectively, by the two social class groups, can be explained in terms of the difference in the relevance of the skill area and the person area. It might be that middle class mothers can conceive of a variety of ways, other than linguistic, for the acquisition of skills and for this reason these mothers place less emphasis upon language. Whereas the working class mothers can conceive of fewer alternatives to language for the acquisition of skills. This might seem to be a plausible explanation, but we think that it by no means accounts for the differences between the social classes.

We shall argue that the explanation is to be found in the nature of the social relationship when skills and person relationships are transmitted. If it is the case that in the working class knowledge is transmitted through a social relationship in which the receiver is relatively passive and if, in the middle class, knowledge is transmitted through a social relationship in which the receiver is active, then we might expect the distribution of responses which have been revealed. It may be that motor perceptual and manipulative skills are acquired by the child in the middle class by his exposure to varied and attractive stimuli which the child explores on his *own* terms. In other words, in the acquisition of motor, perceptual and manipulative skills, the child regulates his own learning in a carefully controlled environment. It is of significance that despite the relatively greater emphasis placed upon language in the skill area by the working class group, the middle class place greater emphasis upon language in response to the statement, 'Showing them how things work'. It is likely that this statement, for the middle class, raises questions of the transmission of principles, whereas the other three statements within the same area *do not*. If this is the case, then the situation for the middle class child is particularly fortunate. For, on the one hand, he is socialized into elementary skill learning through role relationships which emphasize autonomy *and* he has access to principles.

In the working class group, the concept of learning may well be different and, therefore, the form the social relationship takes when skills are acquired would be of a different order. The concept of learning here seems to be less one of self-regulated learning in an arranged environment and more a concept of a didactic theory of learning implying a passive receiver, in which a mother has little alternative but to tell or instruct a child. Although the emphasis in the working class group, relative to the middle class, is upon language, presumably upon *telling* or instructing, the child is much less likely to receive explanations of principles. Thus it may be that the working class child learns skills in terms only of an understanding of the operations they entail, whereas the middle class child learns both the operations and principles.

Other work of the Sociological Research Unit can be referred to here in support of these hypotheses. Two years prior to the interview in which the present schedule was administered, a sample of 351 middle class and working class mothers (of which the sample used in this paper is a subsample) were given a questionnaire in which the mothers were invited to give their views upon a range of experiences relevant to their child's behaviour in the infant school. We found that when middle class mothers were asked to rank in order of importance six possible uses of toys, they ranked more highly than did the working class mothers 'To find out about things' (Bernstein and Young 1967). Further, middle class mothers saw the role of the infant school child as an active role, whereas the working class mothers tended to see this role as a passive one (Jones 1966). Middle class mothers, relative to working class mothers, indicated that 'play' in the infant school had educational significance (Bernstein 1967).

It would appear then that the difference in the response of middle class and working class mothers to the relevance of language in the acquisition of various skills is more likely to arise out of differences in the concept of learning than out of differences between the social classes in terms of the value placed upon the learning of such skills. The socialization of the middle class child into the acquisition of skills is into both operations and principles which are learned in a social context which emphasizes *autonomy*. In the case of the working class child, his socialization into skills emphasizes operations rather than principles learned in a social context where the child is accorded *reduced autonomy*.

We will now turn to discuss the differences between the social classes in their emphasis upon the use of language in inter-personal contexts. The results are very clear. Where the context is inter-personal, the middle class relative to the working class, move markedly towards the use of language. Further, the shift in the emphasis upon language from the skill area to the person area is very much greater in the middle class than in the working class. Thus, the verbal realization of affects, moral principles and their application to behaviour, and independence in cognitive functioning, is much more likely to be linguistically elaborated in the middle class than in the working class. This is *not* to say that these aspects of socialization do not have the same significance in the working class, only that (according to the mothers' responses) language is of less relevance in the form of the socialization.

Indeed, *both* classes rank the statements (in the person area) in the same order of difficulty.

It is not possible to infer from the mothers' responses what they actually would say to the child, but again we can refer to evidence obtained from the first interview with the mothers two years earlier. This evidence strongly suggests that:

1 The middle class mothers are more likely than working class mothers to take up the child's attempts to interact verbally with the mother in a range of contexts.
2 The middle class mothers are less likely to avoid or evade answering difficult questions put to them by their children.
3 The middle class mothers are less likely to use coercive methods of control.
4 The middle class mothers are more likely to explain to the child why they want a change in his behaviour. (Bernstein and Brandis 1968).

Thus, we have good reasons for believing that not only is there a difference between the social classes in their emphasis upon language in contexts of inter-personal control, but there is a difference in the meanings which are verbally realized. It would seem that the internalizing of the principles of the moral order, the relating of this order to the specifics of the child's behaviour, the communication of feeling, is realized far more through language in the middle class than in the working class. The social is made explicit in one group, whereas the social is rendered less explicit in the other. Where the social is made explicit through language then that which is internalized can itself become an object (Mead 1934). Perhaps here we can begin to see that the form of control over persons in the middle class induces a reflexive relation to the social order, whereas, in the working class, the form of control over persons induces a relatively less reflexive relation to the social order. (See note.)

The question of the relatively greater emphasis upon the use of language in the inter-personal area raises fundamental questions about the nature of middle class forms of socialization which would take us beyond the confines of an empirical research report. In Bernstein (1966 and particularly 1968) there is an extensive discussion of the social antecedents of forms of language use and socialization. The view taken in these and other papers is that linguistic codes are realizations of social structure, and both shape the contents of social roles and the process by which they are learned. In short, it has been suggested that the use of elaborated codes renders the implicit explicit, whereas the use of restricted codes reduces the possibility of such explicitness. Thus the codes and their variants regulate the cultural meanings which are rendered both explicit and individuated through the use of language. Whilst there is not evidence in this paper that middle class mothers use forms of an elaborated code and working class mothers use forms of a restricted code, Robinson and Rackstraw's analysis (1967) of the answering behaviour of mothers in the main sample indicates grounds for believing that these coding orientations are likely to be found. Further, the works of Bernstein and Brandis (1968) and Cook (1968) show that the forms of control used by the middle class and the working class are consonant with the predictions derived from the sociolinguistic theory. We will have further evidence when Miss Cook's analysis of the speech of the mothers is completed.

We have suggested that in the middle class skills are acquired in such a way that the child has access both to operations and principles. He tends to regulate his own learning in an arranged environment which encourages autonomy in skill acquisition. For this reason the middle class mothers place less emphasis upon the use of language in the statements within the skill area. In the case of the working class child, we have argued that he socialized more into the acquisition of operations than into principles through a social relationship which encourages passivity in the learner and so reduces autonomy in skill acquisition. Thus the working class mothers, relative to middle class mothers, place greater emphasis upon the use of language when responding to the statements in the skill area. In the case of control over persons, we have suggested that the forms of such control in the middle class arise out of a social structure which is realized through the use of elaborated codes, whereas the forms of control in the subgroup of the working class under examination arise out of a social structure which is realized through forms of a restricted code. As a result, the form of control in the middle class induces a reflexive relation upon the part of the child towards the social order, whereas in the working class the forms of control induce a much less reflexive relation to the social order.

We should point out that a developed reflexive relation to the social order does not necessarily imply role distancing behaviour. In the same way, reduced reflexiveness to a particularistic social order does not necessarily imply that role distancing behaviour will *not* occur in relation to members of a society holding universalistic status.

We can best summarize our interpretation of the results of this analysis and the more general explanation given in this paper, by the use of the following model:

SOCIAL STRUCTURE

↓

EMPHASIS ON LANGUAGE

Orientation	Role/self—concept	middle class	working class
Persons	Reflexiveness : ⟶	High	Low
Skills	Autonomy: ⟶	Low	High
Implicit theory of learning:		Self—regulating	Didactic

The model should be read *horizontally* in relation to the areas of orientation and consequent emphasis on language, and *vertically* in relation to implicit theories of learning and emphasis upon language. For example, if there is a *high* emphasis upon the use of language in terms of orientation to *persons* then this will tend to generate high *reflexiveness* of the self-concept; if the emphasis on the use of language is *low* then this will generate *reduced reflexiveness* of the self-concept. In terms of the orientation to *skills,* a *low* emphasis on language will generate *autonomy* in the self-concept, whilst a *high* emphasis on language in this area will *reduce autonomy* in the self-concept. At the same time, the relative emphasis upon the use of language in these two areas perhaps implies different implicit theories of learning. Where the emphasis upon the use of language is *high* in terms of orientation to persons or *low* in terms of orientation to skills, then the implicit theory of learning is *self-regulating.* Where the emphasis on the use of language is *low* in terms of orientation to persons or *high* in terms of orientation to skills, then the implicit theory of learning is *didactic.*[4] It is important to add that, in this paper, because of the small sample, we have treated the middle class and working class as homogeneous groups. When the total sample is analysed it may be possible to show that there are sub-groups within each social class group who respond differently in relation to these two areas. It is quite possible that differential emphasis upon the use of language in terms of the acquisition of skills or inter-personal control is related to differences in the form of the social relationships. A subculture may give rise to an implicit theory of learning which is self-regulating in terms of orientation to persons and didactic in terms of orientation to skills, or *vice versa.* The relationship between culture, linguistic codes, implicit theories of learning and differential emphasis upon the use of language is a matter of investigation. An extensive discussion in Bernstein (1968) deals with the relationship between social structure, forms of social relationship, linguistic codes, and different orders of meaning. The hypotheses on which our model is based are derived from this paper.

We can now develop our discussion in regard to possible discontinuities between implicit theories of learning in the home and explicit theories of learning in the school. It is suggested that there may be, for the working class child in the primary school two sources of discontinuity; one in the area of skill acquisition and the other in the area of inter-personal relations. If, for example, the school emphasizes autonomy in the acquisition of skills but the implicit concept of learning in the home is didactic in relation to skills, this will be a major source of discontinuity. Similarly, if the school is concerned with the development of reflexive relations in the area of inter-personal relations but the implicit concept of social learning in the home operates to reduce reflexiveness in this area, then this will be another source of discontinuity. It may be unreasonable to expect children exposed to such discontinuities to respond initially to forms of control which presuppose a culture and socialization very different from their own.

Earlier in this discussion we referred to the fortunate situation of the middle class child in terms of the results of our analysis. His role relationships emphasize autonomy in the acquisition of skills and reflexiveness in the area of inter-personal relations. He is accorded discretion to *achieve* his social role. On the other hand, the role relationships of the working class child, in terms of our analysis, reduce his autonomy in the skill area and reduce reflexiveness in the inter-personal area. He has much less discretion — his social role is *assigned*.

In this paper we have shown that maternal definitions of the role of language as a socializing process are dependent upon the area of orientation, and that this differential emphasis on the use of language is related to different forms of social relationship within the social structure. Further, we have argued that the differential emphasis on the use of language in relation to certain areas of orientation may reflect different implicit theories of learning which affect the self-concept of the child. We have suggested that these different implicit theories of learning in the home may conflict with the theories of learning in the school, and in this way give rise to major sources of discontinuity between the home and the school.

This analysis has enabled us to construct a model which gives a sociological explanation of social learning through the mediation of the linguistic process of socialization.

Conclusion

We must emphasize that our data consists of mothers' reports not of their actual behaviour, and that these reports have been obtained through the use of a closed schedule. The analysis of the degree and type of discrimination on the part of the middle class and working class mothers gives us reasonable grounds for believing that the scaling procedures and the statements were appropriate. We also believe that the situation constructed was such that the 'right' or conventional response was not obvious to the mothers. We have shown that both groups ranked the statements in the person area according to the same gradient of difficulty. However, we cannot present at the moment an analysis of possible differences between the social classes in their interpretation of the statements. We may be able to throw some light on social class differences in the interpretation of the statements when the responses of the mothers to the closed schedule is related to their responses to the other schedules within the language section of the second questionnaire *and* to the results of the analysis of the initial questionnaire.

The findings presented here indicate very clear differences between the social class groups in their relative emphasis upon language. We hope to be able to utilize the model offered in the conclusion of the discussion to show, when the total sample is analysed, intra-class differences in the orientation to the use of language in these two areas of socialization. Perhaps the most important conclusion of this paper is to stress the need for small scale naturalistic and experimental studies of the channels, codes and contexts which control the process of socialization.

In conclusion, it is the case that the three hypotheses given in the introduction have been confirmed. The findings have also revealed that working class mothers relative to middle class mothers place a greater emphasis upon language in the acquisition of basic skills. The inferential structure developed in the discussion makes explicit the relationships

between macro aspects of social structure and micro aspects of socialization.

Note

The diagram below sets out the different relationships between reflexiveness and autonomy which may arise as a result of the cultural meanings realized through language.

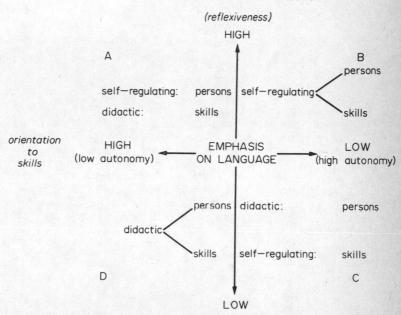

SUBCULTURE CULTURE
ORIENTATION TO PERSONS

(reflexiveness)

The diagram should be read as follows. The vertical and horizontal axes
are scaled in terms of the emphasis upon language. The vertical axis
refers to degrees of reflexiveness in socialization into relationships with
persons and the horizontal axis refers to degrees of autonomy in the
acquisition of skills. The four quadrants contain similarities and
differences between implicit theories of learning. These control the
forms of the socialization into the two basic areas of socialization.
Whilst quadrants 'B' and 'D' would apply to sections of the middle
class and working class respectively, the model indicates the probability
of intra-class variance both at one point and over time.

The model only permits statements about the emphasis upon
language; no inferences can be drawn which refer to the nature of
the information. In order to examine the latter it would be necessary
to know the dominant linguistic code used in each area of socialization.
Whilst it is unlikely that individuals limited to restricted codes would
hold self-regulating theories of learning (except embryonically) didactic

theories of learning may well be held by users of both elaborated and restricted codes. The hypothetical relationships between social structure, family role systems, linguistic codes and person and object verbally realized meanings are set out in Bernstein (1968).

The concept of reflexiveness[5]

It is useful to distinguish between two aspects of reflexiveness; a role and an ideational aspect.

Ideational aspects:

Reflexiveness here refers to the degree to which an individual is able to make explicit verbally the principles underlying object and person relationships. Thus we could have high or low reflexiveness towards objects and/or persons.

Role aspects:

Within role: Reflexiveness here refers to the range of alternatives or options which are accorded to any given role. Thus we could have high or low reflexiveness in terms of the range of alternatives made available. *Between role:* Reflexiveness here would refer to the degree of insulation among the *meanings* made available through role relationships. Roles may be more or less insulated from each other and so may the meanings to which the roles give access. Where the meanings made available through different roles are highly insulated we could say that there is low reflexiveness; where the meanings made available through different roles *reverberate* against each other (low insulation) we could say there is high reflexiveness.

   This formulation indicates that the relationship between language and reflexiveness and the cultural and the institutional order is indeed complex.

Notes

1   The work reported in this paper was supported by grants from the Department of Education and Science and the Ford Foundation to whom, gratefully, acknowledgement is made. Thanks are also given to the local education authorities for their close help and co-operation in the research.

2   The schedule was designed by Marian Bernstein and Basil Bernstein.

3   We are not here elaborating upon the more complex issues of sub-cultural differences in the interpretation of statements within closed schedules.

4   On implicit theories of learnings, see J. Klein, *Samples of British Culture,* volume II (Routledge and Kegan Paul, 1965); Trasler, (ed.) *The Formative Years* (BBC Publication, 1968); R.D. Hess and V.C. Shipman, 'Early Experience and the socialisation of cognitive modes in children', *Child Development,* 36(4) (1965), pp. 869-86.

5   We are very grateful to Dr Michael Young, Lecturer in the Sociology of Education, University of London, Institute of Education, for his comments upon this formulation.

References

BERNSTEIN, Basil, 1961, 'A socio-linguistic approach to social learning' in Julius Gould (ed.), *Social Science Survey*. London: Penguin.

BERNSTEIN, Basil, 1967, 'Play and the infant school'. *Where*, supplement II, *Toys*.

BERNSTEIN, Basil, 1968, 'A socio-linguistic approach to socialization', in J. Gumper and D. Hymes (eds.), *Directions in Socio-linguistics*. Holt, Rinehart and Winston. Also in *Human Context*, I, December.

BERNSTEIN, B., and YOUNG D., 1967, 'Social class differences in conceptions of the uses of toys', *Sociology*, I, (2)

BERNSTEIN, B. and BRANDIS, W., 1968, 'Social class differences in communication and control' in W. Brandis and D. Henderson. *Primary Socialization, Language and Education Volume I: Social Class, Language and Communication*. University of London Institute of Education, Sociological Research Unit Monograph Series directed by Basil Bernstein: Routledge and Kegan Paul.

CICOUREL, Aaron V., 1964, *Method and Measurement in Sociology*. Glencoe, Ill.: The Free Press.

COOK, J., 1968, *Familial Processes of Communication and Control*. To be published in the Sociological Research Unit Monograph Series (see above).

FISHMAN, Joshua, 1966, *Language Loyalty in the United States*. Mouton.

GARFINKEL, Harold., 1967, *Studies in Ethnomethodology*. Prentice-Hall.

GRIMSHAW, Alan, D., 1968, 'Socio-linguistics' in W. Schramm, I. Pool, N. Maccob, E. Parker, L. Fein, (eds.), *Handbook of Communication*. Rand McNally.

HYMES, Dell, 1967, 'On communicative competence'. This paper is revised from the one presented at the Research Planning Conference on Language Development Among Disadvantaged Children, held under the sponsorship of the Department of Educational Psychology and Guidance, Ferkauf Graduate School, Yeshiva University, 1966. The paper is available from the Department of Social Anthropology, University of Pennsylvania, Philadelphia.

JONES, Jean, 1966, 'Social class and the under-fives'. *New Society*.

LOEVINGER, Jane, 1959, 'Patterns of parenthood as theories of learning'. *Journal of Social and Abnormal Psychology, sq.*, pp.148-50.

MEAD, G.H., 1934, *Mind, Self and Society*. University of Chicago Press.

ROBINSON, W.P., and RACKSTRAW, S.J., 1967, 'Variations in mothers' answers to children's questions, as a function of social class, verbal intelligence test scores and sex'. *Sociology*, I(3).

WINER, B.J., 1962, *Statistical Principles in Experimental Design*. McGraw-Hill, chapters 4 and 8.

JULIENNE FORD

Ability and opportunity in a comprehensive school *

If we cannot, at present, draw any firm conclusions about the extent to which comprehensive schools are *productive* of talent, we can at least examine the extent to which they provide increased equality of opportunity for individuals with equal talent potential or 'ability'. For the most common criticism of the tripartite system is that while purporting to effect selection on the basis of ability (operationally defined as IQ) it does not in fact do so accurately.

Despite the conclusion of Floud, *et al,* in 1956 that, if measured intelligence was taken as a criterion, then the social class distribution of grammar school places was equitable,[1] Douglas has more recently shown that a problem of social class bias in selection still does exist. The working class pupil must typically have a slightly higher IQ than the middle class one in order to stand the same chance of selection for grammar school, simply because working class areas tend to have smaller proportions of grammar school places than their IQ distributions would justify.[2] It is widely believed that comprehensive reorganization will go some way towards ameliorating this situation, that the extent of 'wastage of talent' or 'uneducated capacity'[3] will be reduced and that, in fact, *'Comprehensive schools will provide greater equality of opportunity for those with equal talent'.*

Now in order to test this and the remaining three hypotheses a sample of pupils in comprehensive and tripartite schools was required. A number of considerations affected the selection of this sample. In the first place, in order for any generalizations to be valid it was necessary to find a comprehensive school which was both typical of the majority of comprehensive schools in England today, and which had been established long enough for the majority of its pupils to have been attending that school for the whole of their secondary education. In addition to these basic criteria it was considered essential that this school be relatively 'uncreamed', drawing almost all the secondary age pupils in the catchment area. For, while the *typical* comprehensive school today *is* creamed for the top levels of ability by neighbouring grammar schools, the theory that we are examining concerns the effects of large scale comprehensive reorganization. It is therefore desirable to simulate as far as possible the conditions which will obtain when (as seems likely) the whole of the public sector of secondary education is reorganized in this way. In this respect, then, the criterion of typicality

*Reprinted from Julienne Ford, Social Class and the Comprehensive School (London: Routledge and Kegan Paul, 1969; New York: Humanities Press Inc.), pp. 32-45, by kind permission of the author and publishers.

was abandoned in order to do justice to the ideals of the comprehensivists who rightly claim that where creaming occurs the basic principle of comprehensivization — a common education for all[4] — is lost.

The problem thus became one of locating a well-established relatively uncreamed comprehensive school of more or less average size which also embraced three characteristics typical of English comprehensives: some system of horizontal organization on the basis of ability groupings (streams), some system of vertical organization unrelated to ability (houses), and coeducation. *'Cherry Dale' Comprehensive* was just such a school.

Cherry Dale school stands on a relatively isolated housing estate somewhere in the inner London area. Built to serve the children from the estate, it is certainly a neighbourhood school,[5] for only 1 or 2 per cent from every year's production of 11 year olds 'go away' to school. The neighbourhood, like most neighbourhoods in urban England, does tend to be socially homogeneous — the majority of the children come from backgrounds which can be described as working class — however a sufficient proportion of middle class children attend the school to allow comparisons to be made.[6]

Cherry Dale is in its physical appearance typical of modern comprehensives. The buildings are light and colourful, there are sports facilities, a swimming pool, a 'flat' where girls practise domestic science, and all kinds of facilities for scientific, technical and art education. But it is also typical in its academic organization. The school is organized both into academic streams or teaching groups on the basis of ability and into the mixed ability groupings called houses and house-tutor groups. It is important at this stage to note that in Cherry Dale, as in most comprehensives, the actual teaching takes place in academic streams. There are, in effect, seven of these teaching groups in each year group, the first two ('A'$_1$ and 'A'$_2$) being 'grammar streams', the next two ('B'$_1$ and 'B'$_2$) covering the upper-middle ability range and the lower streams ('C'$_1$ and 'C'$_2$) being mainly practical in orientation; the final stream ('D') is a remedial group.[7]

Having selected a suitable comprehensive school, the problem of choosing tripartite schools for purposes of comparison was precisely delimited. For, in order to control as many confounding variables as possible, it was necessary to find two schools which closely 'matched' Cherry Dale in relevant respects. *'Gammer Wiggins' Grammar School* and *'South Moleberry' Secondary Modern* were therefore selected as suitable coeducational tripartite schools in similar working class areas of inner London.[8]

The sample comprised the complete fourth years of these three schools:[9] 320 14-15 year old boys and girls.[10] Questionnaires were administered to the children in their form groups (or, in the case of Cherry Dale School, their academic streams), in an ordinary classroom during lesson time, and were completed under supervision. In this way the problem of bias from non-response was virtually eliminated, for all the children present returned a questionnaire and it was possible to ensure that practically all of these were completed fully.

The most obvious way of testing the hypothesis on this sample is by analysis of the interaction of social class and measured intelligence as determinants of academic attainment in the three schools. For we know that, under the traditional system of secondary education, the impact of social class on educational attainment is greater than can be explained by the covariation of class and IQ.[12] In other words, under the tripartite system opportunities for those with equal ability (defined as IQ) are not equal and the inequalities are related to social class. If the hypothesis were correct, then we would expect IQ to be a greater determinant, and social class a lesser determinant of educational attainment in comprehensive than in tripartite schools.

Now a number of writers have suggested that where comprehensive schools employ some system of academic streaming (as most of them do) this may not be the case.[13] Thus, on the basis of a study of about 800 comprehensive schoolchildren, Holly concluded that 'Streaming by ability within the comprehensive school does not seem . . . to result in producing a new elite based on attainment or intelligence quotients: it seems merely to preserve the traditional class basis of educational selection.'[14] Yet the comprehensive enthusiast might well reply that, since no one would maintain that comprehensive schools eliminate class bias in educational attainment completely, the more interesting question is whether such schools are *relatively* more effective in this respect.[15]

Some light can be thrown on this question by examination of the social class and IQ composition of the fourth year streams in the three schools considered here.

Social class was determined by responses to the simple question 'What is your father's job?', accompanied by the verbal instruction 'Imagine that you are explaining to a new friend what your father does, try to give as much information as you can.' The information given was in almost all cases sufficient to enable responses to be classified according to occupational prestige.[16] Of course father's occupation as reported by a child is not the best possible measure of social class. A more precise classification could be produced from an *index* including assessments of income, life styles and the education of both parents as well as occupational prestige. But occupational prestige is certainly the best single *indicator*. For its use is based on the reasonable sociological assumption that, since the work role is such a time-consuming one, it is in terms of this that people evaluate one another. Furthermore, owing to the necessity to control several variables simultaneously in the following analysis, the social class variable has simply been dichotomized. And several studies have shown that the most socially significant and meaningful social class classification is a simple non-manual/manual division.[18]

The sample was also dichotomized according to IQ scores.[19] Since such scores are artificially created to represent comparable deviations from a norm of 100, those children with scores up to and including 100 were classified as of 'low IQ', and those with scores of 101 or more were classified as of 'high IQ'. However, as there were no children in the grammar school with scores of 100 or less, in order to assess the relationship between IQ and streaming in this school the pupils were dichotomized at the median point. Thus for this group 'low IQ' refers to scores between 101 and 120, while 'high IQ' refers to scores of 121 or more.

Table I shows the relationship between social class, IQ and stream for the three schools.

TABLE I Social class and IQ composition of streams in the three schools

School	Stream	Middle class†		Working class		N= (100%)
		High IQ* %	Low IQ %	High IQ* %	Low IQ %	
Grammar	'A'	84	7	7	3	30
	'B'	60	20	20	0	25
	'C'	41	26	22	11	27
	'D'	20	0	47	33	15
Comprehensive	'A'	33	8	59	0	39
	'B'	4	9	56	31	46
	'C'	8	6	29	56	48
	'D'	0	10	10	79	19
Secondary modern	'A'	31	7	52	12	29
	'B'	11	22	44	22	18
	'C'	0	8	25	67	24

* That is 120+ for grammar school or 100+ for comprehensive and secondary modern schools
† That is non-manual paternal occupation

It can be seen from the table that in all three schools *both* social class and IQ are related to stream. However our interest is primarily in the extent to which the *relative* importance of social class and IQ as determinants of stream differs between the three schools. For this reason Table II has been derived from the above figures.

Table II shows the strength of the relationships between social class and selection for the 'A' stream *when IQ is held constant*. Only children with 'high' IQs are considered and the extent to which social class affects the chances of these children to be placed in the top streams of their schools in analysed. Thus, for example, 46 per cent of the middle class children in the grammar school with 'high' IQs are placed in the 'A' stream, while only 10 per cent of the working class children in the same ability range achieve this placement: a difference which is statistically significant. In the comprehensive school the relationship between social class and placement in the 'A' stream is still statistically significant for the 'high' IQ group; however in the secondary modern school, when IQ is controlled in this manner the relationship between stream and social class is reduced to insignificance.[20]

TABLE II   'High' IQs only: social class and 'A' stream placement in
the three schools

SCHOOL	Middle class % placed in 'A' stream	Working class % placed in 'A' stream	p = *
Grammar	46	10	.01
Comprehensive	68	35	.01
Secondary modern	82	52	n.s.

* 'A' stream compared with all other streams in a 2 x 2χ^2 test of significance

The results of this comparison, then, give no support to the hypothesis.
Indeed they tend to confirm the suspicions of Holly and others that
selection on the basis of streaming in the comprehensive school, like
selection under the tripartite system, tends to underline class differentials in educational opportunity. For in the comprehensive school, as
in the grammar school, there appears to be a relationship between
social class and 'A' stream placement over and above that which can
be explained by the well-known correlation between social class and
measured IQ.[21] In other words, at the same ability level the middle
class child stands a greater change of placement in the 'grammar'
streams of a comprehensive school than the working class child, a
situation in one respect not substantially different from that which
exists under the tripartite system.

Now it might be objected that to show that a class bias in stream
placement exists in the comprehensive school is not necessarily to
demonstrate that there are inequalities in educational attainment which
relate to social class. For just possibly those children who have been
placed in the lower streams of the comprehensive school will achieve
the same eventual educational levels as those in the 'A' stream: stream
might bear little relationship to level of education reached.

A good index of the extent to which this is the case can be derived
by examination of the leaving intentions of the children experiencing
the various forms of education. For, if a substantial proportion of
those in the lower streams of the comprehensive school intend to stay
on at school to follow fifth and sixth form courses, then one could
argue that the class bias in streaming has little consequence for actual
educational attainment. If, on the other hand, children in the lower
streams of the comprehensive school resemble those in the secondary
modern in their leaving intentions then clearly streaming has an impact
on level of educational attainment and the class bias in streaming is
certainly important. In Table III, therefore, the leaving intentions of
children in the three schools are compared.

It can be seen from the table that streaming within the comprehensive
school has a definite impact on leaving intentions, for all of the 'A'
stream children intend to stay at least into the fifth form, while 13 per
cent of the middle class and 40 per cent of the working class children
in the lower streams intend leaving in the fourth year and therefore

TABLE III Leaving intentions by school, comprehensive stream and social class

School	Social class	% leaving in 4th year	% leaving in 5th year	% leaving in 6-8th years	N = (100%)
Grammar	Middle class	0	10	90	68
	Working class	0	28	72	29
Comprehensive 'A' streams	Middle class	0	50	50	16
	Working class	0	87	13	23
Comprehensive 'B-D' streams	Middle class	20	60	20	15
	Working class	40	56	4	98
Secondary modern	Middle class	32	47	21	19
	Working class	40	52	8	52

have no hope of sitting for GCE examinations. This is, of course, hardly surprising. For the 'A' streams have been following five-year courses specifically designed to terminate in GCE, and, while many of those in the 'B' and 'C' streams will sit CSE examinations none of those in the 'D' stream are expected to gain any formal qualifications at all. Streaming within a comprehensive school is thus an important determinant of educational attainment and for this reason the class inequalities in stream placement shown in Tables I and II are important.

Another interesting feature of Table III is the comparison of the comprehensive 'A' stream and the grammar school children. For the former represent the highest ability group in the comprehensive, children who might well have gone to a grammar school under the tripartite system, yet only 28 per cent of them intend staying into the sixth form. This compares with 85 per cent of grammar school children intending to stay at least one year in the sixth form — a difference which is highly significant ($\chi^2 = 40.2$, $d.f. = 1$, $p = .001$). This differential holds both for the working class children ($\chi^2 = 18.09$, $d.f. = 1$, $p = .001$), and for the middle class ($\chi^2 = 14.39$, $d.f. = 1$, $p = .001$).

This raises in an acute form the question of 'wastage of ability' which was examined in the *Early Leaving Report*. For the table shows not only that 'home background influences the use which a boy or girl will make of a grammar school education'[22] (18 per cent more middle than working class children staying on into the sixth form), but also that this same effect of home background can be observed in the comprehensive 'A' streams. For half the middle class 'A' stream children in the sample and only 13 per cent of the working class ones intended to stay beyond the fifth. Indeed it seems from these figures that this 'wastage' is even greater in the comprehensive than in the grammar school.

In order to investigate this alarming possibility it is necessary to compare the leaving intentions of those working class children who

are 'able' enough to profit from sixth form courses under the two
systems. For this purpose 'able' children were arbitrarily defined as
those with an IQ score of 111 or more — approximately the average
level for grammar school pupils.[23] The number of such children in
the secondary modern school and comprehensive 'B' to 'D' streams
was, of course, too small to be considered.

TABLE IV   Working class children with IQ scores of 111 or more:
leaving intentions by type of schooling

	Leaving in 5th year %	Staying into sixth form %	N = (100%)
Grammar school	31	69	23
Comprehensive 'A' stream	84	16	19

$$(x^2 = 10.98, d.f. = .01)$$

The evidence from the three schools, then, far from revealing a greater
equality of opportunity for the comprehensive school pupil, shows a
persistence of class bias in educational attainment under the comprehensive system. Indeed there is some indication that 'wastage of ability'
among bright working class pupils may be occurring on an even larger
scale in Cherry Dale comprehensive school than in Gammer Wiggins
grammar school.[24]

For where comprehensive school children are taught in ability groups
or streams as nearly all of them are,[25] the 'self-fulfilling prophecy'
characteristic of the tripartite system is still very much in evidence.
'Ability' is itself related to social class, but middle class children get an
even larger share of the cake than their ability distribution would justify.
The middle class child is more likely than the working class child to
find himself in the 'grammar' stream at the comprehensive school, even
where the two children are similar in ability. And even those working
class children who do succeed in obtaining 'A' stream placement are
four times more likely than their middle class counterparts to 'waste'
that opportunity of leaving school without a sixth form education.
Thus while there is little evidence on the question of whether comprehensive reorganization of secondary education will promote a greater
development of talent, there is some serious doubt whether it will
decrease inequalities of opportunity for those with equal talent.

In short there is little evidence from this study of three schools that
comprehensive education as it is practised at the present will modify
the characteristic association between social class and educational
attainment. Indeed one could argue that it can hardly be expected to
do so. For, as C. Arnold Anderson has said, 'In order for schooling to
change a status system schooling must be a variable.'[26] In other words,
for the relationship between social class and educational success to be
destroyed it would not be sufficient to give every child the *same* chance.
Working class children, disadvantaged by their cultural background and

inferior physical environs, would need to be given not the same but superior educational opportunities. Yet in the typical comprehensive school the average working class child starts off with the same handicaps that would have lengthened the odds against his success under the old system. And the outcome of the race appears to be no less predictable.

However, a number of advocates of comprehensive reorganization would argue that, even in the absence of any evidence in support of the first two hypotheses — even if there is no proof of the *'educational'* superiority of the comprehensive system — the *'social'* arguments in favour of such schools are overwhelming and reorganization is therefore desirable on 'social' grounds alone.[27]

Notes

1 Jean E. Floud, A.H. Halsey, and F.M. Martin, *Social Class and Educational Opportunity* (Heinemann, 1956).
2 J.W.B. Douglas, *The Home and the School* (MacGibbon and Kee, 1964).
3 The notions of talent wastage and uneducated capacity are employed in the Crowther Report *15 to 18* (London, HMSO, 1959) and the Robbins Report *Higher Education* (London, HMSO, 1963).
4 'A Comprehensive school is not merely unselective: it is a school which caters for all levels of ability apart from handicapped pupils needing special education. The term is hardly justified unless there are in fact within it sufficient numbers of pupils in all parts of the ability range to call for and justify proper provision for them': *London Comprehensive School 1966* (ILEA, 1967), p.17, paragraph 23.
5 The notion that comprehensive schools are neighbourhood schools pervades many of the official publications but is discussed most fully in Robin Pedley, *The Comprehensive School* (Pelican, 1963) especially chapter 5.
6 Approximately a quarter of the pupils *in the sample* from Cherry Dale school were middle class and there is no reason to believe that this differs from the proportion for the school as a whole. There is some evidence that LEA areas may become *more* socially homogeneous so to this extent it is not unrealistic to examine a comprehensive school in a relatively homogeneous catchment area.
7 Of course the streams were not *actually named* in such an overtly hierarchical way. The picture has also been oversimplified in that the 'D' stream did comprise two small separate groups. But, as these were equal in status and were often grouped together for timetabling and other purposes (for example they responded to the questionnaire as one group) they will be treated throughout as a single stream.
8 The tripartite schools were chosen from areas more or less similar to that of the comprehensive school with regard to social class composition and general neighbourhood environment. In this way it was hoped to minimize the confounding influence of 'neighbourhood context' on educational attainment, aspirations and attitudes. For the classic discussion of the importance of this variable see Natalie

Rogoff, 'Local social structure and educational selection' in A.H. Halsey, *et al.* (eds.), *Education, Economy and Society* (Free Press, 1961), pp. 243-4. And, for a study of the importance of neighbourhood context in the case of English comprehensive schools, see S. John Eggleston, 'How comprehensive is the Leicestershire Plan?', *New Society* (23 March 1965).

[9] Excluding, of course, those who were absent from school on the day the questionnaire was administered.

[10] The fourth year was selected as this was the oldest group which could be studied before the sample became biased by leavers. Any study of the educational and occupational plans and expectations of such a biased sample would have been highly misleading, c.f. Ralph Turner, *The Social Context of Ambition* (Chandler, 1964).

[12] For good summaries of this position see Denis Lawton, *Social Class Language and Education* (Routledge and Kegan Paul, 1968) chapter 1 and A. Little, and J. Westergaard, 'The trend of class differentials in educational opportunity', *British Journal of Sociology*, 15 (1964), pp. 301-15

[13] For example Michael Young, and Michael Armstrong, 'The flexible school', *Where*, supplement 5 (1965), especially p. 4.

[14] D.N. Holly, 'Profiting from a comprehensive school: class, sex and ability', *British Journal of Sociology,* 16(4) (1965), p. 157.

[15] This point is also made by A. Giddens, and S.W.F. Holloway, 'Profiting from a comprehensive school: a critical comment', *British Journal of Sociology,* 16 (4), (1965), pp. 351-3.

[16] This is the Hall-Jones scale. In those cases where the information *was* insufficient or where the father was dead or had deserted the family (about 3 per cent in all) classification was on the basis of mother's occupation. The open ended format was used in preference to a pre-coded schedule as it has been shown that the extent of misunderstanding of the latter is greater than the likelihood of coding bias in the former. See J. David Colfax, and Irving L. Allen, 'Pre-coded versus open ended items and children's reports of father's occupation', *Sociology of Education,* 40 (1) (1967), pp. 96-8.

[18] Blau, Peter M., developed a measure of occupational prestige according to the amount of bias in judgements of respondents from different social class backgrounds, and found that the break between manual and non-manual occupations was the most important predictor of such bias. 'Occupational bias and mobility', *American Sociological Review,* 22 (1957), pp. 392-9. F. Martin similarly found that when a matrix was constructed between Hall-Jones categories and subjective social class categories the *most* difference between any transition from one grade to the next on the Hall-Jones scale which appeared on the subjective dimension occured in the transition from manual to non-manual. See D.V. Glass (ed.), *Social Mobility in Britain* (Routledge, 1954), pp. 51-75. A more recent review of the English situation also led to the conclusion that 'Two class formulation is much more than an analytical simplification of those who have studied class. It is a simplification which has a profound hold on the perceptions of class found in British society', see Michael Kahan,*et al*

'On the analytical division of social class', *British Journal of Sociology,* 17 (2) (1966), p. 124.

[19] The scores were obtained from school records.

[20] Obviously tables showing class chances of 'A' stream placement for children of relatively low IQ or of, say, 'D' stream placement for those of relatively high or low IQ can also be calculated from Table I. However these have not been presented as the strong correlations between the three variables render the numbers involved in such tabulations too small to be meaningful.

[21] I say 'appears to be' because in order to make a categorical statement to this effect it would be necessary to produce partial correlations which would indicate the extent and direction of the relationships between the three variables *over their whole range.* The analysis here presented is necessarily crude because the numbers involved preclude anything but dichotomization.

The lack of a statistically significant relationship between class and stream in the secondary modern school may also be explicable by the small numbers involved. For this reason no attempt at *ex post facto* explanation of this has been attempted.

[22] *Early Leaving:* a report of the Central Advisory Council for Education (London HMSO, 1954), p. 19.

[23] See Jean Floud, and A.H. Halsey, 'Social class, intelligence tests, and selection for secondary schools', in A.H. Halsey, *et al.* (eds.), *Education, Economy and Society* (Free Press, 1961), pp. 212-13.

[24] This finding conflicts with that of Miller. He found that, in response to the more evaluative question 'Do you want to leave school as soon as possible?', 83 per cent of grammar, 93 per cent of 'comprehensive grammar' ('A' stream), 72 per cent of 'comprehensive modern' (Lower streams) and 57 per cent of modern school children answered in the negative. See T.W.G. Miller, *Values in the Comprehensive School* (Oliver and Boyd, 1961).

[25] Pedley noted in 1963 that 'Out of 102 comprehensive schools recently questioned on this subject, 88 "stream" the children on entry, 11 during or at the end of the first year. The remaining three do so after two years.' op. cit., p. 88.

[26] 'A sceptical note on education and mobility' in Halsey, *et al.,* op. cit. (1961), p. 252.

[27] For example Peter Townsend, in his 'The argument for comprehensive schools', *Comprehensive Education,* 1 (1965). Townsend himself concedes that the distinction between 'social' and 'educational' arguments is somewhat spurious, as the 'social' arguments (about occupational placement, social 'mixing' and class ideologies) are really extensions of the 'educational' argument.

ROBERT W WITKIN

Social class influence on the amount and type of positive evaluation of school lessons*[1]

A great deal of research, theory, and plain speculation has been centred in recent years on the relationship between social class and education (Jackson and Marsden 1962; Bernstein 1960, 1965; Douglas 1964; Lawton 1967; Floud, Halsey, and Martin 1957; Klein 1965). The research reported below is intended to throw some light on important questions arising out of the work of these investigators and writings based on this work. Does the working class child evaluate his school experience less positively than the middle class child? Furthermore, given free choices among different evaluative indices in respect of a given lesson, does he make different choices as compared with the middle class child? Finally, does the relationship between working class and middle class pupil evaluation of school experience differ as between types of school (comprehensive, grammar and secondary modern)? Because the results of this study question certain recently established 'orthodoxies' in education thinking, it is necessary to provide a little background. What follows is a somewhat oversimplified view which sketches in a few broad lines to frame what is really a highly confused and complex field of study.

The class-culture conflict model

The educational orthodoxies referred to have fostered the view that there is a 'dissonant' relationship between 'middle class' culture and 'working class' culture in respect of the social system of the school. The dominant cultural ethos of the school, particularly the grammar school, is said to be middle class. This is very much the situation suggested by Jackson and Marsden (1962) in their famous study of working class pupils in the grammar school. For these investigators, the middle class culture of the grammar school negates the working class culture of a large number of its pupils which leads the child from a working class background either to reject the 'school culture' and conform to his own (early leaving, rebellion, etc.) or to reject his own culture and conform to that of the school. The middle class child, of course, experiences no such conflict since 'school culture' is seen as an extension of 'home culture'. As Bernstein has put it (1961, p. 296), 'The social structure of the school, the means and ends of education,

*Reprinted from Robert W. Witkin, 'Social class influence on the amount and type of positive evaluation of school lessons', Sociology, 5(2) (May 1971), pp. 169-89, by kind permission of the author and publishers, the Clarendon Press.

create a framework that the middle class child is able to accept, respond to, and exploit.' Bernstein's work has lent a great deal of support to what I have called the class culture conflict model. In a series of remarkable researches and theoretical papers he has demonstrated the quite divergent consequences for the child's experience depending upon whether he is socialized into the elaborated linguistic encoding strategies utilized within middle class social structures or is confined to the use of restricted codes prevalent in working class social structures. When we come to consider the consquences of this for the formal learning situation within the context of the lesson, the implications seem clear enough (Bernstein 1961 p. 304): 'The attempt to substitute a different use of language and to change the order of communication creates critical problems for the lower working class child, as it is an attempt to change his basic system of perception, fundamentally the very means by which he has been socialized.' Elaborated and restricted codes constitute only one of several dichotomies developed over the years to define 'working class' and 'middle class' cultures in oppositional terms (cf. Klein 1965). By describing the school itself in these terms, however, the child's experience is assumed by many investigators to reflect the consequences attendant upon this 'conflict' between class cultures in the wider community.

Perhaps the most impressive support for the 'class culture conflict model' of the school has stemmed from the major statistical studies (Crowther 1959, Robbins 1963, Douglas 1964). These reports have given a clear and unequivocal picture of wastage of working class talent in terms of early leaving and poorer academic performance. Crowther found that 87 per cent of children with above average IQs have left school by the age of sixteen; and that of grammar school boys whose fathers were professional or managerial workers 38 per cent had left school by age sixteen, whereas for the sons of skilled and less skilled manual workers the figure was as high as 72 per cent. Robbins found that a working class boy in the top quartile of the ability group selected for grammar school at eleven would not do as well in the GCE as a middle class boy in the bottom quartile of the group. It can hardly be denied that class related factors are at the root of this very considerable wastage of ability within our educational system. What is problematical, however, is the part played by the school as a social system. There is a distinction, invariably overlooked, between the relationship of children to wider educational values (and their utilization of resources in pursuit of these values) and the children's relationship to the school as a social system and their experience within it. It is my contention – argued elsewhere[2] but supported here – that it is possible for social class differences in the community as a whole to produce these educational effects (early leaving, lack of motivation for achievements, failure to utilize educational opportunities, etc.) *without* there being conflict between the ongoing school culture and that of its working class pupils. In short the 'class culture conflict model' may indeed describe a 'community wide' situation and yet be inadequate in describing the socio-cultural system of the school. If this model does describe the school system, then we would expect the following three hypotheses to be supported in respect of pupil evaluation of both school in general and the English lesson in particular. For the purposes of this study the English lesson was thought to be a particularly suitable test case.

Hypotheses to test the 'class culture conflict model'

1   That there are significant social class differences in respect of the pupil's general orientation to school, with working class children less positive towards school and middle class children more positive.

2   That there are significant social class differences in respect of a particular lesson (e.g. the English lesson), with working class children less positive in their evaluation of that lesson and middle class children more positive.

3   That the discrepancy between middle class and working class evaluation of school in general and the English lesson in particular should be greater in the more middle class institutions — the grammar and independent schools — than in the secondary modern or comprehensive schools (especially bearing in mind the high wastage of working class ability in the grammar schools).

The counter-argument: the 'articulated systems model'

The point of view advanced in this paper is a somewhat different one from the orthodoxy outlined above. It is argued that an important difference between middle class and working class children in respect of evaluation of school experience arises as a result of a quite different relationship between the child and the school for each of these categories. For the middle class child, the social system of the school is articulated with that of the home on one side and the community on the other to a much greater extent than is the case for the working class child. It is important to be clear as to what is meant by 'articulation' in this context. It does not refer to the compatibility or relevance of the child's experience within school to his experience within the home or community. It refers to the integration of home, school, and community within a single super-ordinate system of generalized expectations governing the child's relationship to physical, social and cultural objects. It is usual to treat social roles as the units of social systems and to refer them to the particular system of which they constitute a part. Nevertheless, some social roles (or at least generalized parts of them) are more 'demanding' than others in terms of the amount of the actor's social time and social space they occupy. That is to say, some sets of expectations (e.g. generalized aspects of certain professional roles) are not confined to a particular social system but extend both through social time and social space, linking and controlling the actor's behaviour in different social systems. The social systems in which the actor participates within this area of social space and social time occupied by such roles may be said to be articulated for the actor to the extent that he is subject to the generalized aspects of these roles. Where a high level of articulation exists, the actor's response within these systems is controlled by the 'superordinate' system of generalized roles. Where the level of articulation is low, the actor is subject to the control of specific sets of expectations generated within the particular social systems in which he participates. In certain social systems the level of articulation can be high for some actors and low for others. The viewpoint presented here is that for middle class children in schools the level of articulation is high relative to that for working class children. Where the level of articulation is high, the probability that an actor's experience and interaction within a particular system will diverge from the expectations he holds is that much greater. This is so simply because the expectations he holds are generated within the context of a super-ordinate system and he is thereby *less* subject to the particular exigencies of a given social system. The opposite is the case for the actor for whom the level of articulation is low. His expectations are generated within a particular social system and he is *less* subject to the general exigencies of a superordinate system. The question of 'more' or 'less' is an important one because it is assumed here that some level of articulation exists for all actors.

I have made the point that the levels of articulation as between middle class and working class children differ with reference to the social system of the school. In terms of the time out of the life of the child (i.e. the school day) and the quantity of active response required, however, there are no great differences as between middle class and working class children. They all attend lessons between certain hours and the pattern of a lesson, with its demands in terms of quantity of response relative to ability, is much the same for all groups of children albeit pitched at different levels and within different schools systems. I hypothesize, therefore, that over a wide range of schools the social classes ought not to differ in respect of their general orientation to school. The amount of positive orientation to school will be a function of the level of involvement and participation of the child.

When we come to evaluation of the English lesson (as the particular lesson chosen for this study) I predict that there ought to be significant social class differences, but in the *opposite* direction to those that would be expected using the class culture conflict model. The reason is simply this. Because the articulation of school with other social systems is so high for the middle class child there is a greater likelihood that his expectations *in* school will not be fully met. Within the school itself very particular expectations are generated and interaction situations offer possibilities for considerable variation. The child who refers his experience to a superordinate system for evaluation is less free to exploit the possibilities within particular interaction contexts. He will be much less 'set' to perceive the particular lesson in terms of any intrinsic gratification that is offered and will be more concerned to evaluate it in terms of the extent to which it meets his generalized expectations. The working class child, on the other hand, is more likely to have his expectations met. Because school has a low level of articulation with other systems for him, expectations are largely generated within the school itself. He is thus more free to exploit the possibilities within variable situations, and to respond to the opportunities for immediate gratification. This should increase the likelihood that the working class child will evaluate the particular lesson in a more positive way than the middle class child.

In addition we need to consider the part played by the type of school. It would seem reasonable to suppose that the level of involvement and participation encouraged by the school will influence the general orientation of its pupils. We ought to find therefore that comprehensive schools and grammar schools register a rather higher level of positive orientation to school than secondary modern schools, since the general level of participation and involvement demanded by both types of school is usually greater than is the case for secondary modern schools. When it comes to predicting the amount of positive evaluation of the English lesson by type of school, the situation is somewhat different. We would still expect comprehensive schools to register the greatest overall amount of positive evaluation, since the evaluation of the particular lesson is likely to reflect the level of immediate gratification available and the amount of pupil dependence on value definitions generated within the school. These will bear more effectively on working class children because their lack of a superordinate reference prevents them putting distance between themselves and the value definitions of the school. In comprehensive schools where the newer methods used in teaching English in a more 'conversational' and 'enjoyable' manner are employed to a much greater extent, and interaction situations are frequently novel, experimental and variable, the opportunities for immediate gratification are maximized. However, the middle class child will be less free to exploit these than the working class child because of the higher level of articulation of school for him. Therefore, although the overall amount of positive evaluation should be highest in comprehensive schools, the social class differences should be most evident here in respect of evaluation of the English lesson. Secondary modern schools probably provide a somewhat lower level of possibilities for immediate gratification but the large working class element should mean that there is a great deal of pupil dependence on school value definitions. We would expect them to be somewhat below the comprehensive schools for overall positive evaluation of the English lesson and also in the extent to which social class differences are evident. Grammar schools are expected to reveal the lowest overall amount of positive evaluation of the English lesson, and social class differences in respect of evaluation are expected to be minimal. This is because for the greater proportion of children within the grammar schools, the level of articulation of school is high. Furthermore, the school itself tries in a quite self-conscious way to meet these superordinate expectations. These two factors greatly restrict the possibilities for immediate gratification compared with the other two types of school. Further still, because the expectations generated within grammar schools approximate more closely to the superordinate expectations of the middle class children, social class differences are likely to be much less in evidence. For the working class child is subject to those expectations generated within school and will tend to become dependent on the school's value definitions.

The three alternative hypotheses set up to test this latter theoretical viewpoint involve the complete contradiction of the three hypotheses set up to test the class culture conflict model.

Hypotheses to test the 'articulated systems model'

1 That there are no significant differences between the social classes in respect of the amount of positive orientation to lessons in general.

2 That there are significant differences in respect of pupil evaluation of the English lesson, with middle class pupils being less positive and working class pupils more positive.

3 (a) That the rank order for the overall amount of positive orientation to lessons in general as between types of school should be, first, comprehensives, followed by grammar and then secondary modern schools.

(b) That the rank order for the overall amount of positive evaluation of the English lesson as between types of school should be, first, comprehensives, followed by secondary modern and then grammar schools.

(c) That the rank order for the most evident social class differencies in respect of evaluation of the English lesson as between types of school should be, first, comprehensives, followed by secondary modern and then grammar schools.

Research design

A questionnaire was administered to some 3,400 pupils constituting the entire fourth year of thirty-six schools. Children in remedial classes were excluded. There were six grammar schools, three direct grant schools, one private school, eight comprehensive schools and eighteen secondary modern schools. They were chosen to include single sex and coeducational urban and rural, large and small schools. Schools were selected to provide the widest possible variation in educational environments. The range included schools as socially distant as, for example, a modern school in 'dockland' and a grammar school in north London. Although a very wide range of socio-cultural environments was sampled, there were obvious limitations. The sample size, large by normal standards, is far too small to be representative. The schools selected were confined to the south of the country, being chosen from London, Bristol, Cambridge, and the south-west. For the purposes of grouping by type of school, direct grant, private, and grammar schools are classified together as grammar/independent. It was thought advisable to include approximately equal numbers of boys and girls in the total sample and to include a breakdown by sex of social class in relation to pupil evaluation, but the theoretical viewpoint advanced here has nothing as yet to offer in terms of predicting what differences, if any, should arise.

The child's general orientation to school was measured in terms of his choice of one of four statements about his school experience.

1 School is great. I've got plenty of friends here and I really enjoy my lessons.

2 I like school because I enjoy my lessons, but I don't have many friends here.

3 I like school because I have a good time with my friends but I don't enjoy my lessons.
4 School is a waste of time because I don't like my lessons and I've no friends here.

The statements offer various possibilities for combining having/not having friends with liking/not liking lessons. An estimate of the amount of positive orientations to school was obtained by summing the responses to statements 1 and 2 (liking lessons irrespective of friendship) and statements 3 and 4 (disliking lessons irrespective of friendship). To see whether 'working class' children differed from middle class children in their choice of evaluative statements in respect of a particular lesson, children were asked to evaluate their English lessons by ticking *any number* of six statements (all positive) that they felt were true of their English lessons. The object here was to see whether children differed between social classes both in terms of quantity of ticking and choice of the particular statement they endorsed.

1 In my English lessons there are always lots of new and interesting things to do.
2 In my English lessons I feel I have learned something important to me.
3 In my English lessons I am encouraged to use my own ideas and do things my own way.
4 In my English lessons I am told clearly what I am expected to do and taught how to do it.
5 My English lessons are fun. I really enjoy myself and that's what matters most.[3]
6 In my English lesson the teacher gives me all the help I need to improve my work.

The six statements were intended to cover evaluate possibilities in terms of variety and interest, personal importance, self-expression, clear direction and teaching, fun and enjoyment, and teacher support. Although many methodological objections have been raised to scales using only positive items, it was decided in this case that the advantages outweighed the disadvantages. A primary objection is that one-way items render detection of aquiescence response-set less likely. The positive reason for selecting one-way items was that, in my experience, schoolchildren are particularly susceptible to the 'social desirability' effect when completing questionnaires. This was a far more serious risk. It was felt that one-way items would remove the psychological tension created by negative evaluative statements of the lesson itself. Not ticking was put to the child as a definite alternative to indicate his disagreement with a positive statement. It was clearly stated too that he need not tick any statement for the particular lesson if he felt that all of the statements were ones he could not endorse as true of that lesson. The child was therefore able to indicate negative evaluation in a manner which was unlikely to alert the 'social desirability' defence.

The social class of the child was obtained by classifying the father's occupation in accordance with the Registrar General's (1966) five social classes. Social class 3, however, was split into two groups — 3(a) non-

TABLE I (All thirty-six schools)

Social class	N	Statement (1)	Statement (2)	Statement (3)	Statement (4)	Statements (1) and (2)	Statements (3) and (4)
Middle	1 354	809	172	364	9	981	373
Working	1 968	1 089	184	678	17	1 273	675
Total	3 322	1 898	376	1 042	26	2 254	1 068
χ^2		6·446	9·499	21·248	0·681	22.266*	

* Significant at the 0.05 level and above

TABLE II (Ten grammar/independent schools)

Social class	N	Statement (1)	Statement (2)	Statement (3)	Statement (4)	Statements (1) and (2)	Statements (3) and (4)
Middle	474	252	82	137	3	334	140
Working	193	105	22	64	2	127	66
Total	667	357	104	201	5	461	206
χ^2		0.117	3·550	1·245	—	1·227*	

*Not significant

TABLE III (*Eight* comprehensive schools)

Social class	N	Statement (1)	Statement (2)	Statement (3)	Statement (4)	Statements (1) and (2)	Statements (3) and (4)
Middle	475	306	46	119	4	352	123
Working	767	453	76	231	7	529	238
Total	1 242	759	122	350	11	881	361
x^2		3·668	—	3·786	—	3·712*	

*Not significant

TABLE IV (*Eighteen* secondary modern schools)

Social class	N	Statement (1)	Statement (2)	Statement (3)	Statement (4)	Statements (1) and (2)	Statements (3) and (4)
Middle	405	251	44	108	2	295	110
Working	1 008	531	86	383	8	617	391
Total	1 413	782	130	491	10	912	501
x^2		9·992	2·037	16·609	0·479	17·167*	

*Significant at 0·05 level and above

TABLE V (Boys)

Schools	Positive (1 and 2)		Negative (3 and 4)		x^2
	Middle class	Working class	Middle class	Working class	
All 36 schools	505	642	220	356	5·450*
Grammar/independent	193	75	78	31	—
Comprehensive	179	250	67	110	0·826
Secondary modern	133	317	75	215	1·270

*Significant at the 0·05 level

TABLE VI (Girls)

Schools	Positive (1 and 2)		Negative (3 and 4)		x^2
	Middle class	Working class	Middle class	Working class	
All 36 schools	476	631	153	339	20·259*
Grammar/independent	141	52	62	35	2·657
Comprehensive	173	279	56	128	3·745
Secondary modern	162	300	35	176	24·279*

*Significant at the 0.05 level and above

manual, and 3(b) manual. Social classes 1, 2, and 3(a) were then grouped together and designated 'middle class' and social classes 3(b), 4, and 5 were grouped together and designated 'working class'.

Results

Tables I, II, III and IV above, in the columns from left to right, give the numbers of children in each social class within the thirty-six schools followed by the number of children in each social class responding to each of the four statements about general orientation to school. The last two columns give the numbers within each social class of those children positively oriented to lessons (irrespective of friendship) and those children negatively oriented to lessons (irrespective of friendship). These are obtained by summing responses to statements 1 and 2 and statements 3 and 4 respectively. Results are given for all schools together, and then separately for grammar and independent schools, comprehensive schools and secondary modern schools. χ^2 values are given at the foot of each column.

Tables V and VI above, give the numbers of children who endorse statements 1 and 2 (those positively oriented to lessons) and statements 3 and 4 (those negatively oriented to lessons) for boys and girls separately. Within each column the children are broken down into two groups, 'middle class' and 'working class'. The χ^2 values are given in a separate column to the right.

Schools were compared with respect to positive orientation to school (irrespective of class) and positive evaluation of the English lesson (irrespective of class). The null hypothesis was set up that positive orientation to school and ticking behaviour in respect of the English lesson are independent of type of school. The results were as follows:

Positive orientation to school lessons

The null hypothesis was accepted for comprehensive and grammar schools for boys and girls together ($\chi^2 = 0.596$) and separately (boys: $\chi^2 = 0.020$ and (girls: $\chi^2 = 0.921$). Comprehensive and grammar schools were then grouped together and compared with secondary modern schools. The very much lower level of positive orientation in the secondary modern schools led to the rejection of the null hypothesis for boys and girls together ($\chi^2 = 12.386$) and for boys ($\chi^2 = 19.297$) but the null hypothesis was accepted for girls ($\chi^2 = 0.193$).

Evaluation of the English lesson

The null hypothesis was rejected for five out of six statements both for boys and girls together and separately: χ^2 values for the thirty-six schools are given in Table VII below.

TABLE VII χ^2 values

	Statement (1)	Statement (2)	Statement (3)	Statement (4)	Statement (5)	Statement (6)
All 36 schools (boys and girls)	59·957	65·021	65·859	34·970	2·312	74·132
Boys	58·280	12·871	40·746	22·848	5·235	33·070
Girls	8·699	75·608	18·391	11·838	1·152	45·221

TABLE VIII (All thirty-six schools)

Social class		Statement (1)	Statement (2)	Statement (3)	Statement (4)	Statement (5)	Statement (6)	No tickers
Middle	1 382	414	794	631	656	273	708	85
Working	1 983	715	1 277	945	1 053	473	1 213	64
Total	3 365	1 129	2 071	1 576	1 709	746	1 921	149
χ^2		13·538*	16·504*	1·328	10·494*	8·018*	12·882*	16·237*

*Significant at the 0·5 level and above

TABLE IX (*Ten* grammar/independent schools)

Social class		Statement (1)	Statement (2)	Statement (3)	Statement (4)	Statement (5)	Statement (6)	No tickers
Middle	496	111	252	196	228	98	211	44
Working	194	52	93	79	104	41	83	10
Total	690	163	345	275	332	139	294	54
χ^2		1·427	0·386	0·119	3·475	0·178	—	2·500

TABLE X (*Eight* comprehensive schools)

Social class		Statement (1)	Statement (2)	Statement (3)	Statement (4)	Statement (5)	Statement (6)	No tickers
Middle	480	173	265	279	206	96	269	26
Working	775	337	494	421	367	195	496	24
Total	1255	510	759	700	573	291	765	50
χ^2		6·768*	8·188*	1·653	2·296	4·264*	7·941*	4·325*

*Significant at 0·05 level and above

Results on children's general orientation to school may then be summarized as follows.

All thirty-six schools

General orientation to school did reveal significant social class differences at the 0.01 level. The sex breakdown reveals that these are most evident for girls but that the χ^2 value is still significant for boys. The direction of difference is such that middle class children are more positive and working class children are less positive. A very important qualification is necessary here. Type of school was found to be an extremely important factor in the amount of positive orientation for boys but it was not found to be a factor in the case of girls. The social class differences for boys must be interpreted in the light of this. Secondary modern school boys comprise a very large proportion of working class pupils to middle class, and in these schools the amount of positive orientation was appreciably less for all children than in the other two types of school (60 per cent as compared with 70 per cent in grammar and comprehensive). This fact, alone accounts for the social class differences found in respect of boys, for the eighteen secondary modern schools are contributing more than their share of negative orientation and because of their high ratio of working class to middle class pupils this unbalances the picture for the thirty-six schools. That this is so becomes particularly apparent when we consider the social class differences within types of school taken separately.

Grammar/independent schools

General orientation to school revealed no significant social class differences at the 0.05 level, either for boys and girls together or separately.

Comprehensive schools

General orientation to school revealed no significant social class differences at the 0.05 level, either for boys and girls together or separately.

Secondary modern schools

General orientation to school revealed significant social class differences at the 0.01 levels for girls only. Most of this significance was contributed by the overpositive orientation of the middle class girls (17.158 in 24.279). There were no significant social class differences for boys.

The tables VIII to XI show the numbers of children within each social class in the schools studied, followed by the numbers of children in each social class responding to the six evaluative statements in respect of the English lesson. It will be recalled that the children were invited to endorse any of the statements which they felt were true of their English lessons. A separate column at the end gives the number of children in each social class who chose not to tick any of the statements. The χ^2 values are given at the foot of each column. The results are given first for all thirty-six schools and then separately for the grammar/independent schools, comprehensive and secondary modern schools.

TABLE XI (*Eighteen* secondary modern schools)

Social class		Statement (1)	Statement (2)	Statement (3)	Statement (4)	Statement (5)	Statement (6)	No tickers
Middle	406	130	277	156	222	79	228	15
Working	1014	326	690	445	582	237	634	30
Total	1420	456	967	601	804	316	862	45
χ^2		0·004	0·015	3·614	0·897	2·679	4·834*	0·446

*Significant at the 0·05 level

TABLE XII (Boys)

Schools		Statement (1)	Statement (2)	Statement (3)	Statement (4)	Statement (5)	Statement (6)	No tickers
All 36 schools								
Middle class	746	186	435	309	355	129	378	54
Working class	1007	330	642	436	558	240	599	39
x^2		12·568*	5·403*	0·610	10·069*	11·370*	13·635*	9·801*
Grammar/Independent								
Middle class	289	43	164	104	137	44	127	26
Working class	107	25	56	41	59	23	46	5
x^2		4·457*	0·563	0·221	1·844	2·283	0·052	1·641
Comprehensive								
Middle class	248	92	132	138	102	51	144	17
Working class	365	149	234	186	179	84	233	16
x^2		0·838	7·204*	1·331	3·926*	0·630	2·318	2·144
Secondary modern								
Middle class	209	51	139	67	116	34	107	11
Working class	535	156	325	209	320	133	320	18
x^2		1·624	0·029	3·444	0·985	6·453*	4·597*	1·616

*Significant at the 0·05 level and above

Tables XII and XIII then give the results for positive evaluation of the English lesson for boys and girls separately, broken down by class and type of school.

The results may be summarized thus.

All thirty-six schools

Social class differences in respect of the English lesson are significant at the 0.05 level for five out of the six statements – (1), (2), (4), (5) and (6) – not for boys and girls together and separately. These differences are in the predicted direction. Working class children are more positive and middle class children are less positive. Although not significant, the social class differences in respect of the other statement (3) are in the same direction.

Grammar/independent schools

Social class differences in respect of the English lesson are not significant at the 0.05 level for any of the six statements for boys and girls together or for girls alone. Social class differences in the predicted direction are significant for boys for statement (1) only.

Comprehensive schools

Social class differences in the predicted direction are significant at the 0.05 level for statements (1), (2), (5), and (6) for boys and girls together. Significant differences in the same direction exist for boys for statements (2) and (4) and for girls for statements (1), (5), and (6).

Secondary modern schools

Social class differences in the predicted direction are significant at the 0.05 level for statement (6) for boys and girls together and for statements (5) and (6) for boys alone. There were no significant class differences for girls.

Conclusions

Hypothesis (1): class culture conflict model.

We must reject this hypothesis since no significant social class differences were found for boys in any type of school or for girls in comprehensive and grammar schools in respect of general orientation to lessons. The finding for girls in secondary modern schools would not have been predicted by the model and is therefore irrelevant as a test of the hypothesis.

Articulated systems model. The hypothesis may be accepted, although in part only. The findings for girls in secondary modern schools were not anticipated. It is possible to account for them quite convincingly on a *post hoc* basis but the temptation will be avoided since is is hoped to analyse sex differences fully at a later date.

Hypothesis (2): class culture model.

The hypothesis is totally rejected.

Articulated systems model. The hypothesis is fully supported.

TABLE XIII (Girls)

Schools	Statement (1)	Statement (2)	Statement (3)	Statement (4)	Statement (5)	Statement (6)	No tickers
All 36 schools							
Middle class 636	228	359	322	301	144	330	31
Working class 976	385	635	509	495	233	614	25
x^2	2·159	11·961*	0·328	1·754	0·362	19·225*	6·776*
Grammar/independent							
Middle class 207	68	88	92	91	54	84	18
Working class 87	27	37	38	45	18	37	5
x^2	0·074	—	0·020	1·641	0·797	0·067	0·892
Comprehensive							
Middle class 232	81	133	141	104	45	125	9
Working class 410	188	260	235	188	111	263	8
x^2	7·098*	2·301	0·694	0·079	4·447*	6·347*	2·380
Secondary modern							
Middle class 197	79	138	89	106	45	121	4
Working class 479	170	338	236	262	104	314	12
x^2	1·395	0·034	1·032	0·029	0·132	1·123	0·348

*Significant at the 0·05 level

Hypothesis (3): class culture model.

The hypothesis is totally rejected.

Articulated systems model. The hypothesis is fully supported.

Discussion

There are possible alternative explanations of our findings, and we must say something about these since they challenge the validity of the argument. The first concerns the streaming of the schools. It might be argued that had the children been grouped on the basis of examination classes and non-examination classes, the results might have been different. The bases of streaming were extremely variable between our schools and we are still collecting data relevant to this problem for later analysis. Nevertheless, it is not expected that the results of this analysis will radically alter our basic findings, although some effects are bound to be observed in the case of almost any type of regrouping. There is some evidence, even in the results presented here, which argues against accounting for our findings, in terms of exam orientated classes versus non exam orientated classes. Grammar schools which constitute the most 'academic' schools in our sample reveal a high level of positive orientation to school and a low level of positive evaluation of the English lesson. Even allowing for the fact that this could be an artifact of the two different types of task the child is confronted with, we would still have to explain why comprehensive schools reveal the highest level of positive evaluation of the English lesson. Even allowing for the fact that this could be an artifact of the two different types of task the child is confronted with, we would still have to explain why comprehensive schools reveal the highest level of positive evaluation of the English lesson when they contain so many more examination oriented classes than secondary modern schools; and why they reveal such a high level of positive orientation to school when they contain that many fewer examination classes as compared with grammar schools. Further investigation and analysis of this problem is certainly necessary, especially since the likelihood of interaction effects is so great.

Another possibility is that social class differences in respect of the English lesson are an artifact of a social class response-set, with middle class children ticking less and working class children ticking more. This argument is somewhat easier to dispose of. Although the finding that grammar school ticking is lowest is consistent with this view, the volume of ticking within the grammar school is the same for both social classes and indeed it is much the same for both social classes within the secondary modern schools too.

This raises a third possibility that is somewhat more awkward to deal with. If there is not a social class response-set there may well be an IQ response-set, with children of high IQ ticking less; or worse still, there may be an interaction between IQ and social class. At first glance the idea of interpreting the results in terms of an IQ response appeals quite strongly. We would then expect grammar schools to reveal the lowest ticking level, and because of the homogeneity of IQs we would not expect to find many social class differences. We would also expect secondary modern schools to reveal the highest ticking level, and again because of the homogeneity of IQs we would expect few social differences. In the comprehensive schools where IQs are much more heterogeneous we would then expect many more social class differences to arise (class is correlated with IQ). The weakness of the argument is shown in the comparison of secondary modern and comprehensive schools. There must be many more children of high IQ in our comprehensive schools but the overall volume of ticking is higher, not lower. It is higher for three statements, equal for two and lower for one. Nevertheless, the possibility of an interaction effect between social class and IQ is still a strong contender for an alternative explanation. In the absence of independent estimates of IQ which we were unable to obtain, it must remain so. In the final analysis this could become an argument between competing types of explanation. Both IQ and social class might be highly correlated with the hypothesized 'level of articulation' as indeed would membership of exam oriented classes. The question would then be not whether IQ, social class and exam orientation are correlated with ticking behaviour but whether ticking behaviour is explicable in terms of a response-set that is irrelevant so far as the evaluative content of the statements is concerned. I am confident that there is considerable validity in the children's responses which is reflected in their consistent preferences for certain statements rather than others. Furthermore, they show quite different preferences among the same set of statements, when these are applied to the art lesson, for example. Pupil evaluation of art, music and drama was measured at the same time but the data for these subjects are not dealt with in this paper.

The theoretical viewpoint which I have proposed to account for (and indeed to predict) these results may be summarized as follows. The expectations constituting the roles of the middle class child are largely generated at a superordinate level. They extend far into his social time and social space and serve to link his behaviour in different social systems. The expectations constituting the roles of the working class child are to a greater extent generated within particular social systems which involve him. These systems are not articulated for him, and his behaviour does not have to be referred to a superordinate system for evaluation. He is more free than the middle class child to exploit those opportunities for immediate gratification that may exist and at the same time *because of his lack of a superordinate reference he is less able to distance himself from the definitions of his behaviour and experience as they are generated within the school.* Although this interpretation was not stressed in the counter-argument above, I regard it as being of the utmost importance. When we move from the level of considering gratification, and concern ourselves with evaluation in the wider sense, the power of the school to define values is important. At the same time the power of the school to effect any fundamental change in the child's relationship to Education with a capital E is severely limited. Let us take the two separately. As we stated above the working class child does not possess the superordinate reference that would enable him to distance himself from definitions of conduct and experience generated within the school. Therefore the power of the school to influence value definitions bears more effectively on the working class child. He accepts value definitions but he remains less able than the middle class child to benefit from (in the sense of utilizing) education. Conversely, the middle class child is freer to disagree with the value definitions of the school but he is able to benefit from education because of the higher level of articulation. It is precisely this level of articulation which the school is relatively powerless to effect. Whether school is or is not articulated with other systems is, from the point of view of the child, dependent on whether basic socialization processes bring his behaviour under the control of those generalized expectations which define his relationship to social and cultural objects and *effectively link his behaviour in different social systems.*

The distinction made in this paper between articulated and non-articulated social systems and superordinate as opposed to non-superordinate expectations generated as a consequence of articulation is in no way synonymous with the distinction often made in sociological literature between universalistic and particularistic orders of meaning. The latter distinction relates to the scope of cultural relevance that given items or events have within the individuals systems of meaning. The former distinction does not prejudge in any sense the scope of cultural relevance for the individual. The individual who participates in articulated social systems and whose behaviour is guided by superordinate expectations may nevertheless be oriented in terms of particularistic orders of meaning. Similarly, the meanings generated within non-articulated systems may well be universalistic. It is beyond the scope of this paper to argue the point thoroughly, but this writer believes that the conditions which generate universalistic as opposed to particularistic orders of meaning are to some extent independent of those generating superordinate as opposed to non-superordinate expectations. Certainly, it does not necessarily follow that if an individual's behaviour is guided by a superordinate system of expectations his orientation in terms of the significance that these expectations have for him will be a universalistic one. It is entirely conceivable that for many individuals the expectations generated as a result of social system articulation give rise to particularistic orders of meaning in which the scope of cultural relevance for the individual is a narrow one.

The social and psychological roots of what are essentially different relationships to life go quite deep and it seems unlikely that schools of any type touch them more than superficially. Certainly, the school can make education a more enjoyable and satisfying experience for children. There is evidence even in this study that comprehensive schools are achieving improvements here. Schools can teach in a manner that is more relevant to the child's background, culture and experience. It is important to remember, however, that speaking the child's language does not of itself articulate the world for him in the sense of fundamentally altering his relationship and mode of relating to social reality. However 'enjoyable' and 'relevant' the child's experiences are between 9 a.m. and 4 p.m. the statistics are likely to continue to reflect the wastage of working class ability, just so long as the social conditions generating these basic modes of relating to the world prevail within the wider community beyond the school. It is doubtful as to whether the school controls even the most important associations and influences that occur within it, let alone the vital influences beyond it.

It does not appear that the social structure of schools and the experience of the children within them can be profitably described in terms of the class culture conflict model. The precise nature of the influence of school structure on the experience of the child is obscured rather than revealed by such a view. This writer, at the present time, is personally convinced that Bernstein is probably right in respect of the educational consequences of different linguistic codes, at least in terms of the child's ability to utilize educational opportunities and develop his 'skills' in an academic direction. Nevertheless, the following type of inference is more questionable (Bernstein 1961, p. 306). 'The teaching situation for the lower working class child is often persecutory and exposes him to a persistent attack on his language and so his normal mode of orientation. *He is bewildered and defenceless in this situation of linguistic change.*'[4]

Our choice of the English lesson is relevant here because in terms of the children's evaluation of this lesson, we find nothing to indicate that the 'persistent attack on his language' in terms of 'attempts to extend the child's vocabulary' or 'to alter his mode of sentence construction' results in the negative evaluation by the working class child of his English lessons. The reverse seems to be the case. Furthermore unless school is highly articulated for the child, academic problems are likely to remain purely academic for him and frustration is not an inevitable consequence. Failure to make this distinction has in my view led to a conceptual distortion of the relationship between the child and the ongoing culture and social structure of the school.

Notes

[1] The research reported here was financed by the Schools Council under the auspices of their curriculum development project 'Arts and the adolescent'. I am deeply indebted to the organizer of the project, Malcolm Ross, whose personal encouragement and practical help has been invaluable throughout.

[2] Paper in preparation.

[3] The inclusion of the words '. . . and that's what matters most' was an oversight which I deem to be unfortunate, although I personally do not believe, on the basis of responses to all the statements, that the exclusion of these words would have produced a different result.

[4] Italics are Bernstein's. It is to be noted that Bernstein's remarks in the passage quoted refer to the *lower working class* child. I am not certain as to whether Professor Bernstein really wishes his theoretical distinctions to be limited to the lower working class child. I think not (although he clearly does in the passage quoted above). For those who interpret him, and for those who like myself regard his work as the most significant in the field, its wide social applicability is not the least attractive feature of his theory.

References

BERNSTEIN, B., 1960, 'Language and social class'. *British Journal of Sociology*, Vol. II.

BERNSTEIN, B., 1961, 'Social class and linguistic development: a theory of social learning', in A.H. Halsey, J. Floud and C.A. Anderson (eds.), *Education, Economy and Society*. New York: The Free Press.

'CROWTHER REPORT', 1959, Central Advisory Council for Education (England), *15 to 18*. London: HMSO.

DOUGLAS, J.W.B., 1964, *The Home and the School*. London: MacGibbon and Kee.

FLOUD, J., HALSEY, A. and MARTIN, F., 1956, *Social Class and Educational Opportunity*. London: Heinemann.

JACKSON, B. and MARSDEN, D., 1962, *Education and the Working Class*. London: Routledge and Kegan Paul.

KLEIN, J., 1965, *Samples of English Culture* (2 volumes). London: Routledge and Kegan Paul.

LAWTON, D., 1969, *Social Class, Language and Education*. London: Routledge and Kegan Paul.

'ROBBINS REPORT', 1963, Committee on Higher Education, *Higher Education*. London: HMSO.

JAMES PATRICK

A Glasgow gang observed *

Entrée

I was dressed in a midnight-blue suit, with a twelve-inch middle vent, three-inch flaps over the side pockets and a light blue handkerchief with a white polka dot (to match my tie) in the top pocket. My hair, which I had allowed to grow long, was newly washed and combed into a parting just to the left of centre. My nails I had cut down as far as possible, leaving them ragged and dirty. I approached the gang of boys standing outside the pub and Tim, my contact, came forward to meet me, his cheeks red with embarrassment.

'Hello, sur, Ah never thoat ye wid come.'

Fortunately, the other had not heard the slip which almost ruined all my preparations.

I had not planned to join a juvenile gang; I had been invited. For two years I had been working in one of Scotland's approved schools during my vacations from Glasgow University and Jordanhill College of Education. As a result I applied for a full-time post as a teacher, was accepted and started work in August 1966. During the Easter and summer holidays of that year I had met Tim, who had been committed to the school some months previously. Thanks to some common interests, we quickly became friends; a friendship which was resumed when I returned to the school. In discussion with the boys the topic of gangs and gang warfare constantly cropped up. One particular conversation in the middle of July I remember well. A group of boys were lying sunbathing in the yard during their lunch hour. I was sitting on a bench among them, criticizing boys who got into trouble while on leave. Tim, who had been on the edge of the group and lying face downwards on the ground, suddenly jumped up and asked me what I knew about boys on leave and how they spent their time. The honest answer was very little, nothing at all in fact. At this point the signal for the end of lunch break was given and, as the boys put on their vests and shirts and walked over to their 'line', Tim sidled up to me and asked me to come out with him and see for myself.

This combination of invitation and challenge worried me during the holiday I had before taking up my permanent appointment. While I knew from records that Tim was a gang member, with an older brother serving a sentence for murder, the realization of what an opportunity was being offered me, coupled with a general feeling of well-being

*Reprinted from James Patrick, A Glasgow Gang Observed, pp. 12-17 74-84, 143-4, by kind permission of the author and publishers.

THE YOUNG TEAM, 1966-7

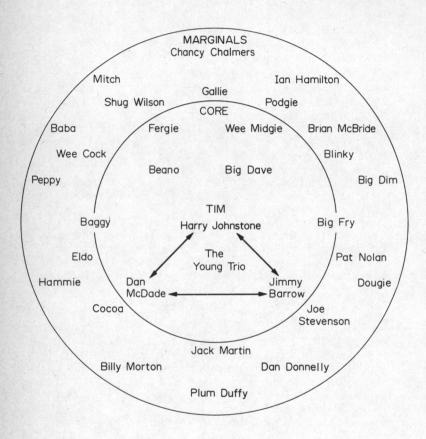

MARGINALS
Chancy Chalmers

Mitch   Ian Hamilton

Gallie

Shug Wilson   Podgie

CORE

Baba   Fergie   Wee Midgie   Brian McBride

Wee Cock   Blinky

Beano   Big Dave

Peppy   Big Dim

TIM
Harry Johnstone   Big Fry

Baggy

The
Young Trio

Eldo   Pat Nolan

Dan   Jimmy

Hammie   McDade   Barrow   Dougie

Cocoa   Joe
Stevenson

Jack Martin

Billy Morton   Dan Donnelly

Plum Duffy

after three weeks in Italy, made me resolve to accept Tim's suggestion. The very fact that Tim wanted someone in authority to see 'whit the score wis' intrigued me. On my return I made use of every possible occasion to discuss privately with Tim-the most suitable time for me to meet him while he was on leave, the type of clothes I should wear, the bond of silence and loyalty which would have to exist between us, ?tc. At first Tim thought that I should be introduced to his mates as an approved school teacher but I soon pointed out the dangers and difficulties of that arrangement. For a start, I would then have been unlikely to see typical behaviour. It was slowly dawning on me that the best solution to the problem would be for me to become a participant observer.

I realized, however, that this method of approach presented its own problems, chief of which was to what extent I should participate. My greatest worry was that incidents might be staged for my benefit, that Tim's behaviour might be radically altered, for better or worse, by my presence. Tim's willingness to introduce me to the gang solved the problem of obtaining entrée. But from then on I would have to play it by ear. I spent the month of September thinking and planning, as the tan on my face slowly disappeared to leave me as pale as Tim and the others. I consulted no one during this period as to what my role should be, my main reasons being a need for total secrecy and a fear of being stopped. Privately I came to the conclusion that I must be a passive participant – a conclusion that became increasingly difficult to abide by, as I shall explain later. I had read but not fully appreciated, Michael Young's thoughts on the 'Interpenetration of observer and observed' in his book *Innovation and Research in Education*. A sentence of his was to remain in my mind: 'The main problem, and excitement, of the social sciences is how to cope with the involvement of observer in observed . . . ' Not only had I to recognize the fact that I was bound to change what I was observing just by observing it, but I had also to contend with the problems of role confusion. The situation of my being a middle class teacher during the week and a member of a juvenile gang at the weekend produced a very real conflict for me. In fact it was the internal struggle between identification with the boys and abhorrence of their violence that finally forced me to quit.

To overcome the problem of background, I decided to present myself as Tim's 'haufer' (i.e. his best friend in the approved school), who was out on leave at the same time, and, 'havin' nae people' (i.e. relatives), had been befriended by Tim. This proved to be a simple but effective answer to questions about where I lived.

A third problem was that of language. Born and bred in Glasgow, I thought myself *au fait* with the local dialect and after two years of part-time work with these boys I considered myself reasonably familiar with their slang– another serious mistake as it turned out. So confused was I on the first night that I had to 'play daft' to avoid too many questions and also to enable me to concentrate on what was being said.

The plan was to meet Tim on the Saturday evening of his next weekend leave. Boys from Glasgow and the surrounding area were allowed home for a weekend once a month and for Sunday leave in the middle of the month.[1] I began to concentrate on making my physical appearance acceptable to the group. I was prepared to give my age as seventeen, although this point was never questioned. In fact I was able to pass myself off as a mate of a fifteen-year-old boy; my exact age remained indeterminate but apparently acceptable. Clothes were another major difficulty. I was already aware of the importance attached to them by gang members in the school and so, after discussion with Tim, I bought the suit I have described in the first paragraph. Even here I made two mistakes. Firstly, I bought the suit outright with cash instead of paying it up, thus attracting both attention to myself in the shop and disbelief in the gang when I innocently mentioned the fact. Secondly, during my first night out with the gang, I fastened the middle button of my jacket as I am accustomed to do. Tim was quick to spot the mistake. The boys in the gang fastened only the top button; with this arrangement they can stand with their hands in their trouser pockets and their jackets buttoned — 'ra gallous wae'.

One point of cardinal importance remains to be explained: namely how an approved school teacher could develop such a close relationship with a pupil. I was the youngest member of the staff and looked it, and this as much as anything else made my relations with the boys easier and more informal. A common set of interests — football, swimming and pop music — helped to further my connection with Tim. He for his part showed an intense curiosity about my home, familyand middle class background and I was equally curious about him. Our conversations during the evenings and weekends when I was on duty, plus the camaraderie engendered by a week's camping with a group of boys including Tim, seemed to ensure a closer relationship than usual between teacher and pupil in a normal day school. But the bond of loyalty thus forged was soon to be tempered in far more testing circumstances.

Finally, Tim and I came to an understanding that, whatever happened, nothing would be disclosed by either of us to other members of the staff or to anybody else. This was seen by both of us as a necessary precaution for our own protection. Tim kept his part of the bargain throughout the four-month period I was involved with the gang (from October 1966 to January 1967) and continues to keep it. I have given a fictitious name to every single character in this book, and any material of an incidental nature which would make participants traceable will be slightly altered or omitted. This leads me to a discussion of the legal advice I have received. Some abridgements have necessarily been made. Unhappily for society, no character in this book is fictional. And, while using pseudonyms, I have retained nicknames of a type likely to be repeated in other gangs throughout the city. I propose to describe the general area in which I worked, to list the gangs in that area, but I shall not identify the name of the gang I joined. Wherever possible, I shall let events and characters speak for themselves. There were twelve outings in all and the first few will be recounted in detail. Then, instead of a blow-for-blow account in strict chronological order of every time I met the gang, key events and representative situations will be described.

But allowing the characters to speak for themselves presents two final problems — those of obscenity and unintelligibility. I must warn the reader that some of the phrases used, apart from predictable swearing and blaspheming, are extremely crude and are only included to convey a total picture of conversations I heard. The second difficulty is more intractable. Whole pages may at first glance appear to be extracts from 'Oor Wullie' or 'The Broons' (characters in strip cartoons of Glasgow life), but such is the dialect. A glossary is included as an appendix to the book to enable the reader to translate the main text into English.

On the Friday night as I left school, I reminded Tim for the last time that I was coming purely as an observer. At first he had been amused and delighted at my acceptance of his offer; latterly, as I made detailed preparations with him, his attitude became one more of incredulity. I now understand why.

Saturday afternoon and Monday evening

I was keen to go out with the gang as often as possible before Christmas. This was only partly because I wanted a rest and time to rethink my position but mainly because a major gang fight with the Barnes Road was being scheduled for the holiday period. Challenges were soon to be issued for a full scale 'ba'le'. The vacation was chosen as both teams would then be at full strength, with approved schools and remand homes releasing large numbers of boys for the festive season.

On that first Saturday night at the pub I gathered that Tim was being given what amounted to a progress report. Since than I had discovered that he was being brought up to date with news of the Fleet rather than of his own gang. I was anxious to see if he held a similar briefing for the Young Team. This would mean meeting Tim early on the Saturday afternoon, shortly after his release from the school. The more Tim resisted the idea, the more I insisted.

At last we compromised. Tim would go home, sleep for a couple of hours, and then meet me at the same time as he regularly met the other boys. He had managed to talk the headmaster into granting him an extra day's leave on the following Monday to visit William, who had been moved to Peterhead. Tim's plan was to travel to Aberdeen on the Sunday, thus leaving Monday free. Seeing the gang's activities on a week night was too good an opportunity for me to miss, so I made Tim agree to meet me on the Monday evening as well.

Fergie was the first boy on the scene that Saturday. He was still bubbling over with the happenings of the previous weekend. Tim arrived to hear Fergie describe a fight between the Fleet boys and the Young Team. No one knew, or, apparently, cared, what had caused the disagreement, but within minutes a brawl had started. Soon it developed into a massive free-for-all which spilled out of the pub and onto the pavement and roadway. The fight had been a clean one, no blades, just heads and boots, all 'square-goes'. What surprised me — and what ended the fight — was the arrival of Dick Stevenson, who had thrown in his lot with the Young Team out of a liking for Wee Midgie, who was being badly beaten up by the older boys. I was glad I had missed that night.

'Big Fry', to whom I was then introduced, and whose nickname was based on a chocolate advertisement, then reported the most recent break-ins. This was the first mention in my presence of any theft or shopbreaking in which the Young Team had been involved, certainly Tim had said nothing. Now he stood, smiled nervously and blushed. From what I listened to, the gang seemed to concentrate on their own area. The local cash-and-carry store had been raided yet again. The normal method of kicking down the back door had failed – the owners had learned from past experiences. This time Dave Malloy had broken in by squeezing a car-jack between two iron bars guarding the windows, raising the jack and bending the bars. Entry had thus been gained and the shop cleared of money and goods. The place was broken into again over the Christmas holidays, and the last time I heard it spoken of, an electronic eye had been installed opposite the doors and windows. Similarly, all the other shops in the gang's territory had been burgled, bar five or six which had been rendered impregnable by their owners. Fergie could even rattle off the names of whole streets which he claimed had been 'done' without exception.

'Big Dim', the acerbity of whose nickname was only tempered by its accuracy, had been caught housebreaking again. He had been so infuriated at breaking into a meter which contained filed-down half-pennies that he had attracted attention to his presence in the house. Perhaps he was complaining about the prevailing dishonesty. This type of crime, I had been told, was beneath the dignity of a gang member.

Big Dim was in a class of his own, Tim assured me. At one time, because of his size and weight, he had taken over the leadership of the Young Team during one of Tim's legally enforced absences. Tim, on his return, had simply met up with his closest mates and had accompanied them to their local pub for a drink. Big Dim had entered and challenged Tim to a 'square-go' outside. Knowing full well that he was no physical match for his opponent, Tim had felled him with a hammer which he just happened to have with him. Big Dim had been carried out and dumped in the street. No other challenge to Tim's authority had since been offered.

Beano then related the outcome of one of the skirmishes between the Fleet and the Young Team. The relationship between Dick Stevenson and the 'Mad Mexican', Pat McDonald, had been strained for some weeks, since Dick's release and resumption of complete command. The Mad Mexican – an awesome sight with his long black hair and sideburns, his scrawny, spindling physique, sunken eyes and hollow cheeks – had sulked at being relegated to the background. But the news that Dick had sided with the Young Team against his own boys was too much for Pat. On Saturday night, after hours of hard drinking, he had 'claimed' Dick. Beano, in a dramatic reconstruction of the scene, re-enacted how Dick ('the fittest boay Ah've ever saw – jist oot o'Polmont,[2] right enough') had crashed to the ground after receiving a kick in the stomach. Without using his hands to propel himself forward, Dick had jumped up and 'rattled Pat wi' his heid'.

More butts with the head and 'boots in the chuckies' (alternatively described in rhyming slang as one's 'haw maws') were delivered before Dick knocked Pat out, leaving Dick undisputed master of the pitch. Tim's feelings were: 'It's gettin' ridiculous; too many square-goes an' no' enough chibbin'.'

Later, I found out that the Mad Mexican had 'given the boays up', taken a job as a conductor on the buses, and had 'settled doon'. (Towards the end of 1967, I read in the papers that he had been murdered by a very small gang in Maryhill who styled themselves the 365 after the wine of the same name. Pat's reputation was redoubtable. In the Fleet's pub, he had asked a stranger for the 1½d. he needed to pay for a round of drinks. 'Fuck off, beardie', had been the reply. 'Pat jist went mad and stuck it oan him.' One of the most far-fetched stories I heard concerned Pat. He was in the dock, charged with possessing an offensive weapon. Something the Sheriff (i.e. the magistrate) said angered him, so he leaned forward, picked up Exhibit A (or rather Production Number One in Scotland), his own hammer, and hit the offending magistrate on the head with it. Subsequent inquiry provided no basis in fact for this story.

As other boys joined us at the corner, more information about gang members 'bein' done fur 'GBH' (grievous bodily harm),[3] or 'OLP' (opening lockfast places) was produced. The conversation veered and turned and stopped. There was little to do except 'staun' aboot' until the pubs opened at five. Tim began walking, with the others trailing behind him. We had been walking for some time, 'jist dossin',' when Tim had an idea. 'Let's get right intae that Lib'ry,' he said, pointing to one of Glasgow's Public Libraries.

Running into the building, we ignored the Lending Section because of its turnstile, and burst into the Reading Room. Dan McDade and Billy Morton began setting fire to the newspapers on display, as Tim and the others pushed books off tables and emptied shelves of encyclopedias and reference books. I 'kept the edge up' at the outer door and shouted 'Polis!' as soon as I dared. Dave Malloy was trying to set alight the newspapers being read by old-age pensioners or down-and-outs. One old man beside the door, wearing woollen gloves with the finger pieces cut out, was reading with his face screwed up against the print which he deciphered with the aid of a magnifying glass. Jimmy Barrow's last act was to knock this glass from his hand as he ran past. En route to the street, a male attendant in a green uniform was punched and kicked out of the way. Some, behind me, could hardly run for laughing.

Claiming that I was 'away up the road tae take a bird oot', I left Tim and Dave Malloy, reminding Tim I would see him on Monday. Dave Malloy was visibly relieved to see me depart.

The rain on Monday night was torrential. Not having an overcoat which 'wis in the style', my suit was soggy by the time I reached the corner. Tim had waited behind for me; the others had decided to go to the pictures and had gone ahead. On the way Tim told me that not only his own team but the Fleet and the Possil Uncle were all planning to go to the same cinema. Over the years Monday had become a ritual night for the pictures with the old Seamore in Maryhill Road the standard venue.

And the standard procedure for entry was for a number of boys to pay themselves in, settle down, and then for one of them to sidle off and admit the other boys by opening the exit doors. Those who were caught were charged with fraud.

In the cinema, the fun had begun. Rows and rows of boys, some with girls, who were more like camp followers than real companions, sat heckling the film. The police had already been called and were stationed in the back row of the stalls. During the interval before the main film began, Big Sheila stood up from her seat near the front and turned to the boys behind her, yelling: 'Ah'll take any wan o' youse Fleet boays.' 'Come up here, ya big man ye,' was Dick's riposte. From the laughter I judged that she was held in some affection by the boys. As the lights dimmed, Tim observed: 'She's a big psychey case.' Times without number she had issued challenges like: 'Come oan then. I'll go *right* ahead wae any o' youse mugs.' The boys would humour her rather than fight with her; she countered by claiming that every such refusal was tantamount to a victory. 'I ran a *right* mock wi' his heid.' Her value to the gang lay in her willingness to secrete chibs in her handbag or even her underwear. 'Ye should hiv' seen her makin' up tae this young busy oot fur the first time in Possil-land! Aw the big boays wir saying "Awae tae fuck", when he says, "Boys, come on, move along please." Big Sheila stepped oot an' in a dead sexy voice said tae him: "You've goat lovely come-tae-bed eyes." Brilliant it wis.' The girl herself was tall, solid-looking and built for comfort, with black hair and bad teeth; in sum, none too prepossessing.

We were watching *Mutiny on the Bounty,* and, looking along the rows, I was soon to see as many weapons being held openly as were visible on the screen. At one stage in the film, Marlon Brando made a comment to the effect that the fleet was approaching the harbour. As though in reply, boys rose to their feet screaming: 'The *real* Fleet's here.' This proved to be the last straw for a middle-aged man on my left. As the lights came on, he shouted across: 'Yir aw a bunch o' fuckin' hooligans.' Missiles were hurled in his direction, the police descended from the back row and I made for the exit. Ten boys were arrested. Running away was keeping me fit.

We returned to our pub, a course of action which under the circumstances I thought, and said, though in different words, was foolhardy. The talk, once we had pints of beer in our hands, proved to be worth the risk for me — for by some means or other the subject of schools was introduced.

A few of the boys had attended Saint Monica's comprehensive school on the outskirts of Maryhill. This school, known quite unjustly to the local police as 'the concrete jungle', I myself had taught at for one year. Beano was withering in his scorn and hatred for the place. He had not been there; he had been a pupil at the same junior secondary school as Tim and the others. His young brothers had, however, all been sent to Saint Monica's. 'Ah punch thir wee heids in everytime Ah see thaem wi' thir uniforms oan — thir daft school tie the thickness o' a scarf, an' thir big daft badges. Ye wouldnae get me intae a uniform.' This from a boy who was wearing the gang boy's uniform with as much attention to detail as any apple-polishing prefect in a school blazer.

Beano now began to wax eloquent on the subject. One of his younger brothers 'wee Frankie, pure mental he is, brass-necked it, walkin' up the road wi' his stupid, mid-grey flannels'; here he simulated the voice of a form teacher at a parents' meeting, 'his stupid big ugly shoes an' his wee handbag fur his books'; now the imitation performed was the mincing steps of the stereotyped homosexual. Beano reverted to this topic on another evening: 'Ah hated school 'cos Ah didnae hiv' the brains. Don't worry. Ma wee brother will learn sense; he'll take a tumble tae hissel' an' leave school. Ah'll guarantee it. Dae youse know whit he wants to be? An electrical engineer! Aw naw! Ah'm ashamed. Imagine earnin' a wage!' This provoked approving mirth even from boys like Fergie, the slater and plasterer, and Dave Malloy, who worked in a local paper mill.

'Podgie' reminded the group of the junior secondary teacher, Big Alec, whose opening words to the class every morning were: 'Right, those who want to work, put your hands up. Those who don't, go and sit at the back with your arms folded.' Predictably, charges of indecency and assault were levelled against all and sundry in authority. 'Heidmasters' came in for heavy criticism. One, known to Baggy, was said to drop cigarettes down the dresses of the senior girls and then spend several minutes retrieving them. A member of the Cowcaddens Toi, who had attended the same junior secondary as the others, and was now attending a senior approved school, had drawn the figure of Leslie Charteris's Saint complete with halo on the bald head of a teacher who had collapsed in front of the class.

Tim himself had conducted a running battle with his science teacher. In reprisals for being belted, Tim had poured acid into the aquarium and, if that didn't kill the gold-fish, he also roasted them with bunsen burners. As a climax to this feud, the teacher had dismissed the rest of the class early, ordered Tim to remain behind, locked the door, and announced that he was going to beat Tim up. As the teacher closed the distance between them, Tim had lifted a stool and split his head open with it. At the time, Tim was fourteen. He had been expelled by the headmaster, an action which he still resented almost two years later. Tim, however, had struck back; he waited for the man to leave the school one evening, and then, surrounded by his team, had followed him along the road, cursing and swearing at him.

'Aw Ah ever goat in that school wis techey drawin',' was Tim's considered opinion of his education. At the beginning of his secondary school career, Tim remembered being keen to work. He had started his homework one night amidst the mockery of his elder brothers. Finally, one of them had become so riled at his persistence that he had thrown Tim's school books into the fire. The following day Tim excused himself by asserting that he had lost the books. Never again did he attempt to do any homework.

Yet all the time he attended the approved school, he was fascinated by the books I was either carrying or reading. Without fail, he asked to look through them, returning most of them within seconds. His regular comment at this point was: 'Aw, Ah couldnae study. Ah'd crack up.'

'Jist dossin' aw day'

Life with the gang was not all violence, sex and petty delinquency. Far
from it. One of the foremost sensations that remains with me is the
feeling of unending boredom, of crushing tedium, of listening hour
after hour at street corners to desultory conversation and indiscriminate
grumbling. Standing with one's back against a wall, with one's hands in
one's pockets, in the late afternoon and in the early hours of the
morning, was *the* gang activity. At times I longed to discard my passive
role and suggest some constructive form of entertainment. Once, I
remember, we were all slouching against the walls of 'wir coarner' when
it began to drizzle. No one made any move to seek the protection of a
close-mouth of a shop-front and so, in my observer status, I had to
stand there and let the rain trickle down my face.

Some boys whispered and at least some snatches of their conversation provided me with valuable information, which is presented later in
this chapter. Others had no interest even in talking and were content
to let their minds go blank. Smoking, chewing gum, recounting past
exploits, deriding passers-by, and indulging in horseplay with each other
and with girls, these were the only diversions from 'dossin'. Neither the
young nor the old escaped their caustic and obscene abuse. Specifically
delinquent activities occupied only a small fraction of their waking
hours.

Late one evening, two old women, one with bloated legs, the other
suffering from rickets, hobbled past us in sandshoes, sucking hot chips
with toothless gums. With insults and curses, the gang pushed them off
their pavement and into the gutter where, I was told, they belonged.

Every so often as we stood 'dossin', a thin jet of saliva would hit the
pavement. The boys had their own 'gallous' way of spitting; they kept
their lips and teeth motionless and squirted out the spittle with their
tongues. The trick is a favourite with approved school boys.

On one occasion to break the monotony I took out cigarettes and
asked a passer-by for a match. My action unleashed a torrent of
criticism: 'Is that no' brass neckin' it, askin' fur a match? Aw naw!
He'll think we cannae afford a boax. Ah'd rather dae wi'oot an' that's
nae kiddin'.' Baggy signalled to me that he would help me out of my
difficulties, so I asked him for a match. 'Don't kerry heavy timber,'
he replied while producing a stolen lighter. His sally at my expense
restored the gang's good humour.

'Wee Cock', who naturally preferred to be called 'Wee Eck', began
recounting his experiences of the last few days. He had been arrested
at two in the morning for breaking and entering, and had spent the
first night in a police cell (or 'peter' as they call it). Unable to sleep, he
had passed the time by whistling to himself to keep his spirits up. The
cell, he claimed, was clearly marked as suitable for 18 year olds and the
injustice of a 14 year old being locked up there rankled with him. In
the morning a policeman had entered with an egg sandwich. "Take as
many as you like," he says tae me an' laughs. Ah pit it doon the pan.
It flushed fae the ootside. Scared ye strangl' yersel' wi' the chain.'

After an appearance in court he had been transferred to a remand home. 'Dubbed up aw day in ma peter Ah wis.' By dint of discreet questioning during the long hours we spent standing at the street corner, I was able to piece together the daily routine in the remand home. The boys were awakened at 5.30 a.m. and, after washing, they cleaned out their cells. Then came breakfast at 7.00, after which they were 'dubbed up' until lunch time. Wee Cock was given a cowboy book to read; he skimmed through two pages and then threw it away. Shortly afterwards he picked it up and began reading again: 'Ah wis scared o' crackin' up.'

He had to eat his lunch by himself in his cell, a punishment for trying to escape. At 5 o'clock he joined the others for evening tea. From 7.00 until 9.00 television was watched but no talking or smoking was tolerated. If a comedian appeared, said Wee Cock, the prisoners were allowed to laugh, but not too much. He had envied the 'passmen', boys who in the afternoon were permitted to leave their cells to scrub floors and polish shoes. But only the 'edgers', the 'benders' were chosen for these tasks, I was informed. Wee Cock's hair had been shorn and he claimed to have had no more than one shower during his one week of imprisonment.

He had also been accused in court of 'goin' on the demand', i.e. stealing clothes from younger boys at the point of a knife. Tim leapt to his defence: 'Its aw thae Tongs an' Shamrock that demand jaikets an' leathers. It wouldnae happen up he're.' Yet Fergie remembered that he and Tim had 'taken liberties wi' boays'. They had forced one youngster into a lane and had made him remove even his shoes. Tim countered with, 'Ah widnae demand gear noo; Ah kin afford ma ain.'

Wee Cock had also met the 'Top Man' of the Tongs in the remand home. Asked why he had been arrested, the King had explained that he had inquired of one of his own gang: 'Are ye goin' doon tae the bookies?' 'Aye,' the boy had replied. 'Weil, Ah want tae pit this line oan.' At this he had cut the boy's jaw open. As the boy left the scene, the Top Man had added a final jest: 'Awae an' staun' in shite' (i.e. for good luck).

There was a second charge for the leader of the Tongs to answer. Having been chibbed by a member of a rival gang, the 'King' had sent a letter to the perpetrator, threatening to kill him. (The boy's mother had delivered the letter into the hands of the police). Not content with that, he had sent representatives from a firm of undertakers to the boy's home to measure him for a coffin. The boy had collapsed at the door. Admiration shone in the eyes of the gang.

Wee Cock had also learned (his phrase for this was 'Ah got tolt', i.e. I was told) the latest password among the Tongs, vital information for anyone who happened to be cornered by any of that gang. One replied to the opening remark, 'Ding, Dong! Ah'm a Tong!' with, 'Ha, ha! So am Ah!'

Apart from some rough and exploratory handling of the girls present, the gang's only other pastime was 'puttin' the mix in'. This was their expression for contriving a quarrel where none existed. Beano's attention for example, was directed to a boy walking on the other side of the street. Though the boy could have given Beano a few inches in height and a stone or two in weight, the gang, at Tim's instigation, began to goad Beano into challenging him to fight.

'You could take him easy.'

'You're dead well built an' that'.

'Pit it this wae, you could go right tae town wi' him.'

At first Beano demurred. 'Naw, Ah'll see youse ra morra', he replied as he attempted to eschew the dare. But the pressure on him increased until he was shouting after the boy: 'Hauf-wit features! Youre gettin' set aboot.' The boy took to his heels and fled. Beano returned in triumph. 'He's aw chuffed wi' hissel',' said Tim.

In the space of a few paragraphs I have summed up *all* the gang's conversation and activities over a number of hours. To relieve my ennui I studied the tattoos on the boys' hands and arms for I could not afford to ask too many questions. By far the most frequent tattoo was pricked into the skin of the four fingers of both hands between the knuckles and the first joint. It spelled out the message 'TRUE LOVE'. Another common one was a heart and a scroll which bore the one word 'Mother'. 'Mum and Dad' also made its appearance on the back of the hand and on the arm, together with girlfriends' names. In large letters, Tim had scratched on his arm the legend 'Born a Loser'. Mick, his elder brother, sported on his forearm a red dagger entering the top of a skull and reappearing through its mouth. It was considered to be the finest tattoo in the neighbourhood, surpassing Dick Stevenson's crucifixion scene where the traditional letters INRI had been replaced by the name of Dick's current girlfriend.

'Jist dossin' aw day' was the gang's ideal. School, employment, reading all took up valuable time which could be better spent in doing nothing. Many people in a word association test would answer to the stimulus 'Glasgow Gang' by some such word as 'violence'. The reply 'dossin' would be nearer the truth, and would sum up more of these boys' lives than any reference to isolated violent incidents.

The repetitive monotony of gang life has been remarked upon by many investigators, and perhaps Bloch and Niederhoffer's (1958, p.177ff.) account comes nearest to my own:

> Actually, the average gang existence follows a fairly monotonous routine. Its activities can be predicted in advance. Night after night, gangs can be found at the same street corner hang-out. Weekend nights may bring a slight variation. They may grace a dance or movie. This regular round of activities is broken by auto trips to pick up girls. This is life in the gang. The fighting, burglaries, delinquency, are a very small part of the total range.

In their description of the Pirate gang in New York, the authors suggest that such repetition is welcome to the boys because of their basic insecurities and inadequacies:

> Not versatility, but this regular patterned existence, the same hang-out, the endless 'bull sessions', the familiar faces day in and day out, these are the very attractions that lure the gang boy. He desperately needs and clings to this security, this anchor, to keep him from drifting aimlessly in the Sargasso Sea of adolescence.

On finishing the fieldwork for this study, I reached two immediate conclusions. The first, and one of crucial importance for approved schools, was that Tim, a gang leader, conformed as best he could within the system and used his leave at weekends to act out his aggression. The school never really witnessed what he was capable of; the staff suspected and guessed the truth of the matter, although they had only occasional outbursts of temper to work on. But of Tim's external conduct, his parental status, and of his own notoriety within the subculture of Glasgow's street gangs, they knew next to nothing.

This brings me to my second conclusion, also of relevance to approved schools. Educational sociologists normally encourage teachers to study the subcultures from which their pupils come. I tacitly agreed with the idea but did not fully comprehend it, until I realized that an approved school through lack of knowledge could endanger a boy's life by sending him to work in the territory of a rival gang. A pupil could be knifed or even killed — and this is not being melodramatic but all too realistic — through the ignorance of those whose professional duty it is to protect him as would 'a good and wise parent'.

An immediate result of my work with the Young Team was that the approved school where I was employed reviewed the leave granted to boys known to be gang members. At that time they were being released every so often on Fridays, Saturdays and Sundays — far and away the most likely times for gang activity. Seasonal holiday periods such as Christmas and Easter and all public holidays are also critical points, during which the whereabouts of gang leaders should be carefully noted and their movements supervised. However, approved schools generally continue to release boys at what appear to me the worst possible moments, even though Mays (1954, p. 153) had already warned of these 'periods of exceptional danger'.

Notes

[1] Boys in approved schools were at that time officially allowed forty-two days' leave each year.

[2] Polmont Borstal, near Falkirk.

[3] Why the boys should use this English term in preference to the Scottish one of 'serious assault' I can only conjecture. Perhaps the use of the English term in crime films and books is the explanation.

References

BLOCH, H.A. and NIEDERHOFFER, A., 1958, *The Gang: a study in adolescent behaviour*. New York: Philosophical Library.

MAYS, J.B., 1954, *Growing up in the City*. Liverpool: University Press.

PIERRE BOURDIEU AND MONIQUE DE SAINT-MARTIN

Scholastic excellence and the values of the educational system

(translated by J.C. Whitehouse)

This study was prompted by a desire to challenge the duality still
dominant in a certain methodological tradition by attempting a
methodical understanding, using completely objective techniques, of
the most unconscious and therefore least apparent values which agents
have recourse to in their practice, and of those apparently completely
subjective criteria which serve to define, within a fixed academic area,
the model of the accomplished man, or, in other words, of excellence
as an inimitable and indefinable way of conforming to models. There
is probably nothing which would enable us to perceive the values which
guide the choice of academic juries, often without their being aware of
it, or dominate all academic practices, as clearly as the system of
statistical relationships characteristic of a group of candidates who
have been successful in competitive examinations and are the products
of a system of selection and presentation with which the whole of the
educational system identifies. Indeed, like any social insight, the judgements that teachers make with regard to students, particularly in examination situations, take into account not only knowledge and know-how,
but also the intangible nuances of *manners* and *style*, which are the

---

Editorial note

Le concours général A national competitive examination taken by the
very ablest pupils in the senior forms of French secondary schools.

L'agrégation A competitive examination qualifying successful candidates
to teach in higher education.

Les grandes écoles These are the most highly respected institutions of
higher education in France. Successful completion of the course at one
of these gives access to the upper echelons of the professions and civil
service.

Le prix d'excellence The prize awarded in a school for all-round academic
merit.

Le Brevet d'Études du Premier Cycle A certificate awarded at the end of
compulsory secondary education.

---

*Reprinted from Pierre Bourdieu and Monique de Saint-Martin,
L'excellence scolaire et les valeurs du système d'enseignement francais',
Annales 1 (January/February 1970), pp. 146-75, by kind permission of
the authors and publishers.

imperceptible and yet never unperceived manifestations of the individual's relationship to such knowledge and know-how and the 'half-uttered or unuttered or unutterable' expression of a system of values which are always deciphered in terms of another system of values which themselves are just as unuttered and as unutterable.[1]

The unconscious principles behind the social definition of scholastic achievement (a definition no less arbitrary, although sociologically necessary, whether we call it 'intelligence' or 'brilliance' or 'talent') are most likely to be clearly expressed or to slip out during those co-option procedures when the academic body sets out to recruit those it judges worthy to perpetuate it, such as the competitive examinations in the *grandes écoles* or the *agrégation* and particularly perhaps the *concours général*, the only function of which is to establish a pure and purely honorific grading and thus to carry out, in terms of strictly academic criteria, the pre-selection of those novices most likely to fit into the institution as they are closest to the ideal of academic excellence and the most convinced of the universal value of academic values.[2]

If sociologists have often been too exclusively concerned with grasping the objective regular patterns or rules governing behaviour to take into account the relationship of individuals to them, it is because an objectivist definition of scientific objectivity induces them to leave to intuition (on which the most completely objectivist rely so often) or to psychology what Malinowski called 'the imponderabilia of actual life', and also because, as the author of the *Argonauts* suggested the details and nuances of behaviour which make the *manner of acting* something irreducible to objectivist description, although they 'can and ought to be scientifically formulated and recorded',[3] are not so immediately available for the rapid and superficial recording of the remote observer who merely analyses documents or who, by using questionnaires administered by a third person, may never have seen or heard any of the people whose practices he claims to describe and analyse. Malinowski is right, and all those ethnologists who make a virtue of necessity, and assume the authority of a pseudo-scientific theory of the epistemological virtues of the detached viewpoint to justify their hastily made records of the most external and ossified characteristics of social life, are wrong.

It would however be going too far to use direct and prolonged observation as the only way of seizing the nuances and the intangible qualities which define the native experience *in its objectivity*. Although everything concerned with the *mode* of behaviour — basically style and manners — is too elusive to be measured experimentally by a school of empirical research which is often as routine-bound in the production of its instruments as it is in the interpretation of its results, it is not impossible to find indices of the mode of behaviour in the most objective relationships between the practices and opinions and the sociologically pertinent characteristics of the subjects who perform or profess them. Unawareness of the distinction between behaviour and the mode of behaviour, which is encouraged by a mechanical use of survey techniques, leads us purely and simply to see as identical practices or opinions which are separated only by their modes, such as in politics, for example, the different manners (linked to social origin and the correlative system of attitudes) that a student has of being or saying that he is left-wing, and which make all the difference between what we might call natural left-wingers and thwarted right-wingers, or, to take another example, the different ways of admiring or liking the same work of art which are shown in the cluster of works admired with it, the manner of standing and looking at the work (alone and in silence, telling the people with one about it, examining it for a long time or a short one, and so on). Nothing is further from arbitrary pronouncements based on an intuitive approach than the painstaking gathering of clues so subtle that taken singly they are ambiguous and only completely reveal their significance when their relationships are analysed statistically.

Social factors involved in scholastic achievement

An analysis of the characteristics of those successful in the *concours général* shows that the selection of this group, established by a two-stage process operated firstly by the secondary teaching establishments choosing their best pupils and secondly by means of juries choosing from among those candidates, obeys the general law governing all processes of selection and elimination,[4] in that the demographic, social and scholastic characteristics of a surviving group and the secondary characteristics of the individuals of the different categories of which the group is composed are increasingly different from the characteristics of the group or of the corresponding categories of the group taken as a whole, as, on one hand, the group or the categories are less likely to be represented at this stage of the school career (precisely because they show to a greater degree and/or in greater number the characteristics which determine elimination), and, on the other, the group or the categories are at a more advanced point in the school career, or, at a given point on it, rank higher in the scholastic hierarchy of establishments, disciplines or sections. It appears firstly that the group of successful candidates is separated from the population of the *classes terminales* by a systematic set of social advantages:[5] the former are younger, come more frequently from a *lycée* in the Paris region, more often started their secondary education in a *lycée,* and also come from more privileged backgrounds from the point of view both of social status and cultural capital.[6]

It also appears that successful candidates from the least-represented categories are distinguished from corresponding categories by a whole range of convergent indices. For example, the sons and daughters of industrial workers, who make up respectively 5 and 9 per cent of successful candidates, come from families which are different from the rest of their class by having a relatively high cultural level (with only 8.5 per cent of the working class fathers of successful candidates having no qualifications and 16.5 per cent having the *Brevet d'Études du Premier Cycle,* while the corresponding figures for the working population as a whole are 58 per cent and 2 per cent). Similarly, girls, who account for only 32.5 per cent of successful candidates although they form 48 per cent of the pupils in the *classes terminales,* differ from boys in having

TABLE I Synoptic table of the variations of some social, scholastic, cultural characteristics and some attitudes of successful candidates by social origin

No. of successful candidates in concours général of a given social class characterized by	Secondary education begun in lycée	Lycée in Paris region year of concours	Have jumped classes	Gained prix d'excellence in year of concours	Average number of countries visited	Listen to France-Musique, France-Culture radio programmes	Very good at geography	Giftedness quoted as factor in success	Teacher ideal: the conscientious pedagogue
Farmers and agricultural workers	46	23	7.5	31	2	20	38.5	23	54
Industrial workers	58.5	25	25	29	2.1	20	33.5	37.5	71
Clerical, skilled craftsmen, small traders	83.5	29.5	11	26	2.3	26.5	55.5	52	66.5
Supervisory personnel	100	36.5	9	45.5	2.5	40	54.5	36.5	63.5
Elementary school teachers	93	26.5	26.5	60	4.3	20	53.5	20	66.5
Managerial/professional	86	40.5	26.5	38.5	3.6	35.5	42.5	44.5	57
Teachers in secondary and higher education	85	38	20.5	36.5	3.3	35.5	23.5	29.5	59
ALL	80	35.5	21.5	37.5	3.1	40.5	42	38	60.5

TABLE II Synoptic table of the variations of some social, scholastic and cultural characteristics and some attitudes of successful candidates by discipline

No. of successful candidates in concours général in each discipline from	Father upper class	Father's qualification higher than baccalauréat	Father teacher in higher or secondary education	Still in classical section of lycée	Have jumped classes	Gained prix d'excellence in year of concours	France-Musique France-Culture radio programmes	Giftedness as factor in success	Teacher ideal: the creative thinker
French	66.5	58.5	16.5	83.5	50	28.5	66.5	50	50
Philosophy	57	47.5	14.5	57	19	16.5	60	28.5	43
Latin-Greek	56.5	36.5	13.5	90	10	63.5	28	40	16.5
Languages	69	52	17.5	57.5	25	32.5	30.5	50	15.5
History-Geography	53.5	39	2.5	73	22	46.5	25	31.5	12
Mathematics	74	64.5	13	77.5	32	48.5	28	29	13
Physics	70.5	64.5	23.5	70.5	35.5	59	22	47	12
Natural sciences	26.5	26.5	13.5	40	6.5	33.5	0	6.5	6.5
ALL	61	47	13	65.5	21.5	37.5	40.5	38	18

FIGURE I   Structure of various school populations

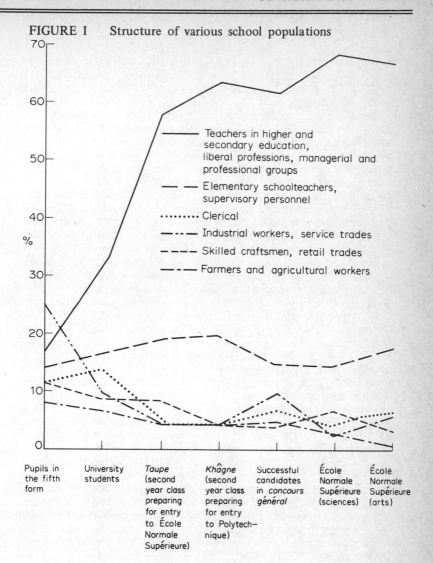

Legend:
- Teachers in higher and secondary education, liberal professions, managerial and professional groups
- Elementary schoolteachers, supervisory personnel
- Clerical
- Industrial workers, service trades
- Skilled craftsmen, retail trades
- Farmers and agricultural workers

X-axis categories:
- Pupils in the fifth form
- University students
- *Taupe* (second year class preparing for entry to École Normale Supérieure)
- *Khâgne* (second year class preparing for entry to Polytechnique)
- Successful candidates in *concours général*
- École Normale Supérieure (sciences)
- École Normale Supérieure (arts)

Sources: Pupils in the fifth form, scholastic year 1967—8: Statistics of Ministry of National Education

Pupils in *khâgne* and *taupe*, scholastic year 1967—8: Statistics of Ministry of National Education.
Successful candidates in the *concours général*: average of scholastic years 1965—6, 1966—7, 1967—8

ENS (Ulm) Arts and sciences, scholastic year 1966—7
Surveys: Centre de Sociologie Européene

a wide range of social and scholastic advantages (67 per cent for example, being of upper class origin as against 58 per cent of boys). The same was also true of successful candidates in mathematics and physics who were relatively more highly selected, came from socially and culturally privileged families, were exclusively male and younger than candidates in literary subjects.

An application of the general law makes it clear that successful candidates have more characteristics rare in their own category (that is, for those from underprivileged categories more compensatory advantages) the younger they are, as they have reached the same level of achievement in a shorter time. They are socially and culturally privileged, and the most precocious of them are also scholastically privileged as more of them (proportionally) have followed 'the noble way' since beginning secondary education and have attended *lycées* in the Paris region. Their precocity, which is in fact very marked, with two-thirds of successful candidates being able to read and count before starting primary school, and which has been maintained throughout their school career, will be rewarded by a place in one of the *grandes écoles* which give those who manage to get into them perpetual precocity by setting them off at once on a social trajectory which will always take them more quickly to the same place, or, to put it another way, further and higher in the same time.

It can be seen that there is no properly scholastic difference which cannot be related to a range of systematically linked social differences, and hierarchies which grow up within the scholastic élite, which itself is separated from the population from which it is drawn by means of a socially biased lottery, can all be ascribed to social differences. Distinctions between the sexes and between age groups and social differences are at the basis of the differences between disciplines, which are arranged in a commonly recognized hierarchical order, from the most respectable disciplines such as French, classics and mathematics, which are socially the most important and carry the most prestige (as shown for example by the coefficients in examinations, by the status of *professeur principal* conferred on teachers in the various disciplines and by the consensus of teachers and pupils) to secondary disciplines such as history and geography, modern languages (which are a special case), natural sciences and marginal disciplines such as art, music or gymnastics. To the extent that various disciplines demand gifts which are unevenly distributed and hence rare to different degrees in different social classes, an increasing degree of selection is observable as one goes up the hierarchy of disciplines. The most respectable disciplines honour pupils from those families who are most favoured by both social position and cultural level, and most favoured in their scholastic career as more of them have followed the princely way through the *lycée* and its classical section throughout their secondary education and have also jumped a class during that period. In these conditions it is hardly surprising that the scholastic hierarchy of disciplines coincides with the hierarchy arising according to the average age of successful candidates, running from mathematics to physics and natural sciences in scientific subjects and from classics to history and geography or modern languages in literary disciplines.

But a complete awareness of these relationships presupposes a realization that they can only be brought to light by operations necessarily excluded from the practice in which they become a reality; the knowledge of the relationship between theoretical knowledge and practice, which here is defined by the exclusion of properly theoretical knowledge of practice, means that the complete study of the object must contain, apart from the study cf objective relationships, the study of the relationship which agents have with these objective relationships, in this case, that is, the study of the ignorance of these relationships and the study of the social determinants of that ignorance.

Among those factors which cause the relationship between the social and scholastic characteristics of a given scholastic group to escape the awareness of agents, pride of place must go to the law governing the process of differential elimination which is that, in a group produced by a selection process allegedly based on purely scholastic criteria but in fact based on social criteria, inequality in selection tends gradually to reduce and sometimes to cancel the effects of inequality with regard to selection. This is both because, as we have seen, the survivors show less and less of the characteristics which meant the elimination of the rest of their category as their chances (linked to their category) of reaching that level of the scholastic career grow less and because the whole system of their attitudes is objectively controlled and, to a certain extent, created by their position as survivors. This explains why, for example, successful candidates of middle class origin and even, though to a lesser degree, those of lower class origin, can find in the exceptional character of their exceptional success reasons for adopting the values of a scholastic system which has recognized their value, and for rejecting the (socially conditioned) 'virtues' which have helped them gain this success in favour of the ideological representation of the causes of scholastic success which successful candidates of upper class origin, who from earliest childhood have been unconsciously trained, by constant exposure within the family, in the subtleties of an extra-scholastic culture and a non-scholastic relationship to it, are also inclined to profess, although for totally different reasons.

Thus, by providing apparently perfectly neutral sanctions for differences which seem to be in no way due to social differences, the educational system obliges both teachers and pupils to seek their cause in natural inequalities. It never discloses the secrets of the alchemy that enables it to carry out that transmutation so completely as in the outstanding value that it accords to precocity, the quality for which there is clearly no absolute or absolutely neutral definition, as it never consists of more than a certain relationship between the age at which something is achieved and the age socially defined as normal or suitable for it (or, more rigorously, the modal age of the corresponding category, which is, in the case of scholastic precocity, the modal age of individuals who have reached the same point in their studies).[7] To show the arbitrary nature of the value put on precocity, we need only consider the reprobation attached to it, often in the same social milieu, in other fields. In the area of sexuality, for example, precocious often means premature. Indeed, if we commonly see precocity as implying more merit or greater gifts than ever and exalt (see the newspapers at examination times) the 15 year old who passes his *baccalauréat* as 'the youngest *agrégé*' or 'the youngest *Polytechnicien* in France' it is precisely because precocity is not seen as increased privilege, but as the clearest manifestation of innate virtues and qualities and natural gifts, since (as we see in the cult of the child prodigy, the extreme form of the Romantic cult of genius), prowess and exploits are all the more likely to be charismatic because, having been achieved at an early age, they seem to owe nothing — and especially not their precocity — to training or hot-house techniques.[8] Thus, the value attached to precocity is only one of the ideological mechanisms by which the educational system tends to transform social privileges into natural privileges *and not privileges of birth.* Intelligence, talent, gifts — these are the titles of rank in bourgeois society which the school blesses and legitimizes by hiding the fact that the scholastic hierarchies which it produces by an apparently perfectly neutral process of inculcation and selection reproduce, in both senses of the word, social hierarchies. In this particular case, the educational system does not only fulfil an ideological function. It gives the authority of its verdicts to one of the least obvious and most effective class privileges, that of what we might call high acceleration. 'What a great advantage nobility confers,' said Pascal 'for it puts a man in a good position at eighteen, as well known and respected as another might be at fifty for his merits. Thus without effort he has gained thirty years.' Like titles of rank, scholastic qualificiations, which are social capital changed into scholastic capital, make it possible to acquire on credit — that is, before the proper time, before others, getting ahead of schedule and dispensing with normal forms of delays — office, honours, profit and pleasure; all the symbolic and material advantages, in short, for which others have to pay on the nail, when they have finally produced their credentials and amassed a capital of real and immediately redeemable guarantees.[9]

Contradictions in the system of scholastic values

This analysis of the scholastic significance and the social functions of the scholastic cult of precocity reveals the hidden affinity which unites the apparently most purely scholastic values and the values of the dominant classes without going right to the principles of the kind of pre-established harmony which causes the scholastic system, even when it seems simply to be obeying its own properly scholastic norms, also to obey external norms at the same time. For a better understanding of the relationship of dependence by means of independence which unites the educational system with a given type of structure of class relationships, we shall have to examine the more refined aspects of distinctions and hierarchies, still based on criteria of mode, which grow up between different forms of scholastic attainment and which can be seen in such objective indices as the hierarchy of disciplines and the attitudes or aptitudes which they demand. On one hand, subjects like French (and, in another register, mathematics) are supposed to demand talent and gifts, and on the other subjects like geography (and to a lesser degree history), natural sciences and modern languages to demand work and study. As opposed to French (or to a lesser degree philosophy) which discourages keenness and scholastic zeal both by the woolliness and imprecision of the work required and by the vague and intangible signs of success or failure, and where (whether it be a question of style or of general culture) often indefinable previous knowledge is required ('candidates are expected to have read widely'), disciplines such as history, geography, natural sciences or languages (both modern and to a lesser extent classical) entail work where there is an opportunity for the student to show his liking for a task carefully accomplished and for careful practical exercises, such as maps in geography and drawings in the sciences, which seem positive and profitable because the effort can be directed and the effect of the work is easily assessable.[10] It is hardly surprising that 'talent' subjects, which offer the best investment for cultural capital (which is 'liberal' as opposed to 'scholastic') and for the easy relationship with culture which can only be acquired by informal exposure to it within the family, attract pupils from a higher social level than those subjects which give working class and particularly lower middle class children a chance to show habits of dedication and industry which, in such subjects more than elsewhere, can fulfil their compensatory role.[11]

Unlike those who are traditionally known in schools as swots or referred to by other similarly pejorative terms, who are concerned about the strictly scholastic profitability of their cultural investments and who, because they are always busy making up their educational 'backwardness', have classic, bookish and scholastic knowledge and preferences directly subordinated to the school even when they are not directly produced by school work, successful candidates in French or philosophy show clearly that they have a wide enough margin of freedom and security to be able to afford an enlightened, dilettante, familiar and eclectic relationship with culture (in the more 'liberal' and less scholastic sense) which can be elastic enough to take in areas not yet recognized or sanctioned by the school. Thus, they go to the cinema more often,[12] and are much more likely to adopt a 'cultured' attitude in those more 'liberal' subjects (films and jazz) which others force themselves to like or treat simply as objects of entertainment.[13]

Thus, all the characteristics by which the French system of education recognizes the élite of its élite and which define the way of true excellence are all concentrated in those living ideals, successful candidates in French (and, a fortiori, those of upper class origin).[14] This is hardly surprising if we remember that there is perfect agreement in this case between the values expressly professed by the whole tradition of literary studies and those observable in the practices and attitudes of students who are successful in them.

Better than any long analysis of the relationship of the well-read person with literary culture, a quick examination of two prize-winning essays from 1969 which deal, by a sort of objective chance, with 'creation' and 'reading',[15] will bring out the profound affinity between the tradition of the humanities steeped in a humanist, personalist and mentalist ideology, and the pedagogic tradition which often carries the academic undervaluation of what is 'pedestrian' and 'lacking in originality' as far as the romantic cult of 'self' expression.

There is in fact a charismatic concept of the writer's activity — described as 'creation'[16] and 'mystery'[17] — and of the deciphering of the work conceived as a 'creative' reading, and as the spiritual identification of the reader's self with the author's self[18] which forms a basis for the irrational and subjective exaltation of the arbitrary nature of sensations or mental states,[19] which is a pretext for the uncritical egoism of personal effusions,[20] romantic mysticism[21] or existential pathos.[22] It would be just as easy to show that the philosophy implicit in traditional philosophy teaching, which oscillates between idealistic intellectualism and personalist spiritualism, is always based on the open or implicit devaluation of what was once called, following Cicero, *plebeia philosophia,* on the devaluation of all 'vulgar' doctrines, like materialism or empiricism, or those too close to 'common sense' and in every case of all 'vulgar' forms of doctrines and particularly of the most 'vulgar' of them.[23] One has only to think of the fate reserved for all those rather boorish philosophers such as Hume, Comte, Taine or Durkheim, apparent even more in lectures than in dreary textbooks, the kind of philosophers who are relegated to a brief introductory mention in essays, and of the many ways of excluding scientific discourse, from ritual excommunication and defamatory anathema to annexing and distorting it ('scientism', 'psychologism', 'sociologism', 'historicism') to be convinced that the 'philosophical *ancien régime',* to use Auguste Comte's phrase, is still flourishing.

Thus everything points to the idea that the 'noble' subjects, French and philosophy, owe their pre-eminence to the fact that the values which they see it as their aim to transmit are in no way in conflict with the values underlying their ways of teaching and coincide to an extremely high degree with the implicit presuppositions of their teaching and the ideologies for which they act as a vehicle. Thus an analysis of the systematic differences which clearly separate the virtuosi of the 'talent' disciplines from the plodders of the second-class subjects shows the principle of a system of parallel contrasts between complementary or opposite qualities and properties which guide pedagogical practices in French education and can be briefly set out as follows: brilliant/dull; unconstrained/painstaking; distinguished/vulgar; cultivated/pedantic; personal/banal; original/commonplace; outstanding/uninteresting; subtle/crude; remarkable/insignificant; elegant/gauche; spirited/heavy; lively/slow; sharp/insipid; wide-awake/sluggish and so on. There are only too many examples one could quote of the use of these categories which are applied to persons, both pupils and teachers, as well as to what they produce, whether it be lectures, work, ideas, speech, and even more so to the style of their practices as well as of their productions. Thus in the language of reports on the *agrégation* an inexhaustible vocabulary used to speak slightingly of the congenital 'mediocrity' of the 'mass of candidates', the 'greyness' of 'dull', 'colourless' or 'dreary' scripts, from which 'thankfully' a few 'distinguished' or 'brilliant' ones stood out.[24] The scholastic definition of the cultured (i.e. non-'pedantic') relationship to knowledge contrasts these two types of relationship to knowledge

FIGURE II   Types of relationship with culture

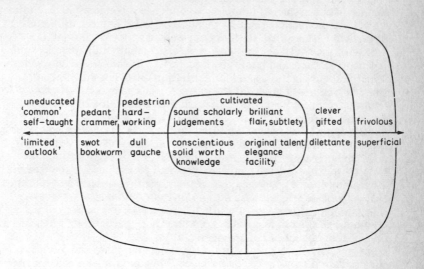

FIGURE III   Types of relationship with school

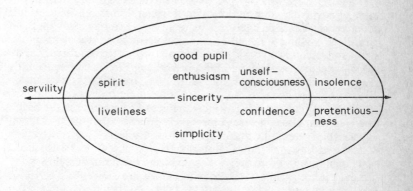

(which are linked, as will be seen, to two different modes of acquiring that knowledge) and two systems of manners, by having recourse to terms which owe their power of suggestion to the fact that each one of them evokes a system of homologous and often interchangeable contrasts.[25]

But the predominance of what might be called charismatic values is so marked in the system that it could well cause us to overlook the indices of the contradictions and conflicts created, in the practice and speech of teachers and pupils, by competition between the two opposing principles of evaluation and hierarchization. Here is another example from the reports of juries for the *agrégation:* 'The exercise of *explication* demands care, close reading of the text and taste, but also *precise knowledge*' (Agr. LM, 1959). The author of that rehabilitation of knowledge, who elsewhere deplored the fact that texts were no longer learned by heart, wrote in the same report: 'The poem, as it stands, if it is beautiful, reaches a higher truth than the anecdotal truth sought carefully by the *scholar* in the author's personal papers', and, a few years later: 'However, it is on the basis of their qualities of taste and judgement that we wish to select candidates, *not merely on the basis of memory.* They should then beware of writing about things of which they are ignorant and they should not scorn knowledge, particularly when it is a case of the foundations of a general culture' (Agr. LM, 1962). There is more to such contradictions and retractions than mere idiosyncracy, for the oscillation between condemning and rehabilitating knowledge and in particular the ambivalent reaction to the idea of university criticism (i.e. the study of a writer's personal papers), accepted by writers, and 'creative' criticism show the ambivalence of the scholastic view of properly scholastic activities.

Another indication of this, more indirect but no less convincing, is to be seen in the lack of certainty about criteria of achievement which seems to show the clash between two types of scholastic honour, the *prix d'excellence*, which is awarded by the whole group of teachers taking a particular class on the basis of a year's work, and success in the *concours général*, a distinction awarded by an external body on the basis of a single examination held on one occasion. Successful candidates in Latin and Greek, who achieve the highest proportion of *prix d'excellence* (63.5 per cent as against only 28.5 per cent in French) differ from other successful candidates by a whole range of systematic characteristics. They see themselves more frequently (60 per cent of cases) than other successful candidates in literary disciplines (42 per cent) as the best pupils in their class; they are more likely to assess their individual work as very good or excellent (26.5 per cent as against 18 per cent) and, when indicating the kind of pupil they would like to be, to use the same qualifiers as those they use to describe the pupil which they are (75 per cent as against 65.5 per cent). These are indices of a *certitudo sui* which matches their scholastic dedication. They have competed in several subjects more often (56 per cent) than all the others (23 per cent) and more of them among the literary candidates claim to be good at mathematics (43.5 per cent as against 20.5 per cent) and never see themselves as very weak. As it is also noticeable that those holding a literary or scientific prize won the *prix d'excellence* more often than those with only one honourable mention as a runner-up, we may suppose that, assuming the aptitudes measured by the *concours général* to be equal in other respects, scholastic evaluation takes extra criteria into account when the *prix d'excellence* is being awarded. And in fact the honour is awarded to the 'good all-rounder' whose docility with regard to the school is not only shown in his willing eclecticism and the care with which he makes his academic invest-ments.[26] Thus, proportionally more successful candidates in classical languages (92.5 per cent) want to enter the Ecole Normale Supérieure than those in philosophy (37.5 per cent), put teaching in secondary or higher education in first place (63.5 per cent as against 41.5 per cent for successful candidates in French, 33 per cent for those in languages and 31 per cent for those in history and geography),[27] can quote the names of former successful candidates (80 per cent as against 33.5 per cent for those in natural sciences) and know a considerable number (all at least seven or eight) of *grandes écoles*. This (the dialectic of reward and recognition) is in fact one of the most important ways that the teaching profession has of ensuring its own continuation. When it is concluded, the school chooses those who choose it because it chooses them.[28] An institution which, like the system of education, completely controls its own reproduction can attract to itself (or repel), by means of the rewards it gives them, those individuals who are closest to what it explicitly and implicitly demands and most likely to preserve it with-out change.[29]

If we note that the distinction between the two types of achievement typified by successful candidates in literary subjects and those in classical languages reproduces, within the field of the 'noble' disciplines, the distinction between them and the secondary disciplines, we see that the application of the same principle will enable us to perceive an almost infinite range of subtle types of systems of attitudes which are almost always attitudes with regard to culture and the school, as, for example, in the case we have considered, the 'laborious' tenacity of the plodder, the free and easy dilettantism of the 'brilliant' pupil and the cautious eclecticism of the good all-rounder. The contradictions between the cult of brilliance, which is the correlative of the scholastic devaluation of 'pedantry', and the recognition of properly scholastic virtues are resolved in the exaltation of the happy mean which defines what could be called *academica mediocritas*, that sum of average virtues, priestly rather than prophetic. Thus, masterly brilliance, is quite different from both the suspect skills of empty virtuosity and the uninspired learning of the *fort en thème*. The nice balance of academic good form, a blend of discreet elegance and restrained enthusiasm, is something quite unlike either the pretentious offhandedness of the presumptuous virtuoso or the pedantic servility of the unduly zealous model pupil, and the originality of a 'person' style or approach contrasts with both the unbridled audacity of creative ambition and with school-masterly platitudes.[30] The qualities which make up academic good form flow naturally from the attempt to reconcile opposites, and it is this amalgam of judgement, taste, balance and subtlety which gives rise to the thoughts, shades and distinctions obsessionally designated as precise and subtle and which protects from effrontery and vulgarity.[31]

Thus, although apparently reasonable and liberal, the code of the happy mean and the *via media* is in reality a cover for a dictatorship of 'good sense', 'tact' and 'taste' which is the basis of the infallible and final judgements a teacher makes both as an examiner and when he is choosing whom to co-opt into his peer group and has, more than once, been the basis for scientific work. What the teachers have to say is based on common, clear assumptions, and could hardly be otherwise, since it is based on criteria such as good sense, which, as we have known since Descartes' day, is the most widespread quality in the world. We can then hardly oppose its judgements without cutting ourselves off from intellectual society and the good taste which belongs by definition to every well-born man whom the whole of good society will support. 'We say this every year without fail. It is, however, a self-evident truth which most candidates obstinately *refuse to see*' (Agr. GM, 1962). Consequently, breaches of good form, taste or judgement are *moral* faults, which show ill-will and spite, perhaps evil nature. ('Too many mistakes are due to a refusal to accept what good sense indicates' Agr. LM, 1962.) The classical manner in which they deplore the student's destructive treatment of everything he touches oscillates between the imagery of barbarity and that of natural calamity. He 'ravages', 'ransacks', 'tortures', 'corrupts', 'ruins' or 'degrades' texts, language, spelling or ideas: 'How often we saw this delicate passage *brutally* abused and offended . . . ' (Agr. LMM, 1965); 'One quite gratuitous Freudian claim degraded a whole beautiful page' (Agr. GF, 1959). One can imagine the great harm done by such over-confident and unsound principles of interpretation and appreciation, based on pure academic flair, when teachers apply them to ideas which do not bear the mark of true French 'good sense' or 'good taste', whether the student be dealing with ancient authors or the contemporary novel.[32]

The contradictions in university ideology are a symbolic expression of the contradiction, inherent in the legitmate conserving and transmitting function of a legitimate culture, between the *objective reality* of scholastic action as the authorized exercise of a lasting, continuous pedagogical process which is *controlled* (*inter alia* by syllabus, by timetable, by school premises), *supported* (by means of standard aids such as set books, textbooks etc.) and *supervised* by the institution, and the *lived reality* of such action, that is, in the ideological representation which gives the person of the pedagogical agent some of the authority automatically given to any official of a scholastic institution by the very fact of his belonging to that institution. Like the priest as the servant of a church, the teacher has an institutional authority, which, unlike that of the prophet or the creative intellectual, absolves him from the need to establish his own authority on each and every separate occasion, as he is preaching to people who already accept the value of his message.[33] Unlike the creative intellectual too, because he, like the prophet, imposes by means of an action of discontinuous and extraordinary influence over a limited area (i.e. his disciples) a message which is original in relation to the range of messages available in the cultural field at a given moment, the teacher, as one charged with conserving a culture considered lawful, reproduces a fixed message following the necessarily routine, standardized norms demanded by the ongoing inculcation needed to produce a cultivated *habitus* and consequently devotion to culture as a durable attitude.[34]

Like the scholastic disparagement of the 'pedantic' and the ideology of the gift, the complementary concept of both mastering and denouncing the scholastic routine — in short, of all that, in Levenson's phrase, goes to make up academic anti-academism[35] — gives an idea of the efforts made to deny, symbolically, the objective reality of the pedagogical situation. The contradictions in the relationship of teachers to the reality of their profession, which, no doubt, become more acute as they rise in it, are never more clearly seen than in the double game they are obliged to play when, as examiners, they want an essay aimed at selecting future teachers to be more than a teacher's, and certainly more than an aspiring teacher's, essay.[36] Although they lay great stress on 'creative' qualities, ('originality', 'imagination' etc.) and those 'personal' qualities which are both intellectual and moral, as opposed to knowledge and technical mastery (which are seen as merely secondary tricks of the trade, textbook knowledge or mechanical productions), they are unwilling to overlook the tiniest infringement of the most minutely codified scholastic observances. But beneath the charismatic image of an ordeal by talent, the prosaic reality of a competitive examination to recruit secondary teachers is always visible: 'Perhaps the best approach would be not to forget for a moment that one is taking an examination (which is impossible), but never to forget that the texts were not written to be questions in an examination. They were calls from one human being to others' (Agr. GM, 1962).

By reminding the examiner too brutally of the fact that it *is* an examination, the good pupil who is no more than a good pupil is not following the rules of the game, which are to forget and to conceal the reality of what he is doing. There can be no other explanation for all these exhortations to pretend, as everything is permissible including fiction, to maintain the fiction. The simulated creativeness and false sincerity of an 'impromptu' essay prepared well in advance are always preferred to acknowledged borrowing or informed teaching.[37] But the objective reality of the 'pedantic' is never more clearly to be seen than in the stereotyped denunciations of scholastic routine: 'Certain candidates seem to believe that an essay can only be good if it can be divided into three sections' (Agr. LM, 1959); 'They (the candidates) simply apply out-of-date formulae, handed down through generations, containing automatic devices expected to save candidates the effort of thought' (ibid.); 'One would think that any text set in the examination is *ipso facto* full of solemnity' (ibid.); 'Candidates should try to realize that the texts set are still products of the human mind and soul' (Agr. LM, 1962). Although candidates are often criticized for their over-didactic approach when in fact that is really why they are there, it is also no doubt for usurping too soon one of the privileges of the teaching profession and exposing too clearly the reality of the exercise.[38]

Dominant and dominated values

But the ruse of the university title, by which the institution induces the teacher to serve it by inducing and authorizing him to use it, should not make us blind to the real basis of the values of the educational system, that is, their link with the values of the dominant classes. Just as the freedom which is left to the teacher is a way of ensuring that he serves the system, the freedom which is left to the system to produce its own values in accordance with the logic of its own inner tensions is perhaps the best way of ensuring that it will serve exterior purposes, because the possibility of this new deviation from its aims is built into the logic of a system which best performs its social functions precisely when it seems to be exclusively pursuing its proper aims.

If, while appearing to recognize no other values than properly scholastic ones, the educational system is really serving the values of the dominant classes, this is basically because the systems of manners distinguished by scholastic taxonomies always refer (with whatever degree of refinement) to social differences, because in cultural matters the manner of acquisition is perpetuated in what is acquired in the form of a certain way of using the acquisition. Thus, when it seems that by means of tiny, infinite and indefinable nuances the 'ease' and the 'naturalness' of certain types of behaviour or speech can be distinguished which, as nothing about them suggests the effort or work involved in their acquisition, are seen as really 'cultivated' or 'distinguished', reference is really being made to a *particular mode of acquisition,* that of unconscious absorption, which is only possible in families whose culture is scholarly culture and consequently only for those who, having scholarly culture as their maternal culture, can have with it the familiar relationship which implies unconscious acquisition.[39] And more generally, the relationship which an individual has with school, with the culture and language it transmits and presupposes (a relationship which is shown in all his behaviour and which all scholastic evaluations and judgements take into account), is more or less 'easy', 'natural', 'tense', 'laborious' according to his chances of survival in the system, that is to say, according to the likelihood objectively attached to his category of his reaching a given position within the system. By laying emphasis on the relationship with culture, which is ideal for giving the illusion of expressing the intrinsic qualities of the person as a system of indefinable manners, and by giving the most privileged status to those types of relationship to culture which are less reminiscent of the period of training, the educational system exceeds to some extent the expectations of the leisured or well-off classes who, by exalting ease, facility, naturalness and casualness, set up an unbridgeable gulf between those who hold the monopoly of good manners, which, by definition, are only acquired as a result of a diffuse and also total process of unconscious and imperceptible absorption in the earliest stages of upbringing, and cultural upstarts who show, in the imperceptible defects of their practices, the subtle elements missing in a badly acquired culture, as they are autodidacts whose ostentatious display of disorganized and discordant knowledge shows a keenness which is both anarchical and stubborn. 'Pedantic' and 'limited', their too exclusively scholastic interest and knowledge show that they owe everything to the school.

Such is the principle which unifies and gives rise to the practices of pupils of lower middle class origin who must, to keep their position in the system, find in the kind of pure and empty keenness which characterizes the relationship with culture and the school of the class from which they come (and which is expressed in a perfectly transparent way in their practices and their preferences) some sure way of compensating for the handicaps linked to the lack of cultural capital by assiduous and often desperately hard work. When successful candidates in the *concours général* who come from the lower middle classes – they are known to be more heavily represented in disciplines which in their present form demand more work (while in French, for example, they are completely absent) – say that their outstanding quality is tenacity, they are directly expressing the objective truth about a whole scholastic practice of necessity, in its taut and tense hardworking mode, marked by the continuous sustained effort they have had to make to keep their place in the system, to 'hang-on', as they say. Another sign of this contrast of two styles of relationship with the school and culture is the fact that successful candidates of lower middle class origin achieved the greatest number of *prix d'excellence* which, as opposed to qualifications like high grades in the *baccaléureat* (in which upper class candidates, from a more or less equivalent group, i.e. pupils in the preparatory classes for the *grandes écoles*, obtain better results), is a recognition of application through the whole school year and no doubt also of docility towards teachers, their teaching and the disciplines they impose.[40] Everything seems to indicate that the longer the period covered by scholastic judgement of knowledge, aptitudes and attitudes, the more likely it is that lower middle class (and also working class) pupils will give proof of their assiduity, tenacity and perseverance and of what they have acquired as a result of them, while upper class pupils impress by their qualities in the shorter space of time occupied by examinations at the end of the year, and particularly in oral examinations which, as they are presently constituted, call for charismatic skill and proof of such qualities as 'style' and 'brilliance'.[41]

We might perhaps expect in these conditions that lower middle class pupils would explicitly demand the means of effectively making use of their disposition to acquire and accumulate knowledge zealously and eagerly and even to profess and proclaim the values implicit in their scholastic practices. In fact, although more of them (65.5 per cent) than children from homes of the managerial classes (57.5 per cent) (but fewer than those of working class origin, 71 per cent) expect the ideal teacher to be conscientious or 'a good teacher', while pupils from managerial families(except those concerned with science) more often expect him to be creative or brilliant (30 per cent as against 22 per cent for the middle classes), they show in many ways their acceptance of the dominant representation of the hierarchy of practices and aptitudes and the half-ashamed relationship which they have with their own culture. This can be seen for example in the fact that they are more likely than the others (47 per cent)to wish to have qualities which they do not see themselves as having, i.e. talent and brilliance, unlike the sons of managerial class families (37.5 per cent) who were both more likely to see themselves as possessing 'charismatic' qualities and to be happy as they are (62.5 per cent as against 54 per cent for middle class and 50 per cent for working class pupils). Similarly, while being more often successful in history and geography or natural sciences and seeing themselves as good at geography (38.5 per cent) more often than children from managerial families and more often liking geography — unlike managerial class children, and more particularly unlike the children of teachers in secondary and higher education, who are the only ones who can afford not to like geography and to see themselves as very weak in it — they accept more readily than any other the dominant idea that they should like French most of all.[42]

Thus, the favourable disposition of lower middle class pupils towards education and their scholastic docility is no less effective than the familiarity of privileged pupils in producing an acceptance of the models of the cultivated mode which implies if not the condemnation at least the disparagement of the practices in which these hardworking attitudes leave their mark. The relationship of lower middle class pupils to their own values (predetermined values which govern their whole practice while they appear to accept eagerly dominant values which their whole practice contradicts and in the light of which it is deprived of any value) is quite similar, as we have seen, to that which unites the values implied in the logic of scholastic action to those recognized and favoured by the scholastic system. This *coincidence* between the contrasting and subordinative relationship which links lower middle class and upper middle class values and the same type of relationship which links properly scholastic values with social values means that all scholastic practices can always be read in two ways — one purely internal one which, as below, brings them back to the logic of the institution itself, and the other, an external one, which takes into account the external functions of internal relationships. It is in this way that we must interpret the half-hearted and slightly ashamed way in which the school recognizes the self-sacrificing inclination of the lower middle classes and the open and to a certain extent forced recognition which it gives to the charismatic manners of the privileged classes.[43] Although only fully recognizing that relationship with culture which can only be completely acquired outside itself, the school cannot completely devalue the 'scholastic' relationship with culture without rejecting its mode of inculcating culture. At the same time, while keeping its favours for those who owe it least in essential things, that is in manner and manners, it cannot reject those who owe everything to it and whose 'pedantic' attitudes, which are devalued in so far as they underlie a 'scholastic' relationship with culture, are given value in so far as they underlie a keenness and a docility which the school cannot absolutely disdain.[44] Thus, the ambivalent relationship of the school to lower middle class and upper middle class attitudes (which are always seen, as we have noted, through purely scholastic categories and therefore never in their social significance) and in particular with petit bourgeois or bourgeois attitudes towards school is superimposed, as an overprint, on the ambivalent relationship it has towards its own objective truth as a mode of scholastic production and of scholastic manners.[45]

The relationship which the educational system has with the different categories of its public and with the values which they import into the system can only in fact be defined independently of the relationship which each of these categories has with the educational system and which is most clearly seen in the dialectics of dedication and recognition. The effect of dedication is evenly distributed over the whole range of successful candidates, as only 11 per cent of those stating their intended career are seeking studies and professions outside the intellectual field (law and political sciences are chosen particularly by successful candidates in history and geography, the Ecole Nationale D'Administration and medicine) and among those saying that they wished to attend a *grande école.* Sixty-three per cent state the École Normale Supérieure, but it is successful candidates from the middle classes and the intellectual sections of the upper classes who show the greatest unconditional acceptance of the values of the school. Thus, successful middle class candidates more frequently put intellectual professions (teaching or research) in the first place, and the same is true of the intellectual segments of the upper classes. Similarly, too, the proportion of pupils in preparatory classes for the literary *grandes écoles* who intend to take up teaching varies in inverse proportion to the position of their family in the social scale. And again, among all the successful candidates in the *concours général* who intend to go on to the École Normale Supérieure and are at a significantly higher social and cultural level than the general range of successful candidates, the sons of elementary, secondary and higher education teachers are, *ceteris paribus,* more heavily represented. Thus the tension contained in the scholastic representation of culture and the relationship with culture, the tension between scholastic values and social values which is superimposed on the tension between lower and upper middle class values, is visible through the logic of the system of relationships between the educational system and the different social classes, or at the higher levels of the school career, the different sections of the dominant classes . . .

As we know on the one hand that scholastic success is a function of the cultural capital inherited from the family (which can be simply measured by the scholastic level reached by ancestors two generations back) and the acceptance of the values of the school, and on the other hand that the effect of 'dedication' (and the correlative 'vocation' for teaching careers) which scholastic recognition by examination produces is, other things being equal, all the stronger when the people to whom it is applied recognize more completely the values of the school and the value of qualifications, or rather, when they have fewer values with which to oppose them, it can be seen that the more directly the interests of the classes and sections of classes on which it exerts its action are linked to the school, or to be more precise, the more completely the marketable value and social position of the individuals who compose them depend on a scholastic guarantee of their worth, the more successful is the school in imposing recognition of its values and the values of its hierarchies.[46]

Although the school can use its relative autonomy with regard to the dominant classes to impose hierarchies whose summit is a university career and to turn to its own profit some individuals from sections of the dominant classes least likely to accept its verdicts, it only ever completely succeeds when it is preaching to the converted such as the sons of teachers or intellectuals or those kinds of submissives whose career, from childhood, is destined to be in the school, an institution which they cannot oppose as they owe everything to it and expect everything from it. We mean, of course, working class boys and *a fortiori* those whose families belong to the teaching section of the lower middle classes.[47]

It is because the objective structure of the relationship between the educational system and the dominant classes, a relationship of dependence by independence, dominates the mechanisms by which the educational system reproduces itself by recognizing those who recognize it and by giving its blessing to those who dedicate themselves to it, that one can see that sort of structural coincidence between the ethos which the agents owe to the social class from which they come and to which they belong, and the conditions for the realization of that ethos which are objectively built into the functioning of the institution and into the structure of its relationships with the dominant classes.[48] The equilibrium between scholastic class values and worldly or intellectual values, between lower middle and middle values, which are visible in the pedagogical practices of secondary teachers and particularly of teachers in higher education, express the tension between aristocratic values, which are a necessary part of the French system of education both by virtue of its own tradition and because of the relationship linking it to the privileged classes, and lower middle class values which are encouraged, even among people who do not have them because of their social origin, by an institution condemning its agents to occupy a lower rank in the hierarchy of the sections of the dominant classes, i.e. in the allocation of power and privileges. Teachers in higher education can thus find, in the very ambiguities of an ideology which express both the social duality of the recruitment of teachers and the ambivalence of the objective definition of the teacher's job, the most suitable tool for repressing without contradiction all deviations with regard to two systems of norms mutually contradictory in more than one respect. It can be seen that scorn for all the hardworking virtues of the intellectual worker, which is the academic version of the aristocracy of talent (which itself, in accordance with the demands of bourgeois heredity, restates the aristocratic ideology of birth) is allied, in practices and judgements on practices, with moral disapproval of success immediately seen as worldly compromise and with the punctilious defence of statutory rights, even if against the rights of competence. These are attitudes which express, in a properly university form, the petit bourgeois propensity to draw comfort from a conviction of their apartness from the universal mediocrity. Thus, because they are the product of an alliance between contradictory demands from the institution and the contradictory models according to which different groups of agents enter into a relationship with the institution, all university norms, whether operating at the level of the selection of students or that of the co-opting of teachers or that of governing the production of lectures, theses or even work claiming to be scientific always tend to favour the success, at least in the institution, of a modal type of man and work defined by a double negation, that is of brilliance without warmth or light and heaviness without scientific weight or alternatively, 'the pedantry of triviality' and the coquetry of learning.

Notes

1 Mention could be made here of the excellent definition of *manners* in which Robert Redfield sees a definition of *life-style:* '. . . a culture's hum and buzz of implications . . . half uttered or unuttered or unutterable expressions of value', Lionel Trilling, 'Manners, morals and the novel' in *The Liberal Imagination,* New York, Viking Press, 1950), pp. 206-7, quoted by R. Redfield, in *The Primitive World and its Transformations,* (Ithaca, New York, Cornell University Press, first edition 1953, fourth edition 1961), p. 52.

2 Similarly a statistical study of the social, scholastic and intellectual characteristics of candidates elected or beaten in elections in a large university such as the Sorbonne would no doubt provide a great deal more information about the values which determine the *homo academicus* and about the academic mind than all the opinion polls and all the contents analysis, especially if it was accompanied by an ethnographic study of the social mechanisms at work in every election (cliques, runs of good and poor performance . . .).

3 B. Malinowski, *Argonauts of the Western Pacific,* (London, Routledge, 1922), pp. 17-20.

4 The survey was carried out by correspondence with successful candidates from 1966, 1967 and 1968, with the rate of reply reaching 81 per cent, 79 per cent and 71 per cent respectively without reminders, which is a good guide to the ethical attitudes of the respondents (especially if it is recalled that the final batch of material was sent immediately after May 1968). The group shows no significant bias from the point of view of any verifiable criteria. For example, 33 per cent of the sample were girls as against 32.5 per cent in the whole group of successful candidates, 23 per cent in both cases were in the scientific disciplines, 35.5 per cent of the sample were from *lycées* in Paris as against 39 per cent in the group as a whole. The distribution of successful candidates by *lycée* and *departement* remained more or less constant throughout the period. P. Maldidier assisted with the analysis of the reports on candidates taking the *agrégation.* J.-C. Combessie and B. Queysanne were associated either with the drafting of the questionnaire or with the analysis of the survey.

5 The two synoptic tables show the chief data, in the form of figures which support the ideas advanced here.

6 The proportion of upper middle class subjects (61 per cent) is much higher among the group of successful candidates than in universities (31.5 per cent) and much nearer than that found in preparatory classes for the *grandes écoles* (i.e. 62.5 per cent in *khâgnes** and 57.5

per cent in *taupes***) and in the *grandes écoles* (i.e. 67.5 per cent for
the Ecole Normale Supérieure (sciences), 66 per cent for that
institution (arts) and the École Polytechnique and 61 per cent for
the École Nationale d'Administration. 74 per cent said that they
intended to undertake further study in the preparatory classes for
the *grandes écoles* and only 26 per cent in universities (although the
preparatory classes accept only some one in twenty of students in
higher education). There are 14.5 per cent of candidates successful
in the *concours général* at the ENS (Ulm), 7 per cent at the Polytechnique, 4.5 per cent at the École des Mines, 3 per cent at the
École Centrale, in contrast to a tiny figure for the faculties of letters
and sciences (information from the survey carried out by the Centre
de Sociologie Européenne on all pupils in *grandes écoles* in 1966).
*khâgne – second year class preparing for competition for entrance
to the École Normale Supérieure.
**taupe – second year class preparing for competition for entrance
to the Polytechnique

[7] The idea of precocity presupposes the existence of a school career
marked off into so many stages (*gradus*) in the gradual acquisition of
knowledge and corresponding to a given age. But, as Philippe Ariès
has pointed out, such a structure did not grow up until the beginning
of the sixteenth century, and the undifferentiated pedagogy of the
Middle Ages did not conceive of the idea of a relationship between
'ability and age structures' (P. Aries, *L'Enfant et la vie de famille sous
l'Ancien Régime* (Paris, Plon, 1960), p.202. As the structure of the
school career has become firmer and more precise, particularly since
the seventeenth century, precocious individual careers have become
rarer and from then on begin to appear to be an index of superiority
and a promise of social success. It would be interesting to follow the
progress during the nineteenth century towards a rigorously defined
career and the correlative development, also linked to the Romantic
ideologies of creation and genius, of the ideology of precocity.

[8] The idea of giftedness is so strongly associated with that of precocity
that youth tends to be *per se* a guarantee of talent. Thus *agrégation*
examiners can spot 'brilliant' results from 'talented young candidates':
'This year we have distinguished performances from several of these
young recruits. Out of twenty-seven successful candidates, fourteen
had not taught and eight of them were among the first ten. . . . Their
success does not make us forget the merits of practising teachers who,
often working in less favourable conditions, made great efforts and
overcame difficulties. . . . But we are grateful to those who stood out
from their first competitive examinations both for having animated the
oral examination with their enthusiasm and their desire to convince
and for having provided such an encouraging experience.' (Agr. GM,
1963). 'In the oral, the *'carrés'* (Younger students) are often the best,
being livelier in discussion, more aware, more receptive and adaptable.
As examinations go on, gravity replaces grace' (entrance examination
for the ENS (Ulm), philosophy oral, 1965). The precocious student
is the apple of examiners' eyes and they are specially indulgent towards
the gaps in his knowledge and his mistakes which can even, under the

heading of 'youthful faults', be a sign of his 'talents'. 'They are younger than in previous years, and it is probably right to assume that their errors are due to lack of maturity and experience and that their mistakes can soon be corrected . . . Their gaucheness and naivety often hide very promising gifts and serious qualities' (Agr.LMF, 1965). 'Finally, there were, as there used to be, candidates capable of doing an *explication de texte*. If they did not obtain the highest marks, it is simply because, here and there, they made minor errors of interpretation because of slips very understandable in a competitive examination or because of youthful faults' (Agr. GM, 1963).

In these texts and those we shall quote later we have italicized those words or phrases which best illustrate scholastic ideology and the fundamental contradictions in terms of which it is structured. We have used the abbreviations (1) Agr. LM (2) Agr. LF (3) Agr. GM (4) Agr. GF (5) Agr. LMG (6) Agr. LMF to indicate respectively (1) and (2) *agrégation* reports, letters, male and female; (3) and (4) *agrégation* reports, grammar, male and female; (5) and (6) *agrégation* reports, modern letters, male and female.

9 Economists commonly forget when studying consumption that the value of a good, and in particular of a symbolic good such as a play (cf. premières and exclusive performances) or a tour abroad is always partly due to the precocity (as defined above) with which it is endowed and which forms part of social rarity at a given point in time. In view of the laws of the differential diffusion of rare goods, inequalities between social classes always take the form of a time-lag. Underprivileged classes are always 'behind'; in other words practices, and particularly consumption, which are the rule in other classes, are the exception in their case, and the individuals who form these classes only obtain the same goods much later at a greater age and therefore for a much shorter time. We could take as an example a house built 'for retirement' as against a flat inherited at the age of twenty.

10 The argument used by successful candidates in literary subjects to show why their homework had been good illustrates this basic difference perfectly.

(1) 'Originality, rigour, sensitivity' (French, son of chemical engineer), 'Spontaneous, not too academic, clear' (philosophy, son of a skilled worker).

(2) 'Perhaps because of the maps, which were fairly detailed, and certain things I knew about the Massif Central and The Vosges. I knew more about these than about the other mountainous areas (geography, son of a clerical worker), 'Clarity, diagrams, references' (natural sciences, son of an art teacher), 'Quality and number of diagrams, carefully thought-out plan' (natural sciences, son of a sales manager).

(3) Classical languages seem to occupy an intermediate position: 'Quite an exact translation and an attempt to achieve good French in it' (Greek, son of a technical manager), 'firstly grammatical accuracy, which is the basic requirement of a good prose, and then a subtle way of translating the complexities of the French text' (Latin prose, son of a doctor).

(4) Successful candidates in mathematics and physics mostly refer to clarity, rigour, accuracy and precision, but remarks about manner are not totally absent: 'Presentation, rigour and the way of presenting the argument' (mathematics, son of a teacher of maritime subjects), 'I think my work got a distinction because it was clear and I quickly reached solutions in the questions I did' (mathematics, son of a teacher in a first-year preparation class for the ENS), 'The speed and elegance of the solutions' (mathematics, son of a doctor).

[11] It has been established elsewhere that differences between students of different social origins which tend to weaken and sometimes to disappear (as inequality between the selection rates of survivors increases) in those areas most rigorously controlled by the school, such as the handling of scholastic language (cf. P. Bourdieu, J.-C. Passeron and M.de Saint-Martin, *Rapport pédagogique et communication* (Paris, Mouton, 1965)) reappear in full force as one moves away from what is directly taught by the school (from, for example, the classical theatre to the avant-garde theatre or the *théâtre de boulevard* – cf. P. Bourdieu and J.-C. Passeron, *Les Etudiants et leurs études* (Paris, Mouton, 1964)). Here it has been noted that successful candidates in the 'noble' disciplines most often listen to cultural stations (with 45.5 per cent of such candidates in French and philosophy regularly listening to France-Musique and France-Culture), whereas successful candidates in geography, and particularly in the natural sciences, only listen to popular stations (France–Inter and outside commercial stations).

[12] 72.5 per cent of them go at least once a month to the cinema as against 61 per cent of successful candidates in history and geography and 53.5 per cent in Latin and Greek.

[13] Some opinions on jazz bring out the basic difference: (1) 'a very rich and attractive form of artistic expression' (French, son of a chemical engineer); 'Jazz is an original means of artistic expression, coming from a fusion of negro religious folklore and European folklore . . . Jazz tunes aren't fixed and unchangeable. They can have variations on them, and new and original interpretations, unlike other musical works, which are fixed by their scores' (mathematics, son of an engineer). (2) 'The rhythm is modern and seems to express all the longings of the modern world, especially when played by negroes' (natural sciences, daughter of a shopkeeper); 'New Orleans blues-age jazz shows something of the Negroes' melancholy' (natural sciences, daughter of a mechanic).

[14] Successful candidates in French are given astonishing attention by the press, and their academic work treated like a literary event. Like speeches made on reception into the Académie Française, the best French essays in the *concours général* or the *baccalauréat* are published in literary papers (in *Figaro Littéraire* or the literary supplement of *Le Monde)*. There is also an indirect indication of the agreed superiority of French in the care taken in the *agrégation* reports in grammar to give some esteem to the discipline. The intention is, by emphasizing the youth of candidates and their 'vocation' and the special qualities demanded by exercises such as translation from Latin, to prove that the *agrégation de grammaire*

is not, as it is commonly seen to be, the poor relation of the
literary one. 'This year it was younger candidates, with a vocation
for grammatical studies who, in the oral at least, set the tone. . . .
They were methodical, had a certain intellectual discipline without
in any way lacking the qualities called for by properly literary
studies. . . .' (Agr. GM, 1963); 'Subtlety, inventiveness, charm . . .
Three candidates showed these qualities, the last of which is by no
means negligible' (Agr. GM, 1963).

[15] See *Le Monde* (literary supplement), 21 June 1969.

[16] 'There is so to speak a phenomenon of spontaneous creation.'

[17] 'the mystery of the artistic gift', 'The magic power (of words)', 'the
mystery of its Beauty'.

[18] 'The mystery of reading', 'It is I who am beside these blue waters,
it is I who meet the gaze', 'The work which we have created', 'It
is *I* who write', 'Marvellously finding my own identity', 'The work
becomes my own creation', 'I can take part in literary creation',
'The character whom I will create'.

[19] 'How many different interpretations of the same character, the
same action, the same sentence!', 'And for each reader the characters
and emotions in the novel will have a particular meaning', 'Can one
make a judgement', '. . . is for me', 'For me the work of literature
creates resonances based on impressions and sensations', 'So that
we can understand them in our own way depending on our own
sensibility', 'We can understand a literary work, explain it, and
above all, react to it!'

The subjectivity of mental states goes naturally with a refusal to
have anything to do with anything which might smack of reductionism: 'It is always dangerous to submit a work of literature to criteria
as though it were an industrial product', 'Can a work be reduced to
a character', 'A work of literature is more than all that.' If anyone
doubts the validity of this analysis and the representative nature
of the documents it is based on, we can merely quote extracts from
examiner's reports on the *concours* in which the principles of
literary *explication de texte* are 'defined' in the hope of showing
that no great distance separates the explicit pedagogical percepts
of *explication de texte* and the wordy disquisitions of their well-
trained pupils in 'creative' reading. For example, simply on the
theme of 'sensibility': 'It shows an astonishing lack of literary
sensibility' (Agr. LM, 1962), 'Sensitivity was required — fresh and
a little naïve perhaps, refusing to try to seek out the secret of a poem
in elaborate and perhaps uncertain complexities ("If you go into the
kitchen . . ." as La Bruyère said) and welcoming with simplicity the
moving intimacy of the "great-hearted servant girl" — a sensitivity
refined by a memory of love', 'It does not take long to discern terms
of value, original tones, densely written passages filled with interior
life, whose aim is perhaps latent but vividly felt', 'The freshness of
mind in a first contact is perhaps a good replacement for over-
detailed knowledge' (competitive entrance examination for the ENS,
French, *explication de textes*, 1966). 'Once the hemistich has been
replaced in its context, we can feel its resonance within us. . . . The

exorcism of poetry has not destroyed the anguish and we feel the last line in our body and soul like an ever-open wound' (Agr. GF, 1959). It will be seen from the above that masters, like their pupils have no fear either of the exaltation of the mystery of poetry or of uncritical narcissism.

[20] 'It is in that reading of oneself, that pouring out of our personality that the novel achieves its aim', 'It is myself that I meet.'

[21] 'Thus, I escape', 'the fleeting sensations which make up the fantastic and marvellous elements of my daily life', 'the fairyland', 'mysterious shadow', 'the work which we have created ourselves by transferring to it our dreams and our imaginings'.

[22] 'All the dreams which incessantly haunt and rend me', 'The desperately pointless railway', 'A man's cry of anguish', 'heartbreak', 'uncertainty'.

[23] We should remember the efforts of several generations of French intellectuals to make Marxism less vulgar.

[24] A report on the competitive entrance examination for the ENA reads similarly: 'Apart from some one or two exceptional candidates who had striking, sometimes dazzling, personalities, the examination left an impression of greyness' (report of the juries on the work of candidates for the ENA, *Épreuves et statistiques du concours de 1967* (Paris, Imprimerie Nationale, 1968), p. 9), as do the reports of juries for the *agrégation* or entrance to the École Normale: 'In short, from the point of view of sound knowledge . . . choice of expression or a feeling for real elegance, the work of most candidates in the *explication* left a disturbing impression of ignorance, confusion and vulgarity' (Agr. LM, 1959); 'The jury is inclined to show indulgence of many *blunders* and even to occasional misinterpretations, but it will never do so in the case of pretentiousness, pedantry and vulgarity' (competitive entrance examinations for the ENS, *explication* (French, 1966); 'In this way it would be possible to go beyond the drudgery of laborious spadework and reach the freedom of a translation combining elegance and accuracy' (ibid.).
The propensity of teachers for rather smug criticism of the faults of candidates means that, as is the case here, the vocabulary centred around the negative pole of the system of contrasts is much richer than that around the positive. It can also be seem from these two examples that the contrasts noted above are not rigid or immutable, many terms being interchangeable (e.g. vulgar, laborious, awkward).

[25] There would be no end to the number (and not only in academic utterances) of judgements formed in conformity with the principles of this system of classification. Of all these contrasts, none is more fruitful than that between learning, which is still suspected of bearing the mark of laborious acquisition, and talent (with the correlative notion of general culture): 'The lack of 'general culture' was most marked . . . it is more useful to candidates than learned works which bewilder them' (Agr. LM, 1959). The distinction between knowledge and talent underlies the devaluation of those disciplines which are supposed to demand only memory, the most despised of abilities: 'Although the effort of *memorization,*

which is so indispensable in philology, cannot of course be neglected, it is nevertheless *culture* acquired by reflection, which gives the facts of language their meaning and, in the end, their pedagogical and human significance' (Agr. GF, 1959).

[26] Although the weight of tests in classical languages in the major literary competitive examinations, for the ENS as well as the literary and grammatical *agrégations,* is commonly known, we too often neglect to examine the effect of subjects considered to be 'of proven worth' ('Grammar pays! — a fact which should not be forgotten', Agr. GM, 1963). As the logic of a competitive examination such as that for the ENS seems to come fairly close to that behind the awarding of *prix d'excellence* they presumably both favour the same type of excellence.

[27] A similar hierarchy can be observed among science candidates, where the figures are 76.5 per cent for successful candidates in physics, 68 per cent for those in mathematics and 52.5 per cent for those in natural sciences.

[28] The effect of dedication is very unequal and varies, as will be seen, according to the socially conditioned attitudes of its recipients towards school.

[29] Any scholastic recognition produces in addition a dedicating effect. The *concours général* in particular is in reality a competitive preliminary recruitment to university teachers, although this is not its avowed aim. An indication of it can be seen in the fact that virtually all successful candidates see it as the most important event of their school lives. Thus a university career can be spent in the atmosphere of amazement produced by a continuous series of university 'events'. 'Very early in the afternoon, I went to the Ministry . . . finally I managed to unearth an obscure official who, on hearing my name, told me point-blank that I had been appointed *maître de conférences* at Grenoble. I was overcome. Along with my admission to the École Normale, it was one of the happiest moments of my life' (R. Blanchard, *Je découvre l'Université,* (Paris, Fayard, 1973), p. 80. 'I was interested in very many other things during my first years in Grenoble, and primarily in the university which had done me the honour of accepting me' (ibid. p. 87).

[30] *Agrégation* reports constantly call for 'liveliness', 'enthusiasm', 'conviction' and 'personal commitment', the opposite of both 'culpable casualness' and 'prudent cunning'. 'She even had the courage to commit herself personally, intelligently and moderately' (Agr. LMF, 1965). Candidates are asked to 'put life into' style and manner of speech, and examiners are pleased by the 'freshness' of young candidates, even when it is a little 'naive.' They also point out that 'a good performance needs tact, skill of course, and enough enthusiasm to make a dull grammatical imposition into a real intellectual pleasure' (Agr. GF, 1959). 'The examiners have too often felt that a pedantic love of linguistic games and verbal complication blunts real insight into the question, critical reaction or realization of the need for lucidity' (competitive entrance examination for the ENS, philosophy oral, 1965). They criticize 'candidates who are

sceptical in literary matters, experts in intellectual gymnastics and in handling *sic et non,* (Agr. LM, 1959), although they cannot find it in themselves to condemn recourse to 'decent rhetoric, not without an unexaggerated warmth or humour' (Agr. GF, 1959). The reports criticize 'excessive casualness', 'cavalier assurance' (with regard to culture and hence with regard to the jury), 'a mixture of negligence and pretentiousness'. They constantly point out that candidates must steer a skilful course between 'too much' and 'too little': 'Every care should be taken to avoid two equally reprehensible attitudes — admiration to order and systematic denigration' (Agr. LCF, 1962). 'Between the opposites of aridity and prolixity there lies a flexible, light, descreet way of gradually coming to basic conclusions' (ibid.); 'After an intelligent reading of the text, without affectation but also without stumbling or making any wrong liaisons . . .' (Agr. GM, 1963); 'We encountered fewer pretentiously or point- lessly abstract expressions . . . fewer "in" words . . . but care must be taken to prevent a commendable striving for simplicity and clarity lapsing into the abandonment of the essay style and replacing it with a slovenly or even vulgar conversational one' (Agr. LMF, 1965); 'We should like to remind future candidates that the *explication* is an intelligent blend of essential literal and literary exegesis . . . a carefully composed amalgam' (Agr. GM, 1957); 'A natural delivery avoiding incorrectness, exaggeration and sweeping generalities' (Agr. LM, 1965); 'The most disturbing and ridiculous aspect is the arrogant and over- bearing tone and an air of deliberate superiority' (Agr. LM, 1965).

[31] 'In difficult cases . . . the only criterion is that of taste, the only possible attitude that of vigilant sympathy' (Agr. LCE, 1962); 'comments made with sobriety and tact' (Agr. GF, 1959); 'a certain nicety of tone must be striven for' (Agr. LM, 1962); 'We expected, most often in vain, what one has a right to expect from future or practising teachers: a certain alacrity, the talent to awaken interest in a translation and appreciation of it, and a taste for rendering not only constructions, but their subtleties too,' (Agr. GF, 1959); 'A French *explication* is privileged to reveal gifts of subtlety, intellectual suppleness and discernment, (competitive entrance examination for ENS, French , *explication,* 1965).

[32] Grammar and good sense compel choice' (Agr. LM, 1962); 'In translation, there is a need of semantic flair' (ibid.); 'The overall translation must give evidence of strength, ingeniosity, taste, in short of an art of finding equivalents. It is the ongoing combination of the taste for geometry and the taste for subtlety' (Agr. GM, 1959).

[33] 'The lay teacher too (like the priest) can and should have something of this feeling. He too is the agent of a great moral person who surpasses him . . .' (E. Durkheim, *Education and Sociology* (New York, Free Press, 1956), p. 89).

[34] 'For what he teaches as a consequence of his office as a representa- tive of the Church, this he considers as something about which he has not freedom to teach according to his own lights; it is something which he is appointed to propound at the dictation of and in the name of another' (I. Kant, *On History* (New York, Library of

Liberal Arts, Bobbs-Merrill, 1963), p. 6).

[35] J.R. Levenson, *Modern China and its Confucian Past* (New York, Doubleday, 1964), p. 31.

[36] 'We must in fact assess scripts on the basis of humbler, if not humiliating, criteria' (Agr. LM, 1959).

[37] 'No candidate may replace the personal development expected of him by reading a page from a critic and modestly declaring that he could not express the matter better' (Agr. LM, 1962).

[38] It would by no means be difficult to show that the same contradictions are present even more clearly in the idea which a student has of his work, his teachers and his own attitudes. Thus, for example, a desire for a narrower, more 'scholastic' framework alternates with the ideal, prestige-laden image of elevated, free work, untrammelled by controls or discipline, and zealous note-taking with an exalted attention to the magic masterly lecture. Yet again, the image of the 'marvellous', 'brilliant' master, with a 'divine spark', not too 'pedantic', 'alive' and 'capable of bringing his subject to life and communicating with his audience' (among expressions used by students in Lille) often coexists in the same individuals with a desire for a 'useful' lecture, 'properly put together', 'with a clear plan', 'easy to follow' and 'well documented'. Although the two types of expectancy have variable weight (as we have seen in the case of successful candidates in the *concours général*) according to categories and in particular according to the social origin of students and disciplines, it is nevertheless true that the predominance of the charismatic values is always marked enough to give a rather shameful and culpable air to all properly scholastic demands.

[39] To the variations in adhesion to a charismatic-style ideology which tends to increase in ratio to a rise in the social hierarchy, account must be taken of, inter alia (docility towards the school being another important factor), the form taken in different social milieux by help given by the family. If help which is positive and seen as such increases as the social level rises (from 25 per cent in the working classes to 36 per cent in the upper classes), although it seems to decrease as the rate of success increases (those with an 'honourable mention' claiming to have received help in 38 per cent of cases as against 27 per cent for prizewinners), it still only makes up the 'visible' part of the gifts of all kinds that children receive from their family. We know, for example, that the proportion of successful candidates who visited museums and art galleries before the age of eleven with their family increases greatly according to social origin (60.5 per cent in the case of lower middle class children and 67.5 per cent for upper middle class children), and this is only one indicator among others of the diffuse and indirect forms of encouragement given by the family. It can be seen that upper class children amass explicit and implicit help, while lower middle class children (in particular those of clerical workers and elementary school teachers) receive in particular direct help, and that working class children can only exceptionally count on any of these scholastically profitable forms of help. Successful candidates in the *concours général* coming from the lower middle classes (70 per cent as against 64 per cent) learned to read before going to school more often than those

from the upper classes, but less often than those from the working classes (85 per cent) this form of direct help being merely one of the compensatory advantages either social or scholastic which explain the success of this very highly selected category.

[40] 40.5 per cent of lower middle class pupils received the *prix d'excellence* during the year as against 38 per cent of upper middle class pupils; 60 per cent of elementary schoolteachers' children as against 35 per cent of those of teachers in secondary and higher education (and 73 per cent of middle class pupils were successful in Latin and Greek as against 67 per cent of upper class pupils in the same category). The fact that the sons of teachers in secondary and higher education come more often (38 per cent as against 28.5 per cent) from *lycées* in the Paris region, where selection and competition are more severe, is not enough to explain the difference. In preparatory classes for the *grandes écoles* (scientific and literary), lower middle class students more frequently (with working class pupils) win the *prix d'excellence* and inversely less frequently obtain a distinction in the *baccalauréat*.

[41] A continuous observation carried out throughout 1965 on eighty students reading for a degree in sociology in the faculty of letters in Lille led to similar conclusions. The substitution of continuous assessment, based on more rigorous and explicit criteria and allowing for a rational organization of preparation, tends to favour relatively students of lower middle class origin as against those from upper classes and women students as against men.

[42] The proportion of students claiming to like French, or like it a great deal, is 73 per cent for lower middle class students (and 79 per cent for the sons of elementary school teachers) as against 68 per cent for pupils from the managerial classes and 62 per cent of working class pupils.

[43] This double relationship clearly takes different forms according to the orders and types of teaching. The subordination to dominant values is never as clearly marked as in the highest ranks of teaching and in those disciplines which, by their content and social and scholastic significance, express in the highest degree the scholastic and social ideal recognized by the French education system. The further one moves from higher literary studies, the cradle of scholastic values (either vertically towards primary education or horizontally towards technical education or in both directions at once towards elementary technical education), the more the agents and their practices are devalued and disparaged, as the representations of it reveal. (These have recently been given new life as a result of the competition between traditional secondary teachers and elementary school teachers.) This can be seen, in the field of primary education, in the 'elementary types' and everything reminiscent of their pedagogy (handwriting 'a dunces' skill', or bothering about spelling) and in the inferior status of all levels of technical education, from the *collège d'enseignement technique* to the Conservatoire National des Arts et Metiers, the poor man's Polytechnique, and the recently created *instituts universitaires de technologie*.

[44] And in fact the school still looks upon a bad relationship with

culture with indulgence when it appears as the price paid for a good relationship with the school. It will be recalled for example that the reports of *agrégation* examiners demand from would-be teachers that they at least profess a loyalty to the institution and the values in its care by the enthusiasm of their words and their manner.

45 That is why teachers can, with the most complete illusion of ethical neutrality, make scholastic judgements which, as shown by the choice of metaphors and adjectives used, are in reality *class* judgements: 'The French spoken by these future *agrégés des lettres* is a mixture of *pretentiousness* and *carelessness, a jargon* which is a *rag-bag of boldly fashionable words* and *vulgar solecisms.* This *clash of styles* is as disagreeable as the sight of *imitation jewellery on a grubby skin.* It is difficult to see how the most intelligent of our candidates can escape being *offended* by it, and how the ideas — often appropriate and subtle — which they have worked out can be expressed in such a way as to *set the teeth on edge* — often in fact, in a *low* way (Agr. LM, 1959). It can be seen how teachers who indignantly refuse any pedagogical action aimed at the overt inculcation of the dominant values can profess these values in the smallest details of their practices, in their declared judgements but also in their expressions of distaste, allusions, hidden meanings, even in their silences and their omissions. Even when taking refuge in an objectivist transmission of factual information, they always transmit more than knowledge, even if it is only the value of that knowledge and of the particular manner of transmitting it which is by definition implicit in the fact of transmitting it.

46 As is shown by an analysis of the social and scholastic characteristics of successful candidates in the *concours général* or of pupils in the *grandes écoles* and, in particular, the comparison between the *écoles normales supérieures,* which are the gateway to reaching intellectual and scholarly posts, and the schools which like the École Nationale D'Administration or the Polytechnique lead to careers in high administrative posts or in business, the different sections of the directing classes can be spread out, according to their relationship with the educational system, between two extreme poles, corresponding to the most heavily represented groups in these two types of institution. At one end of the scale are families with a large cultural capital (measured by the formal qualifications of parents and grandparents), rather small in size, often from the provinces and for a very large part in teaching; at the other, families with a large social capital (measured by the length of time to which they have belonged to the upper classes), fairly large, often from Paris, belonging on balance to the world of power and business. Everything seems to show that, like that of the different social classes, the attitude of different sections of the dominant classes to the school is a function of the degree to which social success depends on scholastic success in each of the corresponding milieux. A statistical analysis of *Who's who* shows that it is in business that social success depends least on scholastic success (23 per cent of employers and managerial classes in the private sector figuring in

Who's Who have had no higher education as against 4.5 per cent of top civil servants and less than 1 per cent of medical practitioners and university lecturers). It would be easy to show that, for the upper middle class world of business and power, the *normalien* who in university ideology is the ideal accomplished man is almost to the pupil of the École Nationale D'Administration, who is the incarnation of an up-to-date worldly culture, what the swot is to the cultivated man according to the canons of the school. Thus, when the jury for the entrance examination for the ENA discover in candidates what others would call 'university qualities' no praise is intended. 'Some candidates, who have certainly worked hard, have left themselves no time to reflect or even to read anything but *Le Monde*. They cannot stand back from what they have studied. They have neither humour nor gaiety, and listening to them inclines one to fear that the administrative system may become a mournful and over-serious institution. If the upper civil service and the great state specialist corps become mathematically exact, lugubrious and pedantic bodies, there is little hope of their creating a happy France' (competitive entrance examination to the ENA 1967).

[47] It can be seen that the school thus helps to reproduce the system of relationships between sections of the dominant classes, by (*inter alia*) deterring children of other classes or other sections of classes from getting as much economic and symbolic benefit from their qualifications as children from the upper middle class concerned with business and power, who are in a much better position to relativize scholastic judgements.

[48] It can be seen for example that the relatively high number of teachers of lower middle class origin decreases as one ascends the hierarchy of grades of teaching, or in other words, as the contradiction implicit in the teaching function becomes more obvious and as the primacy of the relationship to the culture of the privileged classes strengthens. In 1964, 33 per cent of elementary schoolteachers in post were of working class origin, 36 per cent of lower middle class origin and 12 per cent of middle or upper middle class origin, while among teachers in secondary and higher education (no distinction being made between them), 13 per cent were of working class origin, 42 per cent of lower middle class origin and 33 per cent of middle and upper middle class origin. An idea of the social origin of teachers in higher education can be formed by considering the social origin of pupils of the École Normale Supérieure – 6 per cent of working class, 27.3 per cent of middle class, and 66.8 per cent of upper class origin. Although there is no doubt that the different categories of teachers owe a number of their characteristics to the position they occupy in the educational system and the scholastic trajectory, with the correlative type of education, which has brought them to that position, all these characteristics are nevertheless still closely linked to differences of social origin, so that categories of teachers which are scarcely distinguishable by living conditions and professional situation can be separated in their professional and extra-professional attitudes by differences which are not reducible to contrasting categorical

interests. It would not be too bold to propose the hypothesis that, after all due regard has been given to the type of educational career, faculty, discipline etc. (as many characteristics as are no doubt not randomly distributed among different social origins) and to all properly university considerations, there are still some large types of systems of attitudes linked to different social origins. That is why although they are most often constructed according to the categories of a properly intellectual taxonomy, the contrasts noted seem to go back to the contrast between the two intakes — bourgeois and petit bourgeois — into the staff of higher education. For example, the principles according to which R. Blanchard distinguishes, in his memoirs, the 'dim and conscientious' from the 'gentlemen' are in no way different from those which earlier analyses disclosed. Here are a few notes on Blanchard's second category: 'A colleague called him a nobleman of letters', 'more of a *teacher* than a *researcher* and producing little' (op. cit. p.94), 'Surrounded with the glamour of outstanding academic success — *first* in the École Normale Supérieure, *first* in the *agrégation* . . . but he never achieved a great deal . . . and published, once a year, a *brief* note, which at least had the merit of exhausting the subject' (ibid.), 'A real *aristocrat:* firstly by birth: he was the son of a famous professor at the Sorbonne, and his mother was a *grande dame,* a god-daughter of Princess Mathilde. All that was very impressive for plebeians' such as ourselves. He was also very distinguished-looking — tall, slender, elegant, charming, lionized by women and esteeming them highly. His intellectual *gifts* were in accord with his looks and manners, he was intelligent and subtle' (op. cit. p. 95). On the other hand, the dim ones: 'I can recall a group of dim and conscientious teachers and tutors, a "manure heap for genius" as one of my friends jokingly called them . . . ' (op. cit. p. 90), 'and finally the last of the old pupils was an obscure Germanist, the only one not to have been to the École Normale Supérieure (op. cit. p. 94).

INDEX

ability, rising threshold of mediocrity, 27; social analysis of 'latent' distribution, 27-8, 30; tests included, 28; results, 28, 29, 30; reserves of undereducated, 30; influence of group standards on, 35; and entry into selective schools, 79, 88; variance due to differences in educational provision, 79-80; increased correlation with equality of opportunity in comprehensives, 292; and age structure, 360 n. 7

ability grouping, and educational attainment, 148; heterogeneous v. homogeneous, 148; streaming v. non-streaming, 150; in non-streamed primary schools, 246

Acland, H., 'direct' and 'indirect' research, 13 n. 7; variation in ability and school provision, 80

Adams, R.S. and Biddle, B.L., *Realities of Teaching*, 200

adolescents, and peer groups, 23-4; studies in value orientations, 54, 64 n. 15; application to Dublin school leavers, 54-62; influences on staying on, 92-3, 95, 99-100, 105 n. 21; new relationship in comprehensive education, 100; conflict between teacher expectations and independence, 178; adult expectations and 'unacceptable behaviour', 178; role dilemma, 178; realistic ambitions for future occupations, 179, 188 n. 21; conduct variations in similar pupils, 180-1

agricultural workers, chances of university education, 32; family size and educational opportunity, 34; cumulative effect of social handicaps, 35-6

Amidon, E.J. and Hough, J.B., *Interaction Analysis*, 251

Anderson, C. Arnold, need for variable schooling system, 298

Andersson, B.E., *Studies in Adolescent Behaviour* (Göteborg project), 24

Argyris, C., nature of research act, 254

Aries, P., ability/age ideology (*L'Enfant et la vie de famille sous l'Ancien Régime*), 360 n. 7

armed forces, 'latent ability' tests on recruits, 27

Asch, S.E., power of group pressure in altering perception of visual stimuli, 249-50

Association for Comprehensive Education (Corby New Town), 124, 125, and alleged class differentiation, 127, 128; continuing activity, 129

Australia, adolescent value orientation, aborigine/white, 54, 63 n. 13

Barker Lunn, J.C., self-fulfilling prophecy in grouping, 245; *Streaming in a Primary School*, 22, 136, 142 n. 9, 164 n. 9, 165 n. 22

Bartholomew, J., 'The teacher as researcher' (*Hard Cheese*), 254-5

Beck, J., non-participant observation study on classroom behaviour, 261-2; analysis of anxiety problem, 262; and Green, A.G., teacher evaluation of classroom behaviour, 199

Becker, H.S., observing classroom behaviour, 257-8; role of participant observer, 259; cultural/social group differentiations, 259

Becker, H.S., *et al.*, *Making the Grade*, 197

behaviour. distinguished from *mode* of behaviour, 339

Bellaby, Paul, deviance/school organization relationship, 147; distribution of deviance among 13-14 year olds, 167-81

Bellack, A.A., teacher/student interaction patterns, 203 (*Studies in Classroom Language*)

'social arguments' in favour of comprehensive schools, 269; 'Ability and opportunity in a comprehensive school', 292-9; *Social Class and the Comprehensive School,* 22, 269, 292 n. 2

France, 1; socio-cultural class and school entry, 32-6, 344; children and choice of school, 33-4; family size and entry into *lycées,* 34, 44 n. 4; attachment to ideology of educational equity, 37; literary tradition and use of language, 40; faith in *l'école libératrice,* 42; factors affecting working class entrants, 340; structure of school population, 343; aristocratic ideology of birth, 358; moral disapproval of success, 358

further education, 102 n. 2; patterns of uptake, 110, 119-20

Gahagan, D.M. and Gahagan, G.A., *Talk Reform,* 10

gang behaviour, 325-37; participant observation, 327; clothes, 328, 332-3; language, 329; fights, 329, 330-1, 335; shopbreaking, 330; cinema, 331-2; school experience, 332-3; sense of boredom, 334, 336; before the courts, 334-5; tattooing, 336; approved school ignorance, 337

Garfinkel, H., *Studies in Ethnomethodology,* 4, 272

Garfinkel, H. and Sacks, H., 'On formal structure of practical actions*,* 256, 257

Girard, A. and Bastide, H., family size and access to secondary *(lycée)* education, 44 n. 4

Glass, D.C., *Social Mobility in Britain,* 7, 102 n. 6

Goldberg, M.L. *et al., Effects of Ability Grouping,* 148-9, 164 n. 6

Good, T.L. and Brophy, J.E., *Analysing Classroom Behaviour,* 201

Gorbutt, D., teachers' concept of intelligence, 9

Gouldner, A.W., on a 'reflexive sociology', 5; *The Coming Crisis in Western Sociology,* 62

grammar schools, higher education recruitment, 79, 88; holding power over pupils, 89, 98; pattern of early leaving, 98; student dropout, 102

n. 4; single sex, 123-4; 'pressured academic environment', 149; absence of role vulnerability in staff, 219, 222; analysis of role and educational qualifications of headmaster, 229, 242; social class distribution of places, 292; influence of home background, 297; middle class ethos, 302; wastage of working class talent, 303, 304; social class and level of evaluation of English lesson, 306, 315-18, 320; (compared with comprehensive and secondary modern), 293-8; social class/IQ composition, 294-5, 300 n. 14, 301 n. 21; social class/A stream composition, 296, 301 n. 20; leaving intentions, 297 *see also* Hightown Grammar School

grant-earning schools, social origins of male teachers, 232

Gray, J.L., and Moshinsky, P., *Political Arithmetic,* 7

Green, A.G., *Theory and Practice in Infant Education,* 262-3

Gross, W., *et al.,* 193 n. 3; teacher role in innovations, 185; barriers to change, 189

group teaching, in non-streamed primary schools, 245-50

Gue, L.R., 'Value orientations in an Indian community' (Alberta), 54, 64 n. 4

Hajnal, J., *The Student Trap,* 13 n. 7

Halpin, A., 186

Halsey, A.J., concept of 'action research', 6, 81; and EPAs, 130 and n., 142 n. 3, 269; 'Theoretical advance and empirical challenge', 7, 22; *et al., Education, Economy and Society,* 7-8, 243 n. 7, 301 n. 23

Hargreaves, D.H., 'Transmission of value systems through streaming', 146, 198; *Social Relations in a Secondary School,* 10, 169

headmasters, determinant factors in school value orientations, 198; role as seen by staff, 217; concept of own role, 217; subject to outside influences, 221; staff relations, 223, 226; and professional status, 225; and nature of leadership, 228-38; management function, 228; social class, 231-2, 243; school/social